MARK TWAIN AND MONEY

STUDIES IN AMERICAN LITERARY REALISM AND NATURALISM

MARK TWAIN AND MONEY

Language, Capital, and Culture

Edited by Henry B. Wonham and Lawrence Howe

THE UNIVERSITY OF ALABAMA PRESS
Tuscaloosa

The University of Alabama Press
Tuscaloosa, Alabama 35487-0380
uapress.ua.edu

Typeface: Minion

Cover design: Todd Lape/Lape Designs

Library of Congress Cataloging-in-Publication Data

Names: Wonham, Henry B., 1960– editor. | Howe, Lawrence, 1952– editor.
Title: Mark Twain and money : language, capital, and culture / edited by
Henry B. Wonham and Lawrence Howe.
Description: Tuscaloosa : The University of Alabama Press, [2017] |
Series: Studies in American literary realism and naturalism | Includes index.
Identifiers: LCCN 2017001116 |
ISBN 9780817319441 (cloth) | ISBN 9780817390877 (e book)
Subjects: LCSH: Twain, Mark, 1835–1910—Knowledge—Economics. |
Economics in literature.
Classification: LCC PS1342.E25 M37 2017 | DDC 818/.409—dc23
LC record available at https://lccn.loc.gov/2017001116

Contents

Figures

Acknowledgments

The essays by Lawrence Howe, Judith Yaross Lee, and Christine Benner Dixon first appeared in a special issue, "Mark Twain and Economy," of *American Literary Realism* 47.1 (Fall 2014). They are reprinted here with the permission of the University of Illinois Press. Henry B. Wonham's essay, "The Art of Arbitrage: Reimagining Mark Twain, Business Man," first appeared in *ELH* 82.4 (Winter 2015): 1239–66. Copyright © 2015 by The Johns Hopkins University Press. We would like to thank the Oregon Humanities Center and Roosevelt University for their support of this project.

MARK TWAIN AND MONEY

Introduction

Henry B. Wonham

In his September 1870 column for *The Galaxy*, Mark Twain took on a topic of unusual gravity. "Political economy is the basis of all good government," the narrator begins ("Political Economy" 21). "The wisest men of all ages have brought to bear upon this subject the—[Here I was interrupted and informed that a stranger wished to see me down at the door. . . .]" The stranger is a lightning-rod salesman, whose aggressive sales pitch detains the author for half an hour, after which he resumes his unfinished sentence: "—richest treasures of their genius, their experience of life, and their learning. The great lights of commercial jurisprudence, international confraternity, and biological deviation, of all ages, all civilizations, and all nationalities, from Zoroaster down to Horace Greeley, have—[Here I was interrupted again and required to go down and confer further with that lightning-rod man. . . .]" And so on, through a hilarious sequence of prose fragments, interrupted by heated negotiations, resulting in the narrator's ill-considered purchase of "three thousand two hundred and eleven feet of [the] best quality zinc-plated spiral-twist lightning-rod stuff, and sixteen hundred and thirty-one silver-tipped points" (27). Needless to say, Mark Twain's treatise "Political Economy" becomes a casualty of the author's absorption in an actual economic transaction for which his theoretical musings have left him unprepared.

The *Galaxy* sketch provides an intriguing point of departure for the volume *Mark Twain and Money* for several reasons, the most obvious of which is that, like the sketch's narrator, Mark Twain never got around to formulating a comprehensive statement of his economic views, much less a consistent theory of political economy. He certainly had no shortage of opinions about economic affairs. His early fame, after all, rested in large part on his matchless satirical portrait of the get-rich-quick spirit underpinning the culture he and Charles Dudley Warner dubbed the Gilded Age. In the novel of that name, as in *Roughing It* and countless other works, Mark Twain poked fun at America's romance with the almighty dollar, a theme he never tired of, and yet no American writer has ever been more smitten with the dream of material wealth than Twain himself. He may have railed against "the lust for money which is the rule of life to-day," but that rule largely governed his notoriously unsuccessful financial activities and, in important respects, his creative life as well ("Villagers of 1840–3" 100). One need only recall the dubious salesmanship of Tom Sawyer and Hank Morgan to appreciate that Mark Twain was as deeply invested in the critique of Gilded Age capitalism as he was in the possibility of its limitless extension. Robert Sattelmeyer conveys the same paradox more succinctly when he explains that, whatever Mark Twain "may have said about the American economic system in satirical works such as *The Gilded Age*, his own practices constituted an uncritical endorsement of it" (89).

Perhaps the reason Mark Twain never offered a coherent statement of his economic views is that, like the jack-leg theorist of the *Galaxy* sketch, he was too busy with real-life economic affairs. In fact, much like his *Galaxy* narrator, Mark Twain was thoroughly embroiled in business negotiations of various sorts throughout his long writing career, and their claims on his attention were a major distraction from literary work. The story of his business adventures apparently does not include a misguided investment in "lightning-rod stuff," but many of its episodes are at least as outrageous, and some of them bear repeating in a brief overview of his financial preoccupations.

The first serious entrepreneurial scheme to ignite Sam Clemens's fiscal imagination took shape in 1859, when he learned about the surprising properties of a now-infamous South American leaf. Four years earlier, German scientists had learned to extract cocaine as the active agent in the coca leaf, and at twenty-four years old, Sam Clemens saw an opportunity to get in on the ground floor of what he hoped would be a vast new industry by sailing to the Amazon basin in order to establish an American trade in coca. Within a decade, of course, Americans were ingesting cocaine in soft drinks, toothache remedies, and other household products, and Clemens might have been rolling in legal drug money by that time, except for the fact that no ships were scheduled to leave New Orleans for the Amazon in 1859.

This was a lucky break for American literature, for he next signed on with Horace Bixby to learn the riverboat piloting trade, and soon thereafter, with the outbreak of the Civil War, he accompanied his brother Orion Clemens to Nevada, where Sam Clemens's ambition was still to strike it rich, if not in coca, then in silver or gold. In letters home he claimed that in Nevada a man with initiative could expect to spend no more than six weeks "to make $100,000, if he had $3,000 dollars to commence with" (SLC to Pamela Moffett and Jane Clemens 25 October 1861, *Mark Twain's Letters*). And this is what he expected to do as a mere beginning, for when Sam Clemens used the word "rich," he had in mind names like Comstock, Carnegie, Frick, and Rockefeller—massive industrial fortunes, not the sort of "wealth" that could ever be expected from piloting a steamboat or writing books (Wilson and Rees 109).

Probably the only jackpot he ever actually did hit was in marrying Olivia Langdon in 1870, but that certainly did not put an end to his relentless search for the scheme that would make him phenomenally wealthy. Throughout the 1870s he poured money into the projects of various inventers, and he dabbled with his own inventions, receiving his first patent in 1871 for a device called "Improvement in Adjustable and Detachable Straps for Garments." He received two other patents during his lifetime, one for "Mark Twain's Self-Pasting Scrapbook," the other for a memory-building history game. As his many biographers have detailed, the list of other inventions and gizmos he either dreamed up or invested in includes a fire extinguisher that worked like a hand grenade, a perpetual calendar, a bed clamp for keeping blankets in place, a steam brake for railroad cars, and a riverboat paddle wheel designed for icy conditions. At one point he considered purchasing a vineyard and invested $600 in the manufacture of a new type of grape scissors that had been invented and patented by the father of his close friend William Dean Howells.

In addition to dreaming up gadgets that would make him rich, he took an almost equal interest in Orion Clemens's usually zanier schemes, about which they corresponded with frantic energy. One of Orion's more plausible inventions was a wood-carving device that almost seemed likely to succeed, but most of his plans were considerably more visionary, such as a flying machine that Howells and Twain later mocked in one of their Colonel Sellers plays. In the early 1870s, Orion was working on a massive machine that remains a mystery today, except for his intriguing description of it in a letter to his wife: "The clockmaker has made about 3000 links for my chains, and has about 2000 more to make. About 800 connecting parts have to be turned; and I suppose they have not been commenced. . . . I have to get them before the cogwheels intended for the chain can be made. While waiting on these things I am fixing over the pulleys, putting them on brass plates, temporarily, instead of wood, experimentally" (quoted in Kaplan 151).

Sam Clemens sometimes ridiculed his brother's impractical designs, but it is hard not to notice a resemblance between Orion's mystery device, with its thousands of parts, and the Paige typesetting machine, which would soon become Mark Twain's primary technological and financial obsession, and which would ultimately bankrupt him. Not including the fatal typesetter, he probably invested about $200,000 on the ventures mentioned, a huge sum in today's terms, perhaps as much as $4 million. When we include the typesetter, by far his greatest financial blunder, that number increases to at least $6 million in today's money.

There are other major episodes in this well-known story of financial aspiration and disaster, such as the initially successful but short-lived publishing firm Charles L. Webster & Company, and Plasmon, the powdered milk extract that cost Mark Twain another $32,000 in squandered investment. But the basic storyline should be clear: Mark Twain was obsessed with striking it rich, to the point that it is hard to imagine he had time or attention left over for anything unrelated to business. Justin Kaplan, perhaps Twain's greatest biographer, puts a finer point on the significance of the story when he describes Twain's "fatal addiction . . . to drowning his important goals and also his judgment in some . . . tipple of speculation." Kaplan continues: "He was in the grip of a compulsion to think and act always in terms of exploitation and profits; even [the history game], intended to teach chronology to little girls, had to become a commercial venture right away. This is not to say that Mark Twain could have written another *Huckleberry Finn* or two in the time and with the energy he gave to such ventures. But these ventures eroded and colored his literary interests, and by trapping him into such irreversible involvements as his publishing house and the Paige typesetter they often made any writing, of any quality, next to impossible" (253).

Kaplan's powerful assessment of this "fatal addiction" to the dream of wealth *is* the story of *Mark Twain and Money*, as we have been used to hearing it for one hundred years. As that story goes, Twain spent too much time thinking about money, and he would have written more and better books if he could have outgrown the Tom Sawyer–like compulsion to see everything in terms of speculation and profit. One of his earliest and most influential critics, Van Wyck Brooks, made essentially this argument as long ago as 1920, explaining in *The Ordeal of Mark Twain* that the crass materialism of Sam Clemens's frontier environment stunted and perverted his inclinations as an artist. For Brooks and some later psychoanalytic critics, Clemens's personality was substantially formed at the side of his father's coffin, where, according to family lore, his mother exacted a promise that he would "retrieve his father's fortune . . . [and] realize that 'mirage of wealth' that had ever hung before his father's eyes" (52). The whole unfortunate saga of Mark Twain's "ordeal" originated, for Brooks, in this acceptance of financial obligations that distorted Sam Clemens's incipient capacity as an artist. Kaplan is more generous than Brooks about the ultimate effects of Twain's money lust, but they basically agree, as do most of the critics who have come along since, that nothing good came from Mark Twain's fascination with the world of business. It was a world for which, according to Harold Kolb's 2015 assessment, Mark Twain had "too much imagination and too little sense" (248).

The critics who have collaborated to produce *Mark Twain and Money* accept the basic biographical story of his financial misadventures as a matter of record, and yet they take a different view of his "fatal addiction." While each contributor comes to the topic from a unique angle, all tend to concur in treating Mark Twain's compulsive engagement with issues of economy less as a regrettable distraction than as a surprisingly rich source of literary creativity. No one can deny that Mark Twain's attitudes toward wealth were wildly contradictory or that his experiences with money produced more anguish than insight. These critical truisms have understandably discouraged Twain scholars from treating his economic views with the same seriousness that literary critics of the last generation have given to such writers as Daniel Defoe, Charles Dickens, and Henry James—novelists who presumably had something more meaningful and coherent to say about economic life than did Mark Twain.[1] Yet for the contributors to this volume, Mark Twain's contradictory attitudes and misguided enthusiasms provide an illuminating window on the complex and rapidly changing financial culture that so often dominated his attention. Yes, he was a hopelessly inconsistent theorist and a poor investor, but his writing sheds extraordinary light on Gilded Age conceptions of the nature of money, on the operations of credit and debt, on the concepts of real and intellectual property, on the nascent power of the marketing and advertising industries, on the economics of authorship and the literary marketplace, on the politics of bimetallism and the Free Silver movement, on the nature of commodities and the commodity form, on the economic forces of production and consumption, on economic panic and bankruptcy, on capitalism and capitalists, on progressive politics and socialism, and on much more. As the contributors to *Mark Twain and Money* suggest, Mark Twain—for all his pudd'nheadedness on financial matters—had something fascinating to say about all of these topics. Only an age-old and perhaps now antiquated habit of assuming that he would have been better off not thinking about money has prevented scholars from paying careful attention to the way such fiscal concerns animate his fiction.

Coeditor Lawrence Howe opens the volume with "Narrating the Tennessee Land: Real Property, Fictional Land, and Mark Twain's Literary Enterprise," a chapter that aligns Mark Twain's evolving attitudes toward property ownership with a large-scale shift in the way "the concept of property in nineteenth-century America was being reimagined." Contrasting the Clemens family claim to the infamous "Tennessee Land" with the sort of abstract legal arrangements that were emerging in nineteenth-century America to govern the "ownership" of mineral rights, Howe teases out Mark Twain's ambivalent responses to a paradigm shift affecting the very meaning of property in America. Twain was ahead of his time in grasping that "property consists not simply in objects themselves but in a relationship between owner and object that is codified in language, in a system that is as bound up in rhetoric as it is in material." Noting that Twain was unusually sensitive to "the problematic intersection of language and economics," Howe suggests that "his lifelong engagement with words, and especially with storytelling, attuned him to the narrative basis of property rights and the contractual arrangements that governed them."

Judith Yaross Lee also mentions "The Mark Twain Enterprise" in the title of her chapter, though whereas Howe focuses on Twain's relationships to real and imagined property, Lee uses the phrase to identify his stewardship of the most important asset Samuel Clemens ever held, namely, the "Mark Twain" brand. In "Brand Management: Samuel Clemens, Trademarks, and the Mark Twain Enterprise," she draws on concepts that are probably more familiar to MBAs than to literary scholars in describing the multiple strategies Clemens pursued to "manage" his brand, arguing that he "carefully mined, deployed, and directed the commercial value of his products (especially his copyrighted works) and his reputation (which he saw as a business asset)." Readers who are used to sighing over Mark Twain's legendary incompetence in business affairs will be surprised to learn that, within this particular zone of commercial culture, he was not only competent, but innovative and highly successful. Lee explains that his efforts at brand management focused on two themes, one known today as "brand extension" (the projection of his literary identity onto other commercial ventures); "the other approach, by contrast, entailed distancing activities from his role as Mark Twain, mainly by spinning them off, as we would say today, under other labels, as with the anonymously serialized *Personal Recollections of Joan of Arc* (1896) and the imprint of Charles L. Webster & Company." His efforts in both directions, Lee concludes, "showed marketing savvy well ahead of his time, protecting his enterprises from unprofitable controversy and exploiting his name when worthwhile."

Mark Schiebe is another critic interested in Mark Twain's marketing savvy, although, unlike Judith Lee, he insists that "Twain's interest in the power of branding is expressed most significantly in his fiction," especially in *A Connecticut Yankee in King Arthur's Court*. Noting that Twain scholars usually dwell on Hank Morgan's industrial innovations, Schiebe contends that the Yankee's real achievement lies in creating a market for his unprecedented wares. In "'Society's Very Choicest Brands': Hank Morgan's Brand Magic in

Camelot," he argues that the success of Hank's industrial innovations depends upon "a revolutionary shift of consciousness" in Camelot, whose benighted feudal citizens must be transformed into prototypes of the insatiable American consumer. According to Schiebe, Mark Twain understood "the problem of demand" long before economists considered it a problem, and he also understood that its solution lay in "the harnessing of the power of the brand, and the development of branding practices which . . . highlight the mystical rather than the material qualities of a given commodity."

In "The Quality (and Cost) of Mercy: Mark Twain's Evasion of the Poor," Ann M. Ryan redirects our attention from Twain's fascination with wealth toward the very different question of his attitudes toward poverty. Drawing on a wide range of sources, including the "begging letters" Twain received from needy admirers throughout his career, Ryan argues that Twain was haunted by the problem of poverty and beleaguered by the needs of the poor. Moreover, she explains that he responded to the ubiquity of late-nineteenth-century poverty by crafting a disturbing lexicon to describe beggars: "they 'swarm' and 'infest'; they behave like 'vermin' and disease'; they wear 'rags,' and covering their 'monstrous' bodies are always 'layers of dirt.'" Regardless of whether the beggars he describes are "Goshoot Indians" or Italian city-dwellers, the pervasive dirt on their faces "erodes previous markers of race, ethnicity, and nation and replaces those identities with a new kind of economic pigmentation." Poverty thus ironically becomes a more inflexible marker of identity than does race or nationality, for "the dirt that covers [the beggar's body] becomes, for Twain, the sign of an emerging, global underclass." These troubling reflections inform Ryan's reading of *The Prince and the Pauper*, a novel that apparently argues for institutional remedies for the suffering of the poor, but that simultaneously asserts their innate moral inferiority. For Ryan, the novel's ending suggests that "Twain longs . . . to uplift the poor with his philanthropy, all while keeping his white suit, white shirt, and white hands very, very clean." While the novel's ending suggests that King Edward's experiences of pauperism led to benevolent reform, Ryan insists that "the poor remain a dangerous presence in the novel, less a problem to be solved than a neighborhood to be avoided."

Gregg Camfield's chapter, "The Robber Barons' Fool? Mark Twain and the Four Ps of Patronage," opens by acknowledging that we usually associate "literary patronage" with a pre-1800 model of aristocratic or royal support for individual artists. Mark Twain was presumably in the vanguard of a new breed of writers who answered directly to the marketplace, and indeed some of the chapters in this collection (Lee, Schiebe) examine his innovative approaches to marketing his "brand" to the consuming public. Yet Camfield insists that patronage, in the sense of political and economic dependency, does not disappear under market conditions; it simply assumes new forms and makes new demands on literary performance. He examines four kinds of patronage that in different ways, and at different moments, shaped Mark Twain's creative efforts: public, political, peer, and plutocratic patronage. In each instance, Mark Twain took to heart the cynical wisdom he attributed to the slave orator Jerry in "Corn-pone Opinions": "You tell me whar a man gits his corn pone, en I'll tell you what his 'pinions is." Literary performance is always shaped by self-interest, Jerry suggests, and yet Camfield explains that "the subtext of Jerry's argument is that "while opinions are created in reaction to the source of corn-pone," those opinions are often "both conformist and subversive." Mark Twain played this game of subversion-masked-as-conformity throughout his career as a response to the limitations imposed on his art by his public, political, peer, and plutocratic constituencies. According to Camfield, while Twain "often did espouse the opinions of his patrons, the more dependent he was on a source of income, the more indebted to a particular kind of patronage, the more radically divergent were his opinions about that kind of patronage." The rhetorical dexterity needed to sustain this game of flattery and resentment became, in Camfield's view, "one source of his radical inconsistency" on political, social, economic, and ethical issues, for his writing always reflected a "divided sense of having to praise those he depended on while he deeply resented the obligation."

Joseph Csicsila's contribution, "'These Hideous Times': Mark Twain's Bankruptcy and the Panic of 1893," interrogates one of the most fundamental assumptions in Mark Twain studies, namely, the belief that he brought financial ruin on himself through his reckless and impulsive business practices. Csicsila contends that Twain was largely responsible for popularizing an exaggerated image of his own fiscal ineptitude, and he challenges Twain scholars to square that image with the historical record. After examining the circumstances of Twain's business affairs leading up to his bankruptcy filing in April 1894, Csicsila disputes "the notion that Twain was hopelessly irresponsible with his wealth, making poor financial decisions one after another throughout much of his adult life." Contrary to the usual story—and with the support of detailed evidence—Csicsila maintains that "it is not the case that Twain bled his publishing firm dry in order to fund the investment in the Paige typesetter." A more accurate narrative of Twain's business failure, he contends, would acknowledge that the Panic of 1893 was different in scope and magnitude than any of the business catastrophes that preceded it, and that Mark Twain acted rationally in response to conditions that were beyond his control. Over the years, Twain blamed his bankruptcy on various individuals, including himself, and yet Csicsila's careful analysis of the extraordinary economic circumstances of what Twain called "these hideous times" tells a more complicated story about his legendary failure.

In "'Drop Sentiment, and Come Down to Business': Debt and the Disintegration of 'Manly' Character in 'Indiantown' and 'Which Was It?,'" Susanne Weil returns to the scene of Mark Twain's bankruptcy, though with a very different critical agenda in mind. Whether or not Twain was responsible for the failure of Charles L. Webster & Company and the loss of his own significant personal fortune, he blamed himself for these events. Weil picks up the story in 1898, when Twain finally paid off the last of the debts required by his bankruptcy settlement, but doing so, according to Weil, "did not heal the wounds of bankruptcy." Noting that his letters of this period are branded by an "excruciating shame, depression, and feeling of lost manhood," she turns to the "dream fragments" he worked on sporadically between 1895 and 1902 to measure the extent of his ongoing psychic injuries. Weil reads "Indiantown" and "Which Was It?" as brutally confessional accounts of Twain's suffering over the permanent loss of "manliness" he felt as a result of his financial embarrassment. The 1899 fragment "Indiantown" sketches "a thinly fictionalized portrait of Twain's relationship with Olivia, reflecting genuine anxiety [over her role as] his preferred creditor and copyright holder," while in "Which Was It?" Twain narrates the demise of George Harrison, whose bankruptcy leads to "neurasthenic physical wasting," followed by "a total loss of autonomy, as he becomes the blackmailed 'slave' of his mulatto cousin." For Weil, Mark Twain's work on these tales performed an important psychological function, allowing him to lay the "ghosts of guilt and debt" aside in order to grapple with the loss of identity he felt as a result of what Justin Kaplan has called the "symbolic failure of manhood" brought on by bankruptcy (332).

M. Christine Benner Dixon agrees with Weil that Mark Twain's late stories of economic crisis produced a form of emotional relief, for she sees such exchanges of pain and pleasure—the "earning" of pleasure through the endurance of pain—as essential to his creative process, not only in the aftermath of bankruptcy, but throughout his career. In "The Pain Economy: Mark Twain's Masochistic Understanding of Pain," she suggestively broadens the collection's focus on monetary issues by depicting his art as a perpetual "reckoning" of the "pain economy." "Without a down payment of pain," she explains, "ease and pleasure translate into debt," and so "the author stands ready with his balance sheet to track the debtors and creditors, and, when necessary, to set the accounts straight." If these negotiations appear excessively abstract, one need only recall Twain's curious insistence in "Down the Rhône" that "a nerve-stab" from the dentist's scalpel "produces pleasure; and not only that, but the most exquisite pleasure, the most perfect felicity which we are capable of feeling"; or the equally enigmatic claim of the Old Man in *What Is Man?*, who says that the loving mother "takes a living *pleasure*" in suffering for her child: "'*She does it for that reward*—that self-approval, that contentment, that peace, that comfort. *She would do it for your child* IF SHE COULD GET THE SAME PAY" (*A Tramp Abroad*, 1025–26; *Collected Tales, Sketches, Speeches, and Essays, 1852–1890*, 744). Clearly, a compensatory logic is at work in these economic transactions over pleasure and pain, a logic that Benner Dixon associates with masochism. By owning pain and submitting to it, "the masochist takes control over his or her experience" and thereby accumulates a kind of capital that can be held in reserve. Twain's art, she suggestively argues, grows out of the masochist's urge to keep the balance sheet in his or her favor, to suffer at least enough pain to offset unpaid obligations.

Blackface minstrelsy is often cited as a key source of Mark Twain's humor, but few critics possess the expertise to give this general observation a usefully sharp edge. In "Minstrel Economics: Mark Twain, the San Francisco Minstrels, and Folk Investment in the American Dream," Sharon D. McCoy contends that the San Francisco Minstrels (SFM), who moved to New York City in 1865, were the touchstone for Twain's appreciation and literary assimilation of minstrel antics. More importantly, she insists that his "increasingly nuanced and complex satiric uses of minstrel masking are traceable to the commercial and critical success" of that particular troupe. What distinguished the SFM as postbellum America's most popular minstrel company, according to McCoy, was "a signature satiric performance style" that responded to "the particular economic, moral, and racially inflected anxieties of the postwar generation, celebrating economic aspirations while exposing cultural pretension and political and financial corruption." The element of burnt-cork racial masking remained the definitive feature of the genre, of course, but the issues, anxieties, and scandals that dominated public attention during the late 1860s and 1870s—and that received their most outlandish treatment on the SFM's New York stage—were predominantly economic: the "Erie Wars of 1868" that pitted robber barons against one another for control of the Erie Railroad; Jay Gould and James M. Fisk's attempted corner of the gold market in 1869; bribery scandals that reached to President Grant's brother-in-law; debates over the gold and silver standards versus government greenbacks and privately issued paper money; the Crédit Mobilier scandal of 1872–1873, which triggered the Panic of 1873; and the ensuing depression that presaged the end of federal Reconstruction. All of these issues were bound up in the racial politics of the day, as their mediation on the blackface stage made painfully clear, and yet the performance style of the SFM employed racial comedy to ignite economic satire, rather than the other way around. According to McCoy, "Mark Twain developed a parallel satiric use of blackface minstrel masking in his own work." She explains that "his minstrel mask is similar to the SFM's in its topical focus, its multiple and often conflicting satiric targets, and its sympathy with both poverty and aspirations for economic advancement." Focusing on several works Twain produced at the height of the SFM's popularity, such as *The Gilded Age* (1873), "A True Story" (1874), and the hit play *Colonel Sellers* (1874)—which ran for delighted crowds just a few blocks from the SFM's opulent new theater—McCoy argues that the SFM's racially inflected economic satire became a key source of what we now recognize as Mark Twain's most distinctive humor.

Jonathan Hayes takes an even closer look at Mark Twain's first extended satire of the late-nineteenth-century American economic system in "'A House of Cards': Fictitious Capital and *The Gilded Age*." Critics of the novel have traditionally faulted the coauthors for their scattered attention to several major plot lines, including the satire of frontier development efforts by self-interested Wall Street companies and the seemingly unrelated melodramatic love plot featuring Laura Hawkins and the disreputable military officer Colonel Selby. Hayes disputes the charge of shoddy narrative construction by contending that these parallel narratives reveal "a homology between fictional sentimental melodrama and finance-inspired enterprises." Noting that the novel's economic satire centers on the phenomenon of "fictitious capital," or what David Harvey calls "money that is thrown into circulation as capital without any material basis in commodities or productive activity," Hayes argues that melodramatic elements in *The Gilded Age* emphasize a parallel form of distortion within the realm of social life (Harvey 95). Laura's excessive novel-reading and absurdly romanticized conception of actual life, in other words, drive the melodrama toward much the same inevitable ruin that awaits the fraudulent development schemes of the Salt Lick Pacific Extension and the Columbus River Slack-water Navigation Company. "Fictitious capital" and melodramatic fiction are two versions of the same game of deception, for Hayes, whose reading suggests that *The Gilded Age* holds together more effectively than critics have generally acknowledged.

In "'By and By I Was Smitten with the Silver Fever': Literary Veins in *Roughing It*," Jeffrey W. Miller proposes that "the act of mining—the archetypal act of taking money out of the earth—is a symbol for literary production in *Roughing It*." He notes that critics usually locate the book's coherence in the narrator's transition from innocent expectation to seasoned experience, a transformation that corresponds to his overland journey from the bookish eastern states to the vernacular western territories. Miller objects that such a reading constructs "a dichotomy between the 'rough' world of mining and the 'civilized' world of letters," a dichotomy that robs the text of its most compelling metaphor for literary creativity. Miller's reading of *Roughing It*, by contrast, "collapses that dichotomy, arguing that Twain can conceive of what it means to be a literary man only through the rhetoric of mining." His analysis demonstrates that the narrator's mining failure and literary success are two sides of the same coin, as the text emphasizes through its amusing use of proper names for mining claims, and as the narrator further confirms with his manipulative "reporting" on the potential of certain mines to hit pay dirt. Rocks and words are indistinguishable raw materials in Miller's reading of *Roughing It*, which finally insists that the figurative extraction of valuable meaning from lifeless words is the only viable route to western riches. Twain confided to his *Autobiography* many years after the publication of *Roughing It*, "all through my life my facts have had a substratum of truth, and therefore they were not without preciousness. Any person who is familiar with me . . . knows how to get at the jewel of any fact of mine and dig it out of its blue-clay matrix" (269). As a reflection on Mark Twain's complex understanding of the sources of wealth, and on his closely related conception of literary creativity, Miller's chapter reminds us of how persistently he returned to and elaborated the image of mineral extraction.

Coeditor Henry Wonham's chapter, "The Art of Arbitrage: Reimagining Mark Twain, Business Man," rounds out the collection by arguing that something more specific than the dream of phenomenal wealth stood behind Mark Twain's obsession with money. Acknowledging that critics and biographers "have generally concurred in portraying Clemens/Twain as a chronically divided personality, one part reckless business man, given to building castles in the air, the other part worldly-wise writer, skeptic, and ironist, ever alert to sham and fraud," he claims that the business dimension of this dual personality was "more intricately related to Mark Twain the writer and ironist than we have been capable of appreciating." Wonham's consideration of various works, including *The Adventures of Tom Sawyer* and *The Prince and the Pauper*, suggests that underlying both Twain's business activities and his creative aspirations is an image of the "sedentary accumulation of unearned literary and financial assets," or unearned income—an image that is nowhere more indulgently contemplated than in the famous whitewashing scene, where Tom Sawyer sits in the shade, eating an apple, while his fortune in trinkets accumulates. According to Wonham's analysis, Tom has performed a feat of arbitrage, and the lesson of his success—which speaks directly to the sources of Mark Twain's art—is that the workers and players in Tom's world are "destined to remain poor, while profit awaits the sedentary arbitrageur who sits idly in the shade," watching his unearned hoard grow. Wonham concludes that "Mark Twain's entangled careers as writer and business man actually strike a surprisingly harmonious chord" in figuring this image of passive accumulation as "the elusive return on investments of intellectual and financial capital."

The narrator of Mark Twain's sketch "Political Economy" never completes his ambitious treatise, and the cumulative efforts of the contributors to *Mark Twain and Money* are not an attempt to write that essay for him. What the authors *do* hope is that their contributions will initiate a robust scholarly conversation about Mark Twain's relationship to issues of economy, broadly understood, a conversation that does not begin and end with the traditional lament over his "fatal addiction" to speculation. Twain scholars have been slow to engage with the work of literary theorists and economists who are exploring the intersection of their disciplines, probably because money has been considered a dirty word for so long in conversations about his art and achievement.[2] The contributors to *Mark Twain and Money* look forward to a new reckoning.

Notes

1. There are some important exceptions to this generalization about critical neglect of Mark Twain's economic thinking. The most sustained discussion remains Henry Nash Smith's *Mark Twain's Fable of Progress: Political and Economic Ideas in "A Connecticut Yankee"* (New Brunswick: Rutgers UP, 1964), in which Smith reads the novel as "a theory of capitalism and an interpretation of the historical process that has brought it into being" (39). Another foundational study is Louis J. Budd's *Our Mark Twain: The Making of His Public Personality* (Philadelphia: U of Pennsylvania P, 1983), which initiated an ongoing conversation about the marketing of his literary identity. More recently, two of this volume's authors have made important contributions: Gregg Camfield has written extensively on Mark Twain's economic views, especially in several entries for *The Oxford Companion to Mark Twain* (New York: Oxford UP, 2003); and Judith Yaross Lee's *Twain's Brand: Humor in Contemporary American Culture* (UP of Mississippi, 2012) is a pathbreaking study of Twain's presence in consumer culture. Other critics who have made important contributions to scholarship on Twain's thinking about finance and economics include Richard Lowry, *"Littery Man": Mark Twain and Modern Authorship* (New York: Oxford UP, 1996), and Peter Messent, *Mark Twain and Male Friendship: The Howells, Twichell, and Rogers Friendships* (New York: Oxford UP, 2009). A number of recent scholarly articles have also enlivened discussion of these issues. Of particular interest is Mary Esteve's "Shadow Economies: The Distribution of Wealth in and around *Pudd'nhead Wilson*," *ELH* 78 (Summer 2011): 359–85, and Matthew Seybold's "*The Neoclassical Twain: The Zombie Economics of Colonel Sellers*," *Mark Twain Annual* 13 (2015): 78–90. Defoe, Dickens, and James are frequently cited by critics interested in the intersection of literature and economics. See, for example, *The New Economic Criticism:*

Studies at the Intersection of Literature and Economics, ed. Martha Woodmansee and Mark Osteen (London and New York: Routledge, 1999). The absence of a single reference to Mark Twain in this important and comprehensive anthology is one of the motivating factors behind the present collection.

2. Since the 1980s, literary scholars such as Marc Shell, Jean-Joseph Goux, and Walter Benn Michaels have been exploring "the historical and philosophical parallels—usually termed homologies—between economic and linguistic systems." For all his striking relevance to these concerns, Mark Twain has played little to no part in their work or in ensuing critical conversations about the intersection of literature and economics. See Woodmansee and Osteen, "Taking Account of the New Economic Criticism," in *The New Economic Criticism* (14).

Works Cited

Brooks, Van Wyck. *The Ordeal of Mark Twain*. 1920. New York: Meridian, 1955.

Budd, Louis J. *Our Mark Twain: The Making of His Public Personality*. Philadelphia: U of Pennsylvania P, 1983.

Camfield, Gregg. *The Oxford Companion to Mark Twain*. New York: Oxford UP, 2003.

Esteve, Mary. "Shadow Economies: The Distribution of Wealth in and around *Pudd'nhead* Wilson." *ELH* 78 (Summer 2011): 359–85.

Harvey, David. *The Limits to Capital*. London: Verso, 2006.

Kaplan, Justin. *Mr. Clemens and Mark Twain*. New York: Simon and Schuster, 1966.

Kolb, Harold H., Jr. *Mark Twain: The Gift of Humor*. New York: UP of America, 2015.

Lee, Judith Yaross. *Twain's Brand: Humor in Contemporary American Culture*. Oxford: UP of Mississippi, 2012.

Lowry, Richard. *"Littery Man": Mark Twain and Modern Authorship*. New York: Oxford UP, 1996.

Messent, Peter. *Mark Twain and Male Friendship: The Howells, Twichell, and Rogers Friendships*. New York: Oxford UP, 2009.

Sattelmeyer, Robert. "Steamboats, Cocaine, and Paper Money: Mark Twain Rewriting Himself." *Constructing Mark Twain: New Directions in Scholarship*. Ed. Laura E. Skandera-Trombley and Michael J. Kiskis. Columbia: U of Missouri P, 2001. 87–100.

Seybold, Matthew. "The Neoclassical Twain: The Zombie Economics of Colonel Sellers." *Mark Twain Annual* 13 (2015): 78–90.

Smith, Henry Nash. *Mark Twain's Fable of Progress: Political and Economic Ideas in "A Connecticut Yankee."* New Brunswick: Rutgers UP, 1964.

Twain, Mark. *Autobiography of Mark Twain*. Vol. 1. Ed. Harriet Elinor Smith et al. Berkeley: U of California P, 2010.

———. *Collected Tales, Sketches, Speeches, and Essays, 1852–1890*. Ed. Louis J. Budd. New York: Library of America, 1992.

———. *Mark Twain's Letters. Mark Twain Project*. Web. <www.marktwainproject.org/xtf/search?category=letters;rmode=landing_letters;style=mtp>.

———. "Political Economy." *Sketches, New and Old*. 1875. New York: Oxford UP, 1996.

———. *A Tramp Abroad, Following the Equator, Other Travels*. Ed. Roy Blount, Jr. New York: Library of America, 2010.

———. "Villagers of 1840–3." *Huck Finn and Tom Sawyer among the Indians and Other Unfinished Stories*. Ed. Walter Blair. Berkeley: U of California P, 2011.

Wilson, James D., and John Rees. "Business." *The Routledge Encyclopedia to Mark Twain*. Ed. J. R. LeMaster and James D. Wilson. London: Routledge, 2011.

Woodmansee, Martha, and Mark Osteen, eds. *The New Economic Criticism: Studies at the Intersection of Literature and Economics*. London: Routledge, 1999.

1
Narrating the Tennessee Land
Real Property, Fictional Land, and Mark Twain's Literary Enterprise

Lawrence Howe

> Property is the fruit of labor. . . . [P]roperty is desirable . . . is a positive good in the world.
>
> —Abraham Lincoln, 21 March 1864, *Collected Works*

> Most inhabitants of a democracy have property. And not only have they got property, but they live in the conditions in which men attach most value to property.
>
> —Alexis de Tocqueville, *Democracy in America*

In the center of *Roughing It*, Mark Twain gives a very prominent place to the episode of the "blind lead." With masterfully paced suspense, he recounts the moment when he and his partner—Calvin Higbie, the man to whom he dedicates the book—examine the rock from the Wide West mine.[1] Observing something suspicious in the specimen, Higbie makes a clandestine descent into the shaft of the Wide West claim and confirms what his examination of the rock had suggested. The mine had more than one vein running through it, and the blind lead—a vein that remains hidden beneath the surface and, consequently, is discovered only by accident—contains ore of a character distinctly different from that in the Wide West vein, and thus it is not protected by the Wide West claim. In addition to the episode's artful composition, Twain's account alludes to peculiarities of the laws of mining rights; a special quirk of the rules enables Twain and Higbie to stake their own claim on the blind lead, but their subsequent neglect of their responsibility to perform work on the claim within a specified period results in the loss of their rights.

Before all goes wrong, though, the two men fantasize about the opulent lives that await them. They discuss their plans to visit Europe and the palatial houses they would build in San Francisco's posh Russian Hill neighborhood. Fueled by the fantasies of his imminent wealth, Twain reports, he wrote home instructing that his share of the family land in Tennessee be sold and the proceeds donated to charity. This is the first published reference to the Tennessee land, which Twain will deploy as a crucial plot element in *The Gilded Age* the next year. But, alas, after the disappointing loss of the blind lead, his unfolding narrative in *Roughing It* recurs to the memory of this elusive wealth, torturing Twain when other opportunities slip away from him in later episodes.

I rehearse this pivotal moment of expectation and disappointment because it denotes a shift in forms of property—from ownership of land in Tennessee to contract rights for mining valuable ore in the Comstock Lode. This shift reflects how the concept of property in nineteenth-century America was being reimagined. While the blind-lead episode condenses this change, the full text goes further to illuminate how Twain himself converted personal losses of property of various forms into literary success, earning him both wealth and cultural capital. Proceeding from the premise that Twain sought to cast himself as an exemplar of United States culture, I argue that his desire for property plays a significant role in his evolving self-portrait of American identity.

The overwrought though persistently motivating notion of the American Dream is founded on the readily assumed virtues of property ownership, which at its furthest extreme is magnified into fantasies of striking it rich. Although the phrase "the American Dream" is attributed to James Truslow Adams in 1931, the concept behind it has a much longer history (441). Clearly operative in texts like Crèvecoeur's *Letters from an American Farmer* and Hawthorne's *The House of the Seven Gables*, it arguably dates back as far as 1492. The extravagant version of this culturally formative concept had significant appeal to Samuel Clemens. However, in characteristic fashion, Twain's writings equivocate between the desire for property and misgivings about the uncertainties and obligations that ownership entails.[2]

My argument about Twain's fascination with property unfolds in three stages. First, I examine the shift of property regimes in *Roughing It*, focusing on Twain's interest in the idiosyncrasies of how property relationships are maintained and forfeited. Next, I investigate the Clemens family's ownership of the Tennessee land, real property that the family expected would provide them with intergenerational security. The story of the Tennessee land encompasses multiple narratives within both the life of Sam Clemens and the career of Mark Twain, all of which reflect the complexities of property as tantalizing. Finally, I show how Mark Twain's writing becomes the means for converting Sam Clemens's personal disappointments into capital gains, both financial and cultural. The further reaches of my argument attempt to show how property consists not simply in objects themselves but in a relationship between owner and object that is codified in language, in a system that is as bound up in rhetoric as it is in material.[3] The assertion and maintenance of ownership is thus enmeshed in a range of discourses and practices that are often abstract, making property, as Joseph Singer has noted, both "contingent and contextual" (10). Despite our commonsense conceptions of property as tangible and durable, property ownership is framed in narratives that rely on their ability to persuade others of their validity. As a writer who saw his life's work in both literary and commercial terms, Twain understood the problematic intersection of language and economics. His lifelong engagement with words, and especially with storytelling, attuned him to the narrative basis of property rights and the textual forms of the laws and contracts that governed them. To the degree that language is a flawed medium susceptible to misunderstanding, if not manipulation, the status of property is subject to interpretive variance.

The Lure of Ownership on the Frontier

The discovery of silver in Nevada Territory induced many fortune seekers to flock to the Washoe desert. But while Sam Clemens would also catch the prospecting fever that swelled the region's population from just a hundred to twenty thousand residents in little more than three years (Liebcap 39), his initial motivation for going west was to avoid the Civil War. The war indirectly headed in the same direction: to finance the war, the Lincoln administration encouraged settlement, mineral extraction, and ultimately formal entry of Nevada into the union as a state. The federal appointment of Orion Clemens as territorial secretary serendipitously presented his brother Sam with the opportunity to serve as the unofficial secretary to the secretary and thus remove himself from the likelihood of conscription in the national conflict. Although prospecting for silver was not initially part of his plan, an interest in property would take hold. Before he would become embroiled in the buying and selling of shares of mining claims, he wandered into a more conventional form of property claim.

His visit to Lake Tahoe, as recounted in *Roughing It*, is first an aesthetic experience. Twain recalls being overcome with delight upon glimpsing the beauty of the alpine lake. After twenty arduous days of overland stage travel and a sojourn of about the same duration in the desolate, desert landscape of Carson City, Tahoe's "noble sheet of blue water . . . walled in by a rim of snow-clad mountains that towered aloft full three thousand feet higher still!" appears to him as "the fairest picture the whole earth affords" (148). Having choked on the dust that the Washoe zephyr raked across Nevada's bleak terrain, Twain marvels at the miraculous properties of the lake's restorative waters. After a brief reconnaissance of the lake by boat, he and his companion, Johnny, decide to stake their claim to a ranch of three hundred acres. They perform the requirements to validate their claim—fencing the boundaries with a few felled trees and establishing a shelter, first with logs, then saplings, finally settling for a pile of brush (humorously diminishing their labors as they successively downgrade their domicile)—and look upon their homestead with satisfaction: "We were land owners now, duly seized and possessed, and within the protection of the law. Therefore, we decided to take up our residence on our own domain and enjoy that large sense of independence which only such an experience can bring" (151). Invoking the American ideals of ownership and independence, Twain rhetorically situates his text within the founding ideology of the nation. But this opportunity to embrace the American ethos turns out to be short-lived; just one day later, their pride of ownership goes up in smoke, literally, when the campfire that Twain had neglected was fanned into a wildfire, making their once idyllic "ranch" an infernal scene. Lamenting their loss, he deadpans: "We were homeless wanderers again, without any property" (156).

In addition to the humor evoked by the swivel to disappointment, this episode reflects the terms and conditions of property ownership in land, reinforced in the otherwise redundant comment of being "homeless . . . without any property." From the era of the early republic, homesteading was conceived as a way to make land accessible to citizens quickly and equitably in order to develop resources and spread prosperity. Lincoln signed the Homestead Act of 1862 into law, similarly, to encourage settlement in the West. But as Twain's experience illustrates, the security of a property claim is vulnerable to any number of threats. The first is from nature; the only thing that remains after the wildfire has ravaged his and Johnny's claim is the picturesque beauty of the unscorched portion of the Tahoe landscape. As Emerson notes in *Nature*, landscape is an aesthetic property, not a material one: "There is a property in the horizon which no man has but he whose eye can integrate all the parts, that is, the poet" (9). Surveying the farms of his neighbors, the Concord sage judges the aesthetic property to be "the best part of these men's farms, yet to this their warranty-deeds give no title." Twain's reaction to the scene of his erstwhile property is not as sanguine as Emerson's, but he expresses delight and awe mixed with his disappointment. For Twain, these aesthetic moments are not simply transitory experiences but also a means to access memory that enables him to recover in writing what was materially lost.

Property rights in minerals were a secondary interest not only for Twain but also in the nation's legal system. Despite the need for clear rules and protocols that arose with the California Gold Rush and again a decade later with the influx of hopeful arrivals to the Comstock region, individual rights to mineral claims on federal land were not officially recognized until 1866.

Prior to the enactment of the Federal Mining Statutes, miners were squatters, technically trespassing, though the federal government had neither means of prohibiting encroachment nor a system for collecting rents from miners or royalties on the value of their strikes. In this ungovernable region, miners may have enjoyed unfettered access to the land, but they also lacked the means to secure their interests. Consequently, rules "devised for establishing, exchanging, and protecting private mineral claims" (Liebcap 30) were drawn up by consensus in the various mining districts, which functioned as voluntary self-policing property regimes in the absence of local, territorial, or federal law. These rules were recognized in courts throughout the region and were adopted later in state law. When the federal government finally acted to codify mining rights, the mining district rules were generally adopted without significant alteration.

Property rights in minerals functioned differently from rights entailed in homestead grants or other conventional real estate purchases. The land on which Nevada prospectors staked their claims was federal property (Anderson and Hill 116). Because the land had little value other than the ore that it might contain, mining prospectors were happy to have access to the potential mineral wealth without having to obtain ownership of the land. Their interests lay not in the surface features of the land or in improving it for permanent residence, but in extracting the ore that lay beneath the surface. Thus, homesteading and mining claims formed entirely different relationships to land. The work required of a homesteader, as seen in the Lake Tahoe episode, was understood as an improvement of the land: establishing a home and a livelihood for the owner and, in exchange, converting wilderness into productive, cultivated acreage that benefited the country as a whole.[4] This improvement provision followed from Locke's principle that property rights are warranted by the mixture of one's own labor with nature, which was echoed in Blackstone's *Commentaries on the Laws of England,* and later by American legal scholar James Kent: "The sense of property is graciously implanted in the human breast, for the purpose of rousing us from sloth, and stimulating us to action. . . . The natural and active sense of property pervades the foundations of social improvement. It leads to the cultivation of the earth, the institution of government, the acquisition of the comforts of life, the growth of the useful arts, the spirit of commerce, the productions of taste, the erections of charity, and the display of the benevolent affections" (2:319–20). Kent's property theory implies a narrative trajectory with a teleological purpose: the natural desire for property gives rise to individual productivity, and government is formed to establish and protect the orderly recognition of property rights.

Legal theorist Carol Rose has argued that property rights in philosophy, legal codes, and individual claims of ownership take the form of storytelling in which a delineated plot embeds ownership within a validating narrative. For example, she shows that the durable influence of Locke's theory relies on a "story line, beginning in a plenteous state of nature, carrying through the growing individual appropriation of goods, then proceeding to the development of a trading money economy, and culminating in the creation of government to safeguard property" (Rose 26). Beyond the Genesis allusion of the story's origin in a "plenteous state of nature," Locke explicitly adopts biblical narrative by tracing property rights over nature to Adam and Noah. Locke's theory of the mixing of one's labor with nature as the act that establishes one's property claim is traced to Adam and Eve's banishment from Eden, which required them to live from the fruit of their labors rather than from the spontaneous bounty they had enjoyed in the garden. Blackstone goes even further, noting that Genesis, "the most venerable monument of antiquity, considered merely with a view to history," does not simply contain the general principles of Judeo-Christian property but "will furnish us with frequent instances of violent contentions concerning wells; the exclusive property of which appears to have been established in the first digger or occupant, even in such places where the ground and herbage remained yet in common" (2:5). Thus, for Blackstone, Genesis is not simply foundational myth but also case law.

Still further, Locke not only bases property-rights theory in biblical narrative but also analogizes that scriptural source to the condition of America while echoing the opening phrase of Genesis: "Thus in the beginning all the world was America" (145), where he locates the plenteous state of nature uncontaminated by an exchange transaction through the currency of money. Although Locke makes this association without ever having seen America himself, Tocqueville draws upon a similar, biblically inflected narrative about the property conditions of the America that he observed firsthand:

> When the Creator handed the earth over to men, it was young and inexhaustible . . . ; and by the time that they had learned to take advantage of the treasures it contained, they already covered its face. . . .
>
> It was then that North America was discovered, as if God had held it in reserve and it had only just arisen above the waters of the flood.
>
> There, there are still, as on the first days of creation, rivers whose founts never run dry, green and watery solitudes, and limitless fields never yet turned by the plowshare. In this condition it offers itself . . . to man who has already mastered the most important secrets of nature, united to his fellows, and taught by the experience of fifty centuries. (280)

Tocqueville's narrative is the equal of Locke's creation story; it relies on the divine warrant of Christian destiny to provide the backstory that validates the abilities of European immigrants to fulfill the potential of the continent through the exercise of property rights. These conflations of Genesis and the story of America are in evidence in Twain's own diaries of Adam and Eve. Their references to Niagara and Buffalo establish America as the site of Eden; more subtly, Adam's references to Eden shift from calling it the "estate" or the "Park" to the "property" after the fall (*Extracts from Adam's Diary* 49), underscoring the Lockean notion that labor establishes property rights.

Mining property rights, as Twain makes clear in the blind-lead episode, also required a specified commitment of labor (Anderson and Hill 111). However, the improvements for a mining enterprise differed considerably from those required in agricultural land grants. Miners' camps were, at best, temporary dwellings, and there was no specific requirement that the miners actually bivouacked at the site of their claim, so there was little sustained domestic and social development that the construction of permanent homes and towns would have developed. More importantly, mining derives value not by cultivation of land and improving its value but by extracting value from it. Where homestead landowners support a continuing process of productivity and thus enable the land to accrue value over time, those asserting mineral rights conceive of the value of the property as a zero-sum game. As the desired mineral is exhausted or the cost of extracting it exceeds the value of the mineral itself, the value of the mining property is correspondingly depleted. This inverse-value ratio is especially true for Nevada, in whose "infernal soil," Clemens observes in a letter to his mother, "nothing but that fag-end of vegetable creation, 'sage-brush,' ventures to grow" (26 October 1861). Even the scorched Lake Tahoe homestead that Twain and Johnny relinquish back to the wilderness would regenerate over time and recover the value that they saw in it; whereas, unless some overlooked mineral lay hidden for later discovery, an abandoned mining claim is worthless either from having been exhausted or never having satisfied the prospector's hunch.

The consensus rules for regulating mining property rights did not prevent disputes from erupting. Avarice was a sufficient cause for claim-jumping or sabotage of others' efforts. But even in the absence of malice, the convolutions of mineral deposits below the surface made it extremely difficult to determine where the rights of one superseded those of another. Unlike with the surface mining of the California Gold Rush, silver was found and extracted from deep-vein mines and milled from the quartz deposits that contained it. If conducting a survey of surface features was difficult, determining subterranean boundaries between claims was even more so. Deep-vein mining was also more technically demanding and costly. It "required tunnels . . .

with elaborate structural support, roads to be built to haul ore, . . . mills to be constructed to separate the ore from its surrounding elements; and extensive aqueducts to be developed to bring water to the mines" (Liebcap 31). The law's indifference to the complexities of ownership of these kinds of improvements is central to the punchline of the Great Landslide hoax.

If the Lake Tahoe episode reflects the requirements of homestead property law, and the blind-lead episode depends on anomalies of mining law, the Great Landslide hoax hinges on the conflation of these two regimes. In this practical joke, the newly arrived United States Attorney, General Buncombe, agrees to act as counsel for Dick Hyde, a rancher, against Tom Morgan, a neighboring uphill rancher. After a landslide relocates Morgan's property, entirely covering Hyde's downhill ranch, Morgan ignores Hyde's plight; he sees an advantage in being "in possession" and "refuse[s] to vacate the premises" (222). All the witnesses called in the trial, even those called by the defense, testify to the "absurdity" (224) of Morgan's argument. His own counsel makes a "singularly weak" defense, and then Buncombe closes eloquently, packing his summation with every cherished American ideal. After making a great show of his deliberations, the judge acknowledges that the "overwhelming weight" of the matter "is in favor of the plaintiff Hyde" (225). However, he recognizes that the landslide is a "decree of Heaven . . . with which the sacrilegious hand and brains and tongues of men must not meddle. Gentlemen," he pronounces, "it is the verdict of this court that the plaintiff, Richard Hyde, has been deprived of his ranch by the visitation of God! And from this decision there is no appeal" (225–26). Buncombe, frantic with indignation, visits the judge later that evening urging him to modify his untenable verdict. After further consideration, the judge offers a way out: Hyde, still holding title to the land buried thirty feet under Morgan's land, "had a right to dig it out from under there" (226). Buncombe gives up; two months would pass before he realized that he had been the butt of the legal hoax.

Now, aside from the extended scale of the prank and the coordinated participation from the entire community, its humor relies on the conflation of incompatible property regimes: land versus mining. General Buncombe argues on Hyde's behalf by appealing to the logic of a rancher's title, whereas the judge's "solution," which clinches the joke, is predicated on the mining concept of "extralateral rights" (Liebcap 33). Deep-vein mining claims in the Comstock granted two-hundred-foot slices along the exposed surface but also extended below the surface wherever a miner could follow one's section of the vein, "even below the property of others" (Liebcap 39). So the principle that the judge absurdly applies to the ranchers' dispute derives from the widely embraced logic of the rules established by the various mining districts in the Comstock region. The residents of the territory, ranchers and miners alike, would have understood the fulcrum of the joke, and no doubt found it hilarious that the U.S. Attorney did not perceive that he was being had.

Moreover, Morgan's insistence that he's simply maintaining the rights to the same ranch that he's always had—the same soil thirty feet deep—approximates the basis of Higbie and Clemens's claim in the blind lead by applying a qualitative measure in mineralogical terms. The other humorous facet embedded in the hoax is that Morgan's ranch, defined by law as real—that is, *immovable*—property, has been literally converted to *movable* property by the landslide. But his remark that he thinks his ranch somewhat improved by its new location ignores legal definitions of property in land. His ranch is not defined by the specific soil on which it rests, but as a particular plot determined by specific boundaries defined as measurable distances and by specific angles to each other and in reference to benchmarks. So he might think of his house as his home, but it now lies within the boundaries defined as Hyde's ranch. By law, his "trespass" onto Hyde's ranch exposes him to a liability decision. In effect, Twain's account of the verdict in the hoax reflects what has been called the "fall of vested rights," in which "courts sacrificed holders of stable forms of property to protect investors in dynamic forms of property" (Alexander 185).

If the Lake Tahoe episode demonstrates how the natural disaster of wildfire frustrates property rights, and the Great Landslide hoax shows how terra not-so-firma similarly complicates property rights, Twain remarks on numerous instances where the flooding river in *Life on the Mississippi* entirely confounded property rights, redrawing not only boundaries of individual holdings but also state jurisdictions (24). His recurrence to these natural challenges to civil law registers his interest in how the social discourse is obstructed, exposing the fragility of a system assumed to be permanently sound. To be sure, Morgan's relocated ranch would represent a comic version of "dynamic property," and the privilege that the court's mock verdict accords it underscores how Twain's text plays with the fluid complexities of property-rights theory. The judge's inclination to apply the rights of mining property rather than property in land is a reflection of the legislative myopia of Nevada. "Between 1861 and 1866," the Nevada legislature "passed 47 mineral-rights laws," focusing "on the procedures for arbitrating disputes, and on the evidence that the courts should use in defending property rights from trespass" (Anderson and Hill 118). This surfeit of laws led to a spike in litigation much like the case burlesqued in the hoax.

Still, even in cases where the regulations of the mining property regime would seem to be more clearly applicable, conflicts could and did arise. One such case is Sam Clemens's own brush with impracticalities of mining rules. In a letter to Orion, Sam explained how he and his partners in Clemens Mining Co. discovered that several miners from the Salina Company had taken possession of the Clemens Monitor ledge, refusing to relinquish it and insisting that the Clemens group should not have left if they'd intended to keep possession. Sam reports that he sought legal counsel only to find out that "according to the d—d laws of this forever d—d country," unless the interlopers used violence against them, they had little recourse but to wait them out and take possession when the others left, and hope for justice in a district court that met irregularly (17 May 1862).

These kinds of conflicts between individuals were replicated on a larger scale between Nevada and California. The entire Esmeralda region, and especially its principal town, Aurora, was at the center of a crisis over the boundary between the Golden State and its upstart neighbor. The boundary dispute had a long history, predating the establishment of the Nevada Territory. The language of the Organic Act founding Nevada Territory did little to define more clearly its western border, establishing the ridgeline of the Sierra Nevada as the boundary between the two (Hulse 1:94). The conflict grew intense with escalating expectations that the Esmeralda region would be the site of the next big mining strike. California acted quickly to establish Aurora as the county seat of Mono County in order to confirm its position within state borders. In response, the Nevada legislature commissioned a survey that showed Aurora clearly within its borders, which California rejected as invalid. Aurora shifted between California and Nevada, not by relocation of the town as in the Great Landslide hoax, but by the redrawn border depending on how contesting parties deemed the merits of the survey. Although the two states intermittently resolved their difficulties over a period of years, in 1863 the dispute became hostile to the point of armed skirmishes (Hulse 1:98).[5]

The 1863 "Sagebrush War" took on the sectional affiliations of the Civil War that was roiling the nation far to the east. Myron Angel, Nevada's first historian, notes that one of the region's three nicknames, the "Battle Born State," enshrines its connection with the Civil War (264–67). Nevada historian Effie Mack noted that many influential Southerners had migrated to the far West, bringing their secession ideology with them: "in 1860 the southern sympathizers in California were estimated to be thirty per cent of the population" (269). And others who were not aligned with the Confederacy viewed secession as necessary for the formation of a far West republic of Pacific coast states. Many of the pro-California residents of Aurora were reported to be aggressively pro-Confederacy, so the boundary dispute was breaking across an ideological fault line that divided the nation. In light of this history, *Roughing It*'s relative silence on the Civil War and the brewing antipathies in Nevada is rather curious. Although Twain's text provides a series of episodes that deal with conflicting property rights between individuals and partners, the broader history behind his account shows that sectional animosities not only compounded the tension of speculating mania but also expanded the property dispute into conflicts over state sovereignty and national identity.

Competing Narratives of the Tennessee Land

When the anticipated fortune from the blind lead prompts Twain to divest himself of the Tennessee land, his gesture suggests that the advantages of property in mineral rights have outstripped the merits of the older form of property in land. However, the blind lead's unrealized windfall and Twain's continued interest in the Tennessee land suggest that the value of property in land persists. Still, even the bedrock confidence in the stable value of real estate comes into question when we scrutinize the facts of the Tennessee land.

Much of what has been known about the Tennessee land comes from Twain's autobiographical writings, and his sources appear to be family lore. Just a year before composing *Roughing It*, Twain wrote what is now a well-known early draft of his *Autobiography*, describing his father's Tennessee property as "a monster tract" of "seventy-five thousand acres" that he bought "at one purchase" for "somewhere in the neighborhood of four hundred dollars" (*Autobiography of Mark Twain* [*AMT*] 1:61). This account describes a primal scene of the family's dubious legacy: "When my father paid down that great sum, and turned and stood in the courthouse door of Jamestown, and looked abroad over his vast possessions, he said, 'Whatever befalls me, my heirs are secure; I shall not live to see these acres turn to silver and gold, but my children will.' Thus with the very kindest intentions in the world toward us, he laid the heavy curse of prospective wealth upon our shoulders" (*AMT* 1:61). In a text that the editors of the *Autobiography* call "Random Extracts" written in 1897–1898, Twain recalls "the vast plot of Tennessee land . . . held by my father twenty years—intact" (*AMT* 1:208). He goes on to note how John Clemens's heirs gradually "managed it all away except 10,000 acres," which Orion traded for a house lot that he finally sold in 1894 for $250. Twain concludes, "That ended the Tennessee Land."

Twain and others elaborated this account further. In 1875 a reviewer of *The Gilded Age* in the Cincinnati *Commercial* claimed to have examined records that show the Clemens holdings to have been 80,000 acres. In a 1906 autobiographical dictation, Twain "corrected" the extent of the holdings upward to 100,000 acres (*AMT* 2:21). Lou Budd has noted that "recent estimates put [the Clemens] holdings of undeveloped land in Tennessee at close to 100,000 acres" (2). If those estimates came from sources other than Twain's *Autobiography*, Budd doesn't say. Taken together, these curious reports attest to a gradual expansion of this property by as much as 33 percent without explanation—an odd development, to be sure, especially in the absence of corroboration. And the highest estimate—a conveniently round number—if accurate, would have made John Clemens the owner of nearly one-third of Fentress County. This proportion might lead us to wonder: if he owned such a significant stake, why would he have ever immigrated to Missouri? To ascertain the reliability of this questionable account, research of the Tennessee land records in Fentress County seemed to be a necessary step. The mosaic of available documentary evidence provides a counter-story that reveals both factual errors in Sam Clemens's knowledge and inconsistencies in the Fentress County records themselves. This counter-story points to the likelihood that the Clemens property narrative was a family mythology, one that Twain was varyingly attracted to, circumspect about, and frustrated by.

The documentary records, summarized below, don't simply undermine Twain's account of the Tennessee land, they contradict it.

JOHN MARSHALL CLEMENS'S PROPERTY TRANSACTIONS, FENTRESS CO., TENNESSEE 1827–1842

JMC, et al. (1827–1830)	20 grants (15,150 acres); JMC share	8,758.8 acres
Purchases (1830–1835)		799.125 acres + 4 lots
Sales (1833–1842)		<2,268 acres>
Purchases (1840)		20,200
Correction for Grant #6402 inclusion		<1,666>
	Total	**25,823.9 acres + 4 lots**

The Fentress County deed books and grant ledgers confirm that John Clemens, shortly after arriving in 1827, leveraged his position as county clerk to acquire quite a bit of land, and he continued to acquire or sell land five years after moving his family to Missouri. But contrary to the story that Twain tells, the elder Clemens's land was obtained not in a single large acquisition but through a patchwork of scattered grants and purchases: most of the twenty separate land grants that he claimed from 1827 to 1830 were in the range of 100 to 200 acres. The smallest parcel was 73 acres, and the two largest were 5,000-acre tracts. In fact, Tennessee law allowed a maximum of 5,000 acres in a single grant. One could acquire multiple grants, as John Clemens did, but acquiring a "monster tract" in one transaction was prohibited by the Tennessee land grant system. Also contrary to Twain's account, his father owned seven of his twenty grants jointly with at least one other individual, including the two 5,000-acre grants. The elder Clemens also filed three grants in the name of his son Orion, a child no older than five during this period. In all, John Clemens's share of land grants totaled 8,758.8 acres (including acreage listed under Orion's name). Adding in 1,203 acres and four town lots purchased from individuals between 1830 and 1835, and subtracting 268 acres that he sold (contradicting Twain's assertion that his father held this "vast plot . . . twenty years—intact"), his holdings by 1838 totaled 9,693.8 acres, slightly less than 13 percent of the purported 75,000-acre "monster tract" that Twain recollects.

Orion is listed as co-grantee on one of the early 5,000-acre tracts with his maternal uncle James Lampton and Ben Quarles, probably a relative of Jane Clemens's brother-in-law, John Quarles. Most notable about this shared 5,000-acre tract is its grant number—6402—because this specific grant involves an unusual documentary history. The deed records from 1840 show a transfer of 10,000 acres from James Clemens, Jr., of St. Louis to his uncle John Clemens of Hannibal for one dollar; but, oddly, half of this is also described as originating as Tennessee Grant #6402. And last, in 1867, Orion deeded to his mother a parcel of land totaling 35,000 acres, described as grant #6402, and only eight months later he executed a second deed that revised the volume of this parcel downward, listing the tract as 23,604.5 acres. We're left to wonder how a particular grant could expand from 5,000 acres to 35,000 and then contract by about one-third to the precise measurement of 23,604.5 acres. The Tennessee State Archives, providing yet another story, lists James Clemens, Jr. (John Clemens's nephew) as the claimant of grant #6402 in 1827, three years before the claim by Orion and others was recorded. So the 1830 claim on this original 5,000-acre grant by two-year-old Orion and a pair of distant relatives appears to have been achieved by an "irregularity" in the records, records that John Clemens was responsible for maintaining.

To complicate matters, the Tennessee Land Grant Index lists only fifteen grants, not twenty, in John M. Clemens's name (spelled variously) totaling 7,441.8 acres, 1,300 fewer acres than are accounted for in the Fentress County Records. To be sure, the accuracy of Fentress County grant records and the State Grant Index were compromised by several factors. Some antebellum records did not survive the Civil War, and many of the Fentress records were transcribed as a WPA project in 1934. In their introduction to *Tennessee Land Grants*, Barbara Byron and Samuel Sistler openly acknowledge the impossibility of compiling a definitive list of grants: "The Tennessee land grant system was marked at its inception by confusion, fraud and litigation" (I, n.p.). Furthermore, the Mountain District in which Fentress County lay, they admit, "perhaps more than any other, was subject to gross fraud and speculative abuse in the issuance of grants." Old records can also yield other surprising discoveries: in 2013 the Fentress County registrar, Loyce Faye Stephens, found a reference to an 1872 chancery court decision that awarded 5,000 acres to the Clemens family based on corroborating testimony confirming that John Clemens had purchased the parcel in 1840, even though either the transaction was never registered or its record was lost. This may not have been as unusual as it appears; the Fentress records often show a lengthy delay—sometimes as long as a year—between a transaction and its official registration. Still, while the corruption in the land grant system and the lack of registration cited in the chancery court decision confirm the inherent unreliability of documentary sources, these factors don't account for the erroneous provenance of grant #6402 and its curious role in the Clemens family's mythology. When a 5,000-acre grant in 1827 miraculously expands to encompass as much 35,000 acres in Orion's deed to his mother thirty-seven years later, it is highly likely that exponential exaggeration, like that of Colonel Sellers in *The Gilded Age*, is at work.

Despite the uncertainty of the Fentress County records, we can add several other known acquisitions by John Clemens to the tally: two purchases both in 1840, five years after the family moved to Missouri, equaling a combined 5,200 acres. Adding these and the recent discovery of the 5,000 acres confirmed in the 1872 chancery court decision to the balance of his other grants and transactions, and adjusting for the third of the acreage in grant #6402 that was attributed to Orion, we can account for total holdings slightly under 26,000 acres before the family embarks on a gradual sell-off. If the Tennessee State Land Grant Index has greater validity, the total decreases to about 24,500 acres. The documents confirm that John Clemens was a man with an appetite for land. However, the galvanizing story of his legacy as a magnanimous gesture to his children is a rather extravagant fiction.

The records do not present an irrefutable history of their own; rather, they point to inaccurate measurements, imperfect record keeping, and perhaps utter fabrications through which land was claimed. Property narratives that depend on unreliable surveys, erroneous titles, and unclear paper trails assert ownership that is merely contingent. Given that the existing records are incomplete or imprecise, the only safe conclusion to draw from the family's property history is that ownership rights are as unstable as the language in which they are expressed, or as fragile as the documents that are intended to secure them.

Orion, who investigated the Tennessee land more than any other member of the family, understood that their holdings were not as secure as the family had believed. However, he contended that the trouble stemmed from the state of Tennessee granting the same land to different claimants (*Mark Twain's Letters*,[6] Orion Clemens to SLC 7 July 1869). This could have been what occurred in a case like grant #6402, except that the State of Tennessee does not appear to be culpable for the duplicate grant or in the expansion of the volume of land assigned to it. Indeed, in a number of instances, Orion himself erroneously assumed title to five parcels that were entered to other grantees or deed holders, though John Clemens was listed as "Locator"—that is, surveyor. As both an active speculator and county clerk, the elder Clemens had measured quite a bit of Fentress County, but locating a parcel does not confer title. Orion's error inflated the family's account of their holdings by nearly 25,000 acres.

After John Clemens's death, his heirs fended off poverty by selling acreage piecemeal, just as the patriarch had obtained it, and always at a fraction of the value they anticipated. Orion or agents he'd empowered executed some nineteen transactions over thirty-five years, conveying to other hands more than 44,000 acres—and it now seems almost certain that some of this acreage was property to which the Clemenses had no clear title.

Twain's satire of speculation in *The Gilded Age* might encourage us to see him as immune to the family's obsession with the land. In that text, the reluctant bargainer Washington Hawkins repeatedly refuses reasonable offers on the family Tennessee land that he views as lowball bids. In a letter to Howells, Twain admits the similarity between the fictional Hawkins and his own brother Orion (10 May 1874). But Sam Clemens's own indulgence in the speculating mania in the Comstock Lode indicates that he could be just as inflamed by speculation as his brother. Sam's interest in the Tennessee land varied according to his circumstances. While he later criticized Orion for clinging to the fantasy of the land's value, he had at times assumed—eagerly, if not desperately—that the Tennessee land would yield a fortune if effectively managed. Writing from Nevada to Orion in 1865, he gushed enthusiastically about a prospect to sell the Tennessee land to Herman Camp for $200,000. The prospective buyer was a Nevada mining speculator with whom Sam had once passed up a lucrative opportunity to sell mining stocks in New York. Having once viewed Camp as savvy, Sam now saw him as a savior. He chided Orion, "Now I don't want that Tenn land to go for taxes, & I don't want any 'slouch' to take charge of the sale of it. I am tired being a beggar—tired being chained to this accursed homeless desert,—I want to go back to a Christian land once more—& so I want you to send me immediately all necessary memoranda to enable Camp to understand the condition, & quantity & resources of the land, & how he must go about finding it" (13 December 1865). In the *Autobiography*, Twain contends that Orion blocked the deal because Camp planned to develop a winery on the acreage, ostensibly offending Orion's temperance sensibilities (*AMT* 1:63). But Camp never visited Tennessee to assess the land, so it's not clear that Orion's scruples had anything to do with why they failed to execute the deal. Indeed, Sam's expectation that "the condition, & quantity & resources of the land" could be easily documented was unrealistic.

Sam's resentment of Orion smoldered. Writing six months later from Honolulu, he complained to Mollie, Orion's wife, and blamed his own continued poverty on Orion: "It is Orion's duty to attend to that land, & after shutting me out of my attempt to sell it (for which I shall never entirely forgive him,) if he lets it be sold for taxes, all his religion will not wipe out the sin. It is no use to quote Scripture to me, Mollie, I am in poverty & exile now because of Orion's religious scruples. . . . I am satisfied Orion will eventually save himself, but in doing it he will damn the balance of the family. . . . He has got a duty to perform by us—will he perform it?" (22 May 1866). Desperation gave rise to persistent anger at the failed deal, goading Sam to describe his sojourn in Hawaii not as an exotic excursion in an island paradise but as a dreary hardship, "drifting on the outskirts of the world, battling for bread." In the next breath, he complains that as a castaway far from civilization, he is unable to stop Beadle from pirating some of his sketches. In other words, he is weaving a new chapter to this property narrative in which he blames Orion of depriving him of valuable property in two ways: by blocking the land deal that Sam eagerly wanted, Orion has deprived him of profit from the sale of the land, and this has consequently forced Sam to wander remote Pacific islands where he is unable to defend his copyrights. Sam's tendency to conflate real property with literary product here is the first note of a refrain that will echo later in his life.

Slightly more than two years later, the pendulum of fortune swings in the other direction, and Sam sees even brighter prospects looming in the foreseeable future. In a letter to his sister, Pamela, written from his new perch in the East on the verge of marrying into polite society, he drops the names of the illustrious people he's met, offers details of his business plans—he's hoping to buy a stake in a Cleveland daily for $60,000 (of Jervis Langdon's money)—and announces that the first edition of *The Innocents Abroad* (a run of twenty thousand copies) is at press. Not having mentioned the Tennessee land in two and a half years, he now finds that selling what's left of it to Langdon for $30,000 would be acceptable. With his literary and business prospects glowing before him, Sam reasons, "The rest of us might afford to hold on for higher prices, but Ma can't—she is growing old, & I do wish I could see her in liberal circumstances," exhibiting a generosity similar to his charity in the flush of the blind lead (23 June 1869). When times were good for Sam, he either forgot about the Tennessee land or could easily agree to dispose of it without much concern for the terms. To be sure, in light of his report that Langdon thought that parting with it for such a discounted price would be "unfortunate," it's entirely possible that Sam Clemens viewed this discount sale as a good-faith, reciprocal gesture for the newspaper investment that Langdon was about to make on his behalf. Yet even this supposedly discounted valuation of $30,000 was considerably inflated. Orion certainly seemed to think so. He cautioned Sam, "Neither you nor Ma nor Pamela know anything about the land. . . . I have laboriously investigated the titles, localities and qualities, and I would put its present value at about five thousand dollars" (*MTL*, Orion Clemens to SLC 7 July 1869). Consequently, Orion blocked Sam's plan to sell the land to Langdon in order to prevent his younger brother from "unconsciously cheat[ing]" his "prospective father-in-law" (*MTL*, Orion Clemens to SLC, 4 November 1880). In direct contrast to Twain's portrait of his older brother as a foolish dreamer, Orion appears to have been the prudent one in this case, protecting Sam from spinning the property narrative in a dangerous direction. As Mark Twain, however, he will find a way to spin the Tennessee land into profitable form as narrative property.

Recasting the Property Narrative

By 1873 Twain had solidified his literary prospects into genuine prosperity and social acceptance. Accordingly, the joint venture with Warner on *The Gilded Age* reflects a degree of ironic distance from the disappointment of the Tennessee land and makes the family legacy, as one reviewer noted, "not simply one of Twain's jokes, but the groundwork of the whole story" (Cincinnati *Commercial*, 25 November 1875). The epigraphs introducing chapter 1 announce the centrality of property to the narrative. The first is a Chippewa adage meaning "He owns much land"; the second, without attribution, reads, "A gallant tract of land it is!"; and the third, from Meercraft, the devious contriver of many get-rich-quick schemes in Ben Jonson's *The Devil Is an Ass*, alludes to a questionable real estate deal (17). The winking irony in the polyglot epigraphs emphasizes landholding and unscrupulous profit at the outset. The story that follows makes nineteen different references to the Hawkins family's Tennessee land, repeatedly satirizing the speculation mania that had infected the Clemens family, as well as the political corruption of the Reconstruction era. The Hawkins family fortunes become entangled in Senator Dilworthy's scheme of Negro philanthropy, with the proposal that the Hawkins acreage be purchased for Knobs Industrial University, modeled on Hampton Institute. The exposure of Dilworthy's corruption brings the shaky enterprise to ruin. Having seen his folly, Washington Hawkins vows, "I am going to begin my life over again, and begin it and end it with good solid work! I'll leave *my* children no Tennessee Land!" (557). He lets the property go for unpaid taxes—the same fate that Sam Clemens had worried would befall his family's land.

While this narrative turn rejects the "heavy curse of prospective wealth" that Twain describes as his father's "burden" on the family, not all speculation is foolish. In an addendum to the preface of the British edition of the novel, Twain describes speculation as "a characteristic which is both bad and good, for both the individual and the nation. . . . Still, it is a trait which is of course better for a people to have and sometimes suffer from than to be without" (n.p.). The novel's stalwart Philip Sterling, his name assuring the value of his character, embodies the salutary form of speculation. He ultimately strikes it rich in a coal mine, after having exhausted his prospective father-in-law's investment in it. Although this character was Warner's contribution, it resonates with Sam Clemens's biography both in his mining experience and his flirtation with selling the Tennessee land to his coal-baron prospective father-in-law. If there is a parallel to be found here, however, it lies in Sterling's successful speculation as a reflection of Twain's imaginative speculation in the popular literary marketplace.

Even more striking are Twain's reflections on writing "in partnership" with Warner. He described their division of labor somewhat humbly to David Croly, explaining that Warner "has worked up the fiction & I have hurled in the facts" (17 April 1873). But this account itself shows his greater facility with fiction than fact. His responsibility for the novel's conception and execution was far greater than he admits. Privately, he came to see the novel as a kind of proprietary venture, while still honoring the spirit of partnership. For example, in a letter to Livy, he comments on his need to step in to supply a description of Laura Hawkins, the novel's tragic heroine, because Warner's efforts were, in Twain's assessment, obvious "plagiarism" of Constance Fenimore Woolson's style (26 April 1873), suggesting both a lack of literary originality and a property violation in Warner's imitative prose. To resolve the problem, they each wrote a version, and, Twain reports, "mine being rather the best, we used it." The coauthors agreed to produce the climax chapter by a similar competition to be judged by their wives, as Clemens explains in a letter to Mary Fairbanks on the eve of the test readings: "the man who has written it best is all right—the other man's MS. will be torn up. If *neither* succeeds, we'll both write the chapter over again" (16 April 1873). Reporting in a postscript added before posting the letter, "My climax chapter is the one accepted by Livy & Susie [Warner]," Twain was eager not only to boast of his success but also to stake a claim to this important narrative territory. Indeed, an unsigned review in the *Scotsman* credits Twain's portion of the novel and questions the decision to write "in double harness," given the unevenness of the joint venture. The reviewer observes that "[Twain's] method or plan, his style, his humour, *belong entirely, or very much, to himself,*" highlighting his distinctive sense of humor as a kind of property (2). *The Gilded Age*, according to Twain's implied proprietary logic, enabled him to convert the Tennessee land disappointment into the production of valuable literary property, just as he had done in reclaiming failed mining adventures as the material of narrative art in *Roughing It*. In the *Autobiography*, he confirms this transformation of failed land speculation into narrative success by reflecting on the fact that his fictional use of the land in *The Gilded Age* netted him $20,000 in print and another $75,000 from the theatrical production. He calculates or, given what we now know about the diminished acreage, undercalculates the value as "just about one dollar an acre" and underscores the irony that he "was the only member of the family that ever profited" by the Tennessee land (*AMT* 1:209).

It would be a tidy gesture of closure if the tangled story of the Tennessee land were to end with Twain having transferred his conceptions of property from land to the products of his imagination. But he didn't entirely turn his back on the Tennessee land as real estate. In 1907 he and his sister Pamela's children, Annie Webster and Sam Moffett, were surprised to learn that a small number of scattered acres remained in their possession as heirs to John Clemens, and they promptly sold them to a development company. In short order, though, some residents of Fentress County, disputing the Clemens title, blocked the sale. Clemens and his niece and nephew joined with the company to whom they had sold the land in a suit against those who opposed them, but, as legal proceedings so often do, the case dragged on until 1912, two years after Clemens died, and four years after Sam Moffett died by drowning. The Clemens case was ruled a non-suit when the defendants successfully countered that it had been filed in a district with no jurisdiction, and the plaintiffs were ordered to pay defendants' costs.[7] Thus, the nearly ninety-year saga of the Tennessee land was punctuated with a rather quiet conclusion.

There is one final property narrative to consider here, though it bears on the Tennessee land only indirectly. In the Ashcroft-Lyon manuscript, Twain alleges that Isabel Lyon had, among other betrayals, expropriated at least ten acres of land from his 200-acre Stormfield estate. As he wrote, "when I gave her the house and 'five or ten' acres of land, she lifted ten more out of me, & put it in the deed" (*AMT* 3:333). He readily admits to having noticed the twenty acres on the deed and to signing it anyway because, he confides, "I was ashamed of *myself* for not having thought of making the allotment

20 acres in the first place. I felt just the shame a person feels who is caught in a stinginess." Then he backtracks, complaining, "But damnation, I had never been used to 20-acre ownerships!" He contrasts the twenty-acre parcel deeded to Lyon with the half-acre Buffalo lot on which he and Livy began their marriage, then remarks that the Langdons' spacious grounds in Elmira were only three acres, as was the whole of his Hartford homestead, and his Tarrytown and Riverdale homes were five and four acres respectively: "And so my old habit of mind was land-stingy, & thought I was pretty liberal in giving away 'five or ten' acres all in one great pile; indeed I was privately proud of myself. But she—well, she knew me. She knew she could pump ten or fifteen extra acres into the deed & I would sign and say nothing" (*AMT* 3:334). Given the controversy surrounding the Ashcroft-Lyon manuscript and its accusations that his once-trusted advisors conspired against him, even hypnotized him, to obtain fraudulent control of his property—manuscripts, copyrights as well as real estate—we should treat this recollection with caution. In playing up how his habit of mind made him susceptible to Ashcroft and Lyons's alleged duplicity, he had an interest in minimizing his real estate experience. But it is certainly surprising that in his mental inventory of his various property holdings, he makes no mention of the "monster tract" in Tennessee, especially in light of his having included it in his autobiographical dictations as late as 1906. Indeed, he was at this time embroiled in litigation over scattered remnants believed to be a couple of thousand acres. A tract that had played such a persistent role in his family's habit of mind, and that he once believed to be 75,000 or even 100,000 acres, is a curious omission when tallying up his earlier holdings of between one-half acre and five acres as context for a dispute over "ten or fifteen" acres.

Several competing interpretations are in play here. The most cynical conclusion would be that Clemens willfully omitted the Tennessee land, thus underplaying his experience with property in order to reinforce his role as victim in the Ashcroft-Lyon scandal. A more generous reading would conclude that the trauma of realizing how vulnerable he was to losing all his actual property created the opportunity of freeing himself of the Tennessee land's curse of imagined property even before the lawsuit had fully unwound the matter. The last, and to my mind most interesting, prospect withholds judgment about the omission and instead acknowledges that the rhetorical conditions of ownership are readily legible in this last of a series of unstable property narratives. Still more poignant is the claim to identity that he performs in this account. For Clemens, his former confidants' alleged land grab is not about the actual acreage or its market value but about a violation of his trust and of his autonomy. Accusing Ashcroft and Lyon of hypnotizing him and of extracting a sweeping power of attorney by subterfuge,

Clemens condemns them for having usurped his rights to control his own affairs, and to exercise the power of his own name and, more importantly, the pen name that he adopted and had registered as a trademark. For it was as Mark Twain that he claimed title to literary property both as products of his imagination and as renewable commodities in print culture. In the end, the Tennessee land was gone, much like the blind lead, but from those experiences he fashioned an identity brought forth in narratives. Had he lost his identity—his property in himself—and the rights to the narratives through which this identity took shape, there would be no other narrative to imagine, and thus no opportunity to recover from such a fatal loss. In the construction and control of his identity and the literary property attached to it, Twain had sought, like his father before him, to leave an intergenerational legacy for his heirs. In having escaped the danger of losing it all, he composed the Ashcroft-Lyon manuscript as a final melodramatic narrative that reasserts his ownership of his legacy.

Notes

1. Many thanks to John Bird, Jim Caron, Ben Click, Kerry Driscoll, Jim Leonard, Bruce Michelson, Linda Morris, Ann Ryan, Gary Scharnhorst, and Harry Wonham for their interest, and to the Mark Twain Circle for support of this ongoing project; to my Roosevelt colleagues Priscilla Archibald, Gina Buccola, and Ji-Hyae Park, whose critical reading of a very early stage helped shape what appears here; to Barbara Snedecor and the Elmira College Center for Mark Twain Studies for a Quarry Farm residency; to Bob Hirst, Vic Fisher, and the editors and staff of the Mark Twain Papers for their expertise and wisdom; to Faye Stephens, Fentress County Registrar of Deeds, for archival assistance; to the Newberry Library for the support provided while a scholar-in-residence; to the Danish-American Fulbright Commission, and to my colleagues in the American Studies Program at the University of Southern Denmark–Odense.

2. While it may seem distracting to those not familiar with the critical convention, I distinguish throughout the chapter between the man Sam Clemens and the writer Mark Twain. Although the biographical man often overlaps with his literary persona, the distinction between the historical man and the textual representation of himself in writings authored under that name is a crucial, if occasionally subtle, one.

3. In this regard, my analysis draws from the insights of what was called "New Economic Criticism" a couple of decades ago (Osteen and Woodmansee 3–50). This form of New Historicism intersects with innovative analyses of economics as a discipline that is shot through with rhetorical tensions. I am grateful to my Roosevelt colleague Steve Ziliak for his insights about economics and rhetoric.

4. The balancing of individual and community benefits is an example of two

conceptions of property that Gregory Alexander investigates. The concept of property as "commodity" appeals to the rights of the individual to profit from one's use or sale of property, whereas the concept of property as "propriety" entails the ways in which the community benefits from regulations governing certain uses for the greater good.

5. Definitive settlement of the boundary question did not arrive until a 1980 U.S. Supreme Court decision terminated the question (Hulse pt. 2:176–78).

6. Letters available online are cited by date alone; those not yet digitized are cited as MTL, followed by the correspondents and the date.

7. In an ironic turn worthy of a sensational novel, the lead defendant in this suit, Bruno Gernt, was a land speculator who had acquired very large portions of Fentress County for delinquent taxes. Today, Gernt's descendants own a near majority of the total of Fentress County, so John Clemens's goal appears to have been achieved by a land speculator responsible for putting the end point on the Clemens stake.

Works Cited

Adams, James Truslow. *The Epic of America*. Boston: Little Brown, 1931.

Alexander, Gregory. *Commodity and Propriety: Competing Visions of Property in American Legal Thought, 1776–1970*. Chicago: U of Chicago P, 1997.

Anderson, Terry L., and Peter J. Hill. *The Not So Wild, Wild West: Property Rights on the Frontier*. Stanford: Stanford UP, 2004.

Angel, Myron. *The History of Nevada*. Oakland, CA: Thompson & West, 1881.

Blackstone, William. *Commentaries on the Laws of England*. 4 vols. London: Brooke, 1811.

Budd, Louis. *Mark Twain: Social Philosopher*. Bloomington: Indiana UP, 1962.

Byron, Barbara, and Samuel Sistler. *Tennessee Land Grants*. Nashville: Byron, Sistler and Associates, 1998.

Cincinnati *Commercial*, 25 November 1875; transcript in Mark Twain's Papers, Berkeley, California.

Emerson, Ralph Waldo. *Nature. Emerson, Essays and Lectures*. New York: Library of America, 1983.

Fentress County Registry of Deeds, Jamestown, Tennessee.

Hulse, James W. "The California-Nevada Boundary: History of a Conflict," Part 1. *Nevada Historical Society Quarterly* 23.2 (Summer 1980): 87–109; Part 2. 23.3 (Fall 1980): 157–78.

Kent, James. *Commentaries on American Law*. 4 vols. Philadelphia: Blackstone, 1889.

Liebcap, Gary D. *Contracting for Property Rights*. New York: Cambridge UP, 1994.

Lincoln, Abraham. *Collected Works of Abraham Lincoln*. Ed. Roy Baler et al. New Brunswick: Rutgers UP, 1953.

"Literature." *Scotsman*, 9 January 1874.

Locke, John. *Two Treatises of Government*. Ed. Thomas I. Cook. New York: Hafner, 1947.

Mack, Effie Mona. *Nevada; a History of the State from the Earliest Times through the Civil War*. Glendale: Arthur H. Clark, 1936.

Osteen, Mark, and Martha Woodmansee. "Taking Account of the New Economic Criticism: An Historical Introduction." *The New Economic Criticism*. Ed. Martha Woodmansee and Mark Osteen. London: Routledge, 1999. 3–50.

Rose, Carol. *Property and Persuasion: Essays on the History, Theory, and Rhetoric of Ownership*. Boulder: Westview, 1994.

Singer, Joseph William. "Property and Social Relations: From Title to Entitlement." *Property and Values: Alternatives to Private and Public Ownership*. Ed. Charles Geisler and Gail Daneker. Washington: Island Press, 2000.

Tocqueville, Alexis de. *Democracy in America*. Trans. George Lawrence. Ed. J. P. Mayer. Garden City: Doubleday Anchor, 1969.

Twain, Mark. "Ashcroft-Lyon Manuscript." In *Autobiography of Mark Twain*. Vol. 3.

———. *Autobiography of Mark Twain*. 3 vols. Ed. Harriet Elinor Smith et al. Berkeley: U of California P, 2010, 2012, 2015.

———. *Extracts from Adam's Diary*. 1904. In *The Diaries of Adam and Eve*. New York: Oxford UP, 1996.

———. *Life on the Mississippi*. 1883. New York: Oxford UP, 1996.

———. *Mark Twain's Letters*. Mark Twain Project. <www.marktwainproject.org>.

———. *Roughing It*. 1872. Berkeley: U of California P, 1993.

Twain, Mark, and Charles Dudley Warner. *The Gilded Age*. 1873. New York: Oxford UP, 1996.

———. *The Gilded Age*. 1873. London: Chatto and Windus, 1897.

2
Brand Management

Samuel Clemens, Trademarks, and the Mark Twain Enterprise

Judith Yaross Lee

Samuel L. Clemens died a rich man, leaving an estate of more than $600,000 in 1910 (over $15 million in 2014 dollars)—a success all the more remarkable in light of his many famous losses, both small (the Kaolatype swindle and the Scott embezzlement) and large (the Paige compositor and the bankruptcy of Charles L. Webster & Co.). His triumphs as Mark Twain, on the other hand, set him apart from authors like Herman Melville, with his famous 1851 lament to Nathaniel Hawthorne, "dollars damn me" (Parker 841), and E. C. Stedman, who complained at the 1886 annual dinner of the Typothetae of New York City: "We professional authors are looking for spoils, and we haven't yet gotten our fair share. The publisher takes 60 per cent of the proceeds, gives 30 to the printer, and generously leaves the author 10. The only safe plan for us is to turn publisher like Mark Twain" ("Disciples" 5). Turning publisher, however, was just one part of a larger strategy by which Clemens directed the Mark Twain business enterprise through what we would now call *brand management*: he carefully mined, deployed, and directed the commercial value of his products (especially his copyrighted works) and his reputation (which he saw as a business asset). His strategy took two main tacks. In one, known today as *brand extension*, he projected his professional identity as a humorous writer and speaker onto other commercial ventures, riding the wave of branded goods and attendant marketing fueled by America's post–Civil War commercial and media expansions and assisted by new trademark laws beginning in 1870. Mark Twain's Patent Scrap Book (patented 1873) and *Mark Twain's Library of Humor* (1888), among other branded products and activities, belonged to this approach, which culminated in the copyright-management strategies of the Mark Twain Company (1908). The other approach, by contrast, entailed distancing activities from his role as Mark Twain, mainly by spinning them off, as we would say today, under other labels, as with the anonymously serialized *Personal Recollections of Joan of Arc* (1896) and the imprint of Charles L. Webster & Company (1884–1894), though occasionally by suppressing them altogether. While both tacks showed marketing savvy well ahead of his time, protecting his enterprises from unprofitable controversy and exploiting his name when worthwhile, they sometimes impeded one another. Just as he eventually claimed credit for *Joan of Arc*, so he had his hands all over Webster & Co., contributing not only to the departure of its overworked and ill namesake, but also to the demise that caused his thoroughly public humiliation during the depression following the Panic of 1893. Across both strategies and their mixed outcomes, however, the quests to expand his income and protect it from pirates and other profiteers proved the value of the Mark Twain brand.

I use the terms *brand* and *brand management* to invoke Mark Twain's approach to economic activity, rather than as metaphors for reputation or synonyms for celebrity. Brands serve three distinct but interrelated information functions: *denotation*, by naming a good or service or image; *differentiation*, by distinguishing one from another; and *connotation*, by symbolizing a set of associated ideas.[1] The branding process fuses these functions semiotically and creates the financial asset known as *brand equity* by converting intangible meanings into tangible value. Today, trademark registration recognizes and protects brand equity as a form of property, but these benefits came too late for Clemens to exploit. Brand names and trademarks exploded in the United States after Congress took action in 1870, near the start of his most productive years as Mark Twain, swelling tenfold between 1871 and 1875 (from 121 to 1,138) and another tenfold by 1883 (Hartman Center; Ohmann 101). He did not lobby Congress on trademarks as he eventually did on copyrights, but he vigorously policed his brand from the 1870s on, challenging what he saw as trademark violations through lawsuits and public complaints.

Behind these efforts lay a conception of his writing and performances, and the comic persona animating them, as commodities for sale. Early jobs that paid him by the piece—by the em, as a printer; the voyage, as a river pilot; the ounce, as a miner; the column, as a journalist; the performance, as a lecturer—may have led him to see authorship in commercial terms, as Alan Gribben has suggested ("Mark Twain" 32). Whatever the reason, Clemens early understood Mark Twain, like other *lyceum personae*, as "a piece of lecturing property" (Clemens to H. M. Stanley), and he jealously guarded the texts of his performances and writings as economic assets, especially after the "Jumping Frog" tale (1865) and the Sandwich Islands lecture (1866–1867) appeared verbatim in newspapers, costing him their copyrights. His era rewarded such a conception. The lecture circuit belonged to the changing post–Civil War economy, when publishing of all sorts boomed and consumer marketing transformed pleasure itself into a commodity—one more mass-marketed good or service hawked in a self-sustaining cycle by commercial mass media, as William Leach has shown (3, 150). By insisting on the commodity value of his work and his ownership as a brand, Clemens may have led what Loren Glass calls "a fundamental transformation . . . in our basic understanding of literary property," although repeated failure in the courts shows that he consistently misunderstood this transformation (79). His conflation of copyright and trademark confused contents with their labels, whose unique design might deserve copyright protection as creative property, but which otherwise merely name the product thereby labeled. His efforts remain notable, however, for their persistence and modernity. It would be surprising indeed had the coauthor of the era's most cynical economic novel, *The Gilded Age* (1873), failed to commodify his own economic activities and their personification in Mark Twain.

Success as a comic performer played an essential role in this process. Like stand-up comedians today, Samuel Clemens had to cultivate and project a distinct, consistent comic identity—that is, a unique brand of humor—in order to move into the figurative and literal spotlight that meant profit in the marketplace. The pseudonym served those denotative, distinguishing, and connotative branding functions by which Clemens reported Mark Twain's experiences in comic newspaper features, then turned those pieces into lectures, lectures into books, books back into performances, and all these activities into cash and fame. The process thus replicated and reinforced the overlap between self-presentation and public reputation, two elements of selfhood that media scholar Eric Rothenbuhler has identified in another context as central to Americans' "cult of the individual" (96). The post–Civil War period gave a new push to the mythology of the self-made man, which mass media and celebrity furthered in the self-perpetuating cycle that made Mark Twain a topic of countless media productions, as well as a contributor to and publisher of them. Yet Clemens's commercial exploitation of the comic confusion between Mark Twain's self-presentation and public reputation also demonstrates this cycle more literally. His career as a writer exemplifies Rothenbuhler's claim that "reputation . . . [is] a key currency in the cult of the individual" as practiced in the age of modern American media (96, 95). The American fetish of the individual therefore finds an appropriate outlet in stand-up comedy, even as it further pressures each comedian to cultivate a unique comic identity as a commodity. Though Artemus Ward (Charles Farrar Browne) and other so-called Phunny Phellows preceded Mark Twain as pseudonymous literary clowns, his persona differed from theirs in the degree to which Clemens performed a pseudo-autobiographical comic self, based on an unstable equation of persona and person. Ward and Petroleum V. Nasby (David Ross Locke) never disappeared behind their creations as Clemens did; much like modern observational or confessional stand-up comedians, he appeared to express himself through his humor, rather than to portray a role.

Performances—on page, stage, and in public—thus constituted Mark Twain as a self, a product, and a brand. Through the constructivist logic that perception creates reality, the merger of Samuel Clemens and Mark Twain exploited the very principles behind twenty-first-century branding, while playing out the pragmatist tenets that his contemporary William James began developing in the 1870s. "By its very essence, the reality of a thought is proportionate to the way it grasps us," James argued in 1878 ("Remarks" 17), anticipating his larger argument in *Principles of Psychology* (1890) that social interaction creates the fiction of a coherent self and identity: "A man has as many social selves as there are individuals who recognize him," but they coalesce by inference into one "*self*-brand" by the same logic that cattle bearing the same ownership marking represent one "herd brand" (*Principles* 1:294, 337). In this vein, the Mark Twain brand hinged on more than a memorable pen name and distinctive comic persona; it involved creating, commercializing, and steering the Mark Twain identity as a business asset, as Clemens sought to do from the start of his career.

Brand equity thus topped his concerns. As early as 1872, he lobbed a public "blast" (as he put it to his wife) at the notorious British copyright pirate John Hotten for harming the Mark Twain brand (*Mark Twain's Letters* [*MTL*] 5:169). At least seven pirated British editions had appeared by then, but Hotten's 1871 collection *Screamers: A Gathering of Some Scraps of Humour, Delicious Bits, & Short Stories* particularly enraged Clemens by attributing other writers' works to him. "My books are bad enough just as they are written," he complained in the 21 September 1872 London *Spectator*; "then what must they be after Mr. John Camden Hotten has composed half-a-dozen chapters & added the same to them? . . . & then, on the strength of having evolved these marvels from his own consciousness, go & 'copyright' the entire book . . . ?" To drive home the point, he imagined a fitting colophon for the pirate: "a picture of a man with his hand in another man's pocket, & the legend 'All Rights Reserved'" (Twain, "Mark Twain and His English Editor" 14). The fantasy highlights how thoroughly Clemens linked the commercial tradition of trademark, long used to authenticate silver and other handiwork—potters' marks date back thousands of years (Schechter 20)—with the textual tradition of copyright protection.

In fact, in an 1879 notebook entry he credited himself with having "really established international copyright" in *Clemens v. Such* (New York, 1873), a trademark case decided in his favor, although he won just $10 for court costs (*Mark Twain's Notebooks & Journals* [*MTNJ*] 2:307; Feinstein 42–44). The judgment upheld the publisher's contract for one Mark Twain sketch and prohibited further sale of the disputed volume (*MTL* 5:368, 370n5). The suit had sought $25,000 in damages based on two claims, both revived a decade later in *Clemens v. Belford*: that a pseudonym constitutes a trademark, and that Mark Twain's pseudonym had a monetary (equity) value to Clemens that warranted management and protection. "My sketches are copyrighted in my own name," he asserted in his handwritten affidavit to the court on 16 May 1873. "I consider a volume of them worth (to me) not less than $25,000, & certainly would not publish a volume of them unless I felt sure of getting that much for it—one of my reasons being that I consider that an author cannot bunch a mass of disconnected humorous sketches together & publish the same without sickening the public stomach & damaging his own reputation" (Feinstein 20–21).

The problem for the courts in *Clemens v. Such* and *Clemens v. Belford* hinged on differences between trademarks and copyright. The 41st Congress created the confusion when it passed the 1870 Act to Amend, Revise, and Consolidate Patents and Copyrights (16 Stat. 198), the first U.S. trademark law, which sandwiched a mere eight sections on trademarks (§77–84) into 103 sections detailing changes to patents and copyrights, effectively conflating all three categories. The U.S. Supreme Court struck down the act's provisions in the Trade-Mark Cases of 1879, partly because the law as written lacked a constitutional basis in the commerce clause, but chiefly because it held that a trademark is not intellectual property: "A trade-mark is neither an invention, a discovery, nor a writing, within the meaning of the eighth clause of the eighth section of the first article of the Constitution, which confers on Congress power to secure for limited times to authors and inventors the exclusive right to their respective writings and discoveries" (100 U.S. 82). A new trademark law passed in March of 1881 offered little improvement, except in international trade and trade with Indian nations; indeed, although the United States joined the International Convention for the Protection of Industrial Property in 1887, functional domestic trademark protection at the federal level did not exist until 1905, when Congress finally provided for trademarks used in interstate commerce (United States, *Story* 16–17, 20). In the meantime, newspapers of the day noted both the contested cases and new registrations that demonstrated the growing importance of brands in American commerce.

Trademark infringement in the nineteenth century typically meant fraud. Alcoholic drinks and patent medicine raised urgent concerns, because the markings or labels on their barrels and bottles provided the chief guarantee of their contents' origins, thereby attesting to their authenticity, quality, and safety. Of the three 1879 trademark cases (*U.S. v. Steffans*, *U.S. v. White-*

mann, and *U.S. v. Johnson*), two concerned counterfeit Mumm and Piper Heidsick champagnes, and the third, counterfeit OK brand whiskey. Contemporary newspapers from coast to coast regularly carried details of less notable suits over trademark infringement. In January 1872 the San Francisco *Daily Evening Bulletin* reported "another suit for infringement," this time by John F. Cutter of Moorman & Co. (Louisville), who asked the court for a "pro-rata share of profits on whiskey sold under the Cutter brand" by "wrongfully using Moorman & Co.'s brand and barrel" ("Whiskey Men"). The example shows that by 1872 brands already functioned to connote quality, not simply to denote contents and differentiate origins.

Lawsuits like these provide the context for Clemens's sense of insult and offense at having unauthorized editions of his work sold under his name. But the same background allowed him to joke in earnest, while in Canada to secure a British copyright for *The Prince and the Pauper* (1882), that "literary property . . . [should] be as sacred as whisky": "if you steal another man's label to advertise your own brand of whisky with, you will be heavily fined and otherwise punished for violating that trademark; if you steal the whisky without the trademark, you go to jail; but if you could prove that the whisky was literature, you can steal them both, and the law wouldn't say a word. It grieves me to think how far more profound and reverent a respect the law would have for literature if a body could only get drunk on it" ("Mark Twain in Montreal"). Such a joking equation of label, whiskey, and literature shows how well Clemens understood the information economy emerging in the years after the Civil War. Compared to an industrial economy, an information economy trades in intellectual property (such as copyrights and patents) and human knowledge (including comic skill and media know-how), instead of material goods (such as paper and ink). He played out this understanding when he combined comic performance, copyright protection, political advocacy, and a sales pitch for his new book in a highly public Canadian visit: "I never saw that box of dynamite till the Police came to inquire whether I had any more of it," he deadpanned to his audience in Montreal, earnestly insisting, "I did not come to Canada to commit crime—this time—but to prevent it" ("Mark Twain in Montreal").

Clemens persisted in conflating trademarks and copyrights even after he failed in *Clemens v. Belford* (Illinois, 1883), in which he protested the republication of *Sketches New and Old* without his permission and without royalties. This suit sought compensation not only for loss of revenue from the sale of what he saw as counterfeit books—a clear parallel to whiskey cases—but also for loss of brand equity, asserting that "his property in the said *nom de plume* or trade mark, of 'Mark Twain' as a commercial designation of authorship has been deteriorated and lessened in value" as a result of fraud by the persistent pirates Alexander, Charles, and J. Robert Belford (Schmidt, "Special"). Here, too, whiskey provided the paradigm. Cutter whiskey's "brand or trade mark was one of the valuable assets" auctioned off on 11 July 1879, after the firm was dissolved, according to the *St. Louis Globe-Democrat*, which reported a winning bid of $51,050 ($1.28 million in 2014 dollars) after nearly a thousand others ("All about a Trade-Mark"). But Clemens lost in *Belford*, his fourth suit, because he charged trademark infringement instead of fraud and because the judge declined to extend trademark protection to literary property, even conceding the originality of the argument that trademark replaces copyright in works originally published without registration (required before 1976), as in the case of Mark Twain's newspaper sketches (Feinstein 116). "Trade marks only protect vendible merchandise, and can not be applied to or protect literary property," Judge Blodgett ruled (Schmidt, "Special"). Nonetheless, on the basis of his limited success in *Such*, Clemens clung to his conviction that his pseudonym "bestowed extra-statutory blessings upon his work," as Herbert C. V. Feinstein put it, "rights in addition to those allowed other authors under the Federal copyright laws" (22). And Clemens continued to press trademark claims into the next century, using terms much like those in his *Belford* complaint to outline his position to the attorney who represented him and Rudyard Kipling in a joint 1901 trademark and copyright suit: "the public & the trade are deceived, & the author appears to be personally responsible for the unauthorized edition or set; confusion is thereby caused in the market . . . & prejudice is likely to be excited against the author" (Clemens to A. T. Gurlitz). An 1891 newspaper reported that Clemens had "testified in court that any book by him was worth $30,000"—equivalent to $740,000 today—"before he had written a line of it," indicating that he had by then put a firm dollar value on the Mark Twain brand's equity ("Round" 22).

The legal stipulation that "the name of a person, firm, or corporation" may not become a trademark if "unaccompanied by a mark sufficient to distinguish it from the same name when used by other persons" (100 U.S. 82, §79) may explain why the 1877 advertisements for Mark Twain's Patent Scrap Book (U.S. Pat. #140245, awarded 24 June 1873) branded the product with the signature and portrait of the inventor, along with his pen name and a full measure of the humor that constituted his more metaphorical trademark (Figure 2.1). The multiple assertions of Mark Twain's provenance imply a determination to claim the product as authentically his, and humor ranked high among them. Two cartoons illustrated sixteen lines of parodic testimonial text, promising, "Barrels and barrels of profanity . . . can be saved and devoted to other irritating things, where it will do more real and lasting good, simply by substituting my self-pasting Scrap Book for the old-

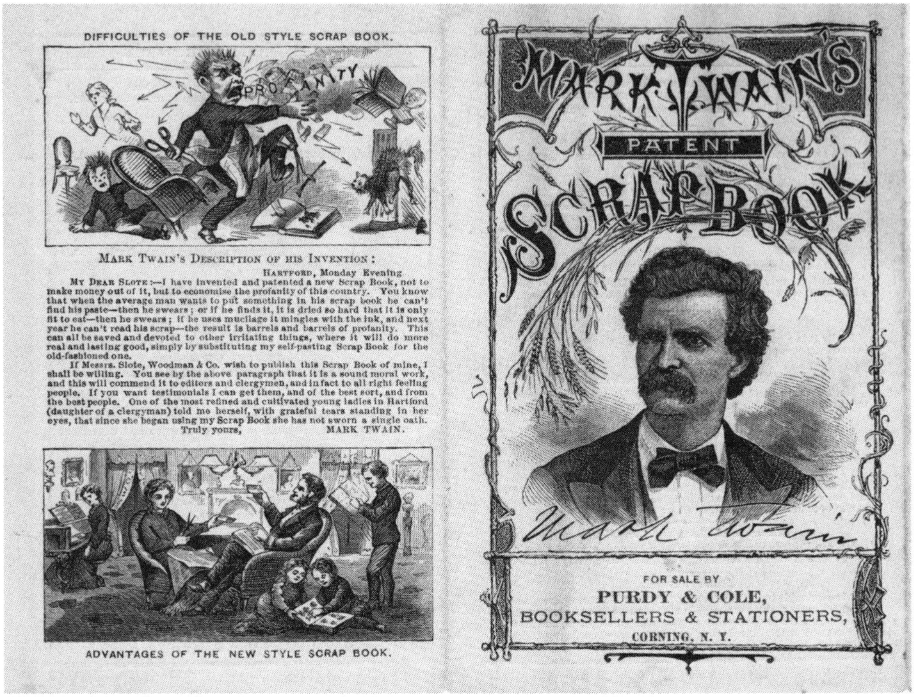

Figure 2.1. This four-page marketing flyer brands Mark Twain's Patent Scrap Book in three ways on each cover. The Mark Twain name and autograph along with Clemens's portrait emphasize the item's authenticity on the front (r), while the name, printed signature, and comic message on the back (l) link this serious product to its inventor's identity as a humorist. Courtesy of Kevin Mac Donnell.

fashioned one." The scrapbook itself carried a trademark notice on a sticker inside the front cover, citing registration on 23 April 1878, but not on the outside, enabling users to brand it themselves. [2]

A more directly programmatic effort followed in 1888, when Clemens published the anthology he compiled with William Dean Howells and Charles Hopkins Clark under the title *Mark Twain's Library of Humor*. The collaborators' division of labor would have more accurately named the book for Howells, had his contract with Harper's not prevented him from publishing under another imprint. Clemens at first proposed abandoning the project in October of 1885 when Howells suggested marketing the book by using Mark Twain in the title, along with the generic *Library of Humor*. "I reckon it would ruin the book—that is, make it necessary to pigeon-hole it & leave it unpublished," Clemens replied. "I couldn't publish it without a very responsible name to support my own on the title page, because it has so much of my own matter in it." Half-joking, he proposed another title on the premise that Providence would rescue them after the manuscript had sat awhile in the pigeon-hole: "He will not desert us now, after putting in four licks to our one on this book all the time. It really seems in a sense discourteous not to call it 'Providence's Library of Humor'" (Twain and Howells 558–59). Putting *Mark Twain* in the title, however, had the double significance of endorsing and branding the project. So did the facsimile handwritten "Compiler's Apology," boldly signed "Mark Twain." The anthology's contents and structure amplified these moves. Clemens's decision to distribute each author's works across the volume replaced Howells's staid chronology with serendipity and asserted Mark Twain's strong presence within. His own "Jumping Frog" opened the book, "How I Edited an Agricultural Paper" closed it, and his byline reappeared every forty pages or so. With twenty entries, Mark Twain appeared nearly twice as often as any other writer, including the now-forgotten Robert J. Burdette, next in line with eleven, and the influential Artemus Ward, just behind Burdette with nine. Whether or not Clark, Howells, and Clemens—who culled the selections in that order (Twain and Howells 399)—intentionally crafted the volume in the genteel context of literary humor and framed Mark Twain accordingly, as Janice McIntire-Strasburg contends, the collection reflects the domestic theme that Camfield and Nickels have discerned. Whatever other editorial motives may have been at work, by stamping the book's cover and contents with his comic identity and sensibility, omitting all other names but illustrator E. W. Kemble's from the title page, Clemens showed his awareness of the commodity value of the Mark Twain brand and his willingness to cash in on its equity value where possible.

But the Scrapbook and *Library* were just two of the many enterprises beyond authorship through which Clemens treated Mark Twain as a comic commodity to be marketed. He had mastered links between publicity and profit and the synergy among various media as early as the summer of 1868, when he promoted an upcoming lecture by inventing scandals about himself and planting a hoax in San Francisco newspapers (*Mark Twain Speaking* 25). Indeed, he emulated, as well as burlesqued, P. T. Barnum's appetite for publicity (e.g., "Barnum's First Speech in Congress" 1867). Across two decades, Mark Twain wrung every drop of commercial value from one of his most successful characters, as he moved Colonel Sellers from the pages of *The Gilded Age* to the theater—first in *Colonel Sellers* (1874), and then in *Colonel Sellers as a Scientist* (1883), with Howells as a collaborator—and thence to newspapers in the serialized novel *The American Claimant* (1892), which was syndicated in the United States and England before appearing between book covers in a volume issued by his own publishing firm. Moreover, with a modern knack for self-reflexivity, he used media as a topic as well as a tool. He lampooned the human interest news report and celebrity interview, two novelty journalistic genres of the post–Civil War period, most notably in "An Encounter with an Interviewer" (1874), while also exploiting them as agents of publicity. Eventually, his hundreds of interviews between 1879 and 1910 amounted to "more than any other human being except perhaps—but only perhaps—for a few statesmen or politicians" (Budd, *Interviews* 401–03).[3] Two early interviews, "Mark Twain as a Pedestrian" and "Mark Twain: His Recent Walking Feat" (both 14 November 1874) in the *Boston Evening Journal* and *Hartford Times*, respectively, exemplified what Daniel Boorstin terms a pseudo-event, an incident created for the purpose of generating media reports. Thus a process that began in the lecture hall eventually moved to less overtly performative venues but continued to trade, in a literal commercial sense, on Mark Twain's brand.

At the opposite extreme from these efforts to capitalize on the Mark Twain brand stood less visible, but no less significant, efforts to divorce his brand from activities inconsistent with its meanings. Like a modern manager, Clemens spun off products inconsistent with the original denotations, differentiations, and connotations of the Mark Twain brand. Three moves stand out as examples of brand management in this vein: suppression differentiated the published Mark Twain from the fullest expression of Samuel Clemens's pen; anonymous publication created alternative denotation, at least temporarily; and branding books under the aegis of Charles L. Webster & Co. gave new identity and meanings to his commercial activity. All three moves hid his role to some degree, though results were mixed.

Suppression created a large space in which the writer could diverge from humor or risk offense. Some works he merely delayed, withholding "Mental Telegraphy" until 1891, for instance, out of worry that readers would dismiss it as humor. But always he kept his eye on the marketplace. In 1880 he boasted of his media savvy to his brother Orion, "*I* take every precaution against unnecessary publicity," precautions that included preventing newspaper transcription of lectures that would compete with the sale of tickets or deprive him of copyright protection (Webster 145–46). In 1899 he volunteered to suppress his four articles on Christian Science if they would "damage the Uniform-edition prospects," advising Francis E. Bliss of Harper's, "They contain nothing offensive against the *lay* Christian Scientist, . . . but they make remorseless fun of his pudd'nheaded little Goddlemighty, Mrs. Eddy, & her jackass 'Key' to the Scriptures" (Clemens to F. E. Bliss). "Christian Science and the Book of Mrs. Eddy" did appear in the October 1899 *Cosmopolitan*, but he did not consult with editors about withholding his uncensored autobiography for a century after his death. He had long since decided, as he told Orion in 1887, "never [to allow] an interviewer or biography-sketcher to get out of me any circumstance of my history which I thought might be worth putting some day into my *auto*biography" (Webster 389). The surprising success of the first volume validated the strategy when it was finally issued in 2010, and the University of California Press rushed more than 300,000 copies into print within weeks of publication to satisfy the demand from readers and Christmas gift-givers eager for a new book by Mark Twain. By early 2014 revenues had run into the millions of dollars (Kirch et al.; Hirst). Here, too, public response reveals the author's savvy. When reviewers complained of too few shocks in the first volume, their objections betrayed unawareness of the taboos he broke in criticizing relatives and friends. Their disappointment ironically highlights how well Clemens managed his brand in anticipating that later generations would accept what his contemporaries could not.

Posthumously published works, such as those collected in Bernard DeVoto's *Mark Twain in Eruption* (1940), John S. Tuckey's *Which Was the Dream?* (1967), and *How Nancy Jackson Married Kate Wilson* (2001), show that the sardonic voice and thematic ambiguities of late-published works such as *King Leopold's Soliloquy* (1905) or "Was It Heaven? Or Hell?" (1902) were no anomalies. Yet variations in publication strategy also illustrate an overall approach to brand management. "The Man That Corrupted Hadleyburg" (1899), one of Mark Twain's great tales, appeared first in *Harper's Monthly*, then as the title story in a 1900 book collection, and a third time in a 1903 collection. The far more slight but despairing "Five Boons of Life" (1902), first published in *Harper's Weekly*, reappeared just once, in the middle of *The $30,000 Bequest and Other Stories* (1906), whereas he did not reprint his anti-imperialist satire "To the Person Sitting in Darkness" (1901) after it ran in the *North American Review*, and he withheld his scathing fable "The War Prayer" (comp. 1905) altogether. A somewhat different brand calculus prevailed when Mark Twain publicly broke sexual rather than political or social taboos. He presented his mock oration on masturbation, "Some Thoughts on the Science of Onanism" (1879), in Paris to an informal club that left no written records, rather than to a New York or Hartford group that might have attracted journalists, while the elaborate scatological and sexual jokes in Elizabethan dialect that made up *1601* circulated only in private editions after its composition in 1876.

Anonymity provided an alternative to suppression, and Clemens tried that, too. He published the *Personal Recollections of Joan of Arc* in thirteen anonymous installments of *Harper's Magazine* from April 1895 to April 1896, in order to broaden his brand identity. "I shall never be accepted seriously over my own signature," he had complained to wife Olivia and daughter Susy, in Albert Bigelow Paine's report. "People always want to laugh over what I write and are disappointed if they don't find a joke in it" (Paine 959). So serious was he about hiding his identity that his terms with Harper's stipulated that his royalty rate would rise if the publisher leaked it (*Mark Twain's Letters to His Publisher* [*MTLP*] 132–33). The jig was up, however, after he filed for copyright on the volume in March 1896, and the book appeared later that year with the Mark Twain brand on the spine and cover—surely the plan all along, considering its marketing value—even though the title page identified the author as "the Sieur Louis de Conte (her page and secretary)."

His publishing ventures under the auspices of Charles L. Webster & Co., on the other hand, let him hide in plain sight. Some scholars have seen the activities of Webster & Co., like his obsession with the Paige compositor, as a distraction from Clemens's real business of authorship, debasing his legacy with crass celebrity memoirs and jeopardizing his finances through mismanagement (Kaplan 295; Loving, *MT Adventures* 273; Gold 1, 6). But the entrepreneurial Clemens saw the publishing house from the standpoint of someone long since convinced of the commodity value of his writing, pen name, and public persona. "The author 'Mark Twain' was dragged into this world by businessman Samuel L. Clemens," Hamlin Hill declares (*MTLP* 3), and indeed Webster & Co. added another arrow to a quiver of mutually reinforcing media activities. As in the 1860s and 1870s, when Clemens discovered how to turn wanderlust and fame into new social and commercial opportunities, so in the 1880s he sought to capitalize on an exploding publishing industry and Mark Twain's authorial success in it by becoming, as the firm proclaimed on its stationery, "publishers of Mark Twain's books."[4] Forming Webster & Co. as a subscription house not only maximized his profits by earning him the author's and the publisher's shares of sales but also lowered the risk of publication to both parties by securing down payments (the subscriptions) beforehand. Subscription sales became less important over the next decade, as railroads increasingly brought bookstores to smaller communities and urbanization increased, and Webster & Co. adapted to this changing landscape by expanding into trade sales in 1890 (Sanderson 38–39).[5] But in 1884 and 1885, anticipating the publication of *Adventures of Huckleberry Finn* and Grant's *Personal Memoirs*, Clemens mistrusted trade publication, which represented just one of five standard publication models at the time, and he was determined to reach readers en masse (Anderson and Hill 117–19; Hill 37–40). More to the point, as Bruce Michelson has explained, America's two dozen subscription houses reaped some 75 percent of all book sales from 1865 to 1890 by hawking books from door to door. Notable subscription titles included the important *Life and Times of Frederick Douglass* (marketed directly to African Americans) and Harriet Beecher

Stowe's *American Woman's Home*, as well as Twain's *Innocents Abroad* and *Huckleberry Finn* (Michelson 17, 81). Subscription publishing's populist ethos also appealed to an author willing to see sales as a form of status, as he put it in an 1886 notebook entry: "My books are water; those of the great geniuses is wine. Everybody drinks water" (*MTNJ* 3:238; Twain and Howells 587).

In any event, the vast subscription audience enabled Webster & Co. to wrestle Grant's book from the Century Co. by offering the dying author twice as much money: 70 percent of net profits (*MTLP* 185n2). The contract not only relieved Grant's financial distress following the failure of his Wall Street firm ("Future" 2) but also gave Webster & Co. a brand identity apart from Mark Twain. Grant's work produced $400,000 in royalties to his widow, $1 million in profit for the firm, and bragging rights for Charles Webster: "It will outsell any book ever issued save the Bible and Shakespeare," he told the *New York Times*, reporting 325,000 subscriptions on publication day (Loving, *MT Adventures* 271; "Demand" 5).

The string of Webster & Co. war memoirs that followed reflected more than the desire to replicate the Grant success. Indeed, contrary to claims that the firm had "little or no effective marketing plan" or stooped to "frank attempts at celebrity publishing" (Loving, *MT Adventures* 273; Kaplan 339), the roster shows a coherent publishing strategy. Webster & Co. sold books of three sorts: firsthand accounts by Civil War heroes, books by Mark Twain, and titles by other notable authors, such as Pope Leo XIII, Tolstoy, Columbus, and Filippini (the celebrated chef of Delmonico's). Stationery envelopes proclaimed the strategy clearly: "CHARLES L. WEBSTER & CO., . . . Personal Memoirs of U. S. Grant and other Biographical Works, Mark Twain's Books, Miscellaneous Publications." This brand strategy explains why Webster briefly entertained acquiring a campaign book for the 1884 presidential race (*MTLP* 177n1), and why, charity aside, the firm sold widows' memoirs, such as Elizabeth Custer's *Tenting on the Plains* (1887) and Almira Russell Hancock's *Reminiscences of Winfield Scott Hancock* (1887), along with *Adventures of Huckleberry Finn* (1884) and *Mark Twain's Library of Humor*.

Clemens spelled out his vision for the list in an 11 November 1885 letter about the volume that became *The Legends and Myths of Hawaii: The Fables and Folk-lore of a Strange People* (1888), reporting to Webster on his reply to a pitch by a former colleague from Virginia City, Nevada: "I told [Rollin M.] Daggett that what was required for success was a *good* book; and that the other nine-tenths of the requisite of success was that there should be a big name back of the good book." And he made clear that Daggett, who had served in Congress before becoming U.S. minister to Hawaii, needed a bigger name than his own. "So I said that if he could get the King to let his name appear as part author, we *wanted the book*. . . . I said we preferred to keep up our standard, and be known in the world as a house that publishes only for Kings and full Generals." Clemens proposed terms that made the inducement concrete: Webster & Co. would pay 15 percent profit above manufacturing costs without "the King's expressed collaboration," 40 percent with royal participation mentioned in introduction, but 60 percent "*with both names in the title page* as authors" (*MTLP* 193).

Nor were kings and generals the only objects of this strategy. Charlie Webster turned to brand names from the religious sphere early in 1887, when he began looking for ways to "switch off of War books if we can" (*MTLP* 213n1), acquiring Father Bernard O'Reilly's *Life of Pope Leo XIII* (1887) and the rights to Henry Ward Beecher's proposed autobiography (*MTLP* 212–13n1, 212–14). The trade list later expanded to include *Stories from the Rabbis* (1893) by the distinguished rabbi and NYU professor Abram S. Isaacs. Here, too, the premium the firm placed on such authors shows in the terms offered to them: for example, a $5,000 advance plus half profits and a $1,500 finder's fee for Beecher's autobiography, though the family eventually returned the advance when he died before delivering the manuscript (*MTLP* 196n2, 197n2, 213n1, 213n1–2, 252n1). Seeing the self as a commodity and a brand let Clemens envision converting celebrity into capital for other authors and for Webster & Co., as well as for himself. Writers on varied subjects evidently found his vision attractive and appeared to enjoy the cachet of appearing on a roster with Mark Twain, U.S. Grant, and the pope.

Clemens showed some discomfort with the spin-off strategy. He claimed very public credit for the Grant contract in 1885, advising the editor of the *Boston Herald*, "I am Webster & Co., myself, substantially" (Clemens, Letter to the editor), although other correspondence shows that Webster proposed the terms that sealed that deal and was the daily public face of the firm until he retired in 1888.[6] For all Clemens's participation (and meddling) in the firm's affairs, it was Webster who secured contracts for overseas publication and copyrights, had an audience with the pope for authorizing publication of his autobiography, pushed a prison sentence for the firm's embezzler-bookkeeper, and discussed books with prospective authors and the press.

The strategy worked. Newspapers only sometimes identified Clemens or Mark Twain as a partner in the enterprise. An 1885 San Francisco news item headlined "Mark Twain: Literary Man with a Good Business Talent," minimized Clemens's public role by noting that "news of the Grant book is provided from the office of Webster & Co., of which he is [only] the 'Co.'" ("Mark Twain: Literary" 2). A later account, headlined "Grant's Luck: How the Hero Narrowly Escaped Selling His Book for $10,000," went further, pointing to Webster's "eye on the alert for the forthcoming work" as the start of the firm's negotiations and the largess of "Webster's relative and business partner" Mark Twain as their finale (5). Coverage of the successful 1888 breach of contract suit against the firm by its printers described Webster as "the senior member of the publishing firm" and "Mr. Samuel L. Clemens '(Mark Twain)'" as "the junior" ("General Grant's Memoirs" 10). Even an announcement of Mark Twain's *Merry Tales* (1892) as the start of a Webster & Co. series enabled by new international copyright law ignored the author's role in the publishing house ("Looking" 4). He likewise remained in the background of a report on Walt Whitman's funeral, which featured E. C. Stedman's memorial poem, as read by his son Arthur, "who, as the editor of the volume of 'Selected Poems,' also represented, by a cabled request of Mark Twain, the firm of Charles L. Webster & Co., the dead poet's publishers" ("Walt" 6). Such marginal presence for someone with Samuel Clemens's love of center stage points to his deliberate intention to distinguish Webster & Co. from the Mark Twain brand.

Mark Twain's fame nonetheless brought more than the usual press attention to the Webster bankruptcy filing on 18 April 1894. Signs of business failure had appeared nine months before, when Frederick J. Hall, who had become a partner in 1886 and bought out Webster in 1888, hoped for improvement while reporting draconian efforts to cut costs and limited options to raise capital: "as things cannot grow any worse," he advised Clemens on 7 July 1893, "they must get better" (Hall 5). Accounts of the failure debate the reasons: the firm "was poorly run" (Loving, *MT Adventures* 273); it clung to subscription sales past their prime (Michelson 183); it published too many books or too many of the wrong books and diverted too much capital to the Paige compositor; its multivolume *Library of American Literature* incurred immediate manufacturing costs for subscriptions paid over time.[7] Despite these problems, business records in the Mark Twain Papers show steady backlist sales and a positive balance sheet through August 1892 (Clemens, Notebook #32, 133; Hall 2), evidence that Webster & Co. succeeded in both publishing books and managing Mark Twain's brand for most of a decade. But in the end, Webster & Co. could not stay afloat through the period of tight credit and reduced sales resulting from the Panic of 1893.

The firm's bankruptcy occurred during what economic historians Douglas Steeples and David O. Whitten have called "the trough of the depression," which lasted through 1897 (43, 61n1). They cite "savage unemployment and demoralizing wage reductions," with jobless rates in the 17–19 percent range for urban workers. Non-farm earnings fell 22 percent due to wage cuts between 1892 and 1894, when prices for wheat and cotton dropped 16 percent and 47 percent, respectively, in an economy estimated to be operating at 20–25 percent below capacity (50–53). This environment hardly supported discretionary purchases, such as books. The *New York Herald* for 20 April

1894 listed several "Business Troubles," including Webster & Co.'s bankruptcy filing, in a long list of court judgments. The paper ranked its story about a firm in which "Samuel L. Clemens ('Mark Twain') is a partner" ahead of the others, even as it announced that "liabilities are much smaller than heretofore reported," estimating less than $80,000 owed against approximately equal assets ("Business" 8). But Mark Twain's stature meant that, within two days, dozens of headlines announced "Failure of Mark Twain," "Mark Twain's Company Embarrassed," and the like. The topic stayed in the news for many months, with headlines such as "Mark Twain Said to Be in Poor Health / The Failure of His Publishing Firm Shock" and "Mark Twain's Affairs," the latter noting, "Mr. Clemens . . . will not think that he will consider himself relieved of the moral obligations to repay his creditors." Nearly six months passed before the court released a full accounting that showed debts substantially less than suspected: $94,101 in liabilities, net assets of $54,164, for a total debt of $39,937 ("Notes" 8). Yet one can imagine the mortification of the author, who had sued Wanamaker and other trade booksellers for undercutting the subscription price of Webster books, at seeing a two-column display ad in the *New York Herald* that boasted in capital letters, "The failure of the well-known publishing house of Webster & Co. rendered it possible for us to close out AT ENORMOUS SACRIFICE PRICES the entire stock of MARK TWAIN BOOKS published by them" (Figure 2.2). Adding insult to injury of this sale without royalties to the author, the ad offered "recent works of this GREATEST OF ALL AMERICAN HUMORISTS . . . at an average of ONE-THIRD OF PUBLISHERS' PRICES" ("Mark Twain books"). The publicity scorched Mark Twain's brand, rubbing Clemens's face in the shame of Webster & Co.'s demise.

His March 1898 fulfillment of a public promise to repay the firm's debts generated international praise for his integrity and honor. Many newspapers quoted a Londoner's tribute: "With the exception of the historical case of Sir Walter Scott, I do not think there is to be found in the records of literature anything quite equal to Mark Twain's conduct" ("London" 8). Clemens had made the promise—itself a form of brand management—on 16 August 1895, as he embarked on the worldwide lecture tour that would fund the repayment of his debts and—in yet another act of brand-name synergy—provide incidents for his next major book, *Following the Equator* (1897). Image repair also came from the distinguished Harper & Brothers, his new publishers, who cemented his literary stature over the next decade by issuing the first uniform edition of his work and hosting his seventieth birthday celebration at Delmonico's. Nine more sets of books issued in the United States and England between 1889 and 1901 testified to the rising commercial value of the Mark Twain enterprise (Schmidt, "History"). Added luster came from the

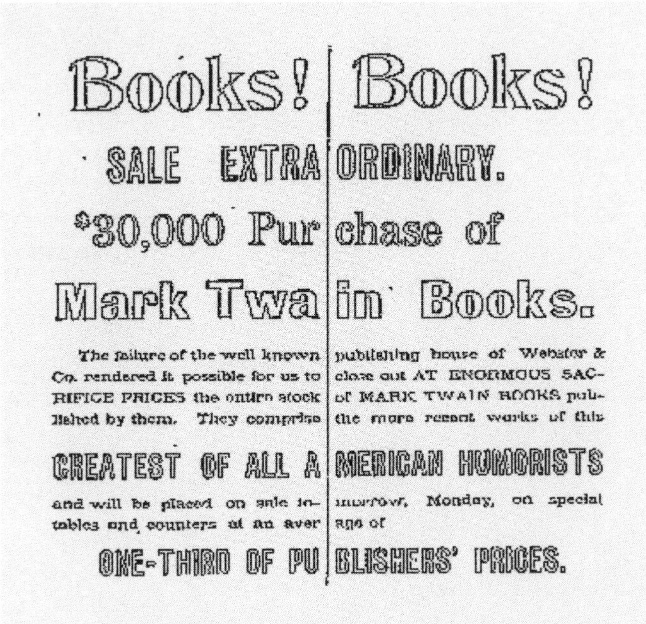

Figure 2.2. The layout and text of this two-column advertisement from the *New York Herald* (25 Nov. 1894, 1) emphasize the marketing value of the Mark Twain brand in hawking highly discounted books following the liquidation of Webster & Co. assets. Leaving aside the bad publicity atop the shame of bankruptcy, the discount sale rubbed salt in the wound of an author who had sued retailers for selling his books below their official Webster & Co. prices.

honorary doctorates bestowed by Yale (1901) and Oxford (1907), the latter set in motion when a friend asked Clemens when he would return to England. His reply—"When Oxford bestows its degree upon me"—indicates once again his careful management of the brand's gradual shift in identification from regional humor to international literature (Baetzhold 368–69n2).

Two final moves to manage the Mark Twain brand took place in the last three years of his life, both aimed at securing Clemens's intellectual property and its equity interests for his surviving daughters, Clara and Jean. Clemens's (self-appointed) business manager Ralph W. Ashcroft conceived and led both moves. In the more ambitious of the two, Ashcroft drove the December 1908 formation of the Mark Twain Company to manage Twain's brand along with his royalties long after the copyright clock ran out. Perhaps to enhance that effort, perhaps for other reasons, during the previous

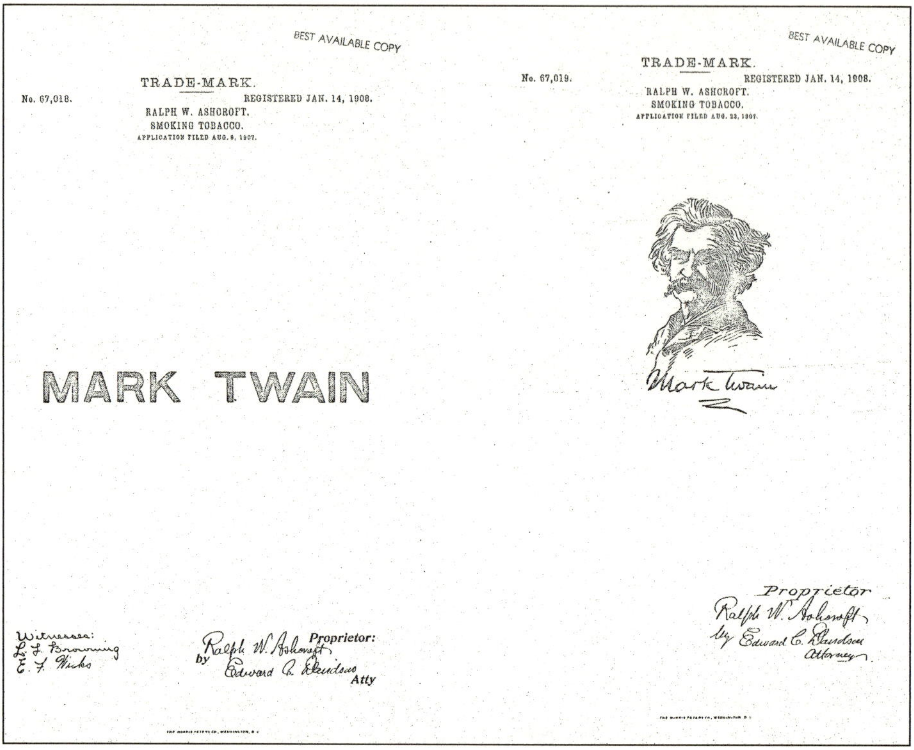

Figure 2.3. Official registrations show that Ashcroft owned the lettering and labeling trademarks for Mark Twain Tobacco, 0067018 and 0067019, issued on 14 January 1908 from applications filed 9 August 1907. Clemens's love of cigars made the anticipated product a good fit for the brand's identity.

winter Ashcroft had secured four trademarks for the name Mark Twain featuring distinctive block letters and an etched image of Samuel Clemens with a facsimile "Mark Twain" signature underneath. Both efforts failed in some ways, although they managed in others to solidify the Mark Twain trademark in myth, if not in fact.

The 1908 registration of the four trademarks would seem to have been the reward for thirty-five years of attempting to claim property rights in the pen name Mark Twain, yet Clemens did not even own them. The original registration documents certifying the marks list Ashcroft, not Clemens, as their proprietor (see Figures 2.3 and 2.4). No extant documentary evidence explains this fact or indicates whether Clemens approved of the filings. Feinstein states flatly, "Neither Clemens nor his family was party to Ashcroft's applications or registrations" (25), although a friend asked Clemens about them during the thirty-day challenge period after seeing the applications

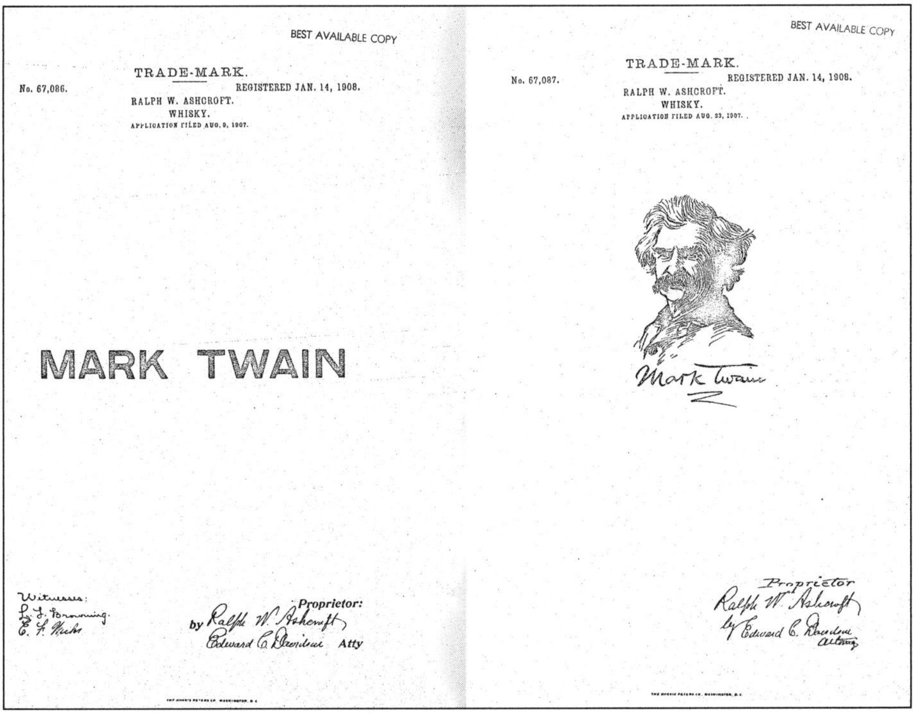

Figure 2.4. Identical designs for the tobacco trademarks in Figure 2.3 and those above for Mark Twain Whisky, 0067086 and 0067087, also issued to Ashcroft on 14 January 1908 from applications filed 9 August 1907, explain public impressions that Mark Twain had patented himself.

listed in the 12 November 1907 *Patent Office Gazette* (Morris).[8] Isabel Lyon wrote, "Answered, Dec. 9, '07," on the face of the letter, but the text of the reply on the verso consists only of a paragraph in untranscribed shorthand, and Lyon does not mention the correspondence in her diary. The declarations accompanying the applications have now been destroyed, but Feinstein's 1968 correspondence with the Trademark Examining Operation of the Patent Office indicates that Ashcroft claimed to have used the Mark Twain portrait commercially beginning on 4 June 1907 and the gothic lettering beginning on 8 August 1907, shortly before filing the applications (Feinstein 25). At least as notable is that neither the trademarks for Mark Twain Tobacco (67,018 and 67,019) nor those for Mark Twain Whisky (67,086 and 67,087) represent—either in word or image—the specific commercial products they aspire to denote. The two sets of trademarks for different products are entirely identical and identically generic: one in each pair denotes Mark Twain through his pseudonym in large block type, while the other denotes

Mark Twain through Clemens's image and Twain's autograph. Together the marks claim brand identity, not product identity, through a triply redundant representation of the public persona crafted and cultivated by Samuel L. Clemens in text and performance, both onstage and in public life.

By designating the embodied Mark Twain as a brand, the registration documents explain the public impression, widely remarked both seriously and humorously in the press, that Clemens-Twain had trademarked or patented himself. Whereas the *Des Moines Daily News* joked about the development as a comic nightmare ("MT Gets"), the *Grand Rapids Evening Press* more philosophically observed, "Mark Twain comes as near being a self-made man as complex modern society permits. . . . [T]he valuable thing which he has made is his personality. And that is what he has had patented" ("'Mark Twain' Patent"; see Figure 2.5). The attention given to Ashcroft in some reports suggests that he encouraged, if not planted, both the coverage and misunderstandings. The latter include not only the *Evening Press* prediction that all celebrities would soon own and profit from commercial use of their names and portraits, but also, and more significantly, Ashcroft's explanation in the *Brooklyn Eagle* that planning for a Mark Twain whiskey and a Mark Twain cigar "is not so much a venture to make money as it is to protect the trade value of Mr. Clemens' name" by "having the name, photograph and autograph patented" ("'Mark Twain' Whisky"). The *Eagle* identified Ashcroft as Clemens's business agent and cited the trademarks as an effort "to keep the use and value of a noted name in the family of the man who made it famous" ("'Mark Twain' Whisky"). The implication was that Ashcroft was acting on Clemens's behalf, but the *Eagle*'s report failed to explain that the registrations issued to Ashcroft designate *him*, not Clemens, as owner.

Contemporary press accounts credited the 1906 Pure Food and Drug Act for the filing, and while that law boosted branding of food and liquor as implied claims to quality, the less celebrated 1905 Trade Mark Act (29 U.S.C. 15 §81–108) must also have played a role. The 1905 law at long last extended federal protection to trademarks in interstate commerce and provided remedies for infringement, but several provisions offered additional benefits to the Mark Twain brand. The act gave trademark protection to commercially used personal names, especially (as in the case of Ashcroft's marks) if "written, printed, impressed, or woven in some particular or distinctive manner or in association with a portrait of the individual," although an application for a trademark using such a portrait of a living individual needed that person's written permission (Greeley 35). That requirement offered Ashcroft an interesting loophole, since Mark Twain was not, strictly speaking, a living individual, but the destruction of the original documents means that we cannot know whether Ashcroft claimed that the requirement was inap-

Figure 2.5. This cartoon from the *Des Moines Daily News* (8 February 1908, 3), three times the size of the article running below it, imagines an overflow of Mark Twain–branded products. The text in the center—"Mark Twain has patented himself, also copyrighted himself, and is going into the cigar and whisky business"—conflates patents, copyrights, and trademarks much as Clemens did, while muddying public understanding of what exactly Ashcroft's trademarks protected.

plicable. Further complications stem from the specification that the official registrant of a mark is its "*prima facie* owner . . . even if the registrant is not in fact the owner of the mark" (Greeley 17).

Given Clemens's early wish that literature could inebriate its users, the choice of whiskey for a first trademark registration made a fine symmetry, if nothing else. And whatever else they mean, the registrations demonstrate the commercial value that Ashcroft, and perhaps the U.S. Patent and Trademark Office, attributed to the Mark Twain brand. Ashcroft may have expected to sell the registered marks to Clemens or the Mark Twain Company, perhaps for a nominal sum simply to establish and formalize a chain of ownership, or for a high price to extort a reward or set a market value. It's difficult to credit noble motives to the registrations in light of the Ashcroft-Lyon controversy (as it became known) that unfolded in the spring of 1909, barely three months after the incorporation and fourteen months after the trademarks came through; yet no evidence of malfeasance exists, either. Despite manuscript, epistolary, and other rants against Ashcroft for violations (actual and perceived) of the personal and fiduciary trust Clemens had placed in him and Isabel Lyon, Clemens left no record of his thoughts on the trademarks. His silence is striking, considering how much and for how long the issue had absorbed him, and considering how actively he lobbied Congress during this same period to improve copyright protection. But he credited Ashcroft with having "invented" the Mark Twain Company, calling it "a stroke of genius" that "may supercede copyright-law some day" (Clemens to Clara Clemens), even as he became suspicious of the reach of the company's tentacles beyond his intellectual property.

Inspired in part by the imminent expiration of the copyright on *Innocents Abroad*, the company claimed as its purview all possible activities involving the Mark Twain brand, with a stated purpose to acquire, secure, license, and exploit in any way "the name, nom de plume, words, or phrase, 'Mark Twain,' especially all the right, title, ownership, and interest of any kind . . . of Samuel L. Clemens, in and to or under in the name, nom de plume, words, or phrase 'Mark Twain'"—especially in conjunction with the Mark Twain brand as I've outlined it here: all forms of intellectual property ("trade names, trade marks, copyrights, patents," and the like), "good will" (i.e., brand image), and "enjoyment or interests, in, to or under the name and words 'Mark Twain'"—brand equity ("Certificate"). However, in order to cover every possible way in which the name Mark Twain might have tangible value, the incorporation document extended the company's claim to rights far beyond intellectual property, including real estate, land and agricultural communities, water use, and trade in financial instruments. Prepared by Ashcroft's lawyer R. A. Mansfield Hobbs, signed on 22 December 1908, and registered the next day with New York State, the document, over the long run, did provide a mechanism for protecting the Mark Twain brand by centralizing all of Clemens's assets—including rights, royalties, and publication of works under copyright or not yet published, as well as tangible holdings—from his death in 1910 through the closure of Clara Clemens's trust in 1978, when the trust's assets passed to the Mark Twain Foundation. But in the short run, it had mixed results. Within his private circle, where brand equity was plotted but not traded, the company's formation fed the conflict between Clemens and Ashcroft that led to charges of theft and fraud when Clemens realized in March 1909 that he had inadvertently given Ashcroft a power of attorney that would permit him to sell any Clemens asset. Soon he was fuming in the notorious Ashcroft-Lyon Manuscript over what he saw as theft and conspiracy by and between Ashcroft and Isabel Lyon (originally Olivia Clemens's personal secretary, then Sam's majordomo, and then Ashcroft's wife). Anger and injury spilled over into his view of the company. Equally enraged by the document's and its creator's overreach, Clemens responded to claims that he owed more money to Hobbs for work on the incorporation with an entrepreneurial humorist's sense of poetic justice: "I am going to do his Organization Paper into a magazine article, and pay his bill out of the proceeds" ("Memorandum for Rogers" 6).

A 1909 memorandum to Henry Huttleston Rogers summarizing the anticipated benefits of the Mark Twain Company shows that it aimed chiefly to preserve brand identity and extend its value. The first benefit on the list had already been achieved: Mark Twain's audacious, novel act of incorporation was "telegraphed all over the world," generating tremendous publicity ("Memorandum"). Longer-term advantages to equity, however, rested on two admittedly untested premises: that the immortality of a corporation "perpetuates *whatever property right there may be* in the name 'Mark Twain,'" and that a corporation explicitly formed to manage such rights "*may* . . . prevent unauthorized publication of Mr. Clemens' books, after the expiration of the copyrights, and after his death" (my emphasis, "Certificate"). Such tentative claims to property rights reflected both the speculative nature of the incorporation and limitations on trademark protection. The company's management of assets entailed arguably beneficial restrictions: on Clemens, by subjecting at least some of his publishing decisions to oversight by the corporate directors; on taxing entities, by converting personal royalties into corporate assets; and on his heirs, by providing "a convenient vehicle whereby his trustees and executors . . . may administer his post-mortem publishing affairs" ("Memorandum"). In contrast to this practical view, newspapers presented the incorporation as the metamorphosis of a person, headlining the story with some variation of "Mark Twain Turns into a Corporation," as the *New York Times* put it, and framing the move as a father's desire to protect his presumably defenseless daughters from "raids by pirates" after their father's death. In the process, such coverage conflated incorporation and trademarks in ways that presented hope as fact. Although he conceded that courts would have the final word, Ashcroft encouraged such a view, telling the *Times* that "when this name [Mark Twain] is the property of a perpetual corporation, Mr. Clemens' heirs will be in a position to enjoin perpetually the publication of all books not authorized by the Mark Twain Company, even after the twentieth-year first copyright and ten-year secondary copyright have expired" ("Mark Twain Turns" 2).

Samuel Clemens had every reason to husband his assets at the end of his life, having finally restored his image and fortune, especially since he believed that insufficient copyright protection had cost him so dearly in his early years as Mark Twain. Moreover, throughout his career, he had struggled to maintain what he considered the integrity of the Mark Twain brand, extending it into enterprises where its associations could reap profits, withholding it from those that might injure them. Even late in life, he needed to police its uses. In 1906, for instance, when Harper's published a *Mark Twain's Library of Humor* vastly different from the earlier humor anthology, Clemens objected in strong terms. "I would not have . . . dreamed of allowing anyone to put my name to a book in whose compilation I took no part," he wrote his editor, Frederick A. Duneka, on 4 June 1906. But with an eye toward managing the brand, Clemens not only insisted, "I must ask you—in fact I must require you—to take this book out of print immediately, & destroy the plates," but also added, "I shall expect—& require—20% royalty on all copies of the book sold between its issue and its suppression" (Clemens to F. A. Duneka). Through such vigilant management, the Mark Twain brand has seen its equity rise for 150 years, even as the significance of the pen name has varied.

Among the problems that arose from the Mark Twain Company, however, not least was the confusion about its claims to ownership of "trade names, trade marks, copyrights, patents, letters patent," and so on. Copyrights and patents that Clemens owned during his lifetime all expired on schedule, and he did not own any trademarks, which in any case did not yet include property rights. But the instinct that led Clemens to claim and exploit the Mark Twain brand across nearly forty years of a rising information economy was hardly off target, as editions from the Mark Twain Project and commercial publishers continue to show. And in the end, myth gave Clemens the trademark protection that lawsuits and incorporation did not. As late as 1956, Harper's sought a 1.5 percent royalty from Houghton Mifflin to license the name Mark Twain for the title page of Henry Nash Smith's edition of *Huckleberry Finn*, a text already in the public domain (Thomas). Absent such licenses, publishers wary of legal repercussions identified Clemens as the author or engaged in what Feinstein calls an "empty ritual" of creating some kind of trademark notice (26).[9] A 1981 memo from University of California English professor Robert D. Hart to Robert J. Hirst of the Mark Twain Papers sharing Harper's letter remarked on its "unscrupulous" action "in exploiting the fiction of the trade-mark 'Mark Twain'"—yet wondered:

"Or is it possible that Harpers [sic] didn't understand the legal situation, but relied on the folklore that the firm had carefully fostered for decades?" ("Memo to Bob"). The myth of the Mark Twain brand testifies to the force of its symbolic value to represent American humor, if not also American literature, as well as to the savvy of the American entrepreneur who created and managed Mark Twain. That value, too, contributes to brand equity. And a final dividend comes from the brand's origins in the same Jamesian constructivist principle that merged Clemens and his comic persona. As "the reality of a thought is proportionate to the way it grasps us," so the equity of the Mark Twain brand made his trademark effectively real.

Notes

I am grateful in general to Robert J. Hirst and the other editors and staff at the Mark Twain Papers for their leadership and example in Mark Twain studies, and in particular to Victor A. Fischer and Neda Salem for their assistance with this project before, during, and after my work in the archives there.

1. For a general introduction to brands, see Arnold and Landa. More detailed analyses appear in Clifton and Simmons, and Holt. I detail the brand dimensions of Mark Twain's humor and its counterparts in contemporary American culture in Lee, *Twain's Brand.*

2. I am grateful to Mark Woodhouse, Archivist for Mark Twain Collection, Gannett-Tripp Library, Elmira College, for photographs of various styles of the Mark Twain Scrap Book, and to Kevin Mac Donnell for the marketing flyer shown in Figure 2.1.

3. Budd identified 278 interviews in his 1977 volume but later estimated in "Interviews" that Clemens gave at least 50 more.

4. According to the U.S. Bureau of the Census (808), the number of book titles published nationwide rose from 2,076 in 1880 to 4,559 in 1890, the period in which Clemens established Webster & Co., and reached 13,470 in 1910, the year he died.

5. Sanderson lists William O. Stoddard's *Inside the White House in War Times* (1890, though sometimes erroneously cited as 1880), illustrated by Dan Beard, as Webster's first trade title.

6. See Webster 302; Twain, *MTNJ 3* 96–97. Gold (162) credits Webster entirely with the Grant acquisition.

7. For accounts of the failure of Charles Webster & Co., see Kaplan 339–41; Gold 132; Loving, *MT Adventures* 295–96. To save costs, Hall stopped manufacturing *Library* volumes in the summer of 1893 but reported that installment payments remained steady, calling them "our salvation" (3).

8. The original applications, declarations, and correspondence from that era have been destroyed by the U.S. Patent and Trademark Office (USPTO). I am grateful to

Ran Raider, President of the Patent and Trademark Resource Center Association, and Government and Legal Information Coordinator and Patent and Trademark Resource Center Representative at the Wright State University Libraries, Dayton, Ohio, for obtaining copies of the registration documents for me and securing confirmation from the USPTO in Washington, D.C., that the original application materials have been expunged from the archives. A 1908 letter to Ashcroft from Edward C. Davidson, the attorney who handled the trademark applications, indicates an ongoing professional relationship (Davidson). I am grateful to Victor A. Fisher, editor at the Mark Twain Papers, for ferreting out the Morris and Davidson letters and sending them to me.

9. For example, the facsimile edition of *A Connecticut Yankee in King Arthur's Court* (1889) edited by Hamlin Hill identifies the author as Clemens rather than Mark Twain and explains in a note that the volume "does not have the name of the author on the facsimile title page because the Estate of Samuel L. Clemens maintains the attitude that 'Mark Twain' is a trademark."

Works Cited

"Agreement." [*No. 1, before the publication of Grant's Personal Memoirs.*] Charles L. Webster and Company. 10 April 1884. Mark Twain Papers.

"All about a Trade-Mark." *St Louis Globe-Democrat* 11 July 1879: col. E.

Anderson, Frederick, and Hamlin Hill. "How Samuel Clemens Became Mark Twain's Publisher: A Study of the James R. Osgood Contracts." *Proof: Yearbook of American Bibliographical and Textual Studies* 2 (1972): 117–43.

Arnold, David. *The Handbook of Brand Management.* International Management Series. Reading: Addison-Wesley, Economist Books, 1992.

Baetzhold, Howard G. *Mark Twain and John Bull: The British Connection.* Bloomington: Indiana UP, 1970.

Boorstin, Daniel J. *The Image: A Guide to Pseudo-Events in America.* 1962. New York: Harper & Row, Harper Colophon, 1964.

Budd, Louis J., ed. "Interviews." *The Mark Twain Encyclopedia.* Ed. J. R. LeMaster and James D. Wilson. New York: Garland, 1993. 401–03.

———. *Interviews with Samuel L. Clemens, 1874–1910.* Arlington: American Literary Realism and the U of Texas at Arlington, 1977.

"Business Troubles." *New York Herald* 20 April 1894: 8.

Camfield, Gregg. "Mark Twain and Amiable Humor." *A Companion to Mark Twain.* Ed. Peter Messent and Louis J. Budd. Blackwell Companions to Literature and Culture. Malden: Blackwell, 2005. 500–12.

———. *Necessary Madness: The Humor of Domesticity in Nineteenth-Century American Literature.* New York: Oxford UP, 1997.

"Century Company Records, 1871–1924." Finding aid. Manuscripts and Archives Division, New York Public Library. New York, 2004.

"Certificate of Incorporation of Mark Twain Company." 1908. Mark Twain Papers.

Chappell & Earl. "New Trademark Law." *Kalamazoo [MI] Gazette* 19 March 1905: 8.

Clemens, Samuel L. *A Connecticut Yankee in King Arthur's Court*. A facsimile of the first ed. Ed. Hamlin Hill. San Francisco: Chandler, 1963.

———. Letter to Augustus T. Gurlitz. 14 September 1901. Mark Twain Papers.

———. Letter to Clara Clemens. 11 and 14 March 1909. Mark Twain Papers.

———. Letter to Francis E. Bliss. 27 February 1899. Mark Twain Papers.

———. Letter to Frederick A. Duneka. 4 June 1906. Mark Twain Papers.

———. Letter to Henry Morton Stanley. 1 September 1872. Henry M. Stanley Archives. Collection King Baudouin Foundation on Deposit at the Royal Museum for Central Africa. Tervuren, Belgium.

———. Letter to the editor of the Boston *Herald*. 6 July 1885. Mark Twain Papers.

———. "Memorandum, S. L. Clemens vs. Mrs. Ashcroft, 15 August [19]09." TS. Documents, 1909, IVL-Ashcroft Controversy. Mark Twain Papers.

———. Notebook #32, July–August 1892 to [22 June 1897] TS transcription. Mark Twain Papers.

Clifton, Rita, and John Simmons, eds. *Brands and Branding*. The Economist Series. Princeton: Bloomberg, 2004.

Davidson, Edward C. Letter to Ralph W. Ashcroft. 1 December 1908. Mark Twain Papers.

"Demand for Gen. Grant's Book." *New York Times* 3 December 1885: 5.

"Disciples of Franklin." *New-York Tribune* 19 January 1886: 5.

"Failure of Mark Twain." *New-York Tribune* 19 April 1894: 1.

Feinstein, Herbert Charles Verschleisser. "Mark Twain's Lawsuits." Diss. U of California, Berkeley, 1968.

"Future of the Grant Family." *Washington Post* 26 July 1885: 2.

"General Grant: Passes a Wakeful Night Sunday." *Boston Evening Journal* 10 March 1885: 2.

"General Grant's Memoirs. Printers and Publishers at War." *New York Herald* 20 May 1888: 10.

Glass, Loren. *Authors Inc.: Literary Celebrity in the Modern United States, 1880–1980*. New York: New York UP, 2004.

Gold, Charles H. *"Hatching Ruin," or Mark Twain's Road to Bankruptcy*. Columbia: U of Missouri P, 2003.

Gopnik, Adam. "The Man in the White Suit [Mark Twain]." *New Yorker* 86.38 (29 November 2010): 78–83.

"Grant's Luck: How the Hero Narrowly Escaped Selling His Book for $10,000." *New York Herald* 16 May 1888: 5.

Greeley, Arthur P. *Registration of Trademarks under the New Trademark Act of the United States: With Notes on the Act*. Washington: J. Byrne, 1905.

Gribben, Alan. "Autobiography as Property." *The Mythologizing of Mark Twain*. Ed. Sara deSaussure Davis and Philip D. Beidler. University: University of Alabama Press, 1984. 39–55.

———. "Mark Twain, Business Man: The Margins of Profit." *Studies in American Humor* n.s. 1.1 (June 1982): 24–43.

Hall, Frederick J. Letter to Samuel L. Clemens. 7 July 1893. Mark Twain Papers.

Hart, James D. "Memo to Bob [Robert Hirst]." 11 November 1891. TS. Mark Twain Papers.

Hartman Center for Sales, Advertising, and Marketing History. "EAA: Timeline." *Emergence of Advertising in America, 1850–1920*. Web. 1 December 2015.

Hill, Hamlin. "Mark Twain: Audience and Artistry." *American Quarterly* 15.1 (Spring 1963): 25–40.

Hirst, Robert H. Personal communication. 20 February 2014. Berkeley, California.

Holt, Douglas B. *How Brands Become Icons: The Principles of Cultural Branding*. Boston: Harvard Business School Press, 2004.

James, William. *The Principles of Psychology*. 2 vols. New York: Holt, 1890.

———. "Remarks on Spencer's Definition of Mind as Correspondence." *Journal of Speculative Philosophy* 12.1 (January 1878): 1–18.

Kaplan, Justin. *Mr. Clemens and Mark Twain*. New York: Pocket Books, 1968.

Keillor, Garrison. "Riverboat Rambler." Rev. of *Autobiography of Mark Twain*, vol. 1. *New York Times Book Review* 19 December 2010: 1.

Kirch, Claire, Judith Rosen, Marc Schultz, and Wendy Werris. "Producing a Holiday Miracle." *Publishers Weekly* 257.48 (6 December 2010): 6–8.

Landa, Robin. *Designing Brand Experiences*. Clifton Park: Thomson Delmar Learning, 2006.

Leach, William. *Land of Desire: Merchants, Power, and the Rise of a New American Culture*. New York: Pantheon, 1993.

Lee, Judith Yaross. "Mark Twain: [Date, 1601.] Conversation, as It Was by the Social Fireside in the Time of the Tudors." *Encyclopedia of Erotic Literature*. London: Fitzroy Dearborn, 2006. 1320–22.

———. *Twain's Brand: Humor in Contemporary American Culture*. Jackson: UP of Mississippi, 2012.

"London Gossip." *Boston Daily Advertiser* 7 March 1898: 8.

"Looking into New Books." *Plain Dealer [Cleveland]* 1 May 1892: 4.

Loving, Jerome. *Confederate Bushwhacker: Mark Twain in the Shadow of the Civil War*. Hanover and London: UP of New England, 2013.

———. *Mark Twain: The Adventures of Samuel L. Clemens*. Berkeley: U of California P, 2010.

MacDonnell, Kevin. "Who Killed Charlie Webster?" *Mark Twain Journal* 51.1&2 (Spring/Fall 2013): 9–37.

Mark Twain books. Advertisement. *New York Herald* 25 Nov. 1894: 1, cols. 1–2.

"Mark Twain Gets a Patent on Himself." *Des Moines Daily News* 8 February 1908: 3.

"Mark Twain in Montreal." *New York Times* 8 December 1881: n.p.

"Mark Twain: Literary Man with a Good Business Talent." *San Francisco Chronicle* 15 June 1885: 2.

The Mark Twain Papers. Bancroft Library, Berkeley, California.

"'Mark Twain' Patent Applied For." *Grand Rapids Evening Press* 13 February 1908: 4.

"Mark Twain Said to Be in Poor Health." *New-York Tribune* 5 May 1894: 4.

"Mark Twain Turns into a Corporation." *New York Times* 24 Dec. 1908: 2.

"'Mark Twain' Whisky under Patent Rights." *Brooklyn Eagle* 5 Jan. 1908: 1.

"Mark Twain's Affairs." *Boston Daily Journal* 10 May 1894: 8.

"Mark Twain's Company Embarrassed." *Springfield [MA] Daily Republican* 19 Apr. 1894: 5.

McIntire-Strasburg, Janice. "'Sivilizing Humor': The Evolution of Mark Twain's *Library of Humor*." *Studies in American Humor* n.s. 3.22 (2010): 11–25.

Memorandum. [Copartnership agreement between Samuel L. Clemens and Charles L. Webster.] 11 March 1885. Mark Twain Papers.

"Memorandum for Mr. Rogers Re. Clemens' Matter." 1909. Mark Twain Papers.

Michelson, Bruce. *Printer's Devil: Mark Twain and the American Publishing Revolution*. Berkeley: U of California P, 2006.

Morris, Edward L. Letter to Samuel L. Clemens. 4 December 1907. Mark Twain Papers.

"The New Trademark Law." *Salt Lake Telegram* 6 April 1905: 4.

Nickels, Cameron C. "Mark Twain and Post–Civil War Humor." *A Companion to Mark Twain*. Ed. Peter Messent and Louis J. Budd. Oxford: Blackwell, 2005. 485–99.

"Notes from the Book World." *Springfield [MA] Daily Republican* 1 October 1894: 8.

Ohmann, Richard. *Selling Culture: Magazines, Markets, and Class at the Turn of the Century*. New York: Verso, 1996.

Paine, Albert Bigelow. *Mark Twain, a Biography; the Personal and Literary Life of Samuel Langhorne Clemens*. 3 vols. New York: Harper & Brothers, 1912.

Parker, Hershel. *Herman Melville: 1819–1851*. 1996. Baltimore: Johns Hopkins UP, 2002.

"Registering Trade-Mark: New Law Reduces the Fee and Makes Other Changes." *Baltimore American* 24 March 1905: 14.

Rothenbuhler, Eric W. "The Church of the Cult of the Individual." *Media Anthropology*. Ed. Eric W. Rothenbuhler and Mihai Coman. Thousand Oaks: Sage, 2005. 91–100.

"Round about Gotham." *Sunday Herald [Chicago]* 20 September 1891: 22.

Sanderson, Kenneth M. "The Books of Charles L. Webster & Co." Unpublished paper for Librarianship 202, U of California, Berkeley, 1979.

Schechter, Frank I. *The Historical Foundations of the Law Relating to Trade-Marks*. With foreword by Munroe Smith. Columbia Legal Studies. New York: Columbia UP, 1925.

Schmidt, Barbara, ed. "A History of and Guide to Uniform Editions of Mark Twain's Works." *Mark Twain Quotations, Newspaper Collections, & Related Resources*. Web. 1 December 2015.

———. "Special Feature: *Samuel L. Clemens vs. Belford, Clarke & Company* (U.S. Circuit Court, 1883, ILL.)." *Mark Twain Quotations, Newspaper Collections, & Related Resources*. Web. 15 November 2015.

Steeples, Douglas, and David O. Whitten. *Democracy in Desperation: The Depression of 1893*. Contributions in Economics and Economic History199. Westport: Greenwood, 1998.

Thomas, Henry F. Letter from Houghton Mifflin to Henry Nash Smith. 1 June 1956. Mark Twain Papers.

Twain, Mark. "Ashcroft-Lyon Manuscript." *Autobiography of Mark Twain. Vol. 3*. Complete and authoritative ed. Ed. Benjamin Griffin and Harriet Elinor Smith. Berkeley: U of California P, 2015. 321–440.

———. "Mark Twain and His English Editor [To the Editor]." *Spectator* [*London*] 21 September 1872: 13–14.

———. *Mark Twain in Eruption: Hitherto Unpublished Pages about Men and Events*. Ed. Bernard DeVoto. New York and London: Harper & Brothers, 1940.

———. *Mark Twain Speaking*. Ed. Paul Fatout. Iowa City: U of Iowa P, 1976.

———. *Mark Twain: The Complete Interviews*. Ed. Gary Scharnhorst. Tuscaloosa: University of Alabama Press, 2006.

———. *Mark Twain's Letters to His Publishers, 1867–1894*. Ed. Hamlin Hill. Berkeley: U of California P, 1967.

———. *Mark Twain's Letters, Volume 5:1872–1873*. Ed. Lin Salamo and Harriet Elinor Smith. Mark Twain Papers. Berkeley: U of California P, 1997.

———. *Mark Twain's Notebooks & Journals, Vol. II, 1877–1883*. Ed. Frederick Anderson, Lin Salamo, and Bernard L. Stein. Mark Twain Papers. Berkeley: U of California P, 1975.

———. *Mark Twain's Notebooks & Journals, Vol. III, 1883–1891*. Ed. Robert Pack Browning, Michael B. Frank, and Lin Salamo. Mark Twain Papers. Berkeley: U of California P, 1979.

Twain, Mark, and William D. Howells. *Mark Twain–Howells Letters: The Correspondence of Samuel L. Clemens and William D. Howells, 1872–1910*. Ed. Henry Nash Smith and William M. Gibson. Assisted by Frederick Anderson. Cambridge: Belknap-Harvard UP, 1960.

United States. Bureau of the Census. *Historical Statistics of the United States, Colo-*

nial Times to 1970. Bicentennial ed. Washington: U.S. Dept. of Commerce, Bureau of the Census, 1975.

United States. Patent and Trademark Office. *The Story of the U.S. Patent and Trademark Office*. Washington: U.S. Dept. of Commerce, Patent and Trademark Office, 1988.

"Walt Whitman Buried." *New-York Tribune* 31 March 1892: 6.

"Wasting Away: General Grant Dying by Degrees of an Insidious, but Fatal Malady." *Cincinnati Commercial Gazette* 2 March 1885: 1–2.

Webster, Samuel Charles. *Mark Twain, Business Man*. Ed. Samuel Charles Webster. Boston: Little, Brown, 1946.

"Whiskey Men at Outs: Another Suit for Infringement of Trade Mark." *Daily Evening Bulletin* [*San Francisco*] 4 January 1872: col. C.

3
"Society's Very Choicest Brands"
Hank Morgan's Brand Magic in Camelot

Mark Schiebe

In her recent study *Twain's Brand: Humor in Contemporary Culture* (2012), Judith Yaross Lee proposes that by inventing "Mark Twain," Samuel Clemens created the seminal American "comic commodity," a multifaceted comic brand capable of being marketed to the public in a variety of mutually reinforcing ways. In doing so Clemens not only powerfully influenced the direction of several twentieth- and twenty-first-century American comic traditions but also shaped the way in which we think about humor's place in the larger economy, a consumer culture where audiences exchange money for humor, and humor for laughter. Clemens's success at developing "brand recognition" for his comedic product, Lee argues, stemmed from his ability to situate his comic brand prominently within an emerging information economy, where public awareness of product and product name—brand equity—becomes as valuable as the product itself, as it greatly increases the probability of future consumer demand (Lee 3–26).

It is in his 1889 novel *A Connecticut Yankee in King Arthur's Court*, I would suggest, that Twain's interest in the power of branding is expressed most significantly in his fiction. This chapter concerns, then, not Samuel Clemens's brand, but Hank Morgan's brands. There is an abiding consensus among Twain scholars that *A Connecticut Yankee* represents the author's most sustained meditation on the dramatic societal changes brought about by industrialization and corresponding shifts in cultural values. Critical attention to economic elements in the novel has thus understandably focused mainly on the Yankee's achievements in industry—that is, on what he produces, rather than on what he sells (and how he sells it).[1] But if Hank Morgan is an industrial pioneer bringing nineteenth-century technology to sixth-century England, he is also a brand pioneer, perhaps the first such character in American letters. I wish to explore this as yet unexamined aspect of Morgan's business career in Camelot.

Hank Morgan's construction of an elaborate network of "Man Factories," an obvious pun on manufactories, indicates that he is engaged in a specific, and morally hazardous, kind of social project, essentially attempting to reeducate an entire populace on a mass production model. In order to sell his wares in sixth-century Camelot, the Yankee entrepreneur must engineer a revolutionary shift of consciousness, turning feudal "animals" (as he habitually refers to them) into American-style consumers; in short, he must mass-produce the men and women who will buy the products he is mass-producing. In this respect, Morgan is ahead of his time in a double sense; a time traveler from the nineteenth century to the sixth, the Yankee also displays impressive foresight in his attention to an economic concern we typically associate with the twentieth century: the problem of demand. The solution to this problem, from a business standpoint, was the harnessing of the power of the brand and the development of branding practices, which, I argue, highlight the mystical rather than the material qualities of a given commodity.

In fact, the capitalist "discovery" of the brand is more aptly labeled a *re*covery; investigation of the etymological history of brand reveals that it is a concept with a rich medieval past. Derived from the Middle High German *brant*, translated as "the act of burning," *brand* once denoted "the blade of a sword or similar weapon, and hence (like blade) the sword itself," a trace of which survives in our modern usage of the verb *brandish* (*OED*). In Arthurian romance *brand* was the term used to describe Excalibur, the weapon whose magical properties were conferred only on those who swore allegiance to the king. Thus, the power of the brand and, more precisely, the notion of brand loyalty, furnishes us with a conceptual link between Morgan's and Arthur's empires, standing in both milieus at the center of a ritual performance that bonds a community: in Morgan's case, his sales force/consumer base, and in Arthur's case his legendary Knights of the Round Table. It also provides support for an interpretation of the novel as a work of radical historical relativism, a "fable of progress" capable of destroying its own premise (Smith).

During the period 1860–1900, America saw not only an unprecedented explosion of industrial growth and subsequent corporate consolidation, but also a "retailing revolution" led by a group of business pioneers who arrived on the scene with the first wave of branded products (Chandler 235–314). The Civil War economy had created demand for a variety of standardized, mass-produced goods whose appeal depended on consistency of product; packaged products like canned goods promised "sealed freshness" to soldiers dependent on sources of food from increasingly distant production sites. The general merchant, the proverbial shopkeeper who sold commodities out of barrels, personally guaranteeing product quality, was being replaced by the commercial merchant, whose emissary arrived with prepackaged, "ready-made" goods, the brand name of the good now functioning as the effective guarantor. The decade following the close of the war saw a dozen or so of the "classic" American brands appear on the market, names like Campbell, Heinz, Quaker Oats, Colgate, and Proctor & Gamble (which provided Union soldiers with a steady supply of soap and candles). By the 1880s customers expected to know the name of the manufacturer who made the product they were purchasing and were becoming increasingly familiar with an associated brand image or logo they had seen in a newspaper advertisement or on a billboard. In *The Incorporation of America* (1982), Alan Trachtenberg comments on this phenomenon: "The mark or name is a peculiar kind of expression, originating not as a spontaneous act of naming on the part of people discovering a new object in their midst but as an act from above, the manufacturer's act, sanctioned and protected by the law of copyright: a fiction underwritten by laws protecting what came to be known as 'intellectual property,' the brand name" (138). There is little doubt that all of this caught the eye (and ear) of Mark Twain, whose immersion in the commercial innovations of his culture, first explored in Van Wyck Brooks's classic 1920 study, *The Ordeal of Mark Twain*, has been a perennially active area in Twain scholarship. Most recently, Loren Glass and Amanda Adams have documented the immense time and energy Twain spent simply attempting to retain ownership of his own work, a frustrating endeavor in an era when copyright law was both elusive and too weak to stem rampant piracy, while the more robust protection of the trademark was reserved, rather idiosyncratically, for "vendible merchandise," a legal category that excluded literary work (Glass 688). It is perhaps no surprise, then, that Hank Morgan's very first administrative order in Camelot is to establish a patent office, "for I knew that a country without [. . .] good patent laws was just a crab, and couldn't travel any way but sideways or backwards" (107).

Brand Loyalty: Modern and Medieval

Out of the handful of rather banal nineteenth-century consumer items Morgan introduces to Camelot, four products are specifically identified by brand name: Persimmon's Soap, Peterson's Prophylactic Toothbrush, Noyoudont toothwash, and St. Stylite tow-linen shirts. With regard to the second of these items, Twain was surely aware of the historical irony: as much as his Yankee scoffs at sixth-century hygiene, the record shows that the modern toothbrush, that great civilizing agent, was in fact *simultaneously* introduced in Connecticut and Camelot.[2] Though the first patent for a toothbrush was granted to H. N. Wadsworth in 1857, mass production in the United States did not begin until 1885 ("Everyday Mysteries"). The Yankee's brand of toothwash appears to have been contemporary (and local), as well. A product by the name of Sozodont was advertised regularly in Twain's hometown newspaper, the *Hartford Daily Courant*. The strangely negative warning implied in the Yankee's twist on the product name is likely a parodic response to an ad that ran in the *Courant* in September of 1888: "When a dealer who happens to be out of Sozodont tries to make you believe that something he has in stock is better or as good, quietly say No, seek the next establishment where that standard tooth beautifier can be obtained" (Briden 74).

Whereas advertising in the first part of the nineteenth century focused on conveying basic information, such as simple product descriptions and availability, reflecting the widespread assumption that demand exceeded supply, by the latter half of the century advertising messages were becoming more abstract and ideological, reflecting awareness among manufacturers that an era of consumer choice was on the horizon (Laird). The rhetoric employed in the Sozodont ad tells Twain's contemporaries nothing about toothwash except that this product is the *only* acceptable toothwash in one's household, the "standard." The rise of advertising agencies in the 1890s suggested that manufacturers were beginning to take seriously the looming crisis of overproduction and the threat of mutually destructive competition for market share, and they aimed to combat these commercial hazards by hiring "professional liars" (Hank's phrase for peddlers of superstition) to weave a magic tapestry of words around their products (166).

Hank's own corps of "professional liars," the knights of Camelot, are ideally suited to drum up brand awareness for the Yankee's products. Here is Morgan explaining his scheme: "In the first place it was a furtive, underhand blow at this nonsense of knight errantry, though nobody suspected that but me. I had started a number of these people out—the bravest knights I could get—each sandwiched between bulletin boards bearing one device or another, and I judged that by and by when they got to be numerous enough they would begin to look ridiculous; and then, even the steel-clad ass that hadn't any board would himself begin to look ridiculous because he was out of fashion" (91–92). To be sure, the "manufacturing" of consumer demand isn't Morgan's only reason for turning the knights of Camelot into an army of galloping billboards; his aim is to eradicate the institution of knight-errantry itself, that "superstitious and chuckle-headed trade," natural rival of the modern order (234). Moreover, the Yankee is convinced that his introduction of soap to the sixth century ("PERSIMMON'S SOAP—ALL THE PRIME-DONNE USE IT") is a step toward undermining the power of the Church, the chief obstacle to the formation of a republic. First soap, "[n]ext, education—next, freedom—and then she would begin to crumble" (190, 191).

The fact that the *purpose* of soap needs to be explained to the skeptical nobility suggests that the relationship between capitalist marketing strategy and the progress of civilization (read: rising standards of hygiene) is a difficult matter to sort out. Progress and profit, as the apologists of capital have it, walk hand in hand, and it's worth remembering Henry Nash Smith's observation that it is plausible to view the Yankee as both "a missionary of the Enlightenment *and* a fraudulent businessman" (Smith, *Development* 159, italics mine).

Among the newly minted salesmen, Sir Ossaise of Surluse has perhaps the most difficult job, that of selling stove polish to the public, since stoves themselves are not yet on the market. His predicament clarifies through comic hyperbole the existential condition of the salesman who *must sell*, whether or not there is a market for his product, and anticipates Arthur Miller's description of America's most famous salesman, a man "way out there in the blue, riding on a smile and a shoeshine" (138). The knight from Surluse is "of a light and laughing disposition," prone to jokes at the expense of his fellow salesmen (and, by implication, consumers), and thus he is the right man for the difficult job (240). Still, while the novel fails to report sales figures, it seems likely that Morgan's stove polish is a commercial flop in Camelot. Unlike the Yankee's tow-linen line of shirts, which "sold like smoke," the explicitly anachronistic stove polish suggests that there may be, after all, a limit to the commercial appeal of the Yankee's branded goods (281). Branding, as Twain clearly appreciated before many of his contemporaries, offered a potential solution to industrial capitalism's inevitable problem of overproduction by lending the commodity an aura of difference associated with a name, a look, a feel, or a smell. Stove polish in the absence of stoves is a comic delineation of the outer limits of brand magic, a limit Twain knew from experience. As famous as he was, his name alone attached to a product wasn't enough to guarantee its success, as his ill-conceived bedcover clamp—an invention for which consumers apparently could perceive no need—proved in 1885, as the initial notes for *A Connecticut Yankee* lay on his writing desk (Loving 273). One wonders to what extent the adventures of Sir Ossaise of Surluse might have been a nod and a wink at his own occasional gift for anachronistic innovations and at the absurdity of marketing useless products.

The lack of critical attention on Morgan's brand-centered business model is understandable. The word *brand* itself appears only a single time in the text and is easily glossed over. Moreover, Morgan utters it in reference not to one of his own lines of consumer items, but instead as way of marking the elite social rank of Camelot's most noble princesses, whom he calls "society's very choicest brands" (177). The phrase occurs as a passing reference, a kind of private joke, in a discussion concerning the relative merits of women of the sixth and nineteenth centuries. Yet, if nothing else, the very fact that the word appears figuratively in this context (Morgan surely wasn't claiming princesses are *literally* brands) indicates that in the Yankee's mind, brand has attained the status of a concept. To be clear, in calling Morgan a brand pioneer, I'm not claiming that he is a self-conscious theorist of the cultural significance of brand, at least not in the sense that he is, say, a self-styled philosopher of republicanism. What I am suggesting is that Morgan, and Twain, demonstrate an instinctive awareness of a wider resonance of brand in sixth-century Camelot, one borne out by etymological investigation.

Gerhard Joseph points to this wider resonance when he draws a connection between Alfred Tennyson's consistent preference for the word *brand* (rather than the more contemporary *sword*) in *Idylls of the King* (1859–1885) and his publisher Frederick Macmillan's attempt to turn Tennyson himself into a "brand name." Joseph traces the etymology of the word back to the Middle High German *brant*, or "the act of burning." In Arthurian legend, the "flash[ing] fire" of the Excalibur endowed the instrument, itself "branded" with Arthur's mark, with the power to brand others (135).

> For though the OED gives 1807 as the date of the first use of "brand" as a trademark denoting proprietorship of goods capable of being "plugged" in the commercial sense, a king's "dubbing" (from the Old High German for "to plug") of his knights is no doubt a ceremonial displacement of a more primitive branding of the skin denoting allegiance to a liegelord—or even to the Lord. [Therefore] while the word "sword" refers to a material object, the term "brand" is more suggestive of the way such an object is also a sign, precisely a blade that may have a message of ownership inscribed or branded upon it and that is itself an instrument of further inscription by its wielder. (135)

In fact, as the OED confirms, in the English language the poetical use of brand as "the blade of a sword or similar weapon" can be traced as far back as Beowulf, and this usage is found in the Arthurian romance *Sir Gawain and the Green Knight*, as well as Milton's *Paradise Lost*; it is employed by Pope in his translation of *The Iliad* ("On his broad Shoulder fell the forceful Brand"); and with conscious archaism in the nineteenth century by Sir Walter Scott and J. A. Symonds, before being picked up by Tennyson (OED). Thus, though the medieval usage of brand is not found in Mallory's *Morte d'Arthur*, Twain's self-professed source of inspiration, it is strongly present in the English canon and is therefore likely to have at least penetrated Twain's semantic unconscious.[3]

Whether or not one gives credence to the notion that Twain made the connection himself, consideration of the genealogy of brand compels us to revise the widely held assumption that there is a fundamental incongruity between the ideologies of Arthurian chivalry and modern capitalism. In fact, in the central myth of Arthurian romance, the undying loyalty of the knights to their king, inspired by his brand Excalibur, one sees a historical antecedent of Morgan's nineteenth-century techniques, a linguistic clue to a set of material practices that link Arthur's instrument of initiation and the Yankee's advertising placards. By this logic, it is the fact of the knights' steadfast allegiance to the Arthurian brand that actually facilitates the entrance of the Yankee, who, rather than doing something altogether new, is merely performing an updated version of the ritual. The knights, we might say, are *rebranded* with the sign of Morgan's consumer goods. They are then charged with the double task of selling the product to the peasantry and rebranding any "wandering knight" they meet on their travels with the sign of the new product, in a manner that parallels the duplicating powers of Excalibur, "a blade that may have a message of ownership inscribed or branded upon it and that is in itself an instrument of further inscription by its wielder." The transaction is exemplified in Morgan's description of Sir Ozana le Cure Hardy, who is in "the gentleman's furnishing line" and specializes in plug hats. "He was clothed all in steel, in the beautifulest armor of the time—up to where his helmet ought to have been; but he hadn't any helmet, he wore a shiny stovepipe hat, and was as ridiculous a spectacle as one might want to see. . . . [His] saddle was hung about with leather hatboxes, and every time he overcame a wandering knight he swore him into my service and fitted him with a plug and made him wear it" (263–64). The double entendre here is expanded to include "plug"; instead of "dubbing" the knights with his brand in order to express proprietorship, Morgan has them "fitted with a plug," the terms connected by the etymological origin of *dub* in its older German variant *plug*. The physical action of placing a hat on someone else, of course, echoes the act of a king's dubbing. This symbolic action, I would argue, stands at the crux of the transformation of Arthur's feudal kingdom into Morgan's capitalist republic. The Yankee will replace swords with hats (and, eventually, kings with cats—if he takes his protégé Clarence's tongue-in-cheek suggestion). A change in material practices has paved the way for changes in the political superstructure. But in another sense Morgan is simply replacing brand with brand—he is rebranding Camelot. The knights and peasantry, turned salesmen and consumers, now signify their allegiance through acts of buying and selling, which in the Yankee's system perform the cultural work of rituals maintaining the new order. The acts have changed, but the new ones bear an oblique resemblance to their forebears, if we follow the semantic trace.

Commodities and Other Enchanted Forms

In the Marxian tradition, brand has long been associated with the commodity, the crucial middle term in the M-C-M' circuit, whereby the owners of capital accrue their profits by exploiting the labor power that goes into its production. The equation works like this: the capitalist invests a certain amount of money into raw materials, technology, and human labor, and the resulting product he brings to market is called a "commodity." Since this commodity is somehow more than the sum of its parts, he then sells it back to those who made it for a greater amount than he initially invested; his capital has been augmented, and he may then begin the process again. When Raymond Williams calls commodity branding "a system of magical inducements and satisfactions," he is in a sense merely paraphrasing Marx's famous remark about the elementary commodity form in *Capital*, volume 1 (Section 4), which Marx calls "a very strange thing, abounding in metaphysical subtleties and theological niceties" (Williams qtd. in Bevan and Wengrow 14; Marx 163). For Marx, the "mystical character" of the commodity derives from the social fact that both buyer and seller ascribe to it an exchange-value that is imaginary and yet entirely objective (because socially agreed upon). The connection between a commodity's value in the marketplace and the value of the labor that went into its manufacture is obscured, and so the values ascribed to commodities take on a fetishistic character—like religious idols, commodities now "appear as autonomous figures endowed with a life of their own" (Marx 165). The Yankee's stovepipe hats are such fetishistic products in the sense that those who purchase them are under the belief that they are acquiring something whose value can't be measured by mere "use." Like the salesmen who sell them, commodities appear as well to be "out in the blue," and in this light not so different from some of the magical things that one finds in Camelot.

What we might call the relative, or perspective-bound, nature of magic is in fact a central motif in *A Connecticut Yankee*, one I illustrate with the following example. The main action of chapters 11–20 concerns Morgan's first chivalric adventure, a quest to rescue forty-five beautiful young princesses who languish in the gloomy castle of three evil ogres and to restore them to their proper castles. In the celebrated comic episode resolving this quest, the Yankee and Sandy, his travel guide (and future bride), discover to their surprise that the ogres' castle is "nothing but a pigsty; a pigsty with a wattled fence around it" (243). Or so Morgan thinks. Sandy's explanation of the situation makes it clear to the initially puzzled Yankee that she in fact sees countesses in a castle, not pigs in a sty, and *it is only he* who suffers from a strange delusion:

> "It was not enchanted aforetime," she said in a musing fashion, as if to herself. "And how strange is this marvel, and how awful—that to the one perception it is enchanted and dight in a base and shameful aspect; yet to the perception of the other it is not enchanted, hath suffered no change, but stands firm and stately, girt with its moat and waving its banners in the blue air from its towers. And God shield us, how it pricks the heart to see again those gracious captives, and the sorrow deepened in their sweet faces!" (243–44)

Taking advantage of Sandy's dogged persistence that it is he who is under a spell causing him to see pigs instead of princesses, Morgan explains to her that his delusion has extended to the terrible ogres, who in his diseased vision appear as three swineherds. The Yankee then heroically saves the princesses by taking out his pocketbook and purchasing the pigs, buying the entire lot of them "at the lump sum of sixteen pennies, which was rather above the latest quotations" (245). In doing so, he solves one set of enchantments by casting a new one. With one fearsome spell, countesses are turned into hogs; with another, hogs are turned into commodities. That is, they've entered the M-C-M circuit. From there it is but a short step, the invention of the refrigerated car, before countesses (read: hogs) are indeed to become "society's very choicest brands."[4]

With capitalist magicians like Philip Armour, not to mention the Yankee's own namesake, J. P. Morgan, a full thirteen centuries away, his chief rival in the casting of enchantments is, of course, Merlin, the sorcerer. Before Morgan's arrival, the inhabitants of Camelot were sent into swoons by Merlin's fantastic prophesies, none of which were subjected to anything like empirical standards of proof. After Morgan terrifies Camelot by "manufacturing" an eclipse of the sun, his next feat is to summon "the fires of heaven" (in other words, "a few bushels of first-rate blasting powder") down upon Merlin's tower, which explodes in front of a huge crowd (88). In the climactic scene in which Morgan miraculously restores the Holy Fountain at a remote monastery, he first lets Merlin have at it. The sorcerer tires himself out with a series of silly "incantations," but the well remains dry. Morgan, lowered into the well by candlelight, and confirming his suspicion that it has merely sprung a leak, nevertheless opts for a theatrical solution, one based on the premise that "[a]s a matter of business it was a good idea to get the notion round that the thing was difficult. Many a small thing has been made large by the right kind of advertising" (277). The secret mending of the leak, a rather prosaic task, is accompanied by an unprecedented smoke and dynamite show in the area surrounding the well, seemingly ignited by Morgan's absurd barrage of verbal nonsense. A great public spectacle has been performed, one confirming Morgan's place as preeminent magician in Camelot. The purpose of the show, of course, is to keep the Yankee's stock high, his brand trusted. As Morgan himself later muses, "a man can keep his trademark current in such a country, but he can't sit around and do it" (311).

By the dawn of the twentieth century, the notion of "brand" had become a central issue in corporate valuation and a subject of vigorous public debate. In June of 1899, a decade after the publication of *A Connecticut Yankee*, the sugar magnate Henry O. Havemeyer testified before the Industrial Commission in Washington on the question of how he went about setting a par value for the stock offered during capitalization of his American Sugar Refining Company. When pressed specifically about his understanding of "value," he argued that future profit forecasts based on the strength of the newly incorporated brand were worth a sum *far above* the total combined assets of the buildings, refineries, and other real estate (Mitchell 62–63). Despite what Lawrence Mitchell calls Havemeyer's "holistic approach to valuation," where expected future earnings and tangible asset value were lumped together, it is clear that Havemeyer's testimony located the "real value" of the company in "the value of the trade-mark, the name Havemeyer as identified with sugar." Asked what it would cost to build all of the refineries then in the company's possession, the sugar tycoon agreed that the sum was roughly between thirty and thirty-five million, but he added that "the brand of Havemeyer & Elder would bring thirty-five millions alone" (65).

At the turn of the century, Havemeyer's method of corporate valuation based on a combination of projected profits, real assets, and brand equity was still viewed with skepticism by the public at large, yet Havemeyer, like Mark Twain, clearly foresaw the formidable power of brand loyalty. Consumers didn't just want sugar—they wanted Havemeyer Sugar. The historical record of the subsequent era, during which a handful of brands rose to kingly status in American consumer markets, more than bore out Havemeyer's reasoning, even if his testimony at the time was manifestly self-serving. On the one hand, branding addressed a sober and pragmatic consumer desire for product consistency. Yet beyond this, the power of the brand revealed the great explanatory power of Marx's analysis of the fetishistic character of commodities. Branding is an attempt by the manufacturer to highlight the "mystical" qualities present in the commodity form, to endow his trademarked goods with autonomous identities, and to forge a consumer group through a powerful ritual of belonging.

Twenty-first-century critics of branding continue to draw inspiration from Marx's insight, which points the way toward alternative forms of belonging based on a critique of the commodity form, refusing, as it were, to substitute a brand (even "society's choicest") for a hog. In the novel's closing sequence, the betrayal of Morgan by all but a handful of his most faithful followers indicates that, like other forms of symbolic power, brand loyalty has its limits. The knights of Camelot may have swapped their helmets for stovepipe hats, embarking on a quest for that new Holy Grail, the paying consumer, but their allegiance to this new form of brand magic proves temporary. "Did you think you had educated the superstition out of those people?" Clarence asks his boss. "Well, then, you may unthink it" (538). The implication here is that a capitalist republic is one whose citizens have dispensed with superstition, yet it is hard not to feel the sharp edge of Twain's cynicism: clearly, Hank's experiment has failed because Camelot's sluggish consumers have resisted his branding efforts, in essence preferring an older brand allegiance (an allegiance to the brand Excalibur) over Hank's modern regime of consumer superstition.

It is difficult to say for certain that the unraveling of Morgan's republic represents an authorial satire of late-nineteenth-century American capitalism, let alone a quasi-Marxian critique of the commodity. As Smith and others have argued, beyond the most obvious satirical attacks, Twain's political and economic intentions in the novel remain unclear and seem to have evolved during the course of its composition (*Fable* 40–56). Nevertheless, *A Connecticut Yankee in King Arthur's Court* is unique among novels of the period for its probing exploration of the power and limits of brand magic. Twain's final plot gambit, the reversal whereby Merlin outwits Morgan and spirits him back to the future, may suggest that Hank's commercial wizardry is too far ahead of its time, but from a twenty-first-century vantage, his prescience is undeniable.

Notes

1. There are two noteworthy exceptions. Ann Douglas compares Morgan's behavior to the showman-like style of performer/businessman P. T. Barnum and the conspicuous consumption of Andrew Carnegie and J. P. Morgan. A decade earlier, Henry Nash Smith pointed out that the Yankee often seems more interested in engaging in a variety of performances solidifying his public image as "the boss" than

he is in attending to the details involved in creating the infrastructure to support industrial capitalism.

2. It was not the first time the author aired opinions on European hygiene. Twenty-two years earlier, Twain and his traveling companions, puzzled and annoyed by the scarcity of soap in France and Italy, took to carrying the treasured item on their persons (*The Innocents Abroad* 140–41, 243–44, 317).

3. In fact, the phrase "A Burning Brand" occurs in *Life on the Mississippi* (1883) as the rather enigmatic heading of chapter 52, which concerns the letter an inmate named Williams covertly writes to himself in an attempt to be released from the penitentiary; the phrase is never repeated, or explained, though we might speculate that Twain was aware on some level that criminals had been historically subject to literal branding of the skin.

4. Philip Armour, Chicago's "monarch of meat," once said, "I like to turn the bristles, blood, and the inside and outside of pigs and bullocks into revenue" (qtd. in Josephson 284).

Works Cited

Adams, Amanda. "Performing Ownership: Dickens, Twain, and Copyright on the Transatlantic Stage." *American Literary Realism* 43.3 (Spring 2011): 223–41.

Bevan, Andrew, and David Wengrow. *Cultures of Commodity Branding*. Walnut Creek: Left Coast Press, 2010.

"brand, n." *OED Online*. Oxford University Press, June 2014. Web.

Briden, Earl. "Advertising in *A Connecticut Yankee*." *American Notes & Queries* 1 (5/6) (January/February 1983): 74.

Brooks, Van Wyck. 1920. *The Ordeal of Mark Twain*. New York: Meridian, 1955.

Chandler, Alfred D., Jr. *The Visible Hand: The Managerial Revolution in American Business*. Cambridge: Belknap Press of Harvard, 1977.

Cox, James. "A Connecticut Yankee in King Arthur's Court: The Machinery of Self-Preservation." *Mark Twain: A Collection of Critical Essays*. Ed. Henry Nash Smith. Englewood Cliffs, NJ: Prentice-Hall, 1963.

Douglas, Ann. "Art and Advertising in *A Connecticut Yankee*: The 'Robber Baron' Revisited." *Canadian Review of American Studies* 6.2 (1975): 182–95.

"Everyday Mysteries: Fun Science Facts from the Library of Congress." <www.loc.gov/rr/scitech/mysteries/tooth.html>.

Glass, Loren. "Trademark Twain." *American Literary History* 13.4 (Winter 2001): 671–93.

Johnson, James L. *Mark Twain and the Limits of Power*. Knoxville: U of Tennessee P, 1982.

Joseph, Gerhard. "Commodifying Tennyson: The Historical Transformation of Brand Loyalty." *Victorian Poetry* 34.2 (Summer 1996): 133–47.

Josephson, Matthew. *The Robber Barons*. 1934. New York: Harvest, 1962.

Kaplan, Fred. *The Singular Mark Twain*. New York: Doubleday, 2003.

Kaplan, Justin. "The Yankee and the Machine." *Mark Twain: A Profile*. Ed. Justin Kaplan. New York: Hill and Wang, 1967.

Laird, Pamela Walker. *Advertising Progress: American Business and the Rise of Consumer Marketing*. Baltimore: Johns Hopkins UP, 1998.

Lee, Judith Yaross. *Twain's Brand: Humor in Contemporary Culture*. Jackson: U of Mississippi P, 2012.

Loving, Jerome. *Mark Twain: The Adventures of Samuel L. Clemens*. Berkeley: U of California P, 2010.

Marx, Karl. *Capital: A Critique of Political Economy*. Volume I. 1867. Trans. Ben Fowkes. New York: Penguin, 1976.

Michelson, Bruce. *Mark Twain on the Loose: A Comic Writer and the American Self*. Amherst: U of Massachusetts P, 1995.

Miller, Arthur. *Death of a Salesman*. 1949. New York: Penguin, 1976.

Mitchell, Lawrence. *The Speculation Economy: How Finance Triumphed over Industry*. San Francisco: Berrett-Koehler, 2007.

Smith, Henry Nash. *Mark Twain's Fable of Progress: Political and Economic Ideas in* A Connecticut Yankee. New Brunswick: Rutgers UP, 1964.

———. *Mark Twain: The Development of a Writer*. Cambridge: Harvard UP, 1962.

Trachtenberg, Alan. *The Incorporation of America: Culture and Society in the Gilded Age*. New York: Hill and Wang, 1982.

Twain, Mark. *A Connecticut Yankee in King Arthur's Court*. 1889. New York: Oxford UP, 1996.

———. *The Innocents Abroad*. 1869. New York: Harper & Brothers, 1969.

———. *Life on the Mississippi*. 1883. New York: Signet Classic, 2001.

Webster, Samuel. Ed. *Mark Twain, Business Man*. Boston: Little, Brown, 1946.

4
The Quality (and Cost) of Mercy

Mark Twain's Evasion of the Poor

Ann M. Ryan

> Amid the greatest accumulations of wealth, men die of starvation, and puny infants suckle at dry breasts; while everywhere the greed of gain, the worship of wealth, shows the force of the fear of want.
>
> —Henry George, *Progress and Poverty*, 1879

> Long ago it was said that "one half of the world does not know how the other half lives." That was true then. It did not know because it did not care.
>
> —Jacob Riis, *How the Other Half Lives*, 1890

> The quasi-peaceable gentleman of leisure . . . consumes freely and of the best, in food, drink, narcotics, shelter, services, ornaments, apparel, weapons and accoutrements, amusements, amulets, and idols or divinities.
>
> —Thorstein Veblen, *The Theory of the Leisure Class*, 1899

> Peasant and noble, worker and factory owner, waiter and banker: each has his or her own unique vantage point and sees important aspects of how other people live . . . these observations shape each person's judgments of what is and is not just.
>
> —Thomas Piketty, *Capital in the Twenty-First Century*, 2014

Before Henry George exposed the myth of industrial progress and its betrayal of the poor, before Jacob Riis focused his camera on the "Other" half, before Thorstein Veblen described a culture of conspicuous consumption, and long before Thomas Piketty warned about unchecked accumulations of wealth, Mark Twain placed the fate of a prince in the hands of a pauper. In a scene worthy of *Oliver Twist*, a poor boy, Tom Canty, stands outside an opulent palace, "face against the gate-bars," hoping to get "a good devouring look" at the prince on the other side. In this archetypical moment from *The Prince and the Pauper*, where rage competes with desire, Twain frames the relationship of beggars to kings. Like Riis and George, Twain divides the economic landscape into the haves and the have-nots. And like Veblen and Piketty, he is suspicious of the mania for "more" that fuels a capitalist economy. Twain's fascination with an American culture of excess—and the human and economic detritus it spawns—both precedes and extends beyond the publication of *The Prince and the Pauper* (1881). In works such as *The Gilded Age* (1873), "The Man That Corrupted Hadleyburg" (1899), and "The $30,000 Bequest" (1904), Twain—no less than Austen, Hugo, Balzac, or even Dickens—dramatizes the transformation of poverty into wealth and wealth into poverty. Often characters in Twain's novels are bought and sold, caught in cycles of gain and loss, and live their lives either from hand to mouth or at the end of a silver spoon.

Despite his consistent critique of the forces that create poverty, however, Twain's sympathy for the poor—that is, for the embodied reality of poor people—is not as steady or uncomplicated as it may seem. This is particularly true in *The Prince and the Pauper*. Much has been written about Twain's love affair with wealth and its trappings, as well as his worry about having been or becoming again a poor man; less has been said about Twain's hostile response to actual poor people. His venomous descriptions of beggars—in Constantinople or New York City or Nevada—have been represented as mere psychological displacement. And while Twain's visceral rejection of the poor certainly has its roots in the lingering specter of poverty in his own life, it also participates more widely in the complicated treatment of the poor during the latter half of the nineteenth century. Indeed, Twain's personal anxieties have a political corollary. Poverty in America was seen at once as a moral failing, the result of individual penchants and choices, and also as a cultural infection, spread by everything from immigration, to poor urban planning, to the rise of great wealth.

Twain opens *The Prince and the Pauper* with an epigraph from Shakespeare's *Merchant of Venice*, in which Portia argues for a generous sense of compassion: "The quality of mercy is not strained / It droppeth as the gentle rain from heaven / Upon the place beneath." By inserting an ellipsis, Twain bypasses these lines and redirects the emphasis of Portia's famous phrase: "The quality of mercy . . . is twice blessed / It blesseth him that gives and him that takes / 'Tis mightiest in the mighty. It becomes / The thronèd monarch better than his crown." Twain edits the speech so that mercy appears to be primarily a boon to "the mighty" and not a blessing to the poor. In this revision the quality of mercy is performative, a visible ornament that "becomes the thronèd monarch" with little advantage to those living in "the place beneath." Twain's King Edward improves by virtue of his newfound sympathy with the poor, but it's a compassion that will die with him; Tom Canty, on the other hand, spends most of the novel forgetting about the poverty of his sisters and his mother, and ends as a powerless totem, not an agent of change. Mark Twain often seems caught between remembering and forgetting the poor, which is precisely the ambivalent response of the culture he lives in. In a letter William Dean Howells writes to his father, in which he describes the politics of both Twain and himself, Howells acknowledges this ambivalence: "We are theoretical socialists, and practical aristocrats" (Howells 231). *The Prince and the Pauper* imagines a world where the poor can be made happy without their poverty being cured. The beggar will not rebel against his oppressor but instead returns his borrowed robes to the rightful king. In a scene that is full of both political and narrative irony, a poor boy happily gives up his power, thus affirming and exposing the practical aristocracy of Mark Twain.

In *The Prince and the Pauper*, Twain represents the poor as sometimes dangerous, sometimes pathetic, and often repellent. While the novel celebrates King Edward's compassion for his people, it does not dismantle—or even weaken—the iron bars that will ensure his kingship. Hearts will change; economies will not. As Lawrence Howe describes its progress, "*The Prince and the Pauper* begins subversively but recoils to a conservatism that accommodates traditional authority" (119). Not quite ready for the "radical novelization of history" that occurs in *A Connecticut Yankee in King Arthur's Court*, here Twain embraces the constraints of the historical romance (Howe 119). He equates the problem of poverty with the finality of the past. So, just as he cannot rewrite history by conceiving of a new fate for the doomed King Edward, the ending of the novel seems to suggest that poverty is similarly fixed and irredeemable. While King Edward will save representatives of the worthy poor, en masse, the poor remain a dangerous presence in the novel, less a problem to be solved than a neighborhood to be avoided. The beggars of *The Prince and the Pauper* communicate Twain's deep anxiety about a free market economy, and not simply or only because of how vulnerable it makes the weakest members of society, but also because it releases a political and economic instability—boom-and-bust speculation, rebellion and resistance in workers, and the dangers of a needy underclass—that will ultimately undermine the security of the rich.

Twain and the (Poor) Man on the Street

The poverty of Twain's Hannibal, Missouri, remained invisible because it was overlain by a system of class that had little to do with actual economic power: "[E]verybody was poor, but didn't know it . . . and there were grades of society—people of good family, people of unclassified family, people of no family. Everybody knew everybody . . . yet the class lines were quite clearly drawn" (*Autobiography* 36). Once the young Sam Clemens left Hannibal, however, poverty become painfully, unavoidably visible. The fictional slum of Offal Court and its gangs of little urchins have their origins on the streets of New York City. In 1853 a seventeen-year-old Clemens wrote home to his mother: "Of all the commodities, manufactures—or whatever you please to call it—in New York, trundle-bed trash—children I mean—take the lead. Why, from Cliff street, up Frankfort to Nassau street, six or seven squares—my road to dinner—I think I could count two hundred brats. Niggers, mulattoes, quadroons, Chinese, and some the Lord no doubt originally intended to be white, but the dirt on whose faces leaves one uncertain as to that fact, block up the little, narrow street; and to wade through this mass of human vermin, would raise the ire of the most patient person that ever lived" (31 August 1853). [1] Twain experiences the poverty of this "mass of human vermin" as a physical assault, a sensation and scenario he will recast in *The Prince and the Pauper* when Prince Edward is followed by a "delighted and noisy swarm of human vermin" (25). Twain metaphorically links this amalgam of racial and ethnic identities with the processes of manufacturing, effectively making "trundle-bed trash" the ugly "commodities" of capitalism. What is a precocious association for Twain at seventeen becomes a seasoned reflection by the time he's sixty-seven. While visiting Nassau in 1902 with Henry Huttleston Rogers, Twain writes in his travel log: "Watchword of the place: 'Let a penny go! . . . *Do* boss!' In all the narrow back-lanes, a pest of small niggers swarms continually after the carriages wailing this abject refrain & making touring uncheerful and irksome. The population is black with a mere sprinkle of whites; the only prosperous industry, the begetting of more niggers" ("Excursions").[2] In both his early and late observations, Twain's metaphors suggest that the machinery of capitalism transforms human beings into commodities and, as Marx writes, "throws workers upon the streets in great masses" (45). Twain's racist vocabulary inscribes him not just as "white," but also as "tourist." His white identity carries with it the expectation of free movement, while as tourist he imagines the island as a kind of playground. When the poor interfere with his movement and pleasure, Twain tosses pennies in the street: a gesture composed equally of charity and contempt. This description of Nassau's poor, black children is followed by a rhapsodic account of the governor's house, which affords "an enchanting view of the many-colored harbor splendors—as wonderful a water-picture as any I have seen anywhere, I think." When Twain ascends to the hilltop home of Sir Gilbert Carter, he sees at a distance the "pale and deep purple," "several shades of green," and "all shades of blue" in the water below. The chaotic contest between white and black, rich and poor, gives way to this Technicolor vision of paradise. In *The Prince and the Pauper*, Twain orchestrates a similar sight line, contrasting the pandemonium of the street against the peaceful and secure vision of it from above: "Tom Canty gazed abroad over the surging sea of eager faces and his heart swelled with exultation, and he felt that the one thing worth living for in this world was to be a king, and a nation's idol. Presently, he caught sight, at a distance, of a couple of his ragged Offal Court comrades . . . his pride swelled higher than ever. . . . Every now and then rose the cry, 'A largess, A largess!' and Tom responded by scattering a handful of bright new coins abroad for the multitude to scramble for" (255). Tossing coins to beggars—ostensibly an act of sympathy—establishes a necessary distance between the rich and the poor, while also recording a certain amount of disdain as they "scramble" in the street for pennies.

Twain often associates poverty with begging and begging with infestation. In *Travels with Mr. Brown* (1867), he describes the tenements of New York as contagious, and the efforts of reformers to improve them as hopeless: "The city is said to contain over a million inhabitants now, and half of them are packed away in these holes and dens and cellars of tenement houses, where unimaginable dirt is the rule and cleanliness is a miracle—would be a miracle, I mean, but they don't have it. They are going to have all these tenement houses all white-washed inside, but that will hardly save the occupants when the cholera comes. It will be here soon, and it will sweep those sinks of corruption like a conflagration" (235). The violence implicit in Twain's vocabulary and the figurative conceits he adopts reflect how deeply threatened he is by the physical presence of the poor and how overwhelmed he feels by the social problem they embody. Twain imagines a plague visited upon the poor for the apparent sin of being dirty. After the ineffectual whitewashing efforts of city officials, cholera will become the inevitable "miracle of cleanliness" that will "sweep" the city clean.

Of the beggars who "swarm" the Duomo in *The Innocents Abroad*, Twain writes: "And for every beggar in America, Italy can show a hundred—and rags and vermin to match. It is the wretchedest, princeliest land on earth." These European beggars are, according to Twain, created by the corrupt institutions—religious and political—that support and venerate "the jeweled frippery" of Italian cathedrals (183). Twain, however, eliminates even the suggestion that the "Goshoot Indians" in *Roughing It* resort to begging as a by-product of cultural and economic injustice. In *Roughing It*, begging is a biologically determined and instinctive behavior, functioning much the same way fingerprints do in *Pudd'nhead Wilson*: as transcendent markers of identity, a part of the Goshoot DNA. Their poverty is not, like the racial status of Roxy or Tom Driscoll, "a fiction of law and custom"; it is written into and on their bodies more permanently even than Twain's conception of race: "their faces and hands bearing dirt which they had been hoarding and accumulating for months, years, and even generations, according to the age of the proprietor . . . like all other Indians; priceless beggars—for if the beggar instinct were left out of an Indian he would not 'go,' any more than a clock without a pendulum; hungry, always hungry, and yet never refusing anything that a hog would eat, though often eating what a hog would decline" (*Roughing It* [*RI*] 127). The insatiable hunger of the Goshoots recalls the clamoring of "trundle-bed trash" on Broadway and the constant refrain of the "small niggers" in Nassau. Twain's hostility is proportionate to the demand for food, for money, or for help that he cannot or will not provide. Of the poor in Magdala, Twain writes: "[T]he horses' hoofs roused the stupid population, and they all came trooping out—old men and old women, boys and girls, the blind, the crazy, and the crippled, all in ragged, soiled and scanty raiment, and all abject beggars by nature, instinct and education. How the vermin-tortured vagabonds did swarm! How they showed their scars and sores, and piteously pointed to their maimed and crooked limbs, and begged with their pleading eyes for charity!" (*IA* 373). Here Twain collapses the "nature versus nurture" distinction that he will develop in *Pudd'nhead Wilson*. The beggars of Magdala—unlike Tom Driscoll or Chambers—are oppressed by the combined forces of biology and culture; "nature, instinct, and education" have all determined the fate of this "stupid population." According to Twain's rendering of them, the poor of Magdala appear to both want and deserve the lives they lead.

Twain employs a common lexicon to describe beggars across cultural boundaries, geographies, and histories: they "swarm" and "infest"; they behave like "vermin" and "disease"; they wear "rags"; and covering their "monstrous" bodies are always layers of dirt. Whether the beggars are "savage," like the Goshoot Indians, or industrial and urban, like the beggars of Italy, the "dirt on their faces" erodes previous markers of race, ethnicity, and nation and replaces those identities with a new kind of economic pigmentation. Twain often represents race as an ironic condition, an inversion of white and black. He further complicates racial identity, using dirt and cleanliness as markers of economic status: Pap is a white man covered in mud; the black-eyed, black-haired Colonel Grangerford wears a clean shirt, "so white it hurt your eyes to look at"; and the seventeen-year-old Sam Clemens threatens to blacken his face, since "in these Eastern states niggers are considerably better off than white people" (31 August 1853). Despite the cultural, ethnic, and political circumstances that distinguish these beggars, the dirt that covers them becomes, for Twain, the sign of an emerging global underclass. Just as little Edward continues to assert, "I am Edward, Prince of Wales," Twain distinguishes himself—as white and/or American and/or civilized and/or clean—from this dirty ethnic morass.

Prince Edward's initial desire to try on the clothing of Tom Canty is deeply embedded within the ethos of the tourist: "If that I could but clothe me in raiment like to thine, and strip my feet, and revel in the mud once, just once, with none to rebuke me or forbid, meseemeth I could forego the crown!" (*PP* 18). Edward's "once, just once" is both a declaration of longing and a kind of stopwatch. Despite his avowed desire to escape from the cares that come with a life of luxury, Edward's language reflects the temporality of that desire. He wishes only to try on the "raiment" of poverty, "once, just once," not to inhabit it permanently. Tom Canty's actual clothing becomes a costume, part of Edward's play. Once Tom puts on the clothes of the prince, however, he's arrived; his dream has been fulfilled. Edward, on the other hand, has just begun his travels. Having been driven from the gates of the palace—only moments after wishing to be free of his royal habiliments—Edward seeks out the family of Tom Canty to "prove that I am none of theirs, but the true prince, and I shall have my own again" (*PP* 24). This quest for his legitimate identity is a zero-sum game for Edward, in which "none of theirs" must lead to all "my own again." At the beginning of the novel, when the baby Prince Edward "lay in silks and satins" while Tom was "lapped in rags," clothing allows Twain to explore poverty as a random, arbitrary fate. Yet the boy's voluntary exchange of clothing drives the plot toward the moment when Edward will recover his "own again": "the sumptuous robe of state had been removed from Tom's shoulders to the king's, whose rags were effectually hidden from sight under it" (*PP* 276). If Edward's wealth is arbitrary, it appears also to be inevitable: the rich stay rich and the poor remain poor. The novel ends with what amounts to a whitewashing: hidden beneath the opulent robes of state are the rags of poverty. Like the barking dog that howls, unseen at the beginning of *Pudd'nhead*, or the cholera germs hidden within the painted tenements of New York, the beggars who harass Prince Edward will continue to swarm outside the gates of the castle, despite his change in wardrobe.

Writing (to) the Beggar

The problem of poverty haunted Mark Twain's fiction and his life. The relationship between his fictional beggars and philanthropists is fraught, framed by self-interest and artifice on both sides. For every vermin-ridden, noisome beggar we find in Twain's work, there is a self-congratulating do-gooder. In "The Good Little Boy Who Failed to Prosper" (1870), Twain explores the narcissism of Jacob Blivens, who "gives a penny to a poor beggar-woman with six children . . . telling her to spend it freely, but not to be extravagant, because extravagance is a sin" (30). In the deterministic experiment *What*

Is Man? (1906), the "Old Man" and the "Young Man" debate the merits of giving "a quarter" to "a gray and ragged old woman, a touching picture of misery," who "puts out her lean hand and begs for rescue from hunger and death." The Old Man is quick to expose the egotism of the philanthropist, who "bought himself free of the tortures of a waiting conscience . . . bought a whole night's sleep—all for twenty-five cents! It should make Wall Street ashamed of itself. On his way home his heart was joyful, and it sang—profit on top of profit!" (343). Yet if Twain suspects that altruism is nothing but disguised self-interest, elsewhere he reveals the theatricality of the beggar's identity as well; the old woman is, after all, a "picture" of misery. Her outstretched hand and the language that describes it are both consciously sentimental and artificial.

Nowhere is the gamesmanship of charity more evident than in the "begging letters" Twain received throughout his career. His responses to them often demonstrate both a visceral suspicion of the outstretched hand and an appreciation for a lie well-told. As early as 1869, Mark Twain began to attract what we would now characterize as fan mail, and it continued until his death in 1910. Many of these correspondents demanded something of Twain: autographs, letters of introduction, explanations of his literature or his life, his time, his advice, his patronage, and finally, his money. R. Kent Rasmussen documents the interpretive dance between the fan/beggar—as earnest, needy, manipulative supplicant—and Twain, as skeptical, harassed, offended patron. One letter asks for a thousand-dollar "loan" to help finance a mortgage; as collateral, the writer offers his $1,400 life insurance policy (*Dear Mark Twain* [*DMT*] 136). Another letter writer, posing as a boy, confides to Twain that he heard a man "say that you deliberately murdered your grandmother in cold blood. This I could not believe and though I am only a boy I knocked the man who thus accused you, down. Was I not right? Please answer & tell me." Of this "transparent bid for an autograph," Twain writes, "Too thin" (*DMT* 100). Another letter dispensed with all pretense, "Gracious Sir;—You are rich. To lose $10.00 would not make you miserable. I am poor. To gain $10.00 would not make me miserable. Please send me $10.00 (ten dollars)." Twain's response: "O my!" (*DMT* 70). In reaction to the demands of one fan, he writes, "The idiots seem to be uncommonly thick, this year" (*DMT* 79). Twain would occasionally respond to a request he deemed worthwhile or to a person whose story moved him. In 1880 Ellen (Mary) Keily, "a resident of the Lancaster, Pennsylvania, county alms house and insane asylum," writes to Twain about her visions of Lincoln, John Wilkes Booth, and Jesus: "Now Mark, I am scribbling too much. I wish some Person would take up my case in hand and give me chance to Prove that I did see Jesus not for my own good but for the benefit of the People" (*DMT*

64). Twain responded with both a letter and five dollars, finally believing the claims of a diseased mind over the less convincing performances of other solicitors.

In responding to these letters, Twain engaged the larger cultural dilemma of how to respond to the poor. *The Prince and the Pauper* arrives at the kind of piecemeal charity we see Twain enact in the "begging letters" and that he often critiques in his fiction. Edward responds to the needs of the poor, but often with a largess that feels either too limited or too late; he "provided good homes for the daughters of the two Baptist women burned at the stake . . . but he was too late to save the man who was convicted of killing a deer in the royal forest" (*PP* 288). Edward's own death, an event that hovers over the end of the novel, is inscribed in his finite acts of charity. Edward's adventure is primarily "to his credit"—a phrase with both economic and moral resonance—and ultimately has more lasting benefit to the king than to his subjects, becoming part of the mythology that will surround his kingship: "as long as the king lived he was fond of telling the story of his adventures" (*PP* 289). Twain's own acts of charity are likewise bound up in his public image and in an emerging celebrity culture. Gregg Camfield writes that Twain was "constantly involved in fund-raising activities. He gave time, money, or endorsements to everything from soup kitchens, a relief fund for Walt Whitman, and the Fisk University Jubilee Singers, and Helen Keller's campaign for schools for the deaf" (82). While Twain would occasionally support these causes and others with monetary gifts, his charitable contribution often took the form of a performance, effectively making his physical presence a kind of largess.

Twain's philanthropy took place in a post-Romantic American culture, in which Emersonian self-reliance had evolved into an "up by the bootstraps" attitude toward the poor. Like many Americans of means, Twain measured how much to give against the risk of giving too much. Camfield refers to a letter written to Olivia during the financial Panic of 1873. Twain writes that there "will be a multitude of tramps & prowlers about. Send Father Hawley a cheque for $50; have all the tramps treated kindly but *sent to Hawley*; give them soup-tickets when they ask for food" [Twain's italics] (21 November 1873). Camfield cites this incident as a sign that Twain "took his charity seriously" (83). Yet while the letter demonstrates Twain's concern for the needy, it also expresses his desire to keep the beggars away from the front door. The soup ticket is a gesture both compassionate and empty, a cold substitute for a hot meal.

Turning away a vagrant may have been a legitimate precaution, but Twain also recognized it as morally suspect and wrote often about how dangerous it can be to ignore a beggar. Injun Joe harbors violent resentments against Doc

Robinson and the Widow Douglas, while in "The Man That Corrupted Hadleyburg," a rejected tramp extends his revenge against the whole town. In "The Facts concerning the Recent Carnival of Crime in Connecticut," Twain playfully acknowledges that twinned with the desire to help the poor is a yearning for them to just go away. Twain's conscience, "a shriveled, shabby dwarf," arrives at the door of Twain's home and demands something like justice from the annoyed narrator: "The pygmy contemplated me awhile with his weasel eyes, and then said, in a peculiarly sneering way: 'You turned a tramp away from your door this morning.'" What follows is a series of painful reminders of all the ways in which the author has failed to be true, kind, selfless, and pure; in the end, however, the narrator kills his conscience and declares: "Out of this with your paupers, your charities, your reforms, your pestilent morals! You behold before you a man whose life-conflict is done, whose soul is at peace; a man whose heart is dead to sorrow, dead to suffering, dead to remorse; a man WITHOUT A CONSCIENCE!" Twain cleverly inverts the *McGuffey Reader* narrative so that the epiphanic moment is not the awakening of conscience, but its wonderful extinction.

Despite their many and apparent differences, "A Carnival of Crime" is as much a pre-text for *The Prince and the Pauper* as *Huckleberry Finn* is its companion. In the former novel, Twain constructs a stage for a conscience that, if not deformed, is at least slumbering; simultaneously, he records the frustration of Prince Edward as he struggles to be fair with a populace that does nothing but torture him. *The Prince and the Pauper* has been read predominantly as a sentimental fiction that celebrates empathy and justice. However, it also represents the anger and resentment felt by those in power when they are forced to contend with a dirty, mean, and sometimes ungrateful populace.

Mark Twain (as) and The Prince

Twain originally planned to publish both *The Prince and the Pauper* and *Adventures of Huckleberry Finn* as a single volume. In a letter dated November 1880, shortly before publishing *The Prince and the Pauper*, Twain writes, "I have 2 stories, & by the verbal agreement they are both going into the same book; but Livy says they're not, & by George she ought to know. She says they are going into separate books, & that one of them is going to be elegantly gotten up, even if the elegance of it eats up the publisher's profits & mine too." One standard reading of *The Prince and the Pauper* is that Twain wrote it as a paean to Eastern respectability. After the publication of *Innocents Abroad*, *Roughing It*, *Tom Sawyer*, and *A Tramp Abroad*, his own cultural maven, Mary Fairbanks, advised Twain to "write another book . . . in an entirely different style. . . . The time has come for your best book . . . your best contribution to American literature" (26 July 1880). Itching for respectability, Twain complied; he wrote to Howells, "I like this book better than *Tom Sawyer*—because I haven't put any fun in it" (15 December 1880). While *The Prince and the Pauper* may have excited the admiration of Hartford literati, his former editor Joe Goodman wrote, "it is the first of your works in which I have been disappointed. . . . You went entirely out of your sphere" (29 January 1882). Generations of critics have agreed, reading *The Prince and the Pauper* as a pale shadow of its more complex and interesting cousin, *Huckleberry Finn*. However, to cast the *Prince and the Pauper* as compulsory "dues paid" to feminine, sentimental culture sidesteps Twain's serious investment in the novel. His decision to write *The Prince and the Pauper*—and even his pairing of it with *Adventures of Huckleberry Finn*—mirrors the economic exchange at the heart of the narrative. *The Prince and the Pauper* functions for Twain like Tom Canty's new clothes: it allows him to divest himself of the American vernacular and to wear the robes of artistic, authorial legitimacy. In his discussion of Twain's first trip to London in 1872, Peter Messent speculates that Twain's conscious evasion of London's less savory neighborhoods reflects a sustained effort to remake himself "as an urbane and well-traveled citizen of the world who had little concern for the city's streets and the brute conditions to be found there" ("Mark Twain and London" 202). No less than Twain's sanitized visit to London, the writing of *The Prince and the Pauper* was an integral part of this authorial "remaking."

By the time Twain began to write both *Huckleberry Finn* and *The Prince and the Pauper*, he had been married to Olivia Langdon, heiress to a million-dollar fortune, for six years, and with the publication of *Innocents Abroad* (1869), *Roughing It* (1871), and *The Adventures of Tom Sawyer* (1876), he was already a successful author in his own right. No longer identifying with the bohemian world of itinerant lecturers and writers, "The Wildman of the Washoe" had begun to characterize himself in royal terms. In a letter to Will Bowen, written shortly after he moved into the home purchased for him by Jervis Langdon, Twain reveled in his new status. He described his new home as the "darlingest, loveliest little palace in America," Livy as his "princess"—"the very most perfect gem of womankind"—and he boasted not only of having servants, but that his books gave him "an income like a small lord" (6 February 1870). And by the time he and his new wife took their first trip to Europe, Twain wasn't just living like a lord; he was spending like one as well.

In her illuminating essay "Mark Twain's Music Box," Kerry Driscoll explores the couple's 1878 European sojourn and finds, in the spending habits of both Twain and Olivia, a record of shared anxiety about their cultural status. Driscoll presents their "deliberate and informed accumulation" of material luxuries as a thoroughly modern story of desire channeled through acquisition (146): "Within a period of sixteen months, she [Olivia] spent nearly five thousand dollars on household furnishings—a staggering sum, equivalent to approximately a hundred thousand dollars in today's currency. The sheer volume of these goods filled some twenty-two freight packages. . . . Many of her acquisitions related to entertaining—table linens, sterling silver, brass chargers, porcelain dishes, Venetian glass—while others were purely decorative in nature: pottery, rugs, mirrors, carved picture frames, and assorted bric-a-brac" (151). As Driscoll makes clear, Olivia and Twain were constructing a home for display, and their purchases made possible the sort of entertaining that would elevate them among their sophisticated Nook Farm neighbors.

Of course, this journey toward respectability was complicated by Twain's equally powerful desire to remain authentic and unconventional, which was doubly complicated by his efforts to market his rough authenticity. The instances of Twain behaving in ways intended to shock the standards of polite company—in his vocabulary, his dress, his views on religion, race, and politics, his taste in music, and food, etc.—are too numerous to relate here. After the disastrous "Whittier Birthday Speech," in which Twain represented Emerson, Holmes, and Longfellow as three drunken miners, Twain sent these Boston Brahmins a letter of apology. He describes himself as an "innocent," unaware that his behavior would cause offense: "But I do not ask you to forgive what I did that night, for it is not forgivable; I simply had it at heart to ask you to believe that I am only heedlessly a savage, not premeditatedly" (27 December 1877). Twain's pleasure at feeling like a "small lord," it appears, carried with it the same social anxieties and fears he chronicled in Tom Canty's experience at court: "Poor Tom ate with his fingers mainly. . . . He inspected his napkin curiously, and with deep interest, for it was of a very dainty and beautiful fabric, then said with simplicity—'Prithee, take it away, lest in mine unheedfulness it be soiled'" (*PP* 54). Attendant upon the golden bowls, silken linens, and velvet furnishings that surround Tom Canty as he dines is the consciousness of his "savagery," and the "heedlessness" that prevents him from discerning how to behave. This is precisely the psychological and cultural crossroads at which Twain found himself in 1878, two years before he began writing *The Prince and the Pauper*.

Twain eventually evolved from western bohemian to "the Belle of New York," and the narrative voice in *The Prince and the Pauper* undergoes just such a transformation. Like Tom, the narrator is also straddling two worlds. When Tom first meets with Prince Edward, the narrator suddenly exclaims, "You should have seen that fickle crowd snatch off their hats then. You should have heard them cheer, and shout, 'Long live the Prince of Wales!'" (*PP* 14). The narrator, speaking confidentially to the reader, sounds like a tourist after spotting a celebrity: "You should have seen . . ." when Edward's attendants "sprang forward to . . . ," the narrator interrupts himself with "I don't know what; interfere, no doubt," not only making himself a subject in the narrative—"I don't know"—but also exposing his limited understanding of the ways of royalty (*PP* 14). As he describes the scenes at court, the narrator quotes from other sources. Like a fashion reporter on the red carpet, he relates what others say about how the prince looks and what he wears. By the midway point of the novel, however, the narrator has shifted his point of view. When describing the inhabitants of the Tower Bridge, the narrator states, "In the times in which we are writing"; and before Tom's first successful performance as prince, the narrator directs the reader, "Let us privileged ones hurry to the great banqueting-room" (*PP* 135). The "royal we" of the narrator mirrors the transformation of Tom Canty from outsider to insider—inherent in the "he can't/ can't he?" tension of Tom's surname. The narrator highlights the distance between the haves and the have-nots—"us privileged ones," and those who "can't" gain entry to the feast.

In *The Prince and the Pauper*, wealth and status are both products of perception. Tom's obsessive desire to *see* a prince, "the one passion of his life," quickly morphs into being *seen as* a prince: "He was 'magnificently habited in a doublet of white satin, with a front-piece of purple cloth-of-tissue, powdered with diamonds, and edged with ermine. Over this he wore a mantle of white cloth-of-gold, pounced with the triple-feathered crest, lined with blue satin, set with pearls and precious stones, and fastened with a clasp of brilliants.' . . . O Tom Canty, born in a hovel, bred in the gutters of London, familiar with rags and dirt and misery, what a spectacle is this!" (*PP* 64). The narrator's exclamation, "what a spectacle is this," collapses several shocking and simultaneous events: Tom is dazzled *by* the spectacle he is witnessing; he has *become* the spectacle he earlier longed to behold; and finally, Tom Canty is also *making a spectacle* of himself. In order to establish his identity as prince, Tom must perform before "the massed world gathered on the river," one of several such events—the state dinner, the river pageant, the reception at Guildhall, and, tellingly, the "Recognition" procession—in which Tom's performance as prince or king essentially creates him as prince or king. The narrator confides to the reader the incongruity of a child "familiar with rags and dirt and misery" performing the role of prince; his exclamation also reveals how easily royal authority can be imitated and reproduced.

Tom's performance as a royal is made convincing by the luxurious clothes, the material riches, and all the trappings of wealth. The nouveau-riche aspirations of the middle class were of course a frequent theme of Twain's, from

The Gilded Age (1873) to "The Man That Corrupted Hadleyburg" (1899). Little of the satiric vein that distinguishes these works, however, is present in *The Prince and the Pauper*. In the 1870s and 1880s, while he was in the midst of building his own palace, Twain targeted both pretentious and shabby displays of wealth almost as often as the pursuit of wealth itself. In the "house beautiful" chapter of *Life on the Mississippi*, or even in the description of the Grangerford parlor in *Huckleberry Finn*, Twain satirizes a failure of taste, rather than the burgeoning consumer culture that fetishizes ostensibly elevated taste. The excessive descriptions in *The Prince and the Pauper* (and the descriptions of excess) are not satiric; they are illustrative. In the court of King Henry and Prince Edward, Twain describes a surplus labor force, an opulence of dress, abundant and exotic food, feasts, parades, and byzantine social codes—yet he stops short of satirizing them. Early on in his adventures, Tom Canty has been dressed, fed, observed, and attended by dozens of servants; like Huck, he initially seems mystified by the ways of the cultural elite: "He made two or three further efforts to help himself, but being promptly forestalled each time, he finally gave up, with a sigh of resignation and a murmured 'Beshrew me, but I marvel they do not require to breathe for me also!'" (*PP* 46) Tom reflects upon how enervating and constraining it is to be rich, which is in keeping with the satire Twain originally planned. In an 1880 letter to Howells, he writes that "the small bogus King has a gilded and worshipped and dreary and restrained and cussed time of it on the throne" (11 March 1880). Yet, in the final version of the novel, far from resenting the trappings of royalty, Tom Canty adapts to them quickly. Unlike Huck, who never fully accommodates himself to the middle-class comforts of the Widow or the Grangerfords, Tom Canty soon acclimates to the luxury of his environment and even develops an appetite for more: "He lost his fears; his misgivings faded out and died; his embarrassments departed, and gave place to an easy and confident bearing. . . . He enjoyed his splendid clothes, and ordered more: he found his four hundred servants too few for his proper grandeur, and trebled them" (*PP* 249–50). Huck may prefer the comfort of old clothes, the simplicity of life on a raft, and the particular sort of freedom that comes from having only a dollar in his pocket, but Tom Canty never expresses a desire to return to a life of poor simplicity—and neither does Mark Twain.

Tom also becomes comfortable with the power of royalty; he enjoys exciting fear in subordinates, giving orders to Princess Mary, doling out justice and wisdom. While Tom learns to become a compassionate king, he also learns to forget the poor who are most immediately affected by his wealth and good fortune: "[T]he vanished monarch faded almost out of his thoughts. . . . Tom's poor mother and sisters traveled the same road out of his mind . . . the thought of their coming some day in their rags and dirt, and betraying him with their kisses and pulling him down from his lofty place and dragging him back to penury and degradation and the slums, made him shudder" (*PP* 252). Tom's comfort with his silk and satin robes parallels his increasing discomfort with the bonds of kinship—represented here in the affectionate kisses of his sisters and mother—that link him to the poor.

Beggars (as) and Bodies

Twain often imagines clothing as a metaphor for identity, making it both an unstable and impermanent commodity. This works in Tom Canty's favor, as he experiences the overnight success characteristic of the self-made American man. Once Twain shifts his attention to the Ruffler's gang, whose bodies function like costumes, this instability suggests darker possibilities for identity. Rather than creating for the Ruffler's gang the postmodern free play that could turn a pauper into a king, the changeable, fluid nature of their bodies suggests a brokenness that is far from liberating. Similar to the monstrous beggars of Constantinople ("the three-legged woman," "the man with his eye in his cheek," "the dwarf with seven fingers on each hand, no upper lip, and his under-jaw gone"), the members of the Ruffler's gang appear to Edward as a collection, not of integrated bodies, but of accidental body parts (*IA* 261). Their physical deformities are performative, as in the freak show of a circus or the oddities made famous by P. T. Barnum. Their various body parts function as theatrical costumes, becoming essential tools in a wider conspiracy to deceive: "One of the blind men got up, and made ready by casting aside the patches that sheltered his excellent eyes, and the pathetic placard which recited the cause of his calamity. Dot-and-go-One disencumbered himself of his timber leg and took his place, upon sound and healthy limbs, beside his fellow-rascal; then they roared out a rollicking ditty" (*PP* 146).

Their arms, legs, eyes, and even the "thieves' dialect" used "when unfriendly ears might be listening" are tools that make possible an elaborate performance of artificial identity (*PP* 147). The Rufflers make both literal *and* ironic Whitman's vision in "Crossing Brooklyn Ferry" that "everyone [is] disintegrated, yet part of the scheme" (150). These fragmented bodies are in fact part of a scheme to steal from and defraud their audience. And what they are "a part of" is not the wider human community, but an organized collective, a "gang" with its own rules, language, and loyalties. The narrator responds to the Ruffler's gang with the same sort of suspicion Twain expresses toward the "begging letters." The "spectacle" created by their appropriation of fake limbs and eyes inspires fear and anxiety in Prince Edward, who awakens to find "the motliest company of tattered gutter-scum and ruffians, of both sexes, he had ever read or dreamed of" (*PP* 145).

The raftsmen from the excised chapter 16 in *Huckleberry Finn* share many characteristics with the members of the Ruffler's gang: they have their own stories and songs, they engage in spectacular performances, and their bodies also have magical qualities—"I split the everlasting rocks with my glance and I squench the thunder when I speak"; "when I'm hot, I fan myself with an equinoctial storm; when I'm thirsty I reach up and suck a cloud dry" (*Huckleberry Finn* [*HF*] 109, 110). However, unlike the Ruffler's gang, the raftsmen exaggerate their individuality—not their group membership—and are made into a community not by economic forces or cultural prejudice, but by the Mississippi River. The Ruffler's gang is conscious of their marginalized status, and they organize their collective actions in response to it. With an almost military sense of purpose, these beggars, mendicants, and tramps assault the peace and stability of a country they deem unjust.

Amid the loose morals and laziness of the Ruffler's gang, Twain presents the righteous anger of Yokel, a farmer driven to beg. Like the other members of the gang, Yokel is dismembered, though in his case not by artifice, but by "English Law": "I begged, from house to house—I and the wife—bearing with us the hungry kids—but it was a crime to be hungry in England—so they stripped us and lashed us. . . . I begged again—begged for a crust, and got the stocks and lost an ear—see, here bides the stump, I begged again, and here is the stump of the other to keep me minded of it. And still I begged again, and was sold for a slave—here on my cheek under this stain, if I washed it off, ye might see the red *S* the branding-iron left there! A SLAVE! Do ye understand that word! An English Slave!" (*PP* 150–51). Yokel is Twain's most sympathetic beggar; through this character, Twain voices the anger of the nineteenth-century wage slave, whose insignia Twain places beneath the dirt—the pigment or "stain"—that colors his face. Just as Jim is "white inside," Yokel embodies invisible contradictions and ironies: a blackened white man, an English slave. Jim experiences a similarly grotesque irony when Huck asks Tom "what it was he'd planned to do if the evasion worked out all right and he managed to set a nigger free that was already free before" (*HF* 360). Yet if Jim and Yokel are alike oppressed by the culture that surrounds them, at least in *Huckleberry Finn* Jim's children and wife are alive and he has a plan for liberating them. Yokel's losses are beyond recovery, and, despite his rage, he doesn't seem fully to understand who is responsible for his suffering. Yokel indicts the impersonal "English Law"; the Ruffler, however, targets the landed gentry for taking the farms of "small husbandmen," who then "turn shiftless and hungry upon the world" (*PP* 149). After hearing the story of Yokel, little Prince Edward stands before the gang and promises to change the laws of England—a simple solution that earns mocking applause from the gang. Implicit in their laughter is the recognition that while a king may be able to change a law, it's unlikely that the power and privilege of wealth will be altered as a consequence. Despite Twain's sympathy for the displaced farmer, the chapter pivots away from Yokel and the systemic injustice suggested by his fate. Instead, Twain closes the scene by echoing the trials of two other kings: Henry V, a disguised monarch insulted by his people; and Jesus on Calvary, crowned "King of the Jews" and scorned during his crucifixion. As the weeping Edward is crowned "Foo-Foo the First," our sympathies shift to the suffering king, and away from the more permanent sorrows of the impoverished Yokel.

Prince Edward struggles to respond to the suffering of Yokel by changing the law and redeeming its inherent injustice. Like the coins of largess tossed in the street, however, this remedy maintains Edward's distance from the ugliness he has just witnessed and expunges his personal responsibility for the poverty around him. While *The Prince and the Pauper* certainly argues for institutional, legal remedies for the suffering of the poor, it simultaneously registers a judgment of those who live in poverty. Edward's refusal to beg or to steal is, in effect, an implicit assertion of moral superiority. While John Canty begs to support any number of vile habits, begging is also the only way the family will survive in "Offal Court." John Canty confronts the little Prince: "'The morrow must we pay two pennies to him that owns this hole; two pennies, mark ye—all this money for a half-year's rent, else out of this we go. Show what thou'st gathered with thy lazy begging.' The Prince said—'Offend me not with thy sordid matters. I tell thee again I am the King's son'" (*PP* 68). By villainizing so many of the beggars Prince Edward meets, John Canty in particular, Twain suggests that the act of begging is as much a character flaw as it is a strategy for survival. By continually asserting his true identity, Edward insulates himself from the "sordid" need to pay the rent, and he distances himself from the community of the poor. As he travels through the lower classes of English society, Edward receives charity from any number of poor and displaced people: Tom Canty's mother, the poor widow, and Miles Hendon. He is fed and clothed and protected from many of the realities that create the criminality and madness that surround him. However, Edward's overwhelming response to the rabble he encounters is disdain and disgust. Hugo insists that Edward "play decoy" by pretending to be his brother, while Hugo fakes an injury to excite the sympathy of a Good Samaritan. The stranger takes the bait: "Now come hither, my boy, and help me carry thy stricken brother to yon house, where—'I am not his brother,' said the King" (*PP* 161). Edward inverts the command Christ gives in Matthew 25: truly, he says unto us, that the "least of these" is not his brother.

Mark Twain (as) and the King

When Mark Twain wrote *The Prince and the Pauper*, wealth was being accumulated at rates unimaginable in antebellum America. Twinned with this wealth was an increase of poverty that was urban, ethnically "colored," and generational. The poverty of *Adventures of Huckleberry Finn* is nothing like what Twain encounters in Europe and New York, or in the lives of Native Americans. St. Petersburg is aristocratic, not democratic, and in *that* world Huck is made a pariah by his lineage more than by his poverty. Huck's Missouri feels more quaint than the sixteenth-century London of Tom Canty, where commerce—the exchange of goods and services for money—is far more visible. Twain's description of London Bridge highlights the various ways in which the "bridge" people earn their livings: "The Bridge was a sort of town to itself; it had its inn, its beer houses, its bakeries, its haberdasheries, its food markets, its manufacturing industries, and even its church" (*PP* 86). The people Huck encounters, by contrast, are defined by location, not occupation: they are townspeople, field hands, raftsmen, or farmers. Huck and Jim avoid urban spaces; they bypass the world of industry and capitalism. Despite occasionally "borrowing" a chicken, they live in a primitive world of hunting and gathering.

On the rare occasions when money appears in *Huckleberry Finn*, it's usually being given, found, inherited, or hidden; we rarely witness money being exchanged for goods. Repeatedly in their travels, Jim and Huck either find hidden money (eight dollars sewn up in the lining of an old coat) or are given money as a gift (two twenty-dollar gold pieces from the white men who refuse to help Huck), or, in a gesture that echoes the largess of the king in *The Prince and the Pauper*, Tom gives Jim a gift of $40 at the end of the "evasion." And the money in *Huckleberry Finn* surfaces in the form of gold or treasure (as in the Wilks girls' $6,000 inheritance) and not as paper money, the currency of a modern economy. The most significant buying and selling that occurs in *Huckleberry Finn* is the buying and selling of slaves, and it's a commercial exchange that the novel resists specifically because of the instability it creates in an orderly community. When Jim describes himself as a rich man because he could be sold for $800, he embodies the irony of a capitalist economy and the life of the wage slave, while also illustrating the corroding effects of slavery itself. Repeatedly, Huck's response to money, and to the economic processes and meanings that attend it, is romantic, Thoreauvian. He wants to go to the woods to live deliberately, to front only the es-

Figure 4.1. *Reforming the Drunkard*, illustration by Edward Windsor Kemble from the first edition (1884) of *Adventures of Huckleberry Finn*.

sential facts of life. Because he does not participate in the world of getting and spending, Huck is not a pauper, nor is he a beggar or a slave.

Of course, there are beggars in *Huckleberry Finn*: Pap Finn, the duke, and the king work to game the system, to con their way into wealth and material luxury. In fact, Kemble's illustration of Pap Finn, standing before the judge with his hand extended, suggests Pap is looking for a handout, not a handshake. And Kemble's representation of Pap after this experiment in redemption, subtitled "falling from grace," reinforces his status as a homeless drunk. The duke and the king construct elaborate, theatrical swindles that they repeatedly describe as "business." In this regard, they are characters who fit more comfortably in Twain's London, specifically because it is a capitalist economy, a place where paupers can become "dukes and kings," and where kings can become indigent. Yet if the world of *Huckleberry Finn* does not seem populated by beggars, late-nineteenth-century America unquestionably is. Twain displaces the hunger and unrest of the post-Reconstruction era onto the London of Tom Canty, and he imagines a solution to that suffering in the form of the redeemed little king.

Three years after publishing *The Prince and the Pauper*, during what the editors at the University of California Press have termed "stint 3," Mark Twain completed *Huckleberry Finn*, including chapter 14. In this chapter

Figure 4.2. *Falling from Grace,* illustration by Edward Windsor Kemble from the first edition (1884) of *Adventures of Huckleberry Finn.*

Huck and Jim debate their respective interpretations of King Solomon, the worth and merits of chopping children in half, and the linguistic habits of cats, cows, and Frenchmen. In the midst of their discussion about "Louis Sixteenth," Jim asks, "[D]ey ain' no kings here, is dey, Huck?" "No," Huck responds confidently (*HF* 96). Readers of the novel may wince at the irony, recalling not just the Morgans and Vanderbilts of Twain's era, but also the Gateses, Kochs, and Bloombergs of our own; still, within the world of the novel, Huck is right. The inequities of *Huckleberry Finn* are not primarily economic; they are the by-products of institutional racism. In this final bit of writing, Twain—through Jim—articulates the lesson that so many readers hope Huck will learn: Jim holds these truths to be self-evident, that all human beings are created equal.

The thematic twin of *Huckleberry Finn*'s chapter 14 occurs at the end of *The Prince and the Pauper*, where King Edward displays a democratic empathy for the poor and downtrodden: "What does thou know of suffering and oppression? I and my people know, but not thou" (*PP* 289). Huck similarly realizes that Jim is a human being, but as an outcast child in a democracy where his voice is only one among many, that empathy will have no force. As satisfying as Edward's moral awakening may be, his kinship with the poor can be expressed only once Edward is clothed in majesty, not in rags; Edward's power lies not in his sympathy, but in his royalty.

Our satisfaction at the return of King Edward to his throne is not simply relief at the recovery of a lost child. Twain creates a vision of benevolent dictatorship, capable of restoring order to the mob and dispensing charity and justice in equal measure. The final chapters of *Huckleberry Finn* feel famously incomplete; critics and readers of all persuasions want for American history the compensations we find at the end of *The Prince and the Pauper*. Unfortunately, "they ain't no kings here." Despite his famous antipathy to monarchy as a political system, Twain is often attracted to the power and style of kings, whether they reign over nations or over Wall Street. When Mark Twain imagines the coronation of Tom Canty and the reclamation of Prince Edward, he has yet to don the white suit, and it will be almost twenty years before Isabel Lyon will call him "the King"; however, what the ending of *The Prince and the Pauper* suggests is that Twain longs to shake off the dust and dirt of Hannibal, to dole out his largess in the street, to uplift the poor with his philanthropy, all while keeping his white suit, white shirt, and white hands very, very clean.

Notes

1. The letters cited in this chapter are available online at the Mark Twain Project, www.marktwainproject.org.

2. I would like to thank Mark Woodhouse, Head Archivist at the Elmira College Center for the Study of Mark Twain, for guiding me to this travel log.

Works Cited

Blair, Walter. *Mark Twain & Huck Finn*. Berkeley: U of California P, 1962.

Driscoll, Kerry. "Mark Twain's Music Box: Livy, Cosmopolitanism, and the Commodity Aesthetic." *Cosmopolitan Twain*. Ed. Ann M. Ryan and Joseph McCullough. Columbia: U of Missouri P, 2008.

George, Henry. *Progress and Poverty*. 1879. New York: Robert Schalkenbach Foundation, 1997.

Gribben, Alan. *Mark Twain's Library: A Reconstruction*. Boston: G. K. Hall, 1980.

Howe, Lawrence. *Mark Twain and the Novel: The Double-Cross of Authority*. Cambridge: Cambridge UP, 1998.

Howells, William Dean. *W. D. Howells, Selected Letters*. Ed. Richard H. Ballinger, Christoph K. Lohmann, Robert C. Leitz III. New York: Twayne, 1980.

Marx, Karl. *Wage-Labour and Capital*. New York: International, 1933.

Messent, Peter. "Mark Twain and London." *Cosmopolitan Twain*. Ed. Ann M. Ryan and Joseph B. McCullough. Columbia: U of Missouri P, 2008.

———. *Mark Twain and Male Friendship: The Twichell, Howells, and Rogers Friendships*. Oxford: Oxford UP, 2009.

Piketty, Thomas. *Capital in the Twenty-First Century*. Cambridge: Belknap Press, 2014.

Rasmussen, R. Kent, ed. *Dear Mark Twain: Letters from His Readers*. Berkeley: U of California P, 2013.

———. *Mark Twain A to Z: The Essential Reference to His Life and Writings*. New York: Facts on File, 1995.

Riesman, David. *Thorstein Veblen*. New York: Transaction, 1995.

Riis, Jacob. *How the Other Half Lives*. New York: Bedford/St. Martin's, 2010.

Trombley, Laura Skandera. *Mark Twain's Other Woman*. New York: Vintage, 2011.

Twain, Mark. "The $30,000 Bequest." *The Best Short Stories of Mark Twain*. Ed. Lawrence Berkove. New York: Modern Library, 2004.

———. *Adventures of Huckleberry Finn*. 1885. Berkeley: U of California P, *1985*.

———. "Excursions." The Mark Twain Papers. Bancroft Library, Berkeley, California.

———. "The Facts Concerning a Recent Carnival of Crime in Connecticut." *The Best Short Stories of Mark Twain*. Ed. Lawrence Berkove. New York: Modern Library, 2004.

———. *The Gilded Age*. 1871. Oxford: Oxford UP, 1996.

———. "The Good Little Boy Who Failed to Prosper." *The Best Short Stories of Mark Twain*. Ed. Lawrence Berkove. New York: Modern Library, 2004.

———. *The Innocents Abroad, or, The New Pilgrim's Progress*. 1869. New York: Modern Library, 2003.

———. *Life on the Mississippi*. 1883. New York: Library of America, 2009.

———. "The Man That Corrupted Hadleyburg." *The Best Short Stories of Mark Twain*. Ed. Lawrence Berkove. New York: Modern Library, 2004.

———. *Mark Twain's Autobiography*. Ed. Albert Bigelow Paine. New York: Harper and Brothers, 1924.

———. *Mark Twain's Travels with Mr. Brown: Being Heretofore Uncollected Sketches of Mark Twain Written for the Alta California*. Ed. Franklin Walker and G. Ezra Dane. New York: Alfred A. Knopf, 1940.

———. *The Prince and the Pauper*. 1882. Berkeley: U of California P, 1984.

———. *Roughing It*. 1872. Berkeley: U of California P, 1995.

———. *What Is Man? The Complete Essays of Mark Twain*. Ed. Charles Neider. Cambridge: Da Capo Press, 1991. 310–50.

Veblen, Thorstein. *The Theory of the Leisure Class*. 1899. Reissue edition. Oxford: Oxford UP, 2009.

Whitman, Walt. "Crossing Brooklyn Ferry." *The Portable Walt Whitman*. New York: Penguin Books, 1979.

5
The Robber Barons' Fool?
Mark Twain and the Four Ps of Patronage

Gregg Camfield

In the sixth installment of "Old Times on the Mississippi," Mark Twain makes this extravagant claim about the "Rank and Dignity of Piloting":

> A pilot, in those days, was the only unfettered and entirely independent human being that lived in the earth. Kings are but the hampered servants of parliament and people; parliaments sit in chains forged by their constituency; the editor of a newspaper cannot be independent, but must work with one hand tied behind him by party and patrons, and be content to utter only half or two thirds of his mind; no clergyman is a free man and may speak the whole truth, regardless of his parish's opinions; writers of all kinds are manacled servants of the public. We write frankly and fearlessly, but then we modify before we print. In truth, every man and woman and child has a master, and worries and frets in servitude; but in the day I write of, the Mississippi pilot had none. (721)

This much-discussed passage has fascinated Twain scholars for some time, primarily because of its ideas about freedom and slavery, or about the art of literary composition. On thinking about Twain's attitudes toward money, I found another word in this screed jumping out at me: patrons. English literary history has long told the story of the decline of patronage in the eighteenth century, with the market taking over as writing became professionalized. But there's the word, addressing one of the most important parts of the publishing *business*, periodicals, which Twain tells us are instruments of party and patronage, which, given that newspapers were often party organs, could mean party *as* patron. One could argue that Twain's use of "patrons" here is a mere vestige, that patronage in this sense was part of the transition to the market, with political parties temporarily replacing the old patrician support of the arts before the public fully took over the role. In this sense, the transition warped the word out of its original sense into the modern meaning, with the term *patronage* becoming synonymous with *custom*, as when merchants tell "customers," "we appreciate your patronage."

Scholars regularly, and rightly, think of Twain as leading this transition to the market, not only because he helped invent ways to market himself, but also because he often wrote that only the public has the right to judge literary merit. In this sense, the *public* as patron becomes the great American ideal. But what if Twain, who prided himself on using the right word, meant *patron* in neither a transitional nor a figurative manner? What if he used it quite traditionally to refer to rich patrons who protected and cultivated writers to serve the patrons' interests? Indeed, in the Gilded Age that Twain and Charles Dudley Warner named, old-style patronage, that of patrician plutocrats, was coming to the United States, even as two transitional forms of patronage—that of party and that of peers—were in full bloom. Not only was Twain aware of all of these forms of patronage, but his success as a writer was affected by them. Not surprisingly, then, his feelings as well as his thoughts about patronage in its many forms inform Twain's oeuvre.

It is not easy, perhaps, to see how profoundly Twain was affected by all four Ps of patronage—public, political, peer, and plutocratic—against the usual history we tell of the demise of patronage. William Charvat's *The Rise of Authorship in America, 1800–1870*, the standard account of writing as business, has a kind of teleological necessity about it that may well obscure some of the countertrends, so it's worth stepping back a bit to appreciate not just the economics but also the ideology of writing during Twain's lifetime. Nineteenth-century American writers carried throughout the century the new American anxiety about what kinds of art would be appropriate for a republic and how a republic should support the arts. Even though the sense that aristocratic patronage had created artistic sycophants was widespread, alternative ways to support the arts were not readily forthcoming in the early years of the republic. Under assault from European cultural critics who saw the lack of a thriving artistic scene as a sign that the United States produced nothing but philistines, Americans tried to find different ways to cultivate the arts, particularly the queen of the arts, rhetoric, in all of its varied verbal forms. That anxiety, however, shaped not just the means by which the literary arts were cultivated but also an ongoing debate about the form and content of literature itself. Not only did Twain participate in this debate, but it has been central to how cultural critics used Twain until fairly late in the twentieth century, with Brooks and DeVoto deploying Twain as a battlefield in their war over what should count as culture, and such heavyweights as Henry Nash Smith clarifying the shape and quality of the argument.

Without recapitulating that discussion, it is worth noting how frequently Twain engaged in the substance of the debate. To my purpose, if one looks at these four different kinds of patronage, how and when Twain entered the debate over culture in America often hinged on the kind of patronage he depended on at the time. I intend to treat patronage in this very narrow sense of political and economic dependency. If one punches "literary patronage" into an American scholarly search engine, most of the thousands of hits will treat literary patronage before 1800. Most of the few treatments of nineteenth-century writers either address non-U.S. writers or expand the definition of patronage to include mentorship. Were I interested in the latter, I'd be adding to a rich collection of studies about the various folk who influenced Twain's career. But I'm interested in bread-and-butter patronage, the kind that created what Twain himself called "Corn-pone Opinions." In that essay, one of his deterministic spasms, Twain told us through his narrator Jerry, "You tell me whar a man gits his corn pone, en I'll tell you what his 'pinions is" (507). It's easy to read this essay as a straightforward statement of dependency, yet the subtext of the article is that, while opinions are created in reaction to the source of corn-pone, the reaction is often contradictory, both conformist and subversive, much as the speaker Jerry is in the essay.

In having a slave describe ways of resisting conformity while appearing conformist, Twain was commenting on his own career. While he often did espouse the opinions of his patrons, the more dependent he was on a source of income, the more indebted to a particular kind of patronage, the more radically divergent were his opinions about that kind of patronage. That is, one source of his radical inconsistency was his divided sense of having to praise those he depended on while deeply resenting the obligation. He often frankly and fearlessly wrote his resentment, usually pigeon-holing his candid remarks and then moving the ideas, modified, into some of his major works. In his reactions to each of these kinds of patronage, we see Twain helping to shape the ways literary artists have come to see their roles in modern and postmodern America.

Public Patronage

Twain's attitude toward the literary marketplace was quite simply that it was the way he made his living. As a young journalist, he worried that he could not marry, because he couldn't "turn an inkstand into Aladdin's lamp" (SLC to Mary Fairbanks, 12 December 1867).[1] Never very good at prognostication, he found with *Innocents Abroad* that book publication of revised journalism turned ink to money quite efficiently. But he eschewed trade publication because he preferred the profits to be found in subscription sales, saying that "anything but subscription publishing is printing for private circulation" (Howells, *Literary* 312). Later, when he found that literary piracy ate into his book profits, he turned to drama as a lucrative alternative: "We find our copywright [*sic*] law here to be nearly worthless, & if I can make a living out of plays, I shall never write another book" (SLC to Moncure Conway, 13 December 1876).

He did continue to write books, though, and he developed a sense of contractual reciprocity with the consuming public. He made this point most clearly in correspondence with Mary Mason Fairbanks, who, as one of his early mentors, pushed him to see his art as something more than a mere commodity. Twain pushed back: "What the societies ask of me is to relieve the heaviness of their didactic courses—& in accepting the contract I am just the same as giving my word that I will do as they ask" (SLC to Mary Fairbanks, 12 October 1868). In short, Twain was saying, "The customer is always right," and that giving the public what it wants is the job of a commercial writer. This attitude persisted, most conspicuously when he was defending *A Connecticut Yankee* against British critics: "I have never tried . . . to help cultivate the cultivated classes . . . but always hunted for bigger game—the masses" (Mark Twain Project [MTP], SLC to Andrew Lang, 1890). Again, the mass public is the appropriate audience, and the author's responsibility is to give the public what it wants and needs. If an author does so, the public reciprocally supports him or her. At least so is the fantasy of a stable contract with the public stated in the *Autobiography* in his discussion of "submerged renown" (*Autobiography* [*AMT*] 1:229). Twain refers to a "Davis" whose books, unknown to the literary classes, sell prodigiously to the working classes. "The man that gets that market, his fortune is made, his bread and butter are safe, for those people will never go back on him" (*AMT* 1:230).

Yet Twain's self-commodification did not sit completely comfortably on him. As early as 1870, he both endorsed this commercial idea and undercut it in his "General Reply" to correspondents who wished to have him review their manuscripts. At first, he seems to suggest that the public is the best and final arbiter of value, but he then undercuts that position, only to reinforce it again:

> I must not and will not venture any opinion what ever as to the literary merit of your productions. The public is the only critic whose judgment is worth anything at all. Do not take my poor word for this, but reflect a moment and take your own. For instance, if Sylvanus Cobb or T. S. Arthur had submitted their maiden MSS. to you, you would have said, with tears in your eyes, "Now please don't write any more!" But you see yourself how popular they are. And if it had been left to you, you would have said the "Marble Faun" was tiresome, and that even "Paradise Lost" lacked cheerfulness; but you know they sell.

> Many wiser and better men than you pooh-poohed Shakespeare, even as late as two centuries ago; but still that old party has outlived those people. No, I will not sit in judgment upon your literature. If I honestly and conscientiously praised it, I might thus help to inflict a lingering and pitiless bore upon the public; if I honestly and conscientiously condemned it, I might thus rob the world of an undeveloped and unsuspected Dickens or Shakespeare. (486–87)

It's easy to imagine Twain's vexed relationship to his audience, for he was entirely dependent on the goodwill of an audience that adhered to no established standard of taste and that provided no rules for marketability. He often noted that different classes of readers had different tastes, and he envisioned market segmentation as crucial to successful literary salesmanship, yet he nonetheless often lumped high and low art together in exasperating and hilarious confusion—as in *Adventures of Huckleberry Finn*, when the king and duke butcher Shakespeare. But there is another aspect to his "General Reply" that speaks, I think, to a deeper sense of anxiety about attachment to the market, namely, that the market rewards a writer only with money; its judgments have nothing to do with a writer's craft, talent, or professionalism. Specifically, Twain follows his suggestion that only the market can judge by mentioning that other trades require apprenticeships; it's only in literature that neophytes believe that they can "serenely take up so dangerous a weapon as a pen, and attack the most formidable subject that finance, commerce, war, or politics can furnish him withal. It would be laughable if it were not so sad and so pitiable." Indeed, we know that Twain found bad writing laughable. From his early burlesque of Elizabeth Stuart Phelps's *The Gates Ajar*, to mid-career mockery of Julia Moore's poetry in *Huckleberry Finn*, to the late-career essays "A Cure for the Blues" and "Fenimore Cooper's Literary Offenses," Twain expressed deep exasperation with and animus toward what he considered inept popular forms and styles. Perhaps one could see this as mere competitive resentment, but Twain's concern for standards of quality suggests that it is something more, the pride of a master craftsman whose patronage is fundamentally controlled by a guild. I address this topic in greater detail in my discussion of peer patronage.

Political Patronage

Political patronage, one of the most common forms of artistic patronage in nineteenth-century America, arose from Jacksonian democracy and the development of the spoils system. Political offices under Jackson were rewards for political support, but the idea was not merely to support cronies; it was ostensibly also to spread the ideals of democracy by pulling people into the administration of the republic. I do not want to get into the arguments over how cynical such justification was in general, but there is no question that to some degree, in using sinecures to support artists, the spoils system did look to create a democratic culture—or at least to show that a democracy could support the arts. Writers were often appointed as consuls, secretaries, postmasters, and customs collectors so that writers could devote at least some of their time to their real craft. Sometimes such political appointments were merely to show the dignity of America in finding a way to support the arts. More often, they were based on some kind of quid pro quo, as when Hawthorne was rewarded with a consulship for writing Franklin Pierce's presidential campaign biography in 1852.

Americans did not invent this kind of political patronage of the arts. Consider, for example, the career of Henry Fielding. He was excluded from his potentially lucrative career as a playwright when Walpole's government, stinging from Fielding's satiric attacks, passed a censorship law that effectively throttled political theater. Fielding assumed he'd have to return to a legal career, but with the patronage of Ralph Allen, Fielding was instead able to work as a journalist and novelist, in both cases continuing satirical attacks on Walpole.

Such a pattern was developed because literature, belletristic or journalistic, was held to be inherently political. The American colonies followed this eighteenth-century pattern, as we can see in the career of Benjamin Franklin, with the difference that the patrons were not so much individual aristocrats as groups of like-minded men on the make, who secured the services of fine writers to further their ends. In this respect, the colonies were already modifying political patronage away from an aristocratic model, and, after the birth of the United States, the power of parties to focus the collective energies of connected and powerful men made them crucial to the development of an American literature.

Twain probably would never have had a literary career at all if American letters were not so deeply involved in a game of political patronage. Would Joseph Goodman have hired Samuel Clemens to write for the Virginia City *Territorial Enterprise* if Sam's brother Orion had not been the secretary to the governor of Nevada Territory? It's hard to say; newspapers needed engaging writers, and in the turbulent West, writers, like nearly everybody else, came and went so quickly that any editor might grasp at straws. But Samuel Clemens was not a straw; he was connected to a man who could decide who would print the proceedings of the legislature (Kaplan 100), who could get access to important information, who might sway the fortunes not just of a newspaper, but of a region or an industry. In the early world of newspapers, political connections were essential to a newspaper's success or failure, so it would have been a shrewd move on Goodman's part to hire a man who could connect his paper to the territorial government.

Regardless of whether or not he owed his start to Goodman's political shrewdness, Twain engaged the practice of political patronage intensely through the 1860s and sporadically for the rest of his life. In the 1860s he boasted in a letter to his mother about his capacity as a reporter to influence patronage: "We shall bud out into a State before many months, which will relieve Orion of his office. If I have influence enough, I mean to get him nominated a candidate for some fat office under the State Government, so that you can come out and live with him. I am a pretty good hand at such things. . . . Oh, I tell you a reporter in the Legislature can swing more votes than any member of the body" (SLC to Jane L. Clemens, 19 August 1863). As a reporter with a flair for fiction, Twain was himself the object of patronage. When he met Anson Burlingame in Hawaii, Burlingame offered him a job, which he turned down, but he later wrote to Burlingame asking for a sinecure that would allow him to write a travel book about China: "I shall have completed my book in the course of a couple of months or so, & then I would like to go with your Embassy as a dignitary of some kind or other, & privately on my own hook as Herald & Tribune correspondent. I want to be a mild sort of dignitary, though, particularly. Pray save me a place. Correspondents will hover about the Expedition anyhow, & so it will be best for the interest of China & the world, that one of them, at least, should be *reliable*" (SLC to Anson Burlingame, 19 February 1868). The comic panache of this letter covers the seriousness of the request, which was to use a government position to support the career of a writer, merely in exchange for good press.

Had such a request bothered him at the time, he would have been quite the hypocrite, inasmuch as he was then working as private secretary to Nevada senator William Stewart, who introduced Clemens to the world of Washington, D.C., affording him the opportunity to sell his correspondence about politics to newspapers across the nation. Here is where we first see the way in which Twain's opinions were at odds with his corn pone. On the one hand, he felt it was legitimate to abuse the power he accrued from access to politicians, boasting in numerous letters that, as a journalist, he was the politicians' master (see, for example, his letter to his mother on 24 January 1868). He knew better, of course. He was unable even to get his brother a job, much less to shape national politics. His comments in chapter 6 of "Old Times on the Mississippi," quoted at the beginning of this chapter, speak more honestly about his powerlessness as a journalist (though some journalists, such as Horace Greeley, did have outsized power, substantially because they did not mix their editorial positions with direct government employment).

On the other hand, he felt that a journalist's real job was to attack corrupt politicians. In a letter to Mary Mason Fairbanks, he wrote: "I am tired of writing wishy-washy squibs for the Tribune, & have joined the Herald staff—2 impersonal letters a week. Mr. Bennett says I may have full swing, & say as many mean things as I please. Now don't say a word Madam, because I just mean to abuse people right & left in case the humor takes me to do it. There are lots of folks in Washington who need vilifying" (SLC to Mary Fairbanks, 24 January 1868). Not surprisingly, it didn't take long for Clemens and Stewart to have a falling-out, jeopardizing the corn-pone train in the short term. Yet Twain's anticorruption stance furthered his career for most of the remainder of his life, gaining him much bread. In particular, *The Gilded Age*, both in the original novel format and in a stage adaptation, was a cash cow for Twain, helping him make a strong break from the journalist's dependence on political patronage.

More importantly, Twain's knee-jerk reaction against being a toady to anyone who had a legitimate claim to his loyalty shaped a principled idea that journalists should be a fourth estate, independent of parties, exposing political malfeasance and promoting good government. I don't mean to say that Twain was alone or first in wanting the press to push for clean government. The constitutional protection of the press shows that many of the founders saw the press as a fundamental check on political power, and the idea that the press was "the palladium of freedom" was already a cliché that Twain frequently mocked, but he mocked it precisely because so many journals were political organs, because political patronage undercut the freedom of the press. As much as he admired the ability of individual journalists, such as Thomas Nast, for their courageous attacks on political corruption, he also resented the overwhelming weight of party influence on the press. His 1870 sketch "Running for Governor" heavy-handedly accuses the "the principal Republican journal[s]" and the "leading Democratic paper[s]" of wholesale slander to further the ends of their parties (493). In this respect, he was laying the groundwork for his own turn to the mugwumps in the election of 1884, when he refused to support Republican James G. Blaine's presidential candidacy, and later his politically inexpedient anti-imperialism, which subjected him to the scorn of many of the major party-connected journals.

After breaking from the Republican Party in 1884, his steady resistance to party politics, his steady attacks on political machines, and his support of George William Curtis's civil service reforms were all of a piece, arising in part out of his reaction against the political patronage of writers. As much as he knew that newspapers did not live up to the ideal, he praised them in *Connecticut Yankee* as vanguards of civilization, and he articulated the ideal crisply in *The American Claimant*, didactically challenging Matthew Arnold's criticism of the American press: "Its mission—overlooked by Mr.

Arnold—is to stand guard over a nation's liberties, not its humbugs and shams" (98). As much, then, as Twain turned against the very political patrons who gave him his start, his profound advocacy for a democratic and independent press seems to bear out the Jacksonian vision that participating in democratic institutions would teach the participants the meaning of democracy.

Peer Patronage

I understand that I title this section with an oxymoron. Perhaps I should instead be talking about a republic of letters. But inasmuch as I'm concerned with how Mark Twain made money, it is important to understand that he benefited from his peer relations not just for encouragement and mentorship, but also because these men shared commercial opportunities as well as intellectual and artistic support. What makes these connections the connections of peers is that they were reciprocal. Charvat talks about the development of the profession of authorship as one in which writers came to see themselves as workers having something to sell. He thus emphasizes the employer–employee relationship between publisher and writer. But for Twain and his peers, these relationships were neither stable nor one-directional. He and many of his peers would swap roles and blur the distinctions between these roles in ways that suggest how much they were trying to find an alternative economic basis for the writing profession.

By Twain's time, there was a long-standing, oft-stated pretense that "letters" were the province of the genteel. If to be genteel were not to be "tainted" by commerce, then those who chose to publish were doing so out of a desire to inform or elevate the public, not out of a desire to make money. Such a pretense had been mocked for over a century by the time Twain started to write—one need only think of Parson Adams, in Fielding's *Joseph Andrews*, trying to sell his sermons to supplement his meager clerical income. Regardless of the reality that most authors wanted to make money, the pretense held, so much so that it was still normal for writers to adopt a nom de plume behind which to hide their genteel selves when entering the market, especially if their writing was of a kind less than genteel itself. So Samuel Clemens had a long list of antecedents when it came to taking a pseudonym before publishing satirical, or even merely comic, work. How to turn a genteel avocation into a paying profession was the challenge for freelance writers. After making the transition from newspaper reporter to freelance author, Twain began to use the metaphor of a craft guild to describe a new economic basis for writing, because it provided a conceptual alternative either to the pure market or to some explicit form of patronage.

We see the complex implications of this metaphor in the way Twain and Howells discussed the economic basis of writing in much of their correspondence. For instance, in the summer of 1874, Twain acted as intermediary between Charles P. Pope, a theatrical producer, and Howells, for Pope to produce Howells's translation of Ippolito Tito d'Aste's *Sansone*. As Twain put it in a letter to Howells:

> I couldn't really make up my mind about a price at first, standing between two personal friends. . . . I came very near telegraphing you, after I got back here, to be sure & charge enough, but it seemed a sort of disloyalty to Pope to be legging for the other side all the time. But I think you made an admirable bargain. No doubt you & I both underrate the worth of the work far enough; but that you are warrior enough to stand up & charge *any*thing above a week's board is gaudy manliness in a literary person. Our guild are so egotistically mock-modest about their own merits.—We make a wretched bargain—caressing our darling humility the while—& then when we come to think how much more we could have got, we go behind the house & curse. —By George I admire you. I suppose "consuling" is not without its uses—it breeds common sense in parties who would otherwise develop only the *un*common. (SLC to W. D. Howells, 22 July 1874)

Three points are worth mentioning here. First, Twain assumes that Howells and the rest of the world understand the genteel basis of the "egotistical mock-modesty" of writers. Second, that Howells was a consul was a result of his working for Abraham Lincoln's campaign, and he did so because his work as a journalist in Ohio connected him to the Republican Party. Thus, Twain is saying that a worldly political connection has at least put Howells in the way of thinking about quid pro quo. The third point is that Twain refers to "literary person[s]" as belonging to a guild.

They didn't in fact belong to a guild, but Twain's own apprenticeship in printing encouraged him to think in terms of guild on a regular basis. I've discussed this elsewhere, so I won't elaborate here, but it is worth noting that the idea of guild labor as a seedbed of democracy was conventional in the United States. As such, Twain was not alone in thinking of writing as a guild in which the reciprocal relationships among the master craftsmen who had earned their status as freelancers were part of an important political and economic tradition that complemented even as it qualified the idea of gentleman writer. The complement was that in a guild, a master rose above the dependence of his apprentices and journeymen, entering into the market not as a laborer alone, but with the elevated status of a master of men, as well as a master of a craft. Indeed, many European cities and towns, dominated by the masters of various guilds, became free of the patronage and protection of nobles, earning a political status outside of the regular feudal order. Part of the political rhetoric of guild labor in the United States was that craft workers, drawing on this tradition of self-government, considered themselves to be, paradoxically, the elites of the commoners.

Writers in the nineteenth-century United States often shared this paradoxical democratic elitism. As Howells put it in a letter to his father, he and Twain were in "accord in our way of thinking: that is, we are theoretical socialists, and practical aristocrats" (W. D. Howells to William Cooper Howells, 2 February 1890, quoted in *Selected Mark Twain–Howells Letters* 273). There is perhaps no better way to put the strange mix of genteel-commonality, or cultured egalitarianism, that characterized a significant portion of the literary world.

In this context Twain could one year be hired by Bret Harte, only to return the favor a few years later by supporting Harte when the two worked collaboratively on a play, which Twain arranged to have produced. Or, one year Twain could be hired and tutored by Joseph Goodman, only to serve later as the publisher of Goodman's book. Or Twain could have his articles published by Howells as editor of the *Atlantic*, only to hire Howells later to edit *Mark Twain's Library of Humor*. Indeed, the long arc of Twain's literary career from journalist, to newspaper publisher, to writer of books, to publisher of books, and back to novelist and journalist, suggests that the profession of authorship was more complex than Charvat allowed. No doubt Twain was a paid professional; no doubt he was also a publisher. The point is that he worked with a group of craftsman peers who shifted between these roles, assisting each other in various professional capacities as they traded around from position to position.

Much has been written about the anxieties created by the unsettled nature of Twain's business relations. Without denying any of this body of scholarship, one suspects it is equally true that Twain gained a sense of autonomy from rubbing elbows as an equal with a body of highly educated and successful men. That sense of autonomy enabled him gradually to find as a literary man some of the freedom he claimed the riverboat pilot had. Indeed, it is fairly well understood that the "Old Times" sketches spoke simultaneously to Twain's development as a pilot and as a writer. When he spoke of journalists, he spoke of them as bound by party, but when he referred to "Writers of all kinds," he spoke of them as servants of the public. That was a duty that he accepted as the price of his real freedom. By the Blaine/Cleveland presidential campaign of 1884, Twain went public with this broader understanding of a writer's power and duty. Given his conviction that James G.

Blaine was corrupt, Twain actively campaigned against him, even though most of his Hartford associates stuck to their party and voted for Blaine. It is useful to understand that the "Australian" system of secret ballot had not yet been adopted in the United States, so Twain knew before election day that if he were to vote for Cleveland, a minor party candidate, or not vote at all for president, his Hartford circle would know. There was no point, if he intended to vote for Cleveland, to remain silent before the election, expecting anonymity to cloak his ultimate action. So he took the plunge, along with Joseph Twichell, actively to campaign against Blaine. Among his efforts was his paper for the Hartford Monday Evening Club "Consistency," in which he explained that his ideas of patriotism excluded blind allegiance to party (or to the nation, for that matter). Such ideas became central to his works, having a profound impact especially on *Connecticut Yankee*, which he was writing at the time.

Twain tried in his correspondence to pull Howells into the mugwump camp, too. While he couched his argument mainly in moral terms, he explained that their moral independence derived from their economic independence as writers: "You know that [the charges against Blaine] are proven, & it seems to me that that bars you & all other honest & honorable men (who are independently situated) from voting for him" (MTP, SLC to William Dean Howells, 17 September 1884; rpt. in *Selected Mark Twain–Howells Letters* 241). While articulated parenthetically, the "independent" situation to which Twain refers is that of the writer whose livelihood depends on a broad national readership. Beholden neither to a political party nor to the subscribers of a local newspaper, the nationally popular freelance writer could, Twain at this point believed, afford to follow his conscience.

Twain elaborated his reasoning in the *Autobiography*, coupling his opposition to Blaine with a fictionalized account of Twichell's experience so as to clarify the writer's independence as another kind of corn-pone consequence. Twain says that of the members of the Monday Evening Club who were appalled by the nomination of Blaine to be the Republican candidate for president, only three actually voted for Cleveland, and all three were privately and publicly abused for their vote. Of himself, he says, he received no hurt, because "I did not draw my living from Hartford. It was quite sufficient for my needs. Hartford's opinion of me could not affect it." Rev. Francis Goodwin, too, was economically and thus politically independent, because his father "was worth seven millions, and was old. The Revered Francis was in the line of promotion, and would soon inherit" (*AMT* 1:318–19). But Twichell was completely dependent on his congregation and so risked his livelihood. Twain claims that the congregation nearly dismissed him, and thus Twichell learned his lesson to dispense with political independence.[2]

Regardless of the particular facts of Twichell's political apostasy in the Blaine affair, Twain's account of his own grounds for political independence is consistent from 1884 to the end of his career. His collaboration with Howells in taking an "anti-patriotic" position in the anti-imperialist league is the natural result of his sense that the guild of writers who could afford to be morally independent had a duty to serve a larger public over a longer horizon than dictated by momentary expediency. He did so even though he expected nothing "but kicks and scoffing, and . . . a diminution of my bread and butter for it" (MTP, SLC to Joseph Twichell, 29 January 1901). Diminution, not elimination—Twain's continued sense of independence relied on a belief that he would not immolate himself on the altar of political duty.

A lack of clear hierarchy among the members of the writer's "guild," coupled with a sense of elitism in service of the people, had a subtle but important influence on Twain's writing, most positively in *Adventures of Huckleberry Finn*. Huck himself barely registers the influence, but four characters who have a degree of financial independence and a sense of noblesse oblige have an outsized positive influence on the action in *Huckleberry Finn*. The Widow Douglas's efforts to acculturate Huck have been the subject of scholarly debate over the years, with many suggesting that Huck's ultimate rejection of efforts to "sivilize" him are equally pointed at the widow and Miss Watson, while others have shown the distinct difference in Huck's reactions to two very different versions of culture and Christianity. If one accepts that the widow has nothing to gain in educating Huck, it's important to see that Twain depicts her as having nothing to lose. Her sister appears to lack the widow's financial independence; is that why Twain depicts her as intellectually shallow and conventional? At any rate, it's worth considering that Twain may well have seen the writer's independence as connected to a larger world of letters, one that embraced cultured women and educated men, especially men in other freelance professions. Consider three other minor characters who shape the action: Judge Thatcher, Dr. Robinson, and lawyer Levi Bell. All three work, without hope of remuneration, to protect the innocent from "deadbeats and rapscallions."

When Huck goes to Judge Thatcher to renounce his money, the judge quickly perceives Huck's need to hide and protect his wealth and then proceeds to use his professional understanding of the law to help. He has nothing to fear from his community's reaction to his efforts, because the community despises Pap. That said, he has nothing to gain, financially or in terms of reputation, by using his deep understanding of human motivations and of the law to serve Huck. Thus does Twain picture disinterested benevolence as the duty of those freelance professionals who can afford it. Later, when the Wilks girls are being cheated by the king and duke, Dr. Robinson does risk his community standing—though probably not his economic independence by any great measure—by alerting the girls to the probable fraud. When they refuse to listen to him, he persists in working in their interest, ultimately enlisting the help of his fellow professional, Levi Bell, a lawyer. Between the two, they uncover the fraud and protect the girls. While these characters are not writers, they represent, I believe, Twain's allegiance to an ideal of freelance virtue, an ideal that returns in a failed sense in the character of Pudd'nhead Wilson, and in a successful sense in that of Doangiveadam, the journeyman printer/gentleman of *No. 44, The Mysterious Stranger*. David Wilson's failure to make a living as a professional mirrors Twain's business failure and the failure of his dream of financial independence. Doangiveadam's independence is more modest; he is able to make a living anywhere and anytime, but his independence derives as much from his frame of mind as from the financial freedom that arises from a lack of dependents and low material expectations. Clearly, Twain's ideal of a republic of letters shifted to some degree over time, even as his vision of the freelance writer's duty toward the public persisted.

Twain's shifting conception of moral independence reflects the reality that the increasing demands of capitalization challenged peer relations among professional men, especially among artists. Perhaps no work of the nineteenth century does a better job of capturing the complex, interconnected, constantly shifting, and always pressured conceptions of authorship than Howells's *A Hazard of New Fortunes*. Fulkerson and March establish a literary magazine on cooperative principles. In that sense, Howells envisions an art created by equals for the common good. But to establish this cooperative ideal, they need the capital of an "angel," or, to use an older term, a patron. The complex arguments about what such a cooperative art should entail against the backdrop of labor disputes and violence in an industrial economy end finally with the gradual withdrawal of the capitalist backer and a more modest, but workable conception of the magazine. This fantasy ending belies Howells's clear sense that big capital was reshaping the republic of letters. For Twain, it was less a sense or an understanding than a lived reality.

Patrician Patronage

I take my chapter's title from the well-known fact that, after his bankruptcy, Twain relied on the support of Standard Oil tycoon and notorious robber baron H. H. Rogers to restore his fortunes. Rogers was willing to help because he so admired Twain's humor, and as the two developed a friendship, the asymmetry in their power could easily have had Twain playing fool to Rogers's king. The evidence exists, at any rate, to support such a conclusion, and even if one were not to go so far, there is no doubt that Twain's financial dependency complicated his relationship with Rogers; even though the two were roughly of an age and had a strong personal bond, Rogers's economic power pulled Twain into its orbit. Twain's public support of Rogers seems to be a blot on his progressive credentials of the period, though this was not the first time he served as a flack for a plutocrat. He supported his father-in-law's anti-union sympathies, too. Yet Twain's fulminations both early and late against just about every plutocrat except Rogers show how uncomfortable he was with these arrangements.

Such discomfort is not surprising. Twain was on record in his European travel books as an inveterate and profound critic of plutocratic and aristocratic patronage. For instance, in chapter 25 of *Innocents Abroad*:

> Andrea del Sarto glorified his princes in pictures that must save them for ever from the oblivion they merited, and they let him starve. Served him right. Raphael pictured such infernal villains as Catherine and Marie de Medicis seated in heaven and conversing familiarly with the Virgin Mary and the angels, (to say nothing of higher personages,) and yet my friends abuse me because I am a little prejudiced against the old masters—because I fail sometimes to see the beauty that is in their productions. I can not help but see it, now and then, but I keep on protesting against the groveling spirit that could persuade those masters to prostitute their noble talents to the adulation of such monsters as the French, Venetian and Florentine Princes of two and three hundred years ago, all the same.
>
> I am told that the old masters had to do these shameful things for bread, the princes and potentates being the only patrons of art. If a grandly gifted man may drag his pride and his manhood in the dirt for bread rather than starve with the nobility that is in him untainted, the excuse is a valid one. It would excuse theft in Washingtons and Wellingtons, and unchastity in women as well. (259–60)

At the outset of his career, Twain called artists whores if they paid for patronage by praising their patrons. In essence, he called himself a whore in the process, in part because he had already accepted politically motivated patronage, and in prospect because he would later accept the patronage of the wealthy in return for promoting their causes.

In supporting Jervis Langdon's coal interests, Twain might have been able to acquit himself of "unchastity" inasmuch as he *married* into a wealthy family. Thus, while Olivia's father did help Twain buy a share in the *Buffalo Express*, and while the Langdons did purchase a house in Buffalo for the newlyweds, it would be a stretch to say that Twain prostituted his artistry to the interests of a wealthy, powerful patron. In writing editorials supporting his father-in-law's business interests, one could say that he was supporting his own, as a junior member in a family business might be expected to do.

It does not seem that Twain found that a comfortable conclusion, however. As with his political patrons, he resorted to a pattern of alternately supporting and attacking the patrician sources of his corn pone. In the case of the Langdon interests, the support may very well have been an embarrassment to a man who had belonged to both a printers' union and a riverboat pilots' union. In a 9 March 1870 editorial in the *Buffalo Express*, Twain attacked a Pennsylvania coal miners' union, whose efforts to improve wages and working conditions were opposed by Jervis Langdon, the owner of mines that the Workingman's Benevolent Association was organizing. Twain's editorial is hysterically opposed to any effort by working men to organize, blames them for trying to steal private property, murder middle-managers, engage in "mob terrorism," and coerce legislatures to serve the interests of labor at the expense of owners (*Letters* 4:544–47). At nearly the same time, however, Twain's public excoriation of the moral poverty of "The-public-be-damned" Vanderbilt ("Open Letter") flatly contradicts his PR for coal-mine owners. And a mere five years later, in "Old Times," Twain could praise his former union for securing the safety of Mississippi riverboat passengers and goods, playing capitalist jiu-jitsu in pointing out that insurance companies came to back the union.

The better-known and more controversial situation in which Twain allegedly prostituted his grand gifts and his "manhood" follows a similar, but more intense, pattern. Rogers took a long time to press for a quid pro quo, having rescued Twain in the mid-1890s but not asking for reciprocity until 1901, when he learned that Ida Tarbell had been commissioned by *McClure's Magazine* to write an exposé of the Standard Oil Company. Rogers asked Clemens for help, not so crudely as to have Twain pen a defense, but rather to have him arrange for Tarbell to interview Rogers. In her memoirs, Tarbell comments ambiguously that Rogers was "as fine a pirate as ever flew his flag in Wall Street," implying that she was taken by his charisma as much as she was contemptuous of his business practices (10). For Twain to have helped Rogers practice his charm on Tarbell was not, then, a trivial service. Perhaps, if we were to extend Twain's own metaphor, he was not so much an unchaste artist himself as he was baud to Rogers's efforts to prostitute Tarbell.

Be that as it may, Twain's unease at being in Rogers's debt shows up repeatedly in his autobiographical dictations and in some of the works he published in his own lifetime. In the dictations, Twain spent an inordinate amount of time and energy attacking just about every American business magnate except Rogers. Even Carnegie, with whom Twain spent a fair amount of time on shared interests, especially the anti-imperialist cause, was not exempt from the stream of abuse that Twain expected to come to light posthumously. He may have been too embarrassed to vent his rage at the oligarchy to which he owed so much, but he seems to have wanted to rehabilitate his reputation for posterity. The ploy largely worked: the autobiographical excerpts that DeVoto published under the title *Mark Twain in Eruption* helped create an image of Twain as a great radical.

I'm also interested in two subtler manifestations of Twain's unease with his dependent position. Precisely when he was most dependent on Rogers, before the Paige typesetter was written off and as Webster & Co. was nearing the end of its rope, Twain wrote *Personal Recollections of Joan of Arc*. Dismissed for most of the twentieth century as one of Twain's weaker works and far from the center of his usual concerns, the book has been somewhat rehabilitated recently because of what it tells us about Twain's partially evolving attitudes about women. I'd like to add one other reason to consider this novel as characteristic of Twain: it speaks, indirectly to be sure, to his concerns about the moral relationship between patron and artist. As he had done repeatedly over his career, Twain turned to the Middle Ages to allegorize contemporary concerns. And as in the case of so many other works, the narrative point of view reveals much about Twain's agenda. The title in this case is particularly revealing. *Personal Recollections* asks us to focus at least as much on the narrator as on Joan of Arc. A transcendent figure, Joan is the ultimate freelance hero, pushing her own moral agenda to support her sovereign. But unlike Roland's Charlemagne, Joan's Charles is an unsuitable patron, unworthy of her moral clarity, unable to rise to the duty of his office. Joan is destroyed, then, because she is unable to find appropriate and sustaining patronage. The novel's narrator, more obviously a figure for literary artists, fails because he is so dependent on his patrons that he cannot find the moral independence to support a righteous cause. The two combined provide, I think, an allegory for Twain's sense in the 1890s that there is no model for the kind of morally independent artistry, the freelance writer, that he had once hoped would serve the largest of public interests.

In part, then, we see Twain retreating entirely from the idea of writing as a profession at all. In his letters to Rogers he says that he is going to leave business behind and devote his days to literature, nothing but literature. Earlier, he saw literature as a kind of business. I don't mean to overstress a few remarks to his patron, but there is a pattern in the autobiographical dictations that shows Twain desiring to redefine literature as outside the realm of ordinary markets. To push the metaphor of pattern a bit, this pattern is made of opposed elements, each of which is odd enough to suggest how much Twain was thinking outside of market-based patronage.

One odd figure in this pattern is Twain's testimony to support changes in

U.S. copyright laws. He wished this change in part to secure the commercial value of his copyrights beyond his death in hopes of providing for his posterity. One can hardly imagine a more emphatic entry into the market as ultimate patron. Yet strangely, Twain seems to back up this idea that literature is not really a business like any other. Indeed, the only reason to provide literature the protections of business is precisely because it is like no other. In his autobiographical dictation of 19 December 1906, Twain pushed the idea that very few books had commercial value that lasted long enough to require protection as intellectual property, so that any change in the law made next to no commercial difference to the authors themselves, because very few books ever make any money, and of those that do, few make money for long.

Twain says in effect, then, that the gentleman author remains the model and will remain the model for the foreseeable future. But when hypothetically asked why Congress should then bother with the concerns of such an economically "trifling" group as commercially successful authors, Twain moved well beyond the realm of economics:

> Almost the most prodigious asset of a country, and perhaps its most precious possession, is its native literary product—when that product is fine and noble and enduring. . . . Nations pride themselves upon the splendors of their deeds of arms, statesmanship, conquest; and when they can point back, century after century, and age after age, to the far-stretching perspective of a great history, their pride is beyond expression in words; but it all exists by grace of one thing—one thing alone—the country's literature. . . . When we call to mind that stately line—"The glory that was Greece, and the grandeur that was Rome"—we should remember with respect and with reverence that if the great literatures of Greece and Rome had by some catastrophe been blotted out, the inspiring histories of those countries would be vacant to the world to-day. . . . It is not foreign literatures that sing a country's glories and give them immortality—only the country's own literature will perform that priceless service. It were worth a Congress's while to spend upon a copyright law time worth the cost of even a hundred battleships if the result of it might some day be the breeding and nourishing of a Shakspeare [sp]. (*AMT* 2:323–24)

This has to be the oddest argument ever made to support a change in national business law. Not one of the writers Twain mentions by name or implication was protected by international copyright. The idea that changed copyright law would in fact be the way to secure a cultural heritage is thus on the face of it absurd. It does not seem that Twain really intended to help create a market for literature so much as to suggest that he, as one of the very few American authors who had an enduring commercial success, had transcended the market in a way congruent with an idealized conception of art as the spontaneous overflow of genius.

The other figure in the pattern says this precisely. Repeatedly in the dictations, Twain refers to "literature from the heart" as real literature. Consider, for example, the dictation of 1 February 1907:

> [W]hen the heart speaks it has no use for the conventions; it can rise above them, and the result is literature, and not to be called by any less dignified name. . . . [S]ometimes, the productions of the unschooled mind get even an added grace and power out of fresh and free and lawless grammar and orthography. If that was my position, I consider it strongly reinforced by a letter which has come to my hands this morning; it was written to Helen Keller something more than three years ago, at the time that she published her history of her life, and it came from a cowboy in the Far West, whose spelling, grammar, and construction do most engagingly set at easy and unembarrassed defiance all the laws that govern those artificialities; but the result is unqualifiedly satisfactory, just the same, and miles and miles above the reach of criticism; it comes out of a sound good heart, and out of a most wise and level head, and is literature—and not commonplace literature, but literature of a high class. . . . It is long since I have seen so delightful a letter as his; it is literature, high literature, and not to be successfully imitated by any art taught in the schools or known to the trained journeyman of the trade. (*AMT* 2:413–14)

By this standard, real literature is, again, spontaneous and likely to erupt where least expected. Thus it cannot be patronized by parties, peers, patricians, or the paying public. If this is true, then in a recurrent mood of his late years, Twain—one of the most successful men of the business of writing, one of the men who helped transform writing from a gentlemanly avocation into a profession—ironically renounced the profession of authorship, even as he continued to sell his works and to create a market for them into posterity. The irony has carried more than a century beyond Twain's death. The scholarly enterprise of preserving Twain's literature for posterity as part of U.S. cultural history has been entrusted to an academic enterprise (of which I am a part as a member of the editorial board of the Mark Twain Project) that eschews the market, looking to patronage from the U.S. government, from wealthy donors, and from the University of California. In putting together one of the most carefully researched and meticulously documented scholarly books imaginable in the first volume of *Autobiography of Mark Twain*, the Mark Twain Project produced a surprise best seller. The market is dead; long live the market.

Notes

1. Letters available online are cited by date alone; those not yet digitized are cited as MTP (The Mark Twain Papers), followed by the correspondents and the date.

2. Kenneth Andrews reports two distortions in Twain's account. There are no parish records, personal letters, or diaries to suggest that any members of Twichell's congregation tried to oust him. Andrews also notes that Twichell did not vote for Cleveland, registering his opposition to Blaine by instead voting for the Prohibition Party candidate. Andrews documents how difficult the decision was for many Nook Farm residents to support Blaine—an account Twain corroborates—and draws from this evidence the conclusion that Twain's account of how difficult it was for Twichell to be politically independent was not accurate. Yet the fact that Twichell voted for a minor party candidate—the temperance candidate at that, even though Twichell loved his beer and made no pretense otherwise—suggests that Twichell was not willing to go too far in expressing his political independence. That is, he threw his vote away on what could be construed as a "moral" alternative, rather than in a way that might have actively undermined Blaine's candidacy.

Works Cited

Anderson, Frederick, William M. Gibson, and Henry Nash Smith, eds. *Selected Mark Twain–Howells Letters*. Cambridge: Belknap-Harvard UP, 1967.

Andrews, Kenneth. *Nook Farm: Mark Twain's Hartford Circle*. Cambridge: Harvard UP, 1950.

Brooks, Van Wyck. *The Ordeal of Mark Twain*. 1920. Revised ed. New York: E. P. Dutton, 1933.

Camfield, Gregg. "A Republican Artisan in the Court of King Capital: Mark Twain and Commerce." *The Oxford Historical Guide to Mark Twain*. Ed. Shelly Fisher Fishkin. New York: Oxford UP, 2002.

Charvat, William. *The Rise of Authorship in America, 1800–1870*. 1968. New York: Columbia UP, 1992.

DeVoto, Bernard, ed. *Mark Twain in Eruption*. New York: Harper and Brothers, 1940.

Fielding, Henry. *Joseph Andrews*. London: A. Miller, 1742.

Howells, William Dean. *A Hazard of New Fortunes*. New York: Harper and Brothers, 1889.

———. "My Mark Twain." In *Literary Friends and Acquaintances: A Personal Retrospect of American Authorship*. New York: Harper and Brothers, 1911.

Kaplan, Fred. *The Singular Mark Twain: A Biography*. New York: Doubleday, 2003.

Moore, Julia. *The Sentimental Song Book*. New York: Platt and Peck, 1912.

Phelps, Elizabeth Stuart. *The Gates Ajar*. 1868. Ed. Helen Smootin Smith. Cambridge: Belknap-Harvard UP, 1964.

Smith, Henry Nash. *Mark Twain: The Development of a Writer*. Cambridge: Harvard University Press, 1962.

Tarbell, Ida. *All in the Day's Work*. New York: Macmillan, 1939.

Twain, Mark. *Adventures of Huckleberry Finn*. 1885. Ed. Victor Fisher and Lin Salamo. Berkeley: U of California P, 2003.

———. *The American Claimant*. New York: Charles Webster, 1892.

———. *Autobiography of Mark Twain. Vol. 1*. Ed. Harriet Elinor Smith. Berkeley: U of California P, 2010.

———. *Autobiography of Mark Twain. Vol. 2*. Ed. Benjamin Griffin and Harriet Elinor Smith. Berkeley: U of California P, 2013.

———. *A Connecticut Yankee in King Arthur's Court*. 1889. Ed. Bernard L. Stein. Berkeley: U of California P, 1979.

———. "Consistency." 1887. Rpt. *Mark Twain: Collected Tales, Sketches, Speeches, & Essays*. Vol. 1. Ed. Louis J. Budd. New York: Library of America, 1992. 909–16.

———. "Corn-pone Opinions." 1901. Rpt. *Mark Twain: Collected Tales, Sketches, 1852–1890*. Ed. Louis J. Budd. New York: Library of America, 1992. 507–11.

———. "A Cure for the Blues." *The $30,000 Bequest and Other Stories*. New York: Harper and Brothers, 1906.

———. "Fenimore Cooper's Literary Offenses." *North American Review* 161 (July 1895): 1–12.

———. "A General Reply." 1870. *Mark Twain: Collected Tales, Sketches, Speeches, & Essays*. Vol. 1. Ed. Louis J. Budd. New York: Library of America, 1992. 484–89.

———. *The Innocents Abroad*. Hartford: American Publishing, 1869.

———. *Mark Twain's Letters*. Mark Twain Project. <www.marktwainproject.org>.

———. *Mark Twain's Letters*. Vol. 4. Berkeley: U of California P, 1995. Print.

———. *No. 44: The Mysterious Stranger. Mark Twain's Mysterious Stranger Manuscripts*. Ed. William M. Gibson. Berkeley: U of California P, 1969.

———. *Notebooks and Journals, Vols. 1–3*. Ed. Frederick Anderson et al. Berkeley: U of California P, 1976–1980.

———. "Old Times on the Mississippi: The Rank and Dignity of Piloting." *Atlantic Monthly* 35.207–12 (1875).

———. "Open Letter to Com. Vanderbilt." 1869. *Mark Twain: Collected Tales, Sketches, Speeches, & Essays*. Vol. 1. Ed. Louis J. Budd New York: Library of America, 1992. 285–90.

——. *Personal Recollections of Joan of Arc*. New York: Harper and Brothers, 1896.
——. *Pudd'nhead Wilson and Those Extraordinary Twins*. 1894. New York: W. W. Norton, 1980.
——. "Running for Governor." 1870. Rpt. *Mark Twain: Collected Tales, Sketches, Speeches, & Essays*. Vol. 1. Ed. Louis J. Budd. New York: Library of America, 1992. 490–94.
Twain, Mark, and Charles Dudley Warner. *The Gilded Age*. Hartford: American Publishing, 1873.

6
"These Hideous Times"
Mark Twain's Bankruptcy and the Panic of 1893

Joseph Csicsila

An old standby of Twain biography is that Mark Twain was a bad businessman. Critics routinely (and perhaps a little too casually) cast him as a reckless speculator, a foolish investor, and a failed entrepreneur as they advance the notion that Twain was hopelessly irresponsible with his wealth, making poor financial decisions one after another throughout much of his adult life, until his well-publicized and personally humiliating bankruptcy in April 1894. Twain would actually help perpetuate this view with his own pronouncements, particularly those made in times when his finances seemed in greatest disarray: "I am terribly tired of business," he wrote to Frederick J. Hall, his partner at Charles L. Webster & Co., in June of 1893. "I am by nature and disposition unfitted for it and I want to get out of it" (Hill 343). And then, of course, there is the seemingly incontrovertible evidence of the failure of his publishing firm and the Paige typesetter fiasco, two among numerous other problematic business ventures Twain pursued in the last two decades of the nineteenth century, ventures that, taken together, appear to leave little doubt that Mark Twain could be astonishingly incompetent in matters involving money.

However, a closer and more careful review of the evidence by scholars over the last fifty years has revealed that Twain may have been a much more adept businessman than the prevailing critical opinion would allow. In 1967 Hamlin Hill, for example, dispelled long-standing allegations perpetrated by Samuel C. Webster in *Mark Twain, Business Man* (1946) and repeated by others (including Justin Kaplan in his 1966 Pulitzer Prize–winning biography) that Twain bankrupted Webster & Co. by removing capital from his publishing firm in order to fund his investment in the Paige typesetter. Alan Gribben's "Mark Twain, Business Man: The Margins of Profit" (1983) extended this corrective argument further by calling attention to the numerous ways Twain exhibited sound business judgment throughout his life. Gribben, for instance, reminds critics that Twain "earned vastly more money than his [literary] contemporaries" directly as a result of his bold decision to market his books through the subscription trade and his facility in negotiating enormously lucrative contracts with his publishers (26). As a publisher himself, Twain was immensely successful, too. We remember the failure of Webster & Co. but tend to forget about Grant's *Memoirs* and numerous other examples of Twain's shrewd and profitable decision making as unnamed head of that firm.

Even Twain's involvement with the Paige typesetter, typically treated as the illustration par excellence of his financial imprudence, has undergone reassessment in the last decade or two. Bruce Michelson's *Printer's Devil: Mark Twain and the American Publishing Revolution* (2006) began the work of exonerating Twain for his belief in the Paige typesetter by both meticulously laying out the ways in which this machine was a bona fide technological marvel and correcting enduring myths about its inability to perform. Michelson, for example, clarifies that the machine, in truth, "functioned reliably during a sixty-day test run at the *Chicago Herald* in the autumn of 1894" (9). Recently, Richard Hopkins, a master artisan printer and letterpress craftsman with more than fifty years' experience overseeing his own printing business, also characterized Paige's complex machine as a true wonder, far superior in design and vision to any of its late-nineteenth-century competitors. In the end, however, it may not have actually mattered whether or not Mark Twain made fundamentally good decisions in the decade leading up to his 1894 bankruptcy. In taking up the question of Twain and his business collapse, Mark Twain studies have yet to consider in any detailed fashion the context of the Panic of 1893 and the considerable role that it played in Twain's financial ruin at the end of the nineteenth century.

"Banking panics were a relatively infrequent feature of the American banking experience during the Gilded Age" (xi), notes economist Elmus Wicker in his recently published history of the post–Civil War era, which only incidentally (though aptly for our purposes) invokes Twain in the context of late-1800s financial crises. But banking panics occurred often enough, four times in the last three decades of the nineteenth century (1873, 1884, 1890, and 1893) for ordinary Americans of the time to regard them as a standard feature of the country's cycle of economic expansion and contraction. These episodes of banking instability generally involved runs on banks by depositors to withdraw hard currency resulting from a general loss of confidence in a particular or several regional institutions, usually brought on by large drops in the stock market. The net effect was an industry-wide tightening of credit, partial suspension of cash payments, and, in the most severe cases, the outright failure of certain banks. According to Wicker's *Banking Panics of the Gilded Age* (2006), the Panics of 1873, 1884, and 1890 were similar to each other in that they all had their origins in the failure of financial institutions that had overextended themselves with questionable investments in the country's railroad infrastructure. The Panic of 1873 was more severe than either the Panics of 1884 or 1890, but all three followed the same pattern of starting in the New York system and then spreading to other parts of the country:

> With the sole exception of 1893, banking panics [of the Gilded Age] had their origin in the central money market and from there spread to the interior. There were at least four channels of transmission: (1) The banking disturbance in New York unsettled the confidence of interior banks, especially the country banks, who reacted by withdrawing their balances and by contracting loans and deposits; (2) as the troubled banks in New York had affiliates in other cities, the closure of the affiliates was a major channel of transmission (for example, the failure of J. Cooke and Co., a merchant bank in New York, led to the suspension of Cooke affiliates in Philadelphia and Washington, D.C., in 1873); (3) the collapse of a large New York bank with a correspondent network diffused the panic geographically; and (4) the suspension of cash payments in New York led to suspension in the rest of the country. (2)

Wicker concludes, however, that the Panics of 1873, 1884, and 1890 were comparatively moderate, averaging fewer than a hundred bank failures each (15). Their greatest impacts were also relatively confined geographically, affecting mainly markets in New York and the Northeast. "The average person living in the interior," he notes, "had little direct experience of bank runs and bank closings" (15).

The Panic of 1893, however, was different. To begin, it was far worse than any of the three panics that had preceded it. In fact, it is arguably more accurate to describe the 1893 financial crisis not as a panic but as a full-blown *depression*, a point Douglas Steeples and David O. Whitten make with the title of their 1998 coauthored study, *Democracy in Desperation: The Depression of 1893*. As they put it, 1893 was the nation's "first great industrial collapse" (129). Only the Great Depression of the 1930s compares, and the shocking statistics bear out this claim. National unemployment, which stood at about 3 percent in 1892, jumped by some estimates to over 18 percent in 1894. In parts of the agricultural Midwest, those figures are thought to have exceeded 30 or 40 percent. Further, as David Whitten points out in a separate article, "the unemployment rate exceeded 10 percent for five or six consecutive years. The only other time this occurred in the history of the U.S. economy was during the Great Depression of the 1930s" (1). By the end of 1893, some 15,242 businesses had failed, including 119 railroads—a staggering 30 percent of the total number of American railroad companies in operation at the time. Another 37 railroads would succumb by the middle of 1894 (Steeples and Whitten 37).

Financial institutions fared even worse during the Panic of 1893. In that first year alone, a total of 642 banks failed, including 69 national banks. As a point of comparison, there were just over seven hundred bank failures during the entire span of the Great Depression (Wicker 15). However, the real story of the Panic of 1893, what sets it off as unique among the financial disturbances of the late nineteenth century, according to Wicker, is the fact that the financial crisis of 1893 began, like the Great Depression, in the interior of the country instead of in New York City, where the earlier post–Civil War panics had their origins. Whereas the Panics of 1873, 1884, and 1890 were brought about by eastern banks investing recklessly in railroads, the Panic of 1893 was fundamentally driven by frantic depositors in the South and West withdrawing and then hoarding cash. But it all seemingly began in a familiar way. In February 1893, the Philadelphia and Reading Railroad failed, leaving behind an unfathomable $125 million in liabilities ($2.9 billion in today's figures[1]). This news sent investors scrambling and the stock market tumbling. Within a few weeks, however, it became clear that the Philadelphia and Reading bankruptcy was something of an isolated incident, and the market soon stabilized. Nevertheless, uncertainty throughout the interior persisted, and banks in Louisville, Kansas City, Denver, and Portland began withdrawing their reserves from institutions in New York, anticipating that credit would soon tighten and depositors would start demanding cash.

After a short recovery later that spring, the stock market crashed again in early May, this time due to concern over the fact that the country's gold reserves had fallen below the safety limit of $100 million. Financial anxiety, which was already high, increased even further and spread rapidly throughout the country. Credit tightened almost immediately, and that set in motion the series of events that led to a full-scale meltdown of the American economy. "As May ended," explain Steeples and Whitten, "depositors for the first time succumbed to their distrust of banks and rushed to convert balances to cash. Interior banks, while reducing loans to strengthen their positions, besieged New York with demands for funds to satisfy the clamor of fearful depositors" (34). But Wicker argues that it was actually the banks themselves throughout the interior that exhibited "panic-like behavior," withdrawing their reserves held in the East "when there was no actual threat of runs by [their] depositors" (82). Whether it was the interior banks or their customers that initiated the panic in May 1893, the strain on eastern banks was so great that by the middle of June, New York City financial institutions began to go under in large numbers. Across the country, banks continued to collapse, and credit all but disappeared. As a result, thousands of American farms and businesses failed in the summer and autumn of 1893, and millions suddenly found themselves unemployed.

This is the historical context of Mark Twain's bankruptcy, which, strictly speaking, occurred on 18 April 1894, when his publishing firm, Charles L. Webster & Co., was officially liquefied. Earlier that month, the Mount Morris Bank of New York, an institution Twain had dealt with going back at least as far as the early 1880s, had suddenly called in the $29,500 in loans (nearly $725,000 in today's figures) it had made to Webster & Co. over several years. Twain, unable to raise the money to satisfy the debt, and ultimately heeding the advice of Henry H. Rogers, filed what is called in the law an "assignment without preference" in the county clerk's office in New York City on 18 April 1894, thereby joining thousands of other American business owners whose companies had recently gone under. An assignment, according to creditor rights and bankruptcy attorney Mark Leipold, is actually "an alternative to bankruptcy." Leipold explains that an assignment is similar to a modern Chapter 7 liquidation proceeding, which also deals with companies beyond hope of reorganization. (A Chapter 11 bankruptcy proceeding, on the other hand, typically allows a company time to reorganize its debt in an effort to emerge as a healthy organization.) However, unlike a formal Chapter 7 bankruptcy case,

> Assignments are structured to save time and expense in concluding the affairs of an insolvent company. Through an Assignment, the insolvent company's assets can be sold quickly and efficiently, and the liquidation proceeds can be distributed to creditors shortly thereafter. In general, after the preferred creditors are paid first, then tax and wage claims are paid. Secured creditors may find an Assignment useful, because it is relieved of the legal costs and risks of the foreclosure and sale of its collateral. (1)

The fact that Assignments recognized the difference between "preferred creditors" and "secured creditors" is what ultimately saved Twain. It was Rogers who saw the opportunity in this distinction and had Livy Clemens declared a preferred creditor of Webster & Co. A preferred creditor includes, among other things, a spouse who has loaned money to the company. Livy had indeed loaned Webster & Co. nearly $60,000 over several years out of what was left of her inheritance. Nevertheless, the Mount Morris Bank, which was declared only a secured creditor at the beginning of the proceedings, sought to assume control of everything of Twain's that might be considered an asset, including the copyrights to his writings and the Hartford home. Rogers first protected the copyrights by having them assigned to Livy as a preferred creditor, then notified creditors that the house was owned by Livy, not her husband, and as such was also protected.[2] Finally, Rogers negotiated a repayment of fifty cents on the dollar, terms that mortified Livy when she learned of them and which led her to appeal to her husband, for honor's sake, to repay the entire debt dollar for dollar. "You know my darling," she would write, "now is the time for you to add to or mar the good name that you have made. Do not for one moment let your sense of our need of money get advantage of your sense of justice & generosity" (Wecter 309). Eventually, Twain—and Rogers—came to see things as Livy did, and Twain would go on to repay the debt, nearly $100,000 ($2.5 million in today's figures), in its entirety.

The Paige typesetter was not actually part of Twain's formal bankruptcy proceedings. Of course, the estimated $170,000 to $300,000 ($4.2 million to $7.4 million in today's figures) Twain invested and eventually lost on the machine between 1881 and 1894 clearly would have affected his overall financial health and, at the very least, did nothing to help matters when money was badly needed in April 1894 (Powers 561). But the fact remains, as Hamlin Hill established in the late 1960s, that Twain did not drain funds from the publishing firm to finance the Paige typesetter, as alleged by Samuel C. Webster and as assumed by subsequent generations of scholars. "After 1888," explains Hill, "when he received his share of the profits from the sale of Grant's *Memoirs*, Clemens took only a very small percentage of his accrued royalties from the organization and none of his working capital of $75,000. Instead he allowed his money to remain in the Company, together with its interest, and supplied more than $60,000 in additional loans from his wife" (6). In fact, 1894, the year of Twain's bankruptcy, seemed in some ways a rather hopeful time for his typesetter investment. In January 1894 Rogers managed to reorganize the investors into a company and to renegotiate Twain's stake in the project, much to his advantage. Rogers even invested a small amount of his own money in the enterprise during this period. Then in the fall of 1894, Rogers arranged for the machine to be tested finally under regular working conditions by the *Chicago Herald*. Early reports were that it performed well. As late as the final week of October, the machine was setting type for eight hours with only seventeen minutes of stoppage, which compared favorably against its chief competitor, the Mergenthaler Linotype machine, a less expensive and less complicated automated printer, which had been in commercial use since the mid-1880s. Ultimately, however, the Paige typesetter did not impress the *Chicago Herald* enough for the newspaper to take a chance with it, and in December 1894 Rogers ended Twain's epic saga with the machine by dissolving the Paige Compositor Manufacturing Company.

So, if it is not the case that Twain bled his publishing firm dry in order to fund the Paige typesetter, how is it that Webster & Co. found itself so far in debt? Where did the money go? And why did the firm need to borrow the money that ultimately led to its demise? The answers to these critical questions lie in an understanding of late-nineteenth-century publishing practices as they relate to the day-to-day operations of Webster & Co. during the ten years or so it was in business.

Twain's career as a publisher, in every practical sense, began long before he founded Webster & Co. in May of 1884. With *The Prince and the Pauper* (1881), Twain left American Publishing Co., the subscription publishing firm he had teamed with since 1869, and joined James R. Osgood and Co. During his twelve years with Elisha Bliss and the American Publishing Co., Twain of course rose to prominence as one of the country's most widely read writers, as well as one of its best-paid. With each successive book, Twain managed to negotiate more lucrative contracts. More importantly, though, he also gradually exerted more control over the production process and marketing of his books during his years with the American Publishing Co. When Bliss died in the fall of 1880, Twain moved on and chose Osgood as his next publisher, and the arrangement he made with the genial former partner at Ticknor & Fields was momentous. Instead of receiving a 7.5 percent royalty, Twain *gave* a 7.5 percent royalty and took responsibility for covering the entire cost of production in exchange for all profits. He would also retain copyright ownership under his contract with Osgood, something he could never get Bliss to allow. Twain, in effect, had assumed the role of publisher, while Osgood adopted that of the contracted client.

As de facto publisher of *The Prince and the Pauper*, Twain personally underwrote the approximately $10,000 ($211,000 in today's figures) in expenses for the paper, the production of the illustrations, the manufacturing of the book's extravagant cover, and finally the process of binding the volumes themselves. Twain was speculating, of course. There was no guarantee, but the payoff for him would be huge if the book sold well. Either way, Twain could afford to finance such a project out of his own pocket in the early 1880s. Times for him were flush. Biographer Ron Powers puts his income in 1880 at $250,000 ($5.3 million in today's figures). Twain and Osgood produced two more books together under this sort of arrangement, *The Stolen White Elephant* (1882) and *Life on the Mississippi* (1883). With the latter volume, Twain moved even closer to self-publication, both installing his nephew Charles L. Webster at Osgood in 1882 "to take pretty full charge of the matter of running the book," as Twain put it, and sharing less of the profits with the firm (Hill 158).

None of the three books Twain published under his arrangement with

Osgood & Co. sold particularly well, however, especially when measured against the figures of Twain's earlier works. Twain blamed Osgood himself. The next step was inevitable: Twain would simply publish his own books. He had the capital and fifteen years of valuable experience in the trade. In May of 1884, just months before the first copies of *Adventures of Huckleberry Finn* were printed and bound, Twain formed Charles L. Webster & Co. as a subscription publishing firm. He placed his nephew and the company's namesake at the helm and paid him a respectable salary of $2,500 annually, plus a fairly decent share of the profits. In the late fall of 1884, as Twain and Webster were preparing for the release *Huckleberry Finn*, Twain learned that Ulysses S. Grant was considering an offer from the publisher of *Century Magazine* to publish his memoirs. In that moment the vision for Webster & Co. was transformed. Twain would venture into the publishing of other writers' work in addition to his own. Just one president had ever published his memoirs before, James Buchanan in 1866. Twain sensed the enormous potential of a presidential memoir from a hero—arguably, *the* hero—of the Civil War, who could take his narrative far beyond the story of his years in office. Moreover, he felt that the *Century* offer of a 10 percent royalty to Grant was appallingly low, given the circumstances. Twain immediately offered a 20 percent royalty, or, if Grant preferred, a contract that would pay him 75 percent of the profits. Additionally, Twain offered a $10,000 advance ($227,000 in today's figures). "Grant," writes Powers, "was incredulous" (493). Publishers simply did not make offers like that. Webster & Co., however, did. In February of 1885, Grant agreed to Twain's terms (but turned down the advance on principle), and together they made history—and a vast sum of money.

Ironically enough, the key to understanding Twain's financial failure lies in the process of bringing forth Grant's *Memoirs* (1885), one of the greatest successes in American publishing history. Throughout the spring of 1885, Webster & Co. solicited presale orders for Grant's *Memoirs*. It would be marketed as a two-volume set. By early May orders were coming in at such a rate that Twain estimated total sales of more than 400,000 sets and a royalty for Grant that "will amount to $420,000, & will make the larges [*sic*] single check ever paid an author in the world's history" (Browning 141–42). Twain, as it turned out, was uncannily spot-on with both predictions. But the production of Grant's *Memoirs* turned out to be enormously expensive. As with his own previous four books, Twain was responsible for underwriting this entire enterprise. However, unlike *The Prince and the Pauper*, *The Stolen White Elephant, Life on the Mississippi*, and *Adventures of Huckleberry Finn*, which each averaged initial printings of thirty thousand copies at a cost of about $10,000 per work to produce, Grant's *Memoirs* would cost more than $200,000 to print and bind the number of copies needed to meet initial demand ($4.5 million in today's figures). By the middle of 1885, all of Twain's personal finances were tied up in the production of the book. And it still wasn't enough. Fortunately, the American economy was in good shape, and banks were loaning money. Twain borrowed additional funds on short-term notes to cover the firm's publishing expenses. The risk for Twain—and the banks—seemed eminently manageable at this point: demand for the book was strong, Webster & Co. had the orders in hand, and volume 1 was on schedule to be published and delivered in December of 1885. Thus Twain borrowed $100,000 ($2.25 million in today's figures) on 21 October 1885, to help cover publishing costs (paper, printing, and binding, etc). The note was signed at 6 percent interest with $15,000 due in January 1886 and the remaining balance of $85,000 due one month later (Browning 204). These types of loans were not unlike today's business lines of credit, used for covering short-term operating expenses.

On the strength of sales for volume 1, Twain was actually able to begin paying off the loans for the entire production of Grant's *Memoirs* early. The project was turning out to be a tremendous success, and Twain's instincts were proving to be correct. No royalties had been paid to Grant's family yet, but in February 1886 Webster & Co. reported $260,000 in its bank account, with another $50,000 in receivables due at the end of the month (a total of $7 million in today's figures). On 26 February 1886, Charles Webster presented Grant's widow a check for $200,000 ($4.5 million in today's figures). Twain's prediction that the firm would deliver the largest royalty check in the world's publishing history had come to pass. In total, Webster & Co. would pay Grant's family $394,000 (nearly $9 million in today's figures). And despite the unorthodox terms of the contract, Twain and Webster would make large sums of money from Grant's *Memoirs*, as well. By the spring of 1886, Twain's share of the profits was $93,000 ($2.2 million in today's figures), and his nephew's $26,000 ($610,000 in today's figures). Twain, as it turned out, exercised sound judgment throughout the Grant undertaking, even deciding in April 1885 to take out expensive insurance policies against fire and theft of the books as they were bound and stored. On 14 January 1886, fire broke out in one of their New York warehouses and destroyed more than 1,300 unshipped books and fifteen thousand costly frontispieces for volume 2. All of the losses were covered by that policy.

Webster & Co. would operate in similarly sound fashion for the next two or three years. The cash on hand (some $250,000, for example, in July 1886) meant that the firm was generally less dependent on outside funding for publishing projects throughout much of the late 1880s. Twain's ideas for book projects to publish in 1886 and 1887 were promising. On the success of the Grant book, he took a chance with General George McClellan's memoirs.

Then, in May 1886, Twain secured permission from Rome to publish the biography of the reigning pontiff, Pope Leo XIII. The following year, he signed contracts with the country's most celebrated minister, Henry Ward Beecher, for his autobiography and the reissue of his popular 1871 book on the life of Christ. Each one of these projects arguably had the potential to be a runaway best seller. The biography of Pope Leo XIII, in particular, with its possible worldwide demand, had the promise of outselling even the Grant book. But neither volume ended up doing very well. The market for Civil War books had been saturated (as Twain and his nephew rightly feared might be the case), and while the pope's biography actually turned out to be marginally profitable for the firm, sales fell far short of Twain's expectation of 100,000 copies in the first year. As for the Beecher project, it experienced an even more staggering setback when the famed minister died suddenly in March 1887, before any writing had begun. The Beecher family returned the $5,000 advance, but Twain estimated the combined losses of projected revenue at $100,000 ($2.3 million in today's figures) (Hill 221).

That same month Twain and Webster first discussed taking over the publication of a project titled *A Library of American Literature*, an eleven-volume series edited by Edmund Clarence Stedman and Ellen Mackay Hutchinson. *A Library of American Literature* figures prominently in the story of Twain's financial demise, but the tale is full of twists and turns, and the scholarly record is in need of some clarification. Critics have called *A Library of American Literature* an albatross, a white elephant, a millstone, and—perhaps the most artful appellation of all—"*The Paige Typesetter of Publishing*" (Powers 525). There is more than a grain of truth to these characterizations, particularly the comparison with the Paige investment, but the problem is that these largely pejorative descriptions tend to leave the impression that the project was devoid of merit. It was not. *A Library of American Literature* was a visionary undertaking. A handful of anthologies of American writings had appeared before, including Evert and George Duyckinck's much-admired *Cyclopedia of American Literature* (1855), but the Stedman and Hutchinson collection was groundbreaking in its scope and coverage of the country's literary heritage. "The encyclopedic comprehensiveness of these volumes," explains Terry Oggel, "was stunning": "ballads, folklore, oratory (Frederick Douglass and John C. Calhoun), noted sayings, platform lectures (Anna Dickinson), Civil War songs, Negro hymns and songs, personal narratives (Andrew Carnegie). Though it was enormously expensive to produce, draining the resources of Clemens's publishing company, it sold well and was well reviewed. Its importance for writers of school texts and literary histories, including the landmark *Cambridge History of American Literature* (1917–1921), lasted more than half a century" (51). Stedman and Hutchinson's collection, with its six thousand pages featuring 2,500 selections by more than 1,200 American writers, was so well done that it served as an essential resource for the emerging field of academic American literary studies through World War I. The trouble, as Oggel rightly points out, and as Alan Gribben argues even more succinctly, is that *A Library of American Literature* was a "worthy but expensive project" (27).

Twain was hesitant from the very beginning. "I think well of the Stedman book," he wrote to his nephew in March 1887, "but I can't somehow bring myself to think *very* well of it" (Powers 525). Despite his initial assessment, Twain approved the project, and Charles Webster purchased the plates of the first five volumes later that fall for $8,000 ($186,000 in today's figures) from the publishing firm in Cincinnati that had originated the project. Webster & Co. began to sell the collection by subscription in 1888, but, because it was too expensive for average consumers to purchase all at once, customers were allowed to buy the eleven-volume set on installment. This would cause major problems for Twain over the next five years. First, nobody except Thomas M. Williams, the individual overseeing the project at Webster & Co., apparently understood the hopelessly confusing installment arrangements. Second, the firm would need to print and warehouse multiple volumes with each order. The storage of tens of thousands of books until they were paid for and could be shipped added significantly to the overall cost of the project. Third, installment payments came in slowly, if they came in at all. "By 1893," according to Powers, "the *Library* had run up more than $62,000 [$1.5 million in today's figures] in uncollected installment payments from customers" (525). As with the production of the Grant book, Twain took out loans to cover expenses. But the early 1890s were very different times. "Signs of recession," report Steeples and Whitten, "began to appear in 1892" (23). Among other things, that meant money was getting harder to come by. And then it was discovered that with the purchase of the plates for the first five volumes for the original publisher, someone (likely Webster himself) had failed to secure copyrights for Webster & Co. This mistake cost Twain at least $6,000 ($140,000 in today's figures), probably much more, when the Cincinnati firm demanded three thousand sets (33,000 books in total) in exchange for the copyrights, which they promptly advertised and sold to the public, costing Webster & Co. a significant number of potential sales.

Still, Frederick J. Hall reported to Twain throughout the remainder of 1892 that sales of the series were strong. But with every order for *A Library of American Literature* that Webster & Co. took, the company effectively went deeper into debt. The costs of production and storage, exacerbated by delays associated with the installment plan, were devouring money faster than it was coming into the firm. The project was now so far in the red that sales alone, even if they were robust, could do nothing in the short term to rescue Webster & Co. Back in November 1888, just a year into the project, Twain had entertained thoughts of selling off *A Library of American Literature*. By the middle of 1892, with the economy beginning to teeter, expenses continuing to grow, and loans becoming more difficult and expensive to secure, he was looking to get out of not only the anthology venture, but the publishing business altogether: "The *Library of American Literature* and some of the other books were selling well enough; but the continuous increase of capital required by a business conducted on the installment plan had steadily added to the firm's liabilities, while the prospect of a general tightening in the money-market made the outlook not a particularly happy one. Clemens thought he might be able to dispose of the *Library* or an interest in it, or even of his share in the business itself, to some one with means sufficient to put it on an easier financial footing" (Paine 946–47). Twain spent the next year and a half looking for ways to either fully fund production of *A Library of American Literature* or to sell off the project. One plan involved approaching Andrew Carnegie for a $100,000 loan ($2.4 million in today's figures), half of the estimated $200,000 ($4.8 million in today's figures) Webster & Co. believed it needed to put the series in the black. As economic conditions worsened over 1893, Twain even approached extended family for money, but nobody was able to offer the kind of funding that had seemed so readily available just seven or eight years before. It was this perfect storm: a critical lack of capital for a costly project in a historically bad economy ultimately forced Twain to liquefy his publishing firm in the spring of 1894.

It is impossible to know, of course, whether Webster & Co. could have survived in different times. The simple fact remains, however, that Twain was able to borrow $200,000 in 1885 to complete production of the Grant volumes, whereas he could not secure financing for the same amount in 1893 to see the Stedman and Hutchinson series through to completion. Did other factors contribute to the failure of Webster & Co. that had nothing to do with the economy and the Panic of 1893? Certainly. Scholars have rightly pointed out that the market for subscription books had all but disappeared by the early 1890s, and then there are the numerous manuscripts of questionable merit the firm took on in its final years. That said, there is a case to be made that the collapse of Webster & Co. and Twain's financial ruin were primarily the results of economic forces well beyond his control. The Panic of 1893, which Twain referred to in a letter to his partner at Webster & Co. in July 1893 as "these hideous times" (Hill 348), took down thousands of businesses and ruined millions of Americans in truly historic fashion. The country would not see that level of economic turmoil again until the 1930s. Over the years, Twain would variously blame his bankruptcy on several different people, including himself. But by framing his financial collapse as the fault of one individual or another, Twain inadvertently focused critical conversation on matters of personal agency. Twain studies have participated in that somewhat limited debate for more than a century. The time has come to consider the full range of forces bearing down on Mark Twain and his business interests in the early 1890s.

Notes

1. Throughout this chapter, I convert nineteenth-century dollar figures into their 2013 estimated values (the most recent figures available) using the calculator at measuringworth.com, a website operated by Samuel H. Williamson, Research Professor of Economics at the University of Illinois at Chicago. The website's calculators are refereed by leading researchers in the field, and its board of advisors is composed of seventeen international academic economists.

2. The Library of Congress Historic Buildings Survey of the Mark Twain House in Hartford, Connecticut, reports that "all land" associated with the Farmington Avenue residence was placed in Olivia L. Clemens's name on 2 June 1879, according to a deed recorded at the city clerk's office in Hartford, Connecticut, on that day (http://lcweb2.loc.gov/master/pnp/habshaer/ct/ct0300/ct0332/data/ct0332data.pdf). It is not clear, however, that the home was placed in Olivia's name as well. The deed recording the sale of the Farmington Avenue "house and land" to Richard M. Bissell dated 11 May 1903 lists both Samuel L. Clemens and Olivia L. Clemens as owners.

Works Cited

Browning, Robert Pack, Michael B. Frank, and Lin Salamo, eds. *Mark Twain's Notebooks & Journals*. Vol. 3, 1883–1891. Berkeley: U of California P, 1979.

Gribben, Alan. "Mark Twain, Businessman: The Margins of Profit." *Studies in American Humor* 1.1 (1982): 24–43.

Hill, Hamlin. *Mark Twain's Letters to His Publishers*. Berkeley: U of California P, 1967.

Hopkins, Richard. *The Tragic Saga of James W. Paige's Marvelous Typesetting Machine*. Terra Alta: Hill and Dale Press, 2014.

Kaplan, Justin. *Mr. Clemens and Mark Twain: A Biography*. New York: Simon and Schuster, 1966.

Leipold, Mark. "Assignment for the Benefit of Creditors." <apps.americanbar.org/buslaw/committees/CL160000pub/newsletter/200908/leipold.pdf>.

Michelson, Bruce. *Printer's Devil: Mark Twain and the American Publishing Revolution*. Berkeley: U of California P, 2006.

Oggel, Terry. "In His Own Time: The Early Academic Reception of Mark Twain." *Mark Twain Annual* 1 (2003): 45–60.

Paine, Albert Bigelow. *Mark Twain: A Biography*. New York: Harper & Brothers, 1912.

Powers, Ron. *Mark Twain: A Life*. New York: Simon and Schuster, 2005.

Steeples, Douglas, and David O. Whitten. *Democracy in Desperation: The Depression of 1893*. Westport: Greenwood P, 1998.

Webster, Samuel Charles, ed. *Mark Twain, Business Man*. Boston: Little, Brown, 1946.

Wecter, Dixon, ed. *The Love Letters of Mark Twain*. New York: Harper & Brothers, 1949.

Whitten, David. "The Depression of 1893." <http://eh.net/encyclopedia/the depression-of-1893/>.

Wicker, Elmus. *Banking Panics of the Gilded Age*. New York: Cambridge UP, 2000.

7
"Drop Sentiment, and Come Down to Business"
Debt and the Disintegration of "Manly" Character in "Indiantown" and "Which Was It?"

Susanne Weil

It is impossible to discount the number and effects of bankruptcies caused by the Great Recession in the wake of the 2008 financial crisis. USCourts.gov reports an average of 1,314,697 bankruptcies per year since the fiscal meltdown of 2008. In 2013, some 2,960 Americans a day filed for bankruptcy ("It's in the Numbers"), despite legislation to stem the tide of filings (United States). Studies have shown that those who struggle with debt are three times more likely to suffer from mental illness ("Debt Linked," par. 1): one international meta-analysis controlling for the effect of mental illness on fiscal decision making found that among the indebted, suicidal thinking and risk of self-harm increased by a factor of two to three (Fitch et al., par. 35–36). A new wave of organizations and counselors, like the Financial Therapy Association, has risen to help debtors handle their psychological as well as economic stress: these emphasize that to recover, bankrupts must move through shame's debilitating effects (Bortz).

When Samuel Clemens's publishing company and typesetter venture failed in the Panic of 1893, he and myriad fellow bankrupts could not turn to such social networks.[1] Clemens had succeeded as a self-made man; his father and older brother Orion both had failed. Though his marriage to Olivia Langdon, with her connections and coal inheritance, certainly aided his rise, Twain earned their living through writing, lecturing, and, essentially, managing his own business. However, as Michael Kimmel argues in *Manhood in America*, linking one's "identity as a man" to the rollercoaster marketplace during the post–Civil War era of panics risked not only one's financial autonomy, but the self-respect it bolstered: "The flip side of this economic autonomy [was] anxiety, restlessness, loneliness. Manhood [was] no longer fixed in land or small-scale property ownership or dutiful service. Success must be earned, manhood must be proved—and proved constantly" (22–23). Losing autonomy through bankruptcy was crushing and shaming. In

Born Losers: A History of Failure in America, Scott Sandage notes that "stock imagery of individual moral blame infused the culture of American capitalism"; as one contemporary newspaper commentary argued, "'men succeed or fail . . . not from accident or external surroundings' . . . but from 'possessing or wanting the elements [of manly character] in themselves'" (92). Failure drew "contempt, misery, and disgrace," and only redoubled work demonstrated that bankrupts deserved redemption (Rotundo 180–81).

Twain did that work, writing his way out of much of his debt, showing strenuous effort by undertaking his round-the-world lecture tour, past sixty and suffering gout. Yet despite moral and practical support from Standard Oil vice president Henry Huttleston Rogers, a loving family, and an adoring public, as well as the talent and determination to write his way out of much of his debt, Twain's post-bankruptcy letters are branded by the excruciating shame, depression, and feeling of lost manhood that he, like other bankrupts, suffered. Further, they show him uncertain whether he could still write to his own standards. For example, on 21 January 1895, adjusting to his changed circumstances, Twain wrote Rogers that

> the thing for me to do is to begin to teach myself to endure a way of life which I was familiar with during the first half of my life but whose sordidness and hatefulness and humiliation long ago faded out of my memory and feeling. With the help of my wife this will not be very difficult, I think. I think, indeed, that she and I could adjust ourselves to the new conditions quite easily if we were alone,— in fact I know it— but the reflection that they are going to be hard on the children (and incomprehensible by them) will string out the probation of course. . . .
>
> . . . [To Olivia's income and income from his books] I must add $5,000 a year by work, and that will keep the tribe alive.
>
> This last item would be quite easy if I might venture to raise it by magazine articles, but that is dangerous and to be avoided if possible. A man who is on the down grade must not print too often,—he must keep out of the public view as much as he can; and when he prints be sure he is not printing anything that is not up to his very best. (*Mark Twain's Correspondence with Henry Huttleston Rogers, 1893–1910* [*MTHHR*] 118–19).

Twain's letter shows that then, as now, the imperative to "keep the tribe alive"—to provide for one's family—was a key marker of manliness. This "breadwinner ideal" of the nineteenth century (Kimmel 20) persists in the *Yankelovich Monitor*'s 2009 survey: in twenty years' data on how those polled define masculinity, the most common response was "being a good provider for his family" (qtd. in Faludi 79). During Twain's 1895–1896 lecture tour, small setbacks could spark comments like this, to Rogers (6 June 1896): "I don't think it is any use for me to struggle against my ill-luck any longer. If I had the family in a comfortable poor-house I would kill myself" (*MTHHR* 216). As Sandage notes, "'I feel like a failure' [is] an expression [that] comes so naturally that we forget it is a figure of speech: the language of business applied to the soul" (5).

In 1898 Twain paid the last debts required by the settlement Rogers had negotiated, but that did not heal the wounds of bankruptcy. The "dream" fragments, texts he worked on from 1895 through 1902 and deliberately withheld from publication during his lifetime, reveal his continued sense of shame. Peter Messent has shown how Twain's autobiographical fragment "Which Was the Dream?"—written in the wake of his bankruptcy—reflects anxiety about masculinity and authorship, noting that the "topic . . . has been relatively neglected" in Twain studies ("Mark Twain, Manhood" 57). For Twain, a writer deeply involved in both companionate marriage and publishing work, Messent argued that the supposedly "'female' realm of sentiment" and "the 'male' world of business" were linked, not severed, leaving his "sense of male identity" particularly vulnerable when his ventures failed (65), and that "turn-of-the-century anxieties about American manhood suffuse Clemens's late work" (73).

This chapter will extend Messent's analysis of "Which Was the Dream?" to the next two "dream" fragments, "Indiantown" and "Which Was It?" These manuscripts suggest that Twain's sense of what Gail Bederman calls "manliness"—"the mingled honor, high-mindedness, and strength stemming from . . . powerful self-mastery" (12)—was not renewed by solvency. Rather, they show how intensely bankruptcy's "symbolic failure of manhood" (Kaplan 332) festered. "Indiantown" (1899) sketches a thinly fictionalized portrait of Twain's relationship with Olivia, reflecting anxiety about his manhood and integrity after she became, despite her objection, his preferred creditor and copyright holder. From 1899 through 1902, Twain wrestled with "Which Was It?"—his next manuscript. Here, his avatar George Harrison fails to act "manly" when faced with bankruptcy, leading first to neurasthenic physical wasting, and, finally, to total loss of autonomy as he becomes the blackmailed "slave" of his mulatto cousin.

Twain's prolonged struggle with the "dream of disaster" story was the process by which he symbolically accepted personal responsibility for his business failures.[2] First Twain projected a divided representation of himself in Tom X, the innocent Boy General, and Jeff Sedgwick, his evil business manager. But that division dissolves when bankrupt Tom X is accused of forging letters that Jeff had written about the nonexistent "Golden Fleece" mine. Though readers know that Tom X's childish neglect of his finances allowed his agent to get away with this scam, the creditors' charge of forgery shows their belief that, in effect, Tom X *is* Jeff. This revelation hurls the accused into a two-year coma, suggesting how painful even symbolic steps toward taking responsibility for bad business choices could be. In the next two manuscripts, a similar shame resurfaces in successive protagonists' pervasive imagery of "counterfeits" and "shams," public misrepresentations that mask inner weakness and loss of manhood (Requa; Weil, "Reconstructing" 91–99).

As John S. Tuckey has explained in his editorial preface to the text, Twain abandoned work on "Which Was the Dream?" in August of 1897 (31). But in 1899—*after* his debts were paid—he outlined and began to write a new version of the "dream of disaster" story (151): "Which Was It?" In this manuscript, Twain's chosen protagonist is not "fine Virginia stock" like Tom X, but an impoverished midwesterner living in a Mississippi river town; the characters surrounding him represent not Twain's wife and daughters, but his father, brother, and a host of inhabitants of Hannibal he knew as a child. In "Which Was It?" the protagonist, George Harrison, discovers that he will do anything, even commit murder, to escape insolvency's shame. Harrison's bankrupt father, Andrew, has mortgaged the family mill to the local "Squire" Fairfax. Mistakenly believing that the Squire plans to foreclose, Harrison sneaks into his mansion to steal the notes of indebtedness and accidentally murders another intruder; the Squire is accused of the murder, and Harrison, torn between his conscience's promptings to confess and his desire to protect himself and son Tom from scandal, remains silent, consumed by guilt. Like "Which Was the Dream?," "Which Was It?" traces the sense of moral degradation that bankruptcy could provoke in men who see themselves as upright, locating that conflict in the land of Twain's origins, the source of his richest creative material.

When Twain began writing this second "dream of disaster" story, he detoured into a third fragment: "Indiantown." His notebook jottings list the same cast of characters as "Which Was It?" (151), and he employs the same narrative device: a time lapse after which the main character would not know whether his disastrous reversal was real or a dream. The text's first two chapters describe the town and its people, but then Twain veers into describing the marriage of two minor characters, David and Susan Gridley, whom he identified in his working notes as himself and Olivia. Indeed, Twain's original plan called for Gridley to be named "Sam," and the Gridleys' three daughters are Susy, Clara, and Jean (151–52). Even without the "key" in Twain's notebooks, readers can easily play who's-who, as the veil between fiction and autobiography in "Indiantown" is gossamer-thin: Susan Gridley is an "educated, utterly refined, scrupulously high-principled . . . religious" woman who tries to "reform" her writer husband's "native affection for all vulgarities," his inattention to debts, and his "devil's spasmodic temper" (167–68). As Olivia did Sam, Susan "dusts [David] off" after such offenses as swearing in the bathroom, in an episode reproduced almost verbatim in Twain's *Autobiography* (1:346–48). There is no Gridley plot in "Indiantown," only description of the David/Susan relationship.

Why did Twain's exploration of the "dream of disaster" take this tangent? "Which Was the Dream?" ends after Tom X wakes up and learns that for the past two years, his wife has had to work to support their family. As Messent notes, "the fact that . . . Olivia had (on March 9, 1894), as part of a maneuver by Rogers to protect the family interests, been assigned all Clemens's property, including his book copyrights and his Paige-machine holdings, must have supplemented [his feeling of dependency and "depleted masculinity"]" (*Mark Twain and Male Friendship* [*MTMF*] 132). Of course, Twain had accepted Rogers's plan: it was a shrewd means of retaining financial control over the proceeds of his years of creative work.[3] Although Olivia would not have done anything with those copyrights without her husband's direction, the copyrights were, nevertheless, no longer in his name. Ironically, the man who had made headlines pursuing lawsuits over his copyrights had relinquished control, in legal terms at least, over his intellectual property.

"Indiantown" suggests support for Messent's conclusion, as the unresolved conflict from "Which Was the Dream?" resurfaces. Analyzing Susan as "shaper" of David's character in light of comments Twain made in letters and notebooks suggests that, even after settling his debts in 1898, he resented Olivia's insistence on paying creditors in full. Whereas in "Which Was the Dream?" Twain divided himself into two unrealistically good and evil characters, in "Indiantown" Twain introduces David as one man with a double nature, his divided self a fiction crafted by his wife:

> It is not easy to describe David Gridley, there being two of him. . . . The one that God made was a sufficiently indifferent piece of work, but it was at least not a sham—all its parts were genuine; but the other one was all sham; there was not a genuine fibre in it. It was the work of Mrs. Gridley . . . [she] put an entirely new outside on David, a shiny new outside, and fine to consider, and this exterior Gridley was the only one the world knew . . . he was but clay in [her] earnest and able potter's hands. (167–68)

David may be clay, but clay made uncomfortable by the cramping sensation of its mold: "he had no real pleasure in being a sham. The real David, the inside David . . . was of an incurably low tone, and wedded to low ideals; the outside David, Susan Gridley's David, the sham David, was of a lofty tone, with ideas which the angels in heaven might envy. . . . The real David cared little whether an inconvenient debt was paid or not; the sham one would settle it with his last shirt" (168–69).

There seems an edge to "*Susan Gridley's* David." Susan, author of this "sham," is, by implication, responsible for both his failings and successes. Once Susan "repaint[s and] re-gild[s]" David's real nature, she is "pleased with the stunning effects which she gets out of her restorations" (170). Through her "diligent hard work," she keeps David's "exterior . . . in such good repair" that no one knows what he's truly like: "[H]e was just a piece of honest kitchen furniture transferred to the drawing room and glorified and masked from view by gorgeous cloth of gold" (167). Twain's imagery not only feminizes David as *kitchen* furniture but presents him as domestic-labor class: his finery is bestowed by his wife in a bizarre gender switch of Veblen's model, making him a trophy husband in a moral dress-up game that shores up the woman's sense of moral, rather than fiscal, superiority. In a well-known letter to Rogers, Twain commented, "You and I are a team: you are the most useful man I know, and I am the most ornamental" (*MTHHR* 310). Messent points out that "the opposition Clemens constructs here between the businessman and the artist, usefulness and ornamentation, is common in turn of the century America . . . [Clemens's] own acceptance of the 'ornamental' label is, to a degree, comic self-denigration. [However,] the correspondence with Rogers shows the gap between commerce and art, business and sentiment, masculine assertiveness and feminized dependency, to be far more porous and unstable than his words would initially suggest" (*MTMF* 130).

Twain's sense of being less a man is reflected through the gendered terms he employs to describe his "Indiantown" couple: Susan is "firm and strong," whereas David is "lazy and soft"; "when courage was required to back a principle, she had it" (167). Twain's comment that "[t]he real David cared little whether an inconvenient debt was paid or not; the sham one would settle it with his last shirt" (167) may help explain why, working through the problem of responsibility for his debts, he detoured into this telling but distorted representation of his marriage. Despite the optimism expressed in his 21 January 1895 letter to Rogers, his wish to settle the debts by whatever means Rogers could manage had already warred with Olivia's sense of right in ways that put considerable strain on both of them. In a 23 July 1894 letter to Olivia, he framed the strategy that he and Rogers were using to whittle down his indebtedness as the duty he owed his wife and children, placing that central obligation above legal or business ties:

> Mind you, dearheart, nobody can charge me with dishonorable conduct; I have not been guilty of any; I shall not be guilty of any until I desert my family to take care of those others [creditors]. Whenever I do that, it will be time for people to call me names; up to that time they can't call me names. Those creditors forced me to make an assignment [of bankruptcy]—goodness knows I didn't want to do it. They must stand part of the hardship of their own act. . . . My very dearest, I love you, I honor you, and I am not going to do a single dishonorable thing. I am not going to wrong anybody. If ever I should, I am not going to begin with you. (*Love Letters of Mark Twain* [*LLMT*] 306)

Olivia was not comforted, as her reply (31 July 1894) shows:

> You say that Mr. Rogers wanted to ask the creditors 25 cents and that you felt that .20 was enough for Pudd'nhead Wilson. In that case if I were over there I should probably ask them .10 or .15 What we want is that those creditors get all their money out of Webster and Co. and surely we want to aid them all that is possible. Oh my darling we want those debts paid and we want to treat them all not only honestly but we want to help them in every possible way. It is money honestly owed and I cannot quite understand the tone which both you and Mr. Rogers seem to take—in fact I cannot understand it at all. You say that Mr. Rogers has said some caustic and telling things to the creditors. (I do not know what your wording was) I should think it was the creditors place to say caustic things to us. (*LLMT* 308–09)

Neither could Olivia grasp Sam's wish to accept the subscription fund to pay his debts started by James Gordon Bennett of the *New York Herald*: she insisted he refuse the money "as long as he was not disabled" (Kaplan 349). Rogers agreed, but for different reasons—taking charity could have alienated the sympathies of Twain's public, potentially damaging sales of his planned collected works, with their potential to repay the rest of his debts (MTHHR 283–89). Clemens gave in, but his resentment of Olivia's stance leaked out in letters to Rogers. In a 14 April 1895 letter, for example, he wrote Rogers, "We were to have stopped at the Waldorf a few days as Charley Langdon's guests, but Mrs. C's head is too level for that. People would think that we were splurging there on our own footing and it wouldn't look modest for bankrupts. Charley may take the children there if he will see to it that their names do not get into print, but the head of the family and I will stop at the Everett" (*MTHHR* 141).

Calling Olivia "head of the family" in this letter may be a joke between married men, but it has a bitter savor, as does his mocking account of Olivia's notion that staying with her brother at a fancy hotel "wouldn't look modest for bankrupts." Earlier, during the 1894 negotiations, Olivia wanted either to join her husband in New York or to have him join her abroad, leaving Rogers to handle matters. But, citing the doctors who argued that she should nurse her health in Europe, Sam refused to let her come to him, and he limited her contact with Rogers: in one letter he urged his friend not to answer one of his wife's letters, saying, "[Y]ou must not bother yourself to write Mrs. C, indeed you mustn't; your hands are abundantly full, without that. You have sufficiently answered her in what you have said to me" (*MTHHR* 46). Rather than being controlled by his wife, it seems that during these negotiations, he effectively locked her out of the bankruptcy negotiations, in spite of—or perhaps because of—her status as preferred creditor. While dealing with the humiliating process of debt negotiation, Clemens needed to assert masculine control, allying himself with Rogers and relegating Olivia to the status of a redundant correspondent for whom he, as her husband, could speak.

This tension resurfaces in "Indiantown" as the manuscript tackles David's role as writer—and Susan's as editor. Like Olivia, Susan allowed David to "let off steam" at home so that he wouldn't behave badly in public. The use of "steam" echoes Twain's pervasive image for his own creativity: the "imagination-mill," whose "tanks" had to "fill up" before he could write, words shooting out of his mind like "steam" once the mill began to "work."[4] And, like Twain, David turns the imaginative product of his own writing over to Susan for editing: "Sometimes he wrote literature for the eastern press—fierce and bloody Indian tales—and she edited. He complained that he sent his Indians out on the war-path and she ambushed them and sent them to Sunday school. She wouldn't let him make an impromptu speech. . . . He fretted and fumed over these harassments, as he called them. But her hand was steady and firm, and he submitted, and found profit in it in the long run" (174–75).

As Twain wrote in an often-quoted letter, "After my marriage, [Olivia] edited everything I wrote. And what is more—she not only edited my works—she edited me!" (qtd. in Brooks 136). Twain clearly exaggerated this and the characterization of Olivia in "Indiantown." There is no evidence that Olivia made him memorize speeches and recite them to her in advance, as Susan did David, and while he was glad to have Olivia and Howells sniff out improprieties in children's books, he stuck by what he felt necessary. Huck could never have said, "All right, then, I'll go to hell," had Olivia been the censorious tyrant Van Wyck Brooks described—or that Twain makes Susan Gridley. However, after bankruptcy, Twain had some reason to feel "managed," as Olivia was awarded ownership of the copyrights to his books, present *and future*, until the debts were settled (*LLMT* 302).

The letters noted suggest that Olivia did not try to give orders, but rather, asked and urged. Still, if we take Justin Kaplan's point that marriage to Olivia and entry to her social class and income 'licensed' Twain to delve into his Missouri material (114ff), the copyrights' assignment may have rankled because it signaled not only the larger loss of control that came with his financial straits, but also anxiety that she was, in a sense, a co-creator of that fiction, whose income helped free him to write, and whose editorial sensibilities helped him tailor his works to a middle-class audience, contributing to their profitability.

I would not argue that "Indiantown" reveals dark discontent in Twain's marriage, but rather that in abandoning this text, Twain saw that the restrictions he complained of—in both his marriage and editing his manuscripts—were largely self-imposed. Twain ends the fragment with a fictionalized version of the famous autobiographical story of the young wife overhearing her husband swearing—David's sole trait presented as masculine (173). She tries to imitate him, David pretends to cry in penitence, she joins in his laughter, and David realizes that "he was ahead of *the game* now" (173; emphasis added). As Michael Kiskis demonstrated, Twain played games with Olivia's editing, too; he would insert choice phrases in his manuscripts, knowing that she would find and cut them ("House" 11; *Mark Twain's Own Autobiography* 171–72). As deflection of blame for his bankruptcy, "Indiantown" did not answer. Twain focused the next version of the "dream of disaster" on the bankrupt figure himself.

George Harrison, the Twain figure in "Which Was It?," first appears in "Indiantown," described as "conspicuously honest and honorable, yet so humble" that he can't commit to any course of action. He is "the result of his mother's careful and watchful training" (160–61), not his wife's. Harrison's mother "had been a moral sentimentalist all her life, and her son was the monumental result (160–61). When first introduced in "Indiantown," Harrison is described as a man whose "sentiment" saps his strength of character to the point where he is "bag[ged] by the first woman who flattered him wholly without stint . . . she proposed to him . . . and married him with a violence. She was a man" (161). This strange observation reflects the later Twain's tendency to frame women who take initiative as masculine: as Messent observes, he sketched a curious gender role-reversal in "The $30,000 Bequest," where "Saladin Foster, the main male character, is given the 'curious and unsexing' pet name of Sally, while his wife Electra (Aleck) is portrayed as the 'calculating business-woman' of the family. Clemens's anxieties concerning his own male identity, his awareness of his past dependency on his wife's inherited money, and the transfer of his own property into her name, may all be reflected here" (*MTMF* 132).[5] In his marriage, Twain was the one looking for the main chance, pursuing speculations; in "Bequest," the female protagonist takes on the world of finance, spinning plans to invest their inheritance, while her husband is just a passive bystander. This blurring of traditional gender roles anticipates the late twentieth-century shifts analyzed by Mairtin Mac an Ghaill and Chris Haywood: as women increasingly assumed the role of breadwinner, behaviors could not reliably be assigned to "dualistic models of gender," and men experienced a destabilizing "genderquake" (72–73). In "Bequest" this destabilization vanishes along with the inheritance, which turns out to be just a hoax. In "Indiantown" Harrison's destabilizing "man"-like wife is kept offstage; in the next fragment, she will be safely dead before the action even starts.

In his odd introduction of Harrison in "Indiantown," Twain sounds the note of sentiment as weakness; whereas in "Which Was It?," Twain frames both sentimental and businesslike thinking as morally bankrupt. "Which Was It?"—like "Which Was the Dream?"—starts with an aborted narrative by Harrison's wife, presented posthumously by Harrison, who then takes up the tale. However, in "Which Was It? Twain abandons his usual first-person narrative, making Harrison explain why he will tell his own story of moral crumbling in the third person: "I cannot do it in the first person; I must spare myself that shame. . . . I could not say 'I did such and such things'; it would revolt me, and the pen would refuse. No, I will write as if it were a literary tale, a history, a romance . . . about another man . . . whose weak and capricious character I may freely turn inside out and expose, without the sense of being personally under the knife. . . . In the hope and belief that by the protection of this device I shall be enabled to frankly tell everything just as it happened, I will now begin" (183).

Twain's characteristic reliance on boy—or, in Fiedler's term, "good-bad-boy" (130)—narrators and protagonists shifts as he abandons "Boy General" Tom X and makes his successor in the "dream of disaster" sequence tell his tale in an objective voice. Speaking of responsibility directly is too painful: he must "make of myself a stranger" to tell the truth (183). George Harrison's truth will be that his sham virtue led him to commit murder to avoid the public shame of bankruptcy. But as the manuscript unfolds, this horror of public shaming turns out to be a weakness he shares with virtually every other character in the community of Indiantown, a representative village of the antebellum Middle West. Like the contemporaneous "Man That Corrupted Hadleyburg," each character's genuine inner self is completely selfish; each dons a wardrobe of virtuous personae to suit any occasion involving the chance to make some money—usually by "selling" a lie, a story, to someone else. Only those characters who are utterly sentimental—and thus, to the unsentimental, utterly stupid—lack this doubleness and fail to seize the main chance. In this new, tell-all third-person voice, Twain represents sentiment not as the moral sensibility that Kimmel, Bederman, and others identify as the bedrock of "manhood," but as a facade behind which men hide moral weakness from themselves as they struggle for economic survival.

In business correspondence Clemens habitually characterized the division between moral virtues (such as generosity) and economic virtues (such as practicality) as "sentiment" versus "business." In an 1891 letter to Fred Hall, nominal manager of Webster & Co., describing *Library of American Literature* negotiations, he wrote:

> If he had played any generosities on us he would have had me, for that is my weak side; I should have been obliged to meet him half way. But no . . . We have not sold copies enough to pay the book's half of 5 or 6 years' office expenses. Will those royalties ever be enlarged while the book owes us a single nickel? No. Will they then? Only on one condition—that business custom and tradition shall require it. If I ever mix sentiment with business again, I mean to see to it that I don't contribute all the sentiment and the other man all the selfishness. (qtd. in Hill 298)

"Which Was It?" reechoes this binary of sentiment versus business. Parker, one of the fragment's countless schemers, invents a fake heir to intercept the fortune left by old George Harrison, the main character's just-deceased uncle, then urges his partner, Bunker, to "drop sentiment, and come down to business":

> "Be honest, just this once, dear, dear old friend and pal, and recognize this plain unadorned fact: we wish to rob that estate, we mean to rob that estate, we don't care what the means are nor who it hurts, old Harrison's treatment of us isn't our inspiration, sentiment is clean away outside it, we'd skin it, by God, if it belonged to an orphan asylum, and you know it; come out and say it, like a man!". . .
>
> Bunker said, "Well, the truth is, it's as you say; but somehow I could never seem to go into an impropriety without shoring myself up with a kind of a justification, you know."
>
> "That's all right, it's your nature. But you've confessed; sentiment has had its innings; the atmosphere is purged of humbug, now, the

decks are cleared for action, our spirits are up, we're ready for business. Satisfied?" (399)

Bunker's self-justification is reminiscent of how Clemens himself justified whittling down payments to creditors in the name of duty to his family. In that letter, his sentiment rings hollow, as Olivia perceived; in his letter to Hall, selfishness aligns with pragmatic business sense. Later, writing "Which Was It?," Twain contrasts characters like Harrison, who cling to what the text presents as mere illusions of honorable "manliness," with swindlers who, ironically, are presented as the few characters in this fragment capable of being honest with themselves. This motif of sentiment versus business resounds through Twain's myriad subplots, suggesting that moral behavior is not the "manly" virtue it was in the early nineteenth century: rather, it has become a way to lie to oneself, just a veneer in a corrupt world.

Harrison is described by his community as "a *man*. Chock full of noble emotion . . . a *man*, every inch of him" (247). This characterization conforms to the Victorian ideal of "manliness" according to Bederman, as "'character or conduct worthy of a man' . . . synonymous with 'honorable, highminded'" (18). But under the pressure of cyclic economic panics and recessions in the late nineteenth century, this middle-class Victorian formula, Bederman notes, grew shaky. Harrison reflects this shakiness first when he comments on his father's breakdown under debt: "There must be something fearfully disintegrating to character in the loss of money. Men suffer other bereavements and keep up; but when they lose their money, straightaway the structure which we call character, and are so proud of, and have such placid confidence in, and think is granite, begins to crumble and waste away, and then . . . the granite that has been sand once is sand again!" (195). Harrison feels that "the foundations of things were falling out" when he (mistakenly) hears from his father that the Squire is going to call in his mortgage; he immediately begins to fear for his son Tom, too. Bederman notes, "Middle-class parents taught their sons to build a strong, manly 'character' as they would build a muscle, through repetitive exercises of control over impulse" (11–12). After telling Tom that his grandfather has paid the family's debts with a counterfeit note, Harrison begs Tom to uphold his "training," reminding him that this education means there would be no excuse if either of them should "fall": "My father educated me; I have educated you. We have the support of training, teaching, admonition—puissant safeguards that some have lacked, poor souls. *Nothing* could excuse us, Tom . . . nothing—*nothing*. For myself I am not afraid, Tom, let come what may; and you—Tom, you will never disgrace your training?—*say* it, Tom" (212–13).

Harrison's "training" by his own father proves no support. Faced with disgrace (218–19), Harrison decides to burn his mill, take the insurance money, and use it to pay his debts, rationalizing that the insurance will cover the loss, and "the companies would get it all—with interest." He quickly moves from condemning himself as "an exposed sham" to excusing himself: "Why, looked at rationally, instead of sentimentally, what becomes of the crime? Why, it's nothing but a loan!" (219). The Twain figure here concludes that his previous, "manly" way of thinking is mere sentimentality; crime becomes the "rational," businesslike way to proceed.

Twain divides this rational thinking and the sentimental, romantic perspective between two characters: Harrison and son Tom, whose romantic ideas about surprises inadvertently spur on his father's ruin. Like an earlier Tom, this character brims with schemes, dreams, and ways out: by keeping these options secret to orchestrate a "grand effect" of "surprises" that will redeem the family's honor (207, 209–10), Tom unwittingly buys his father time to find a criminal way out. When he enters the story, young Tom has just gotten "started in business" as a junior law partner with a substantial pay raise. Rather than simply tell his father this news, he arranges with his boss

> "that my father and grandfather shall be there [in court], on some pretext or other, and it will be a paralyzing surprise for them when the clerk calls the firm and I rise up."
>
> Then Tom thought of another surprise. Instead of telling his father to-night of the renewal of his engagement [to the Squire's daughter Helen, a sure means of cancelling the Harrison debts], he would save that also for the day after tomorrow; he would spring it on the heels of the first surprise and get large effects out of it. (206–07)

Tom's response to the news of his family's financial problems is reminiscent of Tom Sawyer watching his own funeral, knowing that he can fix his loved ones' grief later: "'Of course, my people are in trouble, now—oh, yes, it's cloudy weather at home, I know it—but if I can hold in till day after tomorrow! Helen, it's a romance! It's good to be alive and in it. I'll sit and listen to them worry, and they'll wonder how I can be so calm'" (207). When the Squire gives the note for the canceled mortgage to Tom, the lad responds, "Another jolly surprise for Wednesday . . . it's going to be a grand day, and nobly theatrical!" (209). Once home, "there was a surprise for Tom, who was doing so large a trade in that commerce just now." The surprise is his father's revelation of the Harrison indebtedness, which Tom now knows the Squire will not collect: even though he hears that this "weighs a ton on [his father's] heart" (212), Tom cannot forgo his "surprises" and "effects" until, unable to sleep, he puts the cancelled papers on the breakfast table, where the cook, predictably, misplaces them; Harrison, believing he is still in debt, breaks into the Squire's mansion, where he commits both theft and murder.

Emphasizing how Tom's boyish, romantic sentimentality serves to catalyze his father's ruin, Twain suggests that romanticism is immature and unmanly, highlighting his rejection of the boy narrators and protagonists of his earlier fiction in these bankruptcy fragments: youth no longer seems to wield redemptive power. From here, Harrison's collapse is swift. When he learns that the Squire has been arrested for the murder he committed, he tells himself, "If I were a *man* I would go and take his place. And I will *do* it, by God I will!"; however, this resolve vanishes with the self-denigrating admission, "I am not a man" (232–33).

Harrison's father's misery over debt leads to *his* death from a "congestive consumption." Harrison himself suffers guilt and anxiety, his continued "wasting and wearing thought," leaving him bedridden. Bederman's comments about neurasthenia cast Harrison's (and his father's) bodily wasting in a new light. In the late nineteenth century, this newly discovered disease became a vector through which "challenges from women, workers, and the changing economy not only affected men's sense of identity and authority, [but] even . . . men's view of the male body. . . . due to the excessive brain work and nervous strain . . . professionals and businessmen endured as they struggled for success in an increasingly challenging economy" (Bederman 14). Harrison's business is a mill—perhaps a metaphoric evocation of Twain's aforementioned "imagination-mill"—so it is significant that Harrison considers setting fire to this mill in order to collect insurance money with which to pay his debts. This may reflect Twain's own sense that during his years as a public bankrupt, he was "forcing the mill to go" (*MTHHR* 73–74). Lecturing his way around the world, writing *Following the Equator* to meet his financial obligations, he masked despair with pronouncements like "honor is a harder master than the law" or quips about "blandly getting ready to unload [his debts] on the whole English-speaking world" (qtd. in Pond, par. 4). Twain's bitter indictment of his avatars in these manuscripts is sadly ironic, given that he himself had faced up to the work demanded to pay his debts.

Harrison's collapsing sense of "manliness" faces its final challenge when Twain introduces Jasper, the freed mulatto slave of Harrison's dead uncle. This uncle had refused to acknowledge Jasper's status after Jasper's cabin burned down with his free papers, then forced Jasper to work to buy his freedom again, leaving Jasper understandably embittered (317–20). Harrison knows nothing of this. Now that Jasper is his servant, Harrison inadvertently inflames Jasper's hate as he orders him around. Twain comments that Harrison's treatment of Jasper "seems harsh, coming from so kind-hearted a man as Harrison was, but it was merely custom, the habit of the time, in dealing with the colored man, and had less depth to it and feeling in it than a stranger to the country would have supposed. The whites imagined that the negroes did not mind it. They judged by the negro's outside, and forgot to inquire within" (408). Finding evidence that Harrison killed Bleecker, Jasper blackmails him. When Harrison resists, Jasper beats and humiliates him in a scene that recalls Salazar's argument in *Bodies of Reform*: while the turn of the century's renewed emphasis on a physically strong body promised to "shore up an enfeebled white masculinity," it also carried the potentially disquieting "promise to override the physiological hierarchies of race, gender, and class" (123). In this fragment, Twain shows that overridden promise when Jasper endures thirty-nine lashes from a cat-o'-nine-tails (having been found out after dark without his papers), then wrestles Harrison into submission: "[Harrison's] wrists were prisoners in the vise-like grip of the yellow athlete's brawny hands. He struggled, and raged, and wept—a vain waste of wind and strength, it was but a case of rabbit and wolf; Jasper held him, waited, and said nothing. When he saw that his prey was exhausted, he crushed him into his chair" (411).

With the realization of his reversed social position, Harrison suffers the ultimate loss of masculine autonomy: "Through [his] half-paralyzed brain flitted the shameful reflection, 'Slave of an ex-slave! It is the final degradation; there is nothing below this'" (413). "Which Was It?" sputters out as Jasper "stor[es] up for sarcastic use" sentimental compliments he hears people pay to Harrison's outward, manly honor (429). Twain said that he had to "work like a slave" to prepare the lecture tour that was the first step toward paying his debts (*Mark Twain's Correspondence* 151); here, his avatar experiences de facto slavery. In this dark fantasy, Harrison's freedom could be stripped from him if Jasper reveals what he knows. Citing Leslie Fiedler's contention that "[the] tradition of cross-race male bonding [is] a search for redemption for white guilt," Michael Kimmel argues that bonding "is also a way to present screens against which white manhood is projected, played out, and defined" (66). The perverse and secret bond between Jasper and Harrison makes them foils. As Jasper gazes at the confession of murder he has coerced Harrison to write, Twain writes, "[Jasper] was visibly a changed man. The meek slouch of the slave was gone from him. . . . He looked the master; but that which had gone from him was not lost, for his discarded droop and humble mien had passed to his white serf, and already they seemed not out of place there, but . . . pathetically proper and at home" (415). In contrast, Harrison not only looks but feels emasculated and servile, lamenting, "*Why* was I born with a man's form and a rabbit's heart? why haven't I the courage to kill myself?" (418). In the thrall of the determined power of the freed slave, Harrison fully realizes how much humiliation he will privately accept to avert public shame.

Twain wrote in his *Autobiography* that it was a pity he wouldn't finish "Which Was It?," as it "would spring a handsome surprise" on the reader (3:196). At the point where Twain stopped work on this fragment, readers know something that Harrison does not: Jasper is actually his cousin. Though Jasper refers repeatedly to his white father, he does not name Harrison's uncle in his hearing, evidently saving this bombshell for subsequent torment. This revelation could make Jasper, the freed slave, a claimant for old George Harrison's fortune, the object of so many characters' schemes: as an illegitimate child, Jasper's claim would not hold legal weight, but it would add weight to Harrison's guilt. Although Twain shows admiration for Jasper's having worked to buy his freedom twice, it is unlikely that this particular revelation would be that "handsome surprise," as the tale is told from Harrison's point of view: more likely, that surprise would have been a final reveal that Harrison had only dreamed all this misery—making the entire tale sentimental romance, rather than the honest storytelling that Harrison's deliberate shift from first- to third-person voice was to guarantee.

Twain's comment about this "handsome surprise" should make us wonder why he *didn't* finish "Which Was It?" after writing over three hundred pages from 1899 through 1902. With Jasper poised to take revenge on Harrison, "Which Was It?" would change course drastically, dramatizing the freed slave becoming master over the white family that has repeatedly wronged him. Instead of a drama about what a man will do to escape bankruptcy's shame, the focus would shift to the broader moral bankruptcy of the slave economy. Twain treated racial questions in many prior novels; it seems doubtful that combining race with issues of masculinity would have made "Which Was It?" a more volatile mix than *Pudd'nhead Wilson*, for example. Here, however—unlike *Pudd'nhead*, where white supremacy is reasserted, however ironically, at the novel's close—Jasper's vengeance places him firmly in control of Harrison, and perhaps that was a surprise that Twain was reluctant to spring on an audience in 1902.

It's worth asking why Twain didn't finish *any* of his "dream of disaster" stories (not only those treated here, but "The Great Dark" as well). In his later years, Twain often made repeated attacks on issues that vexed or inspired him, most notably in the *Mysterious Stranger Manuscripts*, begun in 1897 and taken up in multiple versions until finally, in 1909, he jotted, on the next-to-last chapter of *No. 44, the Mysterious Stranger*, that he had finished that novel (Gibson 10–11). Settling the collected works agreement with

Harper's made his finances secure and effectively freed Twain from the need to write for profit. He could choose what to share with the public, what to withhold, what to experiment with, complete, or lay down. Some texts, such as *Letters from the Earth*, he felt were too shocking to publish, and he voiced concern in letters about the possible impact this could have on his surviving family.

As Peter Filene has observed, amid the dislocating changes at the century's turn, "[w]ithout [work] a man was emasculated, bereft of identity" (79): laboring on these autobiographical texts, Twain grappled with his depression and disgust through writing. But publishing them to the world seems to have been a different matter. One would have to love Twain not wisely but too well to place the "dream" manuscripts on the level of the *Mysterious Stranger* texts or *Letters*. The record of what he did choose to publish in his last decade, and what he pushed to complete, suggests that he realized his dream tales' shortcomings. Certainly their excruciatingly personal content would have made publishing them uncomfortable. Having symbolically accepted responsibility for decisions that contributed to his bankruptcy through the process of writing them, by 1902, with his finances secured, he could lay these manuscripts down for good, and with them, the ghosts of guilt and debt. Twain could now—to borrow the words of No. 44—"dream other dreams, and better" (404).

Notes

1. In December 1893 the comptroller of the currency announced that "158 national banks, 172 State banks, 177 private banks, 47 savings banks, 13 loan and trust companies, and 6 mortgage companies" had failed (Dewey 446). Data were not kept on personal bankruptcies, but estimates of unemployment ranged from 17 to 19 percent; over fifteen thousand businesses failed ("Panic" par. 6).

2. For a detailed argument of this point, see Weil, *Reconstructing the Imagination-Mill: Mark Twain's Literary Response to Bankruptcy.*

3. Camfield notes, "A typical post-bankruptcy year's copyright statements from Chatto & Windus and Harper & Brothers shows the wisdom of [Rogers's] plan, with Chatto & Windus paying the Clemenses over 181 pounds (worth about $25,000 current U.S. dollars) and Harper & Brothers, $1,500 (work about $31,000 current dollars). Royalty statements from the American Publishing Company no longer exist, but would presumably have been substantial, too" (223).

4. See, for example, Leary 105–6.

5. Linda Morris's *Gender Play* contains numerous examples of strong-willed female characters Twain wrote who cross-dress and manifest masculine characteristics.

Works Cited

Bederman, Gail. *Manliness and Civilization: A Cultural History of Gender and Race in the United States, 1880–1917*. Chicago: U of Chicago P, 1995.

Bortz, Daniel. "Surviving the Emotional Toll of Bankruptcy." U.S. News & World Report: Money. 18 Jan 2013. Web. 21 June 2014. <money.usnews.com/money/personal-finance/articles/2013/01/18/surviving-the-emotional-toll-of-bankruptcy>.

Brooks, Van Wyck. *The Ordeal of Mark Twain*. 1920. New York: E. P. Dutton, 1970.

Camfield, Gregg. *The Oxford Companion to Mark Twain*. New York: Oxford UP, 2003.

"Debt Linked to Mental Health Problems." Targeted News Service. 26 September 2013. Research Library Proquest. 21 June 2014. Web.

Dewey, Davis Rich. *A Financial History of the United States*. London: Longman, Green, 1922 (1902). Rpt. Elibron Classics, Adamant Media Corp., 2005. Web. 21 June 2014. Full text: <books.google.com/books?id=l30aAAAAMAAJ&printsec=frontcover#v=snippet&q=panic%20of%201893&f=false>.

Faludi, Susan. *Backlash: The Undeclared War against American Women* (The 15th Anniversary Edition). New York: Crown, 2009.

Fiedler, Leslie A. "As Free as Any Cretur . . ." Mark Twain: A Collection of Critical Essays. Ed. Henry Nash Smith. Englewood Cliffs: Prentice-Hall, 1963. 130–39.

Filene, Peter G. *Him/Her/Self: Gender Identities in Modern America*. 1974. Baltimore: Johns Hopkins UP, 1998.

Fitch, Chris, Sarah Hamilton, Paul Bassett, and Ryan Davey. "The Relationship between Personal Debt and Mental Health: A Systematic Review." *Mental Health Review* 16.4 (2011): 153–66. Research Library Proquest. Web. 21 June 2014.

Gibson, William M. "Introduction." *Mark Twain: The Mysterious Stranger Manuscripts*. Ed. William M. Gibson. Berkeley: U of California P, 1969. 1–34.

Hill, Hamlin, ed. *Mark Twain's Letters to His Publishers, 1867–1894*. Berkeley: U of California P, 1967.

"It's in the Numbers." Bankruptcy-America.com. Bankruptcy-America. 2014. Web. 21 June 2014. <www.bankruptcy-america.com/>.

Kaplan, Justin. *Mr. Clemens and Mark Twain: A Biography*. New York: Simon and Schuster, 1966.

Kimmel, Michael. *Manhood in America: A Cultural History*. New York: Free Press, 1996.

Kiskis, Michael. "A Man's House Burns Down: Father/Daughter Collaboration in Mark Twain's Autobiography." Paper presented at Modern Language Association conference, Chicago, December 1990.

———, ed. *Mark Twain's Own Autobiography: The Chapters from the North American Review*. Madison: U of Wisconsin P, 1990.

Mac an Ghaill, Mairtin, and Chris Haywood. *Gender, Culture, and Society: Contemporary Femininities and Masculinities*. New York: Palgrave Macmillan, 2007.

Messent, Peter. *Mark Twain and Male Friendship: The Twichell, Howells, and Rogers Friendships*. Oxford: Oxford UP, 2009.

———. "Mark Twain, Manhood, the Henry H. Rogers Friendship, and 'Which Was the Dream?'" *Arizona Quarterly* 61.1 (Spring 2005): 57–84. Research Library Proquest. Web. 8 August 2012.

Morris, Linda A. *Gender Play in Mark Twain: Cross-Dressing and Transgression*. Columbia: U of Missouri P, 2007.

"Panic of 1893." Saylor.org. The Saylor Foundation, 2014. Web. 21 June 2014. <www.saylor.org/site/wp-content/uploads/2011/08/HIST312-10.1.2-Panic-of-1893.pdf>.

Pond, Major J. B. *Eccentricities of Genius*. New York: G. W. Dillingham, 1900. "Mark Twain in His Times." Stephen Railton and the University of Virginia Library. 1996–2012. Web. 20 Aug. 2014 <twain.lib.virginia.edu/onstage/pondecc.html>.

Requa, Kenneth. "Counterfeit, Currency, and Character in Mark Twain's Which Was It?" *Mark Twain Journal* 17.3 (1975): 1–16. JSTOR. Web.

Rotundo, E. Anthony. *American Manhood: Transformations in Masculinity from the Revolution to the Modern Era*. New York: Basic Books, 1993.

Salazar, James B. *Bodies of Reform: The Rhetoric of Character in Gilded Age America*. New York: New York UP, 2010.

Sandage, Scott. *Born Losers: A History of Failure in America*. Cambridge: Harvard UP, 2005.

Twain, Mark. *Autobiography of Mark Twain: The Complete and Authoritative Edition*. 3 vols. Ed. Harriet Elinor Smith et al. Berkeley: U of California P, 2010, 2012, 2015.

———. "Indiantown." 1899. *Mark Twain's Which Was the Dream? and Other Symbolic Writings of the Later Years*. Ed. John S. Tuckey. Berkeley: U of California P, 1968: 151–76.

———. *The Love Letters of Mark Twain*. Ed. Dixon Wecter. New York: Harper and Brothers, 1949.

———. *Mark Twain: The Mysterious Stranger Manuscripts*. Ed. William M. Gibson. Berkeley: U of California P, 1969.

———. *Mark Twain's Correspondence with Henry Huttleston Rogers, 1893–1910*. Ed. Lewis Leary. Berkeley: U of California P, 1969.

———. "Which Was It?" 1899–1902. *Mark Twain's Which Was the Dream? and Other Symbolic Writings of the Later Years*. Ed. John S. Tuckey. Berkeley: U of California P, 1968. 177–429.

———. "Which Was the Dream?" 1899. *Mark Twain's Which Was the Dream? and Other Symbolic Writings of the Later Years*. Ed. John S. Tuckey. Berkeley: U of California P, 1968. 31–73.

United States. U.S. Courts. "Bankruptcy Statistics." Administrative Office of the U.S.

Courts on behalf of the Federal Judiciary. 2014. Web. 21 June 2014. <www.uscourts.gov/Statistics/BankruptcyStatistics/2014-bankruptcy-filings.aspx>.

Weil, Susanne. *Reconstructing the Imagination-Mill: Mark Twain's Literary Response to Bankruptcy*. Diss. University of California, Berkeley, 1991.

——. "Reconstructing the 'Imagination-Mill': The Mystery of Mark Twain's Late Works." *Mark Twain's Humor: Critical Essays*. Ed. David E. E. Sloane. New York: Garland, 1993.

8
The Pain Economy
Mark Twain's Masochistic Understanding of Pain

M. Christine Benner Dixon

Mark Twain peddles his stories of pain with only a perfunctory apology to the sensitive reader. About to launch into a description of one man's exceptional tolerance for physical pain in *Following the Equator*, Twain writes, "Do not read the following instances if horrors are not pleasant to you" (553). It is a fair warning. What follows is quite grisly: living bodies plunged into fire, limbs amputated, and other such legitimate "horrors." So what makes Mark Twain think that "horrors" are "pleasant" to anyone? Because they are pleasant to him. He admits, "[The third story] is my favorite. Whenever I read it I seem to enjoy all that the patient enjoyed—whatever it was" (554). What, indeed! In the vignette that follows, the "patient" amputates his own leg in a fire, hobbles ninety-six miles on the stump to see a doctor, and then discards the false leg he acquires because he finds it inconvenient. *Enjoyment* is hardly the word.

Twain doesn't need to define what, exactly, that man enjoyed about his pain. The author could see that this pain was valuable, not only to the patient but to readers as well. "We all like to see people in trouble if it doesn't cost us anything," Twain writes (*Equator* 713). But finding pleasure in pain does cost something. For Twain, the exchange of pain and pleasure is a transaction within a system that I will call the "pain economy,"[1] and it carries with it a strict reckoning. The energy surrounding the pain economy, as well as its insistent return to balance, underwrites Twain's creative efforts while also providing a rudimentary moral measure. Only those who suffer may trade in the pain economy. Without a down payment of pain, ease and pleasure translate into debt. The author stands ready with his balance sheet to track the debtors and creditors and, when necessary, to set the accounts straight.

Throughout his writing, Twain documents, manages, even practices the pain–pleasure exchange. The basic functions of the pain economy are essential to human nature, Twain argues. In a fantasy about his own infancy, Twain makes the pain economy the primary lesson:

> I was nine days old at the time, and had noticed that if a pin was sticking in me and I advertised it in the usual fashion, I was lovingly petted

> and coddled and pitied in a most agreeable way and got a ration between meals.
>
> It was human nature to want to get these riches, and I fell. I lied about the pin—advertising one when there wasn't any. ("My First Lie" 439)

Eventually Twain learned to work this system professionally, sometimes selling a counterfeit pain, at other times offering authentic tales of his own suffering.

Without remuneration, however, the author would have no reason to dwell in his own pain. Without the pain economy, Twain's account in *Roughing It* of his foolhardy purchase of a "Genuine Mexican Plug" from an oily horse salesman (178–84) is mere self-insult. Within the text the narrator suffers everything from a mild jealousy for the straight-backed horsemen of the American West to the loss of dignity (and $27) in falling for the salesman's pitch of the "Genuine Mexican Plug" to actual physical injury during his first bone-rattling attempt to mount the horse. "Imagination cannot conceive how disjointed I was—how internally, externally and universally I was unsettled, mixed up and ruptured" (181). A "sympathetic crowd" gathers around the young man, but their words of consolation do not console: "Stranger, you've been taken in. . . . Why, you turnip, if you had laid low and kept dark, there's chances to buy an *American* horse for mighty little more than you paid for that bloody old foreign relic" (181–82). Our narrator/turnip leaves the tale having paid dearly in cash, discomfort, and dignity. His one solace is that he manages to pass the old plug off to a stranger whose pain is sure to equal his own.

The embarrassment of this episode touches Twain the author as well as his narrator. Twain claims association with this naive young man, this being an ostensibly autobiographical account, and thus takes on his shame as well. Twain is conscious of the judgment of his audience, even welcomes it. He ends the tale with this disclaimer: "Now, whoever has had the luck to ride a real Mexican plug will recognize the animal depicted in this chapter, and hardly consider him exaggerated—but the uninitiated will feel justified in regarding his portrait as a fancy sketch, perhaps" (184). The reader judges him either a fool or a liar. Either way, they have purchased his book. Twain has made an exchange with his reader—his pain for their amusement—and everyone comes out the richer for it. Twain is keen on seeing that that pain is paid for.

The pain-pleasure exchange does not always enrich, however. Taking unpaid-for pleasure can run up a hefty bill. In "A Mysterious Visit," the Twainian narrator learns that puffing up one's social accomplishments and earthly rewards (at least in front of the taxman) comes with a hefty price tag. In this sketch, the narrator, unfamiliar with the interests of the "Internal Revenue Department," attempts to lure his officious visitor into revealing his business "with a deep, deep ruse"—that is, the author will brag about his own business successes until the other man cannot help but talk about his. Ultimately, the narrator reports an exaggerated income to the taxman and is left with a bill for $10,650. The author does get out of his bill, but only by cheating on his taxes, which bears its own consequences. "I stood up and swore to lie after lie, fraud after fraud, villainy after villainy, till my immortal soul was coated inches and inches thick with perjury and my self-respect was gone forever and ever" (344). There is no pleasure without a price.

As these examples show, Twain works out the rules of the pain economy in the laboratory of his own experience.[2] In this way, his understanding of pain and pleasure is essentially masochistic. Leaving aside the conventional sexual associations with the term "sado-masochism" (SM), masochism is an enacted moral reckoning and a process of making meaning. And it is in this latter sense that we find productive resemblance to Mark Twain's pain economy.

When I claim that Twain demonstrates a masochistic relationship to pain, I put him in the company of people who are intimate with pain, who experience the transformation of suffering into pleasure, release, or some kind of transcendence. Twain was unable to endure life's pain by sheer force of will. By making his pain an exchange currency, he was able to have control over his pain and release of control at the same time. Engaging with pain and investing in it enriches the suffering subject. Twain's indulgence of this masochism teaches us to profit in our disappointment, our confusion, and our pain.

Lyn Cowan, a Jungian analyst, describes masochism as a function of the soul and a tool for constructing reality: "Masochism is essential, less for sexual pleasure than for the very life of the soul. . . . Masochism, before it is anything else, is essential reality. It is not a mere perversion, not a distortion or deviation, but essence: a reflection of the soul in its tortured, most inarticulate moments. These are moments of exquisite pain, imminent death, intolerable images, of unbearable passion that ignites both body and soul" (xi). The pain-ridden world does not dissolve into the masochist's fantasy. In fact, masochism faces the unpleasant elements of life straight on, without flinching or dreaming. The masochist understands that human beings *will suffer* and so preemptively welcomes pain and finds the means to process it into something worthwhile and beneficial. In the SM scene, this means attaining the blissful "subspace" that resembles Mihaly Csíkszentmihályi's concept of "flow": a transcendent experience of deep concentration and heightened consciousness (Newmahr 96). In Twain's pain economy, the payoff manifests sometimes as laughter, sometimes monetary recompense, sometimes revenge, sometimes glory. As with the masochist, Twain's interest in pain springs from a kind of commercial acumen, not pathological self-deprecation. The author is making use of life's most readily available resource and capitalizing on it.

Trade is possible, however, only when pain and pleasure are out of balance. Twain inclines toward pain imbalance as if by nature, and there he sets up shop. As Twain lessens his pain investment, the value of his writing decreases. Forrest Robinson argues that *A Tramp Abroad*—a book that Twain himself greatly disliked—is Twain's least interesting travel book, because, in part, "the traveler disburdened of inflated expectations is no longer prey to painful disenchantment," which so electrifies *Roughing It* and *Innocents Abroad* ("Innocent" 42). Distancing himself from pain, Twain undercuts his own creative funds.

But imbalance is not only a creative opportunity for Twain; it is a moral issue, as well. Pain capital, if unspent, turns to moral capital. One who suffers without recompense stands on the moral high ground in Twain's eyes. One who gleans pleasure from the suffering of others, on the other hand, is the definitive sinner. This rigorous division between right and wrong speaks to Twain's membership in an "individualistic, rule-based, and universalist" Western culture that, according to moral psychologist Jonathan Haidt, scorns "mere convention" as a measure of morality and seeks a more measurable morality (97, 17). In other words, if pain and pleasure are not balanced, no other moral considerations matter—not loyalty, not authority, not sanctity.

Voluntary submission to pain as practiced by masochists sends a shockwave through "conventional" morality. Mimicking real-world scenarios of "wrongdoing" produces a fruitful pain for a bottom, and the SM scene draws the eye to immorality. So much so that—because scenes may imitate morally reprehensible acts like physical beatings, betrayal, verbal abuse, blasphemy, or even slavery—the practice itself is sometimes condemned as immoral. According to Staci Newmahr, a researcher within the SM scene, an awareness of power relationships is an essential part of masochism: "The common link across all activities and relationships represented in the self-defined SM community is not a sexual content, nor the adoption of roles, but the quest for experiences of imbalanced interpersonal power" (74). In SM, however, everyone is a willing player, simulating injustice or abuse but free to call an end to the scene at any time, thus distinguishing the SM scene from real-world injustice. At least from a liberal Western perspective, consent solves the moral dilemma.

But for Twain, there is no players' contract. Every person participates in the pain–pleasure exchange whether she or he wants to or not. Everyone suffers, and everyone seeks to trade one's pain for something more desirable. But what if one receives a permanent pain that cannot be traded away? Newmahr distinguishes between "pain," "hurt," and "harm" in masochistic play. In the pain economy, "pain" and "hurt"—manageable and familiar—are the most easily commodified. Only "harm" implies an unredeemable permanence, impossible to exchange for pleasure, a kind of frozen asset. For Twain, inflicting permanent, nonconsensual pain is not a game; it is a sin—the only sin.

There is plenty of fungible suffering left to go around, however. We will begin with the most obvious: physical pain. On the surface, physical pain seems difficult to exchange, being so visceral and bodily. But physical pain paradoxically intellectualizes the body. As philosopher Simon Critchley puts it, "In pain, I attempt to take a distance from my body, externalize the discomfort and insulate myself in thought" (42). This distance is enough to enable the exchange of the pain economy. Twain demonstrates a distanced exchange of physical pain in "Down the Rhône." With a mock-scientific intellectuality, Twain records his thoughts from under the dentist's drill:

> It is believed by people generally—or at least by many—that the exquisitely sharp sensation which results from plunging the steel point into the raw nerve is pain, but I think that this is doubtful. It is so vivid and sudden that one has no time to examine properly into its character. It is probably impossible, with our human limitations, to determine with certainty whether a sensation of so high and perfect an order as that is pain or whether it is pleasure. . . . I have every confidence that I can eventually prove to everyone's satisfaction that a nerve-stab produces pleasure; and not only that, but the most exquisite pleasure, the most perfect felicity which we are capable of feeling. (1025–26)

Twain recognizes that converting pain to pleasure is an extraordinarily valuable activity. "I would not ask more," the author proclaims, "than to be remembered hereafter as the man who conferred this priceless benefaction upon his race" (1026). But, of course, Twain hasn't been able to transform the pain of a root canal into purest pleasure—at least not by thought alone. Though he can still expect our eternal gratitude, because he does let us turn our pain to pleasure in the pain economy. But we must suffer first.

Physical pain is not the only kind of currency accepted. Twain was intimate with physical pain—he suffered rheumatism in his writing hand, lay bed-ridden by illness for long stretches of time, and had more than his share of barked shins and saddle sores—yet he seemed to rate financial losses among his most painful experiences. A poor businessman and an inveterate speculator, Twain often found himself hurting for money. Not all of Twain's financial misery was self-inflicted, however. Twain kept careful track of the people he felt had cheated him financially and reserved for them a particularly uncomfortable corner of hell. When speaking of Elisha Bliss, whom Twain believed had cheated him out of $60,000 (Hill 153), Twain seethes with animosity. Twain calls the publisher "a Yankee of the Yankees . . . tall, lean, skinny, yellow, toothless, bald-headed, rat-eyed professional liar and scoundrel" (*Autobiography* 1:370). As usual, Twain uses the text as his means of settling accounts.

Twain would employ the same reckoning tactics to those who swindled not only himself but the greater public. Businessmen and politicians who made personal gains through the financial hardship of others were lumped in with Twain's personal enemies. For example, Twain's diatribes against Rev. William Scott Ament, a missionary to China during the Boxer Rebellion, and Mary Baker Eddy, the founder of Christian Science, center on their apparent willingness to profit financially at the expense of the poor (though he begrudgingly admits that they do offer some benefit in return). *The Gilded Age*, of course, stands as Twain's great condemnation of the greed and self-interest that he saw corrupting politics and business alike.

Physical and financial pain factor large in Twain's pain economy, but perhaps the most poignant and persistent form of pain is psychological—shame, humiliation, and guilt. As a literary masochist, Twain could hardly neglect these pains. What would a masochistic scene be without a little humiliation, after all? Twain was so sensitive to the power of shame that it formed the basis of his concept of the human psyche. From "Corn-Pone Opinions" to *What Is Man?*, Twain preaches that the pursuit of external approval (and therefore self-approval) is the single greatest aim of human life; the failure to attain these things results in unbearable pain.

Twain gravitates to scenes of humiliation, knowing that there is trade to be done there. His frequent return to the scene of his sometime service in a Confederate militia illustrates this point. In 1877 Twain delivered a speech called "My Military History" at a dinner for "The Ancient and Honorable Artillery Company of Massachusetts." For the entertainment of former Union soldiers, Twain mocked a fellow Confederate soldier, Ben Tupper, for his big feet, his bad luck with horses and rats, and especially for his city-boy indolence. He extended his mockery to the entire company of young Rebels who tired themselves out by moving incessantly in order to avoid engaging the enemy. When ordered to hold their ground and fight, they disbanded immediately. Twain wisely prevented his shabby Confederate company from attacking "the enemy," since "the enemy" of yesteryear now composed Twain's listening audience. Twain pandered to the assembled Union veterans, delivering the cowardice of their enemies as entertainment.

Twain's intense focus on humiliation and guilt may seem unhealthy, but in utilizing these feelings Twain builds basic pain capital to fund his writing effort. Guilt, after all, is rich in pain. "Often the deepest suffering comes not from bearing punishment, but from bearing *gnosis*, a constant burdensome knowledge of one's own truths and one's capacity for all manner of evil and destruction" (Cowan 25). That knowledge is itself painful, but it also justifies the suffering position assumed by the masochist. The guilty deserve punishment, after all—the pain becomes theirs by rights. From the sufferer's position, a person can "choose from sometimes competing discourses to contextualize, recast, make sense of, and enjoy the pain, anguish, or subservience of bottoming" (Newmahr 89). Paradoxically, by owning the pain and submitting to it for the sake of reward, the masochist takes control over his or her experience. The empowered masochist makes it more difficult for an outside force to inflict lasting harm. Likewise, Twain chooses his position, accepts his humiliation, and turns his "punishment" into pain capital.

Unsurprisingly, the pleasures and "rewards" of Twain's pain economy can come in as many different forms as pain itself. Like the pain economy, masochism offers participants "investment pain" (Newmahr 138). It is an extreme "no pain, no gain" philosophy: "Pain is understood not merely as an unfortunate byproduct, but as a means to a particular end" (138). For the select few, like the self-sacrificing mother of *What Is Man?* who willingly suffers for the sake of her child, pain alchemizes to pleasure through a satisfied self-concept. "She takes a living *pleasure* in making these sacrifices," the Old Man explains. "*She does it for that reward*—that self-approval, that contentment, that peace, that comfort. *She would do it for your child* IF SHE COULD GET THE SAME PAY" (744). For others, like Huck and Tom at the end of *Tom Sawyer* or any of the numerous unfortunates pitied and then elevated by Edward Tudor in the "Justice and Retribution" chapter of *The Prince and the Pauper*, money is the balm that soothes raw wounds. And for still others—think of Merlin in "a delirium of silly laughter" as he sends Hank Morgan to his thousand-year sleep at the end of *Connecticut Yankee* (443)—pain's payoff lies in the pleasure of a retaliatory blow. Perhaps most importantly for Twain, pain may also be paid off with humor.

Twain's humor depends on a stockpile of pain. In *Proper Mark Twain*, Leland Krauth suggests that Twain's desire for social approval urged him to construct connections between humor and more "serious" subjects—such as human suffering. Twain, however, was not inventing a relationship between pain, humor, and morality for propriety's sake alone. As Twain saw it, pain was essential to humor. "I maintain that a man can never be a humorist, in thought or in deed, until he can feel the springs of pathos. Indeed, there you have a basis of something material to go upon in trying to comprehend what this impalpable thing of true humor is. Trust me, he was never yet properly funny who was not capable at times of being very serious. And more: the two are as often as not simultaneous" (qtd. in Krauth 11). The relationship between pathos and humor is neither coincidental nor contrived. Twain's creative energies are funded by his investment in pain.

Granted, the magnitude of suffering, fear, humiliation, poverty, and powerlessness that Twain addresses in his writing can make laughter seem an illogical response. But Twain's humor does not negate the pain or deny its origin; it transforms pain. Humor is a tool of exchange. "Twain's genius is that he turns the 'dark and terrifying' elements of reality into 'ludicrous monstrosities,'" writes Joe Fulton, echoing Bakhtin's phrasing (54). Twain manages to transform pain from a burdensome but abundant natural resource into commodity, even currency. Twain accepts suffering, amplifies it, and spends it, thus regaining a modicum of control in a world that is racked with unavoidable pain.

That Mark Twain tracked his own ailments and embarrassments with an accountant's precision is not to say that he enjoyed his suffering as it was happening. But he knew that real pain was a reliable currency with which he could purchase pleasure. Like masochism, humor employs a "psychological shift [that] is felt as pleasant" (Morreall 248). In the case of masochism—and Twain's masochistic humor—the original psychological state is frequently painful. Gilles Deleuze writes, "It is argued, justifiably, that the masochist is not a strange being who finds pleasure in pain, but that he is like everyone else, and finds pleasure where others do, the simple difference being that for him pain, punishment or humiliation are necessary prerequisites to obtaining gratification" (71). Twain's humor requires that we have experienced pain. We best enjoy the hassles and humiliations if we identify with the pain—if we too have fallen victim to a snake-oil salesman, if we too have been caught in a brag to our utter shame, if we too have suffered through readings of awful poetry. Only then will Twain provide that humorous/masochistic shift from pain to hearty laughter.

The transformation of pain to pleasure resets the balance on the pain account. "Humor, at its best," writes Neil Schmitz, "forgives and resolves a grievous wrong. It admits it, full measure, receives it, and expresses the immediate experience in humorous language. With verbal dexterity, in some comical voice, it economizes pain's impact" (74). Laughter promises to transform pain, but to build credit, the pain has to actually *hurt*.

For Sigmund Freud, the humorous shift is also a matter of economy. We are accustomed to putting "psychical energy" into appeasing the demands of our conscience and our inhibitions (manifest in feelings of guilt), writes Freud, but the "gain in pleasure" from joking redirects that energy away from those oppressive forces (114–15). In other words, the tension created by our inhibitions—the pain, as it were—fuels the joke itself. When Twain breaks through the restraints of social inhibition, those who are most constrained by the social inhibitions are privileged to laugh the loudest. Take, for example, the culminating joke in "The Man That Corrupted Hadleyburg." Although there are some out-of-town reporters (representatives of the broader social gaze that enforces the inhibition) present at the revelation of the fraud perpetrated by the most "incorruptible" citizens, the majority of the audience members are Hadleyburgers, themselves pressed into false honesty from a young age, who know the Incorruptibles by sight and name. The raucous laughter at the town hall as the principal citizens fall, one after another, is a punishment for the haughty and a reward for those who have long been sidelined and constrained by the behavioral demands of their society. It is a radical transformation of unpleasure into pleasure. Only those who resist the exchange—Mary and Edward Richards—are unable to laugh, and they continue to suffer. Although their share in the inhibition offers them the opportunity to share in the laughter, they are stagnant in the pain economy; they experience no shift at all. They neither accept payment for the pain of their inhibitions nor settle their debts amassed from their various benefactors.

Humor is one of Twain's primary tools for moving readers, characters, or the author himself from pain to payoff—or vice versa. As we laugh at bloated monarchs, braggadocious dandies, and hysterical housewives, we participate in the economy. On the one hand, our laughter may punish with a dose of humiliation one whose pleasures have gone too long unpaid. On the other hand, Twain may provoke our laughter at an innocent victim, giving us a pleasure we did not earn and leaving us on the hook for the bill. Twain makes it easy to glean pleasure from iniquity and pain, but it is always an exchange. Tom Sawyer's guilt—accrued by his infamous whitewash trick—is reduced exactly in proportion to how much joy we derive from laughing at his victims. We have accepted the pleasure of his sin, and so some of the debt becomes ours as well.

The king and the duke's defrauding of the Wilks girls in *Huckleberry Finn* provides another such laughter trap. As readers we thoroughly enjoy the absurd posturing of the king and the duke as grieving English brothers. Their ploy is transparent, and we rightly (and righteously) laugh at their shabby imitation of genuine human emotion: "[T]hey bent over and looked in the coffin, and took one sight, and then they bust out a crying so you could a heard them to Orleans, most" (212). Readers slip into debt when we begin to laugh not only at the self-serving criminals but at their innocent victims as well. The king and the duke's ostentatious performance of tender piety, Huck reports, "worked the crowd like you never see anything like it, and so everybody broke down and went to sobbing right out loud—the poor girls, too" (212). Huck denounces the whole scene as "disgusting." We laugh with him at the lot of them.

When Dr. Robinson finally arrives as the sole clear-sighted citizen, the treachery of our laughter becomes apparent. His censure of the credulous and emotional nieces—this disapproval echoes the essence of our laughter—pushes them into the arms of their deceivers, along with a bag of money worth $6,000 (219). By the end of the scene, Robinson's lack of pity prevents his further intervention—"I wash *my* hands of the matter," he resolves (219). The reader is left with no comfortable place to stand. Our amusement at the king and the duke's fraud makes us complicit either in the villains' schemes or in the doctor's unsympathetic disapproval, perhaps both. Laughter tangles us together in a jumble of guilt, judgment, pain, and pleasure—which is to say, leaves us fully invested. Twain once said, "I have only amused people. Their laughter has submerged me" (Keller 51). But it submerges us, too.

Pain is a kind of commodity currency that Twain knows his readers will accept. Freud reminds us that "the activity of joking cannot be said to have no aim or purpose, for it has set itself the unmistakable aim of arousing pleasure in the listener" (91). But pleasure cannot be had for free, and Twain will often exact his payment in the very moment of amusement. American readers cannot laugh at the irony of the patriotic Ah Song Hi's abuses by employer, policeman, and legislator without accepting the implicit condemnation of a passive American public ("Goldsmith's Friend Abroad Again"). Many of the "Pudd'nhead Wilson's New Calendar" maxims function on a similar principle—if you laugh at a joke, you are the target of it. Look, for instance, at this maxim: "If the desire to kill and the opportunity to kill came always together, who would escape hanging?" (*Equator* 694). To laugh at this joke is to admit that one has, at some inconvenient time, harbored a murderous thought or two, and it is only those who laugh whom Twain threatens with the gallows.

This text is designed to be participatory. The closer we engage with Twain's writing, the more likely it is that our pain accounts will be laid open for examination. It is Mark Twain's masochistic scene, and we play by his rules. Our laughter may deliver humiliation to the guilty, but Twain might prove momentarily that we are just as guilty as those we ridicule—yet our pleasure remains, an outstanding debt. To settle up, we must enter the pain economy; we must play a part in Twain's scene.

Twain steers us away from the edges of the pain economy—the extremes of pain where "harm" dominates. Although Twain idolizes harmed victims as morally unassailable, they are largely inactive in the pain–pleasure exchange. They have accumulated a store of pain that they cannot or will not cash in for their pleasure. For those who practice this "sacrificial pain," Newmahr informs us, there is no pleasure (137). Their suffering is a loving act, an unrequited gift. Gleaning no pleasure, the martyrs' pain is pure moral capital. Refusing their right to retaliate or complain, they rise above the baseness of their fellow human beings to a moral pinnacle. Twain meticulously catalogues, even exaggerates, the suffering of his heroes. He refuses to correct the balance and erase the moral fortune represented by their unrewarded pain.

In part, Twain preserves and exaggerates their pain because he saw himself as the cause (or beneficiary) of it. Working through the agony of throat cancer, Ulysses S. Grant produced a book that buoyed Twain's fledgling publishing company. The suffering and death of Joan of Arc, Twain's purest hero, provided him with a saint to worship and a subject through which, he felt, his writing was elevated to its highest purpose. Their goodness underlines his iniquity and gives him permission to punish himself without restraint.

And then there was Livy. "Livy darling," he once wrote, "you are so good & dear & steadfast & fine—the highest & finest & loveliest character I have ever known; & I was never worthy of you. You should have been the prize of a better man—a man up nearer your own level" (*Love Letters* 318–19). Quick to blame himself for his failures of character, Twain worried he caused Livy unending pain. His hot temper, his failed business decisions, his tendency toward public faux pas—all of these, he believed, were torments to Livy. "I am full of remorse for things done and said in these thirty-four years of married life that hurt Livy's heart" (Clemens 253), Twain wrote in the aftermath of Livy's passing. Livy had died from heart disease; he is literally accepting blame for her death.

The immense debt of Twain's pain associates him with his foremost villains, who willingly profit from the pain of others. As likely as not, they themselves were the source of that pain. The villains purchase comfort, honor, and power with other people's suffering. They commit the most basic sin in the pain economy and commit it flagrantly. The accumulated debt becomes so large that they can never repay it. Twain writes more about his villains than he does about his heroes, and what he writes is far more entertaining, perhaps because their enormous pain debt provides Twain with an almost unending supply of creative potential. Do what he may to charge the villains for their unearned pleasures, the imbalance remains.

Among these villains are the moneyed elite, who bring the pain economy and literal finance together. Ever ready to bribe or cheat, regardless of the harm they inflict, these villains have only one objective: "To get rich . . . dishonestly if we can; honestly if we must" ("Revised Catechism" 539). The lure of domination, Twain believed, was equally strong for capitalist, king, and ideologue. "Power," writes Twain, "when lodged in the hands of man, means oppression—*insures* oppression: it means oppression *always*" ("New Dynasty" 883). And no power was exempt. Religious power, Twain believed, was just as dangerous as political power. He despised corrupt priests and bishops of the Church, who "preached (to the commoner) humility, obedience to superiors, the beauty of self-sacrifice; she preached (to the commoner) meekness under insult; preached (still to the commoner, always to the commoner) patience, meanness of spirit, non-resistance under oppression; and she introduced heritable ranks and aristocracies, and taught all the Christian populations of the earth to bow down to them and worship them" (*Yankee* 67).

But chief of all villains is God himself, who violates the pain economy with a consistency unequaled by any other. God, who allegedly controls even the minutest elements of human life, nonetheless allows miserable misfortune —poverty, illness, and violent accident—to befall his "children." And despite this behavior, he garners unmitigated worship, damning any who refuse to give it to an eternity of suffering.

When Twain's precocious Little Bessie asks her mother why there is suffering in the world, her mother replies: "It is for our good, my child. In His wisdom and mercy the Lord sends us these afflictions to discipline us and make us better" ("Little Bessie" 864). Yet the mother's examples of God's justice show one person suffering for the crime of another, a sinner dying without the opportunity to reform, and the doer of good acts punished. When measured in the pain economy, the actions of this God appear unjust and reprehensible.

Twain does the accounting on God's abuses. His audit centers on the problem of disproportion: "He is always punishing—punishing trifling misdeeds with thousandfold severity" ("Reflections" 332). Twain increases the offense to "ten-thousand fold" and "ten-billionfold," never doubting that God could stop hurting human beings if he wanted to. But he doesn't want to, because—despite relentless torment—God is worshipped by his victims. It is the cardinal sin of the pain economy. Over and over—throughout his autobiographical dictations, in *Letters from the Earth*, "Little Bessie," the Mysterious Stranger tales, and countless other examples—Twain returns to the figure of an unfair (and therefore immoral) deity. Twain never exhausted his supply of indignation on that account.

But Twain's attention on the sins of others does not distract him from his own. Even as he strives to find a source of moral failing outside of himself—in a God who has invented a conscience-riddled but morally weak human creature, for instance—Twain cannot shake his sense of guilt for his personal sins (Quirk 243). Twain knew that he lacked God's cosmic power, but he feared that he shared God's character. Even W. D. Howells, whose *My Mark Twain* is the epitome of loving apologism, had to acknowledge Twain's attraction to self-accusation: "At the last day he will not have to confess anything, for all his life was the free knowledge of any one who would ask him of it. The Searcher of hearts will not bring him to shame at that day, for he did not try to hide any of the things for which he was often so bitterly sorry" (100). Although Howells paints Twain's self-condemnation as a virtue, it is easy to spot Twain's masochistic tendencies. Twain's identification with the sins of his villains gives him one advantage: knowing their tricks and their weaknesses and having suffered for them, he is well positioned to punish. Deleuze explains that, once having suffered punishment, a person becomes able to practice the "evil" once criticized by their submission (39). Twain will punish his villains, but the disciplinarian's role is tainted. Only a sinner may wield the whip.

And sinner he was. Reminiscing on his childhood, Twain reports that he was beaten twice by his father, "once for telling him a lie—which surprised me, and showed me how unsuspicious he was, for that was not my maiden effort" (*Equator* 642). Twain lied incessantly; he would never equivocate on this point. It was important to him to be worthy of his pain. For this self-proclaimed sinner, the pain economy was a necessity. How else could he repay his debt? He wasn't about to stop sinning.

Twain giddily anticipates the impending payback for his violations, and he surrenders himself to the pain economy through his writing. Tom Quirk notes that over the years Twain moved from retelling other people's stories to using his own life as a text to be analyzed and edited (222). The way that Twain uses his own character to chastise the human race, the way that he treats his life as a text to be picked apart and plagiarized, puts him into the dual position of disciplined subject *and* disciplinarian. When Twain makes himself a subject of his humorous writing, he is literally subjected by his own text. Michel Foucault observes that the case report of a disciplined subject, unlike the detailed biography of a hero, leaves the person objectified and regulated (203). It is a powerful act of self-division. "A comic character is never fully identified with his role," explains Slavoj Zizek; "he always retains the ability to observe himself from outside: 'making fun of himself'" (54–55). Thus, Twain paradoxically plays both parts in the masochistic scene: top and bottom.

Mark Twain repeatedly enacted the pain–pleasure exchange on his authorial body. Recounting his days as a cub pilot trying to memorize the ever-shifting river in *Life on the Mississippi*, Twain offers himself as the vessel for the full gamut of human emotion: mental anguish, triumph, and disillusionment. Suffering abuse at the hands of the pugnacious Mr. Bixby, the young man eventually learns his trade, but not without great cost. He now knew "the language of this water . . . [b]ut I had lost something, too. I had lost something which could never be restored to me while I lived. All the grace, the beauty, the poetry, had gone out of the majestic river!" (119).

Contained within his authorial body, Twain's pain is under control. He can earn and spend his pain in measured amounts. In *Innocents Abroad*, Twain subjects himself to the Parisian barber's chair, which he once imagined to be the height of luxury. It is not, of course. What profit could the author find in telling of a pleasant shave? Instead, Twain dwells on the agony of his experience in vivid detail: "The first rake of his razor loosened the very hide from my face and lifted me out of the chair. I stormed and raved, and the other boys enjoyed it" (114). His body becomes a comedic sacrifice, though hardly sinless. If it were, the economy would be stalled at his martyrdom, and the enjoyment of his comrades would be reprehensible. Here, they (and we) are not villains but investors.

There are no passive observers permitted in Twain's masochistic scene. We must participate. In one of his earliest self-inflicted pain experiments, Twain agrees to take a tonic called the "wake-up-Jake" at a natural springs resort. Dizzying nausea is followed by twelve hours of ceaseless vomiting, diarrhea, and nosebleeds. It bears asking why the writer undertakes his awful experiment in the first place. Twain explains, "I was not aware that I had any use for the wonderful 'wake-up,' but then I felt it to be my duty to try it, *in order that a suffering public might profit by my experience*—and I would cheerfully see that public suffer perdition before I would try it again" ("Letter from Steamboat Springs" 35, my italics). The narrator begrudges his sacrifice, but his experiment has been a success: he has traded in his tale of pain for the benefit of his audience. He will gladly let them pay for the next round, however.

If we are willing to accept our villainy, our punishment, and our debt, as Twain does, then our guilt and our pain may be transformed through humor, paid in cash, or redeemed as righteousness. Treating himself as the quintessential human being, full of greed and selfish drives, vulnerable to his own training and inborn nature, both sympathetic and damnable, Twain shows us how to capitalize on our pain, our sin, and our punishment. Unable to resist, Twain is drawn, and draws us, into the scene where he finds his creative energy in navigating the commerce between pleasure and pain.

Notes

1. This phrase bears an unintended (though not totally unwelcome or meaningless) resemblance to W. D. Howells's "economy of pain" (from *The Rise of Silas Lapham*). Although this chapter will explore the pain economy in Twain's writing exclusively, Twain did not come to his opinions about pain in isolation. I leave the door open to those who would draw Twain into conversation about pain, morality, and justice with other writers of his time.

2. By "his own experience," I refer to Mark Twain's experiences as they occur on the page or in relation to the text. "Mark Twain"—as opposed to Samuel Clemens—is a creature of the text, a literary being, and I refer to this aspect of the author, not necessarily the correlative "real-life" experience (though, of course, those biographical experiences often factor into the text).

Works Cited

Clemens, Clara. *My Father, Mark Twain*. 1931. New York: Harper, 1976.

Cowan, Lyn. *Masochism: A Jungian View*. 1982. Foreword by Jay Livernois. Woodstock: Spring, 1997.

Critchley, Simon. *On Humour*. London: Routledge, 2002.

Deleuze, Gilles. *Masochism: Coldness and Cruelty* and *Venus in Furs*. Rev. ed., New York: Zone, 1991.

Foucault, Michel. *The Foucault Reader*. Ed. Paul Rabinow. New York: Pantheon, 1984.

Freud, Sigmund. *The Joke and Its Relation to the Unconscious*. 1905. Trans. Joyce Crick. New York: Penguin, 2003.

Fulton, Joe B. *The Reverend Mark Twain*. Columbus: Ohio State UP, 2006.

Haidt, Jonathan. *The Righteous Mind: Why Good People Are Divided by Politics and Religion*. New York: Pantheon, 2012.

Hill, Hamlin. *Mark Twain and Elisha Bliss*. Columbia: U of Missouri P, 1964.

Howells, W. D. *My Mark Twain: Reminiscences and Criticisms*. New York: Harper, 1910. Rpt. *Open Library*. Web. 2 November 2011.

Keller, Helen. *Midstream: My Later Life*. Westport: Greenwood, 1929.

Krauth, Leland. *Proper Mark Twain*. Athens: U of Georgia P, 1999.

Morreall, John. "A New Theory of Laughter." *Philosophical Studies: An International Journal for Philosophy in the Analytic Tradition*. 42.2 (September 1982): 243–54. *JSTOR*. Web. 22 May 2012.

Newmahr, Staci. *Playing on the Edge: Sadomasochism, Risk, and Intimacy*. Bloomington: Indiana UP, 2011.

Quirk, Tom. *Mark Twain and Human Nature*. Columbia: U of Missouri P, 2007.

Robinson, Forrest G., ed. *The Cambridge Companion to Mark Twain*. Cambridge: Cambridge UP, 1995.

———. "The Innocent at Large: Mark Twain's Travel Writing." Robinson, *Cambridge Companion*: 27–51.

Schmitz, Neil. "Mark Twain's Civil War: Humor's Reconstructive Writing." Robinson, *Cambridge Companion*: 74–92.

Twain, Mark. *Adventures of Huckleberry Finn*. 1885. Ed. Victor Fischer and Lin Salamo. Berkeley: U of California P, 2001.

———. *Autobiography of Mark Twain: The Complete and Authorized Edition*. 3 vols. Ed. Harriet Elinor Smith et al. Berkeley: U of California P, 2010, 2012, 2015.

———. *A Connecticut Yankee in King Arthur's Court*. 1889. Ed. Bernard L. Stein. Berkeley: U of California P, 1983.

———. "Down the Rhône." 1891–92. *Mark Twain: A Tramp Abroad . . . Other Travels*. 1003–29.

———. *Following the Equator*. 1897. *Mark Twain: A Tramp Abroad . . . Other Travels*. 404–882.

———. "Goldsmith's Friend Abroad Again." 1870. *Mark Twain: Collected Tales . . . 1852–1890*, 1:455–70.

——— "Letter from Steamboat Springs." 1863. *Mark Twain: Collected Tales . . . 1852–1890*, 1:32–36.

———. *Life on the Mississippi*. 1883. New York: Oxford UP, 1996.

———. "Little Bessie" *Mark Twain: Collected Tales . . . 1891–1910*. 2:864–74.

———. *The Love Letters of Mark Twain*. Ed. Dixon Wecter. New York: Harper, 1949.

———. "The Man That Corrupted Hadleyburg." 1899. *Mark Twain: Collected Tales . . . 1891–1910*, 2:390–438.

———. *Mark Twain: A Tramp Abroad, Following the Equator, Other Travels*. Ed. Roy Blount, Jr. New York: Library of America, 2010.

———. *Mark Twain: Collected Tales, Sketches, Speeches, & Essays, 1852–1890*. 2 vols. Ed. Louis J. Budd. New York: Library of America, 1992.

———. "My First Lie and How I Got Out of It." 1899. *Mark Twain: Collected Tales . . . 1891–1910*. 439–46.

———. "My Military History." 1877. *Mark Twain: Collected Tales . . . 1852–1890*. 679–82.

———. "A Mysterious Visit." 1870. *Mark Twain: Collected Tales . . . 1852–1890*. 1:340–44.

———. "The New Dynasty." *Mark Twain: Collected Tales . . . 1852–1890*. 883–90.

———. "Reflections on Religion." Ed. Charles Neider. *Hudson Review* 16.3 (1963): 329–52. *JSTOR*. Web. 17 June 2013.

———. "The Revised Catechism." 1871. *Mark Twain: Collected Tales . . . 1852–1890*. 539–40.

———. *Roughing It*. Hartford: American, 1872. *Project Gutenberg*. Web. 24 August 2012.

———. *What Is Man?* 1906. *Mark Twain: Collected Tales . . . 1891–1910*. 731–804.

Zizek, Slavoj. "The Christian–Hegelian Comedy." *When Humour Becomes Painful*. Ed. Felicity Lunn and Heike Munder. Zürich: JRP|Ringier, 2006. 53–58.

9
Minstrel Economics

Mark Twain, the San Francisco Minstrels, and Folk Investment in the American Dream

Sharon D. McCoy

> First class in modern Moral Philosophy stand up and recite: What is the chief end of man?
> A. To get rich.
>
> In what way?
> A. Dishonestly if we can; honestly if we must.
> —Mark Twain, "The Revised Catechism"

> Mr. Addison Ryman in the good old days of the San Francisco Minstrels used to give advice to young men on the threshold of life. "What does Mr. Samuel J. Tilden say? Make your money honestly, young man; and if you can't make it honestly—go into railroads."
> —Kenneth Ackerman, *Boss Tweed*

During the postbellum era, Mark Twain's writings increasingly explore how economic class and social aspirations intertwine with racial identity in American culture. Not coincidentally, those writings also increasingly incorporate aspects of blackface minstrel masking into their economic, political, and moral satire. Though intensely polarizing from its beginnings, the blackface stage remained one of the only venues in nineteenth-century American culture—and the minstrel mask one of the only tropes—in which issues of race, class, ethnicity, and cross-cultural fear and fascination were all held in simultaneous and ambivalent focus. These possibilities in minstrelsy attracted young Samuel Clemens from the first show he saw in Hannibal as a boy (*Autobiography* 2:296). Yet Twain's increasingly nuanced and complex satiric uses of minstrel masking are traceable to the commercial and critical success of the San Francisco Minstrels (SFM), a (white) blackface troupe he knew in both San Francisco and New York City. The SFM developed a signature satiric performance style in response to the particular economic, moral, and racially inflected anxieties of the postwar generation, celebrating economic aspirations while exposing cultural pretension and political and financial corruption.[1] When the Panic of 1873 stretched into a "long-wave" economic depression that clearly presaged the end of federal Reconstruction,[2] their satire intensified. At this time Mark Twain developed a parallel satiric use of blackface minstrel masking in his own work. His minstrel mask is similar to the SFM's in its topical focus, its multiple and often conflicting satiric targets, and its sympathy with both poverty and aspirations for economic advancement. Yet Twain also grounds his use of the minstrel mask in a more firmly fixed moral vision and in his growing preoccupation with the role of history in current economic and social conditions. Further, the substantial financial success of both Mark Twain and the SFM confirmed ideals of American meritocracy as well as the economic aspirations of their audiences, whose collective patronage constituted the tangible financial foundation of that success.

Nothing but "Trouble": Topical Satire, Minstrel Masking, and Money

The San Francisco Minstrels' particular use of the blackface mask was something new when they burst on the New York City scene in May 1865. Out West the SFM had developed a topical improvisational style exposing absurdity and economic corruption in local and national politics. In the more cosmopolitan, multicultural, and densely urban environment of New York City, where opulent mansions existed cheek-by-jowl with "crowded pens of slaughter" (Ryman 6–7), tenements housing thousands in a single city block, the SFM gave free rein to their irreverence. Rather than relying on old jokes or stale blackface conundrums, they improvised commentary on current events and local matters. Their closing numbers were almost exclusively farces and original skits, mocking the upper-class pretense and economic dominance of the legitimate theater, while incorporating "hits" on political or economic corruption. A popular and recurring number was the "Anvil Chorus," essentially a drinking song from *Il Trovatore*, deflating the "high-brow" pretensions of opera. Other skits such as "The Dying Brigand" and "Arrah Na Pogue" took on luminaries of the legitimate stage such as playwrights James Robinson Planché and Dion Boucicault, mocking their efforts to expose the corruption of the rich and powerful in faraway, exotic settings. Such plays offered great opportunity for the improvised "hits" on local affairs or politics that were the SFM's trademark, with plenty of melodrama ripe for parody (Harvard programs 8 May 1865–29 May 1867).[3] The skit "English Capitalists on a Lark" mocked a British lecture group then on a lucrative tour of the United States. Other farces celebrated local haunts, such as "Scenes in Gotham" or "Troubles at the Metropolitan Hotel,"[4] putting attainable and recognizable locations on a level with exotic, expensive, or pretentious stage settings (Harvard programs 1865–1868). Pretense that separated the "upper" economic and social classes from the "lower" was challenged again and again on their stage.

Nor did the SFM neglect the economics of racial identity. In nineteenth-century America, constructions of "race" were largely about money and competition.[5] During the postbellum years, for the first time in United States history, legally sanctioned slavery was no longer a fundamental force in the national economy, and seats of power among the wealthiest had shifted.[6] Millions of previously unpaid African American workers were poised to enter the labor force, escalating fears of competition among the existing multiethnic working classes. New York's own institution of slavery had ended in 1827, resulting in an influx of freed men and women to the city seeking work and new lives. While there was significant racial mixing among the lower classes, there had also been decades of intensifying economic and racial tension, particularly between freed people and new immigrants. Increasingly violent rioting, culminating in the horrific Draft Riots of 1863, resulted in a mass exodus of African Americans from New York City. During these years, blackface minstrel performances had incorporated increasingly stereotypical and derogatory "delineations" of African Americans. In contrast, when the San Francisco Minstrels arrived after the war, they showcased Charley Backus as their "delineator," or impersonator. His dead-on imitations, however, were of actors, politicians, local celebrities, or people who'd had the misfortune to provoke his ire. In their performances the SFM ambivalently exposed many African American stereotypes as masking *performances*, as competitive strategies for getting ahead in a largely white-controlled world, but also with distinctly lower- and upper-class white parallels. For example, their song "The Dandy Colored Waiters" presents African Americans in a service role but reveals that they "answer ev'ry bell and call" not because they are naturally servile, but rather, like any worker, only "for the money that it brings" (Dumont 2; McCoy "Trouble" 241–42).

New York City embraced their novelty and topical relevance. In their first two months at 585 Broadway, the SFM racked up receipts of $14,970 ($221,000 today),[7] or almost one-third of what the most successful blackface minstrel company in the city, Bryant's Minstrels, had made in the previous thirteen months ("Receipts" 139).[8] When Mark Twain arrived in New York City in 1867, he marveled at and reveled in his compatriots' success. He gleefully reported to his *Alta California* readers, "Our old San Francisco Minstrels have made their mark here, most unquestionably," and that their receipts for the previous year [1866] were "only a fraction under $110,000" ($1.67 million today). They played to packed houses with "dozens" standing every night (*Mark Twain's Travels with Mr. Brown* [*MTTB*] 167). Twain noted that "wisely they try to keep up with the spirit of the times" and that "they deserve a continuance of their success" (*MTTB* 167).

The San Francisco Minstrels and their audiences fully agreed. Even during the economic hard times of 1873 and 1874—when almost 25 percent of the city's labor force was unemployed (Barreyre 408–9; Wineapple 475–503), and almost half of all other minstrel troupes disbanded or went bankrupt (Toll 149; Wittke 89; Estavan 7)—the SFM thrived, traveling around the region for part of the year while constructing an opulent new "opera house," paid for with capital they'd earned through their performances (*New York Tribune* 24 June 1883: 4). Their theater opened on 3 September 1874, after a "social view" celebration with "champagne and salads" to which "friends" of the SFM were invited (*NYT* 3 Sept 1874: 8). Their "new hall" was located several blocks uptown of the Park Theatre, where Twain's play *Colonel Sellers* would open later that same month, a challenge they did not ignore. Their attention to the "spirit of the times" made them one of the most successful residential troupes in New York City until 1883, when Charley Backus died and the company dissolved.

This "spirit" was also one in which Mark Twain found reliable capital for his own voice, impelling his satiric persona to new heights in his lectures, speeches, periodical pieces, and books. Unlike the SFM, however, whose choice of the blackface mask as their métier meant that their satire was always explicitly racially inflected, Twain did not turn his attention to the particular and specifically racial aspects of that "spirit" until 1874. His play *Colonel Sellers*, discussed more specifically in the chapter's third section, presented the African American character of "Uncle Dan'l" in a sharper satiric vein than in his novel *The Gilded Age*. That 1873 collaboration with Charles Dudley Warner was written before the Panic, the market crash, and the beginning of the depression, all of which led inexorably to the dismantling of Reconstruction. These events altered Twain's vision of the economic basis of racial politics, and in his stage play he began to explore a blackface masking comparable to the SFM's.

Further, the highbrow literary acceptance and popularity of his "A True Story," published in the November 1874 *Atlantic Monthly*, revealed avenues through which Twain could meld his desire for literary accolades and financial success with the satiric blackface tradition and its ambivalent and always economically inflected consideration of African American presence in American society. In response to the narrator's callow and callous remark to a servant that she has "lived sixty years and never had any trouble" (591), "Aunt Rachel" explicitly decides to let "Misto C—" (and Twain's readers) glimpse the personal anguish behind the servant's laughing minstrel mask. In doing so, she also exposes the narrator's obtuse hypocrisy and his unconscious collusion with and culpability in the system that continues to overlook or fetishize her anguish and her laughter. Yet Twain moves the story from a didactic morality tale into open and ambivalent satire by his break with the traditional frame narrative, giving "Aunt Rachel" the last word. This strategy elevates "Aunt Rachel," even as she moves from "sitting respectfully below" her white employers to standing "tower[ing] above" them (592), allowing her to break free of the narrator's commentary and emphasize her complexity as a fellow human being distinct from her economic racial position. Immediately after she sings God's praises at her reunion with her long-lost son who was sold away from her many years before, she exclaims with pointed irony: "Oh, no, Misto C—, *I* hain't had no trouble. An' no *joy!*" (594). Giving "Aunt Rachel" the last word, however, also allows the narrator and his equally culpable white readership to move out of the spotlight and out of "trouble"—exposed for a moment, yet slipping safely behind *their* mask once more, freed from the responsibility of commenting on or reacting to her revelations.

Clemens's move to the East in 1867 and his 1870 marriage to Olivia Langdon, the daughter of Jervis Langdon, a committed abolitionist and successful businessman, had brought him in intimate contact with wealth, high social status, and a fresh view of moral and family responsibility. That new life also brought him back in close contact with African American servants and the oral culture, humor, and music that had so attracted him as a youth in a slaveholding society. While there are elements of nostalgia or condescension in his backward glances, they exist side by side with scathing satire and a new moral lens focused on slavery, history, continuing societal hypocrisy, and economic inequity. But more, they reveal a mature view of the ambivalent and sometimes ambiguous interactions across shifting lines of race, social status, economic class, and family. This consistent—and consistently ambivalent—moral core, intertwined with a serious consideration of the implications of history in current events, distinguishes Twain's use of the blackface mask from that of the SFM, whose improvisational style and stage performance responded more immediately to their audience's multiple and often conflicting reactions. Yet the sheer chaotic exuberance of the satiric performer and jester remains constant, as both use the mask to ambivalently and ironically unmask pretense or corruption.

Thus, Mark Twain and the San Francisco Minstrels developed parallel yet distinct satiric voices with an ever-present but often conflicted and submerged moral core. They utilized the blackface minstrel mask in direct response to the economic, social, moral, and political anxieties—and particularly, the ambivalence or multiple perspectives—of their Gilded Age audiences. For those audiences were as varied as their targets. Twain chose subscription publishing for his books with ambivalent deliberation, concerned about the cheaper quality of the books and the dismissive attitudes of highbrow literary reviewers, yet attracted to its income potential and its broad audience base.[9] His performances, forays into playwriting, and periodical pieces all worked to further expand that audience. He wrote for "the masses" rather than "the cultivated classes" (Paine 895) and also believed that his works were like "water" rather than "wine": low, high, or in between, "[e]verybody drinks water" (*Mark Twain's Notebooks and Journals* 238).

The SFM, too, drew their audiences from a broad swath of society. Along with audiences one might expect at blackface performances, the SFM's pulse on local affairs and their parodies of expensive theatrical productions attracted families (Knapp 20; Jones 348), Wall Street brokers (Smith 85), and even some of the public figures whose corruption they exposed but whose rags-to-riches successes they might have celebrated. "Jubilee Jim" Fisk, Jr., for example, was a fairly frequent audience member (Jones 348), at least until his role was known in the attempted corner of the gold market that resulted in the "Black Friday" of 1869. Other public figures seemed less enchanted with their satiric presentation on the blackface stage, reputedly responding occasionally with death threats that the minstrels then shared gleefully with their audiences (Estavan 170–71). Even into the last years of his life, and decades after the SFM had stopped performing, Twain regarded their signature blackface minstrelsy as something unique (*AMT* 2:293–94). Throughout their performance career, he apparently reveled in sharing "Trouble" with the San Francisco Minstrels.[10] Each in their own way, they raised a distinctive voice that spoke to and for large numbers of people in the postwar generations.

And they made a hell of a lot of money doing it.

"How Much Capital Will We Want?": Ephemeral Investments, Intangible Value, and Cold, Hard Cash

Economic opportunity was and is central to social mobility in the United States—a cornerstone of the republic's political ideal of meritocracy and exceptionalism. Early religious conviction emphasized a strong work ethic and promoted the idea that success was a mark of God's favor. Secular belief held that hard work and wise investment would eventually receive their reward. While there was always an element of chance—a gamble, a risk—that acknowledged not everyone received his due, the potential positive rewards and the possibility of attaining them have intrinsic value. Yet the American focus on economic advancement presents an ethical dilemma as well as an ideal. The very belief in its value creates tremendous opportunities for chicanery and corruption. Advancement itself is partly measured by those who remain beneath and who are hired (or, in the antebellum years, often purchased) to serve the advancing class. Uneven distribution of wealth, though, results in social crises. Yet the reform movements that arise cyclically to address these inequities also work to restore belief in the fundamental moral core of the ideal itself. While there are certainly corrupt men of wealth and power, Gilded Age audiences saw nothing inherently corrupt about being wealthy or making money. This central ambivalence is frequently characterized as a contradiction or hypocritical stance,[11] but both Twain and the San Francisco Minstrels understood it as a fundamental part of American character, crucial in national ideals of opportunity and social mobility.

Criticizing corruption or decrying the loss of other moral values in the single-minded pursuit of wealth did not mean that economic advancement itself was at fault. Economic advancement was (and remains) a positive social good in American society. The key was character, and balance. People still believed in the Gilded Age, as a writer in *Harper's New Monthly Magazine* had expressed it during the prewar years, that with "judgment, fortitude," and "fidelity," wise and "practical" men could still find success without "shame." At heart, the nation maintained a belief that "character is the best part of capital" ("Freaks of Fortune" 348–49). And this is key in both Twain's and the SFM's successes: they celebrated the ideals of economic and social advancement and meritocracy while savagely critiquing excesses and corruption. In doing so, they established themselves as men of character in an era when character was sorely needed.

Growing political and economic scandals marked the postwar years. New avenues of credit, technological advances, and the rise of corporations that were intertwined with national and international political interests created a bewildering investment environment that seemed impossible to predict or assess. A strong sense of character was harder to discern or maintain.

In Twain's 1871 "Revised Catechism," he argues that earlier generations had the "models" of Washington or Franklin to emulate. Washington had been a wealthy man of good Virginia stock, and Franklin a man who had risen from humble beginnings to gain great wealth and power by his own industry, ingenuity, and invention. They were men of character, and men of character must still exist. Yet the fidelity to previous generations was severely tested, Twain argued, because the new role "models" were corrupt politicians and financiers like William "Boss" Tweed, Jay Gould, James Fisk, and a dozen others whom Twain specifically names. As the "disciples" of money worship, they found the rewards of great wealth at the expense of ordinary people. Twain's "Catechism" moves out of the social and political realm to focus on the central moral dilemma: "Money is God," Twain wrote. "Gold and greenbacks and stock—father, son, and the ghost of the same: these are the true and only God, mighty and supreme" (6).

Twain's satire in the "Catechism" offers no resolution, yet it recasts the economic questions splitting the nation into their fundamental moral terms, showing tangible value (gold), distribution of wealth (greenbacks, or paper currency), and ephemeral speculation (stocks) all as parts of the same moral challenge to the nation. Money itself was not the problem, nor was political debate about its form the solution, so long as men invested it with deified status. Twain's point in his "Catechism" proves prophetic, particularly after the Panic of 1873. For the next two and a half decades, both political parties would focus national economic debates on the basis of currency—an economic debate framed in moral terms. Yet they never addressed the central moral crisis that the "Catechism" reveals. For "soft-money" (paper currency) advocates, the shift to an exclusive gold standard or "specie payment" seemed to be a direct attack on the people hit hardest by the crisis, the poor and working classes. Yet to "hard-money" advocates, the ephemeral world of investment value, credit, and paper currency itself seemed immoral. Twain ends his piece by asking, "Do we progress?" His answer is: "You bet your life!"—and signed with the assurance "Yours truly, Mark Twain." When "Money is God," it all becomes a gamble, a game of chance, with odds stacked by the house, demanding the highest possible stakes.

While Twain's satire here is specific and pointed, he had not yet begun to mine the racial aspects of the fundamental economic crises of his age. He does not mention that Washington had been a slaveowner, nor does he consider that human beings were chattel sacrificed on the altar of his economic trinity, challenging the previous generation's fidelity. In contrast, the San Francisco Minstrels' response to the specie/greenback crisis is characteristically racially inflected, chaotic, and contradictory, the multiple targets of their satire reflecting the multiple beliefs, classes, and ambivalence of their audiences. Their "Specie Payment: Song and Chorus for the Times" by George Cooper and Harry Miller, enters the debate with apparent celebration:

> Ring the bells, and beat the drum!
> Shake your neighbor's hand today!
> Good old times will surely come,
> —Oh, how long they've been away!

Yet in the midst of the celebration, they proclaim, "Gold and silver take 'a drop,'" referring to Jay Gould's and James Fisk, Jr.'s attempted corner of the gold market in 1869, which exacerbated political debates over the gold or silver standard for currency versus the circulation of paper money. Foiled by President Grant, though, it is "Not a 'drop too much,'" offering a pun on the dizzy, drunken fervor of the times. They proclaim that "Wall Street's going to shut up shop," anticipating the New York Stock Exchange's closure during the 1873 Panic. And while advocates of specie payment might enjoy this celebration, paper currency advocates in their audience can take the same lines ironically, for the next verse reveals that it all matters little anyway: "'Taxes' now will end the strife," because they will "wreak [*sic*] us in a year," regardless.

Corruption on multiple levels leaves ordinary people unsure where to turn or how to judge the confusing and conflicting events:

> Jimmy Fisk his match has found,
> Long has he been 'raising Cain'!
> Female Brokers bro't it round!
> Specie payment's come again!

The minstrel stage rarely presented "raising Cain" as purely negative behavior, though it is central to the shifting ground of race and violence. Numerous blackface routines throughout the century claimed the "mark of Cain" as being either whiteness or blackness,[12] but both versions reveal the violent consequences of uneven favor in God's preference of Abel over Cain: the undervalued have the power to strike back. Thus, Fisk's unbridled past, his finding a "match" in a government itself marked by scandal and corruption, and the swipe at brokers as being "Female" reveal marked, chaotic ambivalence. The "Bulls and Bears" of Wall Street are "in a rage!" the minstrels sing; their imperative "Let them fight it out alone" reflects both the rough-and-tumble "frisky" masculinity of the brokers ("Hazing" 55), and the often corrupt but hopeful confusion of ephemeral investments.

Political interests take their "hits" as well, as President Grant's motivations in blocking the gold corner and restoring specie payment are not altruistic, for now he "will 'buy' young Cuba." The minstrels ask, "[D]on't it make your fingers tingle?" Their cheery proclamation that it is once again "the year of jubilee" invokes the sense of hope, freedom, and healing that Grant brought to the Union at the close of the war, particularly for the formerly enslaved. But these lines also articulate betrayal in the face of his administration's growing scandals and the resulting economic hard times for working people of all races. The minstrels draw on the trope of the blackface mask to express the oscillating hope and disillusionment of ordinary folk in the face of political and financial machinations beyond their control—and the only possible response to both: painful laughter.

"There's Millions in It!": Attraction to Wealth and the Satiric Exposure of Corruption

Such concerns also drive the satire of Twain's 1873 collaboration with Charles Dudley Warner, *The Gilded Age*, so effectively that the novel's title quickly came to characterize their era. But Twain's use of the blackface tropes within the novel draws more on an older, nostalgic, and condescending use of the blackface mask in its presentation of racial issues and African American characters. Slavery and its aftermath are only mildly touched on, mostly in terms of one of Colonel Sellers's early failed schemes, to corner the slave market (27–28), and the central political scandal, the land appropriation scheme that is exposed in one of Twain's chapters as "the great 'Negro University Swindle'" (394). The only difference in the novel's postwar world is which "friends" of African Americans benefit from their sale.

African American characters themselves are used solely for pathos or comic relief and pass quickly out of the novel. "Aunt Jinny" is named only once (35), and at other times simply designated as the "negro woman," whose presence shows "shiftlessness and poverty" (23). Uncle Dan'l is played for laughs when the Hawkins family—white and black—are frightened by their first encounter with a steamboat. Hearing its sounds, Dan'l believes that it is the Lord come for judgment and at first offers himself in sacrifice to save the children (35–37). Yet when the steamboat's nature is revealed, Dan'l still "prays" for them all but also abandons his wife and the white children who are their charges, going "so far" into the woods to pray "that he doubted, himself, if the Lord heard him" (40). "Uncle Dan'l" refers to himself as "ole Uncle Daniel" (40), exposing the shortened version of his name as the narrator's and his owners' condescension rather than as an expression of African American dialect. Yet that is the limit of Twain's exposure of racial stereotype: the rest of the satire is all at Daniel's expense. When the Hawkinses fall on hard times, Uncle Dan'l and his wife "pass from the auction-block into the hands of the negro trader to depart for the remote South," and we are told that it "had seemed like seeing their own flesh and blood sold" (78). Yet, unlike in "A True Story," we don't feel anything of the sort. The pathos is perfunctory, with no real sense of loss or horror at the threat of "the remote South" that will haunt Twain's later works. The sale simply functions to show how far the Hawkins family has fallen economically, and perhaps morally.

The character of Uncle Dan'l in the stage play *Colonel Sellers* is still marginal, but a bit more complex, revelatory of Twain's growing sense of racially inflected satiric possibilities. The connection to blackface, too, is overt. Uncle Dan'l's character on stage would be played by a "legitimate" actor in blackface, and the play's New York City opening would be a few blocks from the San Francisco Minstrels' new hall. Twain's play opened at the Park Theatre in New York City on 16 September 1874, and ran for 119 performances, closing on 9 January 1875. Revived multiple times nationally and internationally before star John T. Raymond's death in 1888 (Loving 207), the play eventually earned Twain about $100,000, or $2.1 million today (Thomason and Quirk 112).[13] Appropriations, bonds, railroads, and investment still represent both hope and corruption in the play. Laura Hawkins's betrayal, political machinations, and trial for murder still form the skeleton of the plot, but the piece is propelled almost exclusively by the character of Colonel Sellers, whose first name is no longer the high-falutin' Eschol or Beriah, as in the first and second editions of the novel, but is now simply Mulberry. Played exclusively by actor Raymond, Mulberry Sellers won the hearts of his audiences as a believable character, who had close parallels in their families, friends, or acquaintances. Audiences, in short, recognized him. The play itself was criticized as structurally weak, and many of the other actors were judged inadequate. A few other performers in the show, however, including Mr. John H. Burnett, the actor who played Uncle Dan'l in blackface makeup, also received positive special mention (Wheeler 650).[14] Unlike in the novel, the blackface stage character is intimately intertwined in the play's satire and moral ambivalence.

From his first appearance on stage, Uncle Dan'l stammers (114), but he is less gullible and more assertive than in the novel. Before the steamboat draws near, Dan'l is already telling the children to "behave" themselves in "a strange country," establishing himself firmly as adult and as their protector: "You stick right clos' to me, don't be afeared, I'se wid you" (116). When they hear the steamboat coming, he regales them with a story of his own fight with "the debbil"—actions that presage the character of Jim in *Adventures of Huckleberry Finn*. And while Dan'l and the children run as the steamboat approaches, the stage directions say simply and without comment: "Dan'l & Children run off the stage." When the Hawkinses' adopted adult son Clay chides Dan'l for his fear, Dan'l contradicts him assertively: "How can you talk dat way to me Mars Clay, I isn't fraid o'nothin." Further, he reminds Clay that the young children are safe *because* he is with them. When Clay responds, contritely or not, that he "forgot," Dan'l says comically, but also with certainty, "I should tink you did forgot sum'fin" (116–17).

Though in both the novel and the stage production, Dan'l provokes amusement, the Dan'l of the play also stands up for the children and himself, and talks back to the young white man. Significantly, when the steamboat race gets out of hand, it is Dan'l who brings Sellers's attention to the fact that ruin is upon him: "Oh, Mars Sellers, what is dis? a whoopin and a tearin down the river —" (119). Dan'l here is not ascribing supernatural significance to the boats, as in the novel. Rather than simply embodying a stereotype of racial superstition, here he is calling Sellers's attention to their wildly reckless behavior and the Colonel's own limitations. The Colonel is too sanguine to worry and at first says confidently that the race will "amuse" his friends. Yet the act closes with Sellers's ruin, for the *Amaranth*, in which Sellers has invested "all [his] capital" (115), is destroyed in the ensuing explosion. Too, the dramatic and explosive end of this act is reminiscent of the climaxes to many of the San Francisco Minstrels' farces, which often dropped the curtain after an extraordinary, chaotic, thrilling, and frankly dangerous indoor show of fireworks and explosions.

Unlike the Dan'l of the novel, who with his wife is sold to the horrors of slavery in the Deep South, the play's Dan'l stays with the family throughout all their trials, even after the war. When Laura falls to the wiles of the unscrupulous and "unreconstructed" Colonel George Selby, she lies to her mother in order to continue seeing him. It is not until Dan'l also expresses concern, though, that Laura starts to have doubts herself. When Selby arrives Dan'l says to Laura, "Miss Laura de war's ober, an I'se only a free niggah now, but if you says so I'll tell Mars Selby, you ain't at home." And without waiting for an answer, he proceeds, "'Deed I'll tell him—," at which point Laura has to interrupt and protest that she will see Selby. But as Dan'l exits, she expresses her first real sense of uncertainty in an aside: "Even Uncle Dan'l is uneasy!" (123). The African American character, or "the Africanist presence," as Toni Morrison puts it in *Playing in the Dark*, is used as a sort of moral compass at the extremes (6, 54–57). Dan'l, now free and apparently unmarried but still working for the family, is still willing to protect her, to lie to the unreconstructed and aristocratic southern gentleman on her behalf. Laura, who feels condescension rather than family ties or mutual interest in her relations with Dan'l (a moral marker), is nonetheless taken aback that "even" he is concerned about Selby's motives and wants to shield her from them.

It is in this very different context that the play introduces the land appropriation scheme for the freedmen's university. Unlike in the novel, the play's Colonel Sellers is actually in favor of the underlying idea. He assures Laura that he now feels that they should "let bygones be bygones: I'm reconstructed and I go in for the old flag, and an appropriation" (126). The latter part of his statement reveals that his commitment to the new government order is economically based and personally interested. He follows what is in his own best interests, and while there is some sting in this, it is also understandable in terms of the climate of economic morality in the Gilded Age. Unlike Laura, Mulberry Sellers is not exclusively self-interested, however. Sellers's attitudes are more sympathetic in his stage presentation, and he exclaims without apparent irony, "This glorious union has set the Negro free," and now the next step is to "[e]ducate him—Make him a skilled workman." The Hawkins family and Sellers have the Tennessee land, perfect for the project, and they will be happy to "Let Congress buy it" (128).

While Sellers clearly expects to benefit, on his own behalf and that of his friends, there is less dishonesty in his character than in the novel, less deliberate calculation and callousness toward African Americans, who remain, nonetheless, tangential to his interest. In comparison, we have no doubt that George Selby is uncompromisingly unreconstructed and amoral. We fundamentally doubt Senator Dilworthy's honesty and his motives. We see clearly that Laura acts out of personal betrayal and misplaced trust. Yet in the stage production, Mulberry Sellers is a gentler, more comic, and simultaneously more tragic figure, a dupe of unscrupulous wheelers and dealers he simply does not understand. As William Dean Howells put it in his review for the *Atlantic Monthly*, "If he wrecks the fortunes of his friends, it is out of pure zeal and love for them, and he is always ready to share the last dollar with them, whether it is his or theirs" (Howells 653). Alone among the characters with whom Uncle Dan'l interacts on stage, Mulberry Sellers considers Dan'l's position and to a limited extent his welfare and the welfare of other freedmen. Despite its significant limits and blatant self-interest, that consideration stands alone.

Dan'l's attitudes toward Colonel Sellers contrast with his pointed distrust of the unreconstructed Colonel Selby, and those attitudes color how we interpret the white man's character, for Dan'l's "Africanist presence" again is used as a moral barometer (Morrison 6), as a canary in the mine. Dan'l returns for two short scenes in the fourth and fifth acts of the play. As the plans are moving to fruition and Laura's political manipulations look as though they are going to be successful, there is an odd comic moment between Sellers and Dan'l. When Sellers comes to visit young Hawkins, he is clearly drunk and carrying a bottle that he thinks will become a successful patent medicine (and ironically, one species of mulberry, *Morus nigra*, or "black mulberry" was common in the homeopathic tonics of the day). Hiccuping, he offers Dan'l a dose, which he says will cure his stammering. Dan'l wisely refuses. Sellers tells Dan'l he has "got no faith," and his problem is easy to fix. He tells a story of a man who whistled to interrupt and therefore "cure" his stammering, and Dan'l exits, "Laughing & Whistling" (140).

What is less clear in this scene is what Dan'l is laughing about—or at—and what he actually thinks of Sellers's story, his advice, or his drunkenness. His exit from the scene frees him from any concrete response, reminiscent of the way the narrator is freed from a response at the end of "A True Story." The audience, too, is free to interpret the scene in the light of racial stereotype or with more nuanced awareness. It is ambivalently clear in *Colonel Sellers* that the white man sees his problems as more significant than the black(face) man's, and equally clear that his drunken schemes are ineffective. The play presents this and leaves the audience to judge. It is an odd comic moment, particularly in 1874, as the elections that fall would clearly reveal the impending political consequences of the lengthening and intensifying economic depression. Republicans that fall lost the House, shifting from a "70 percent majority to a 37 percent minority," dooming Reconstruction efforts and presaging the 1877 "compromise" that would not only end but also dismantle them (Barreyre 416). Radical Republicans were increasingly marginalized as moderate "Liberal Republicans" focused ineffectively on a platform of ineffectual civil service reform, and voters responded resoundingly. Sellers's suggestion to Dan'l—and the nation's political response to postwar African Americans—is essentially that they should "whistle Dixie."

An actor's interpretation and the director's blocking would obviously influence an audience's perception of Dan'l's character. Twain left no record of his reactions to Dan'l's portrayal but was vocal in both parodic and real distress about actor John Raymond's portrayal of Sellers as comic only, missing his fuller character and its tragic aspects (Wheeler 650; Thomason and Quirk 112). Yet there is nothing in the text of the play itself to resolve the ambiguity or the ambivalent feelings that Uncle Dan'l's character might arouse, and Twain's use of the blackface mask reflects fundamental satiric possibilities characteristic of the San Francisco Minstrels. Dan'l's final appearance is at Laura's trial for the murder of George Selby, expressing approval of Sellers's testimony on Laura's behalf (148). His role here, viewed on paper and from the perspective of the twenty-first century, seems ineluctably sad, presaging Jim's later and increasingly desperate support of Huck in arguments against Tom in *Tom Sawyer Abroad* (McCoy, "Cultural" 82–85). Audiences in 1874, though, would have had diverse responses to Uncle Dan'l's character and this final scene. Ambivalence and conflicting interests mark the era.

The play itself ends with the dramatic verdict in Laura's trial—a marked lack of closure compared to the novel, leaving the audience to judge whether the "millions" would—or should—ever be realized. But more, Twain left the ending open to the type of improvisation that the San Francisco Minstrels made so popular. As Twain put it in his remarks during the New York City opening-night curtain call, "I have written this piece in such a way that the jury can bring in a verdict of guilty or not guilty, just as they happen to feel about it" (Wheeler 650), emphasizing his own ambivalence and recognizing the central moral ambivalences of the era. On its opening night at the Park, Laura was condemned to death—but in the next night's performance, she was acquitted (650n3), with the jury's decision presumably affected by the different mood of the house. With this choice Twain deliberately invites the ambivalence of both cast and audience to find joint expression and allows both a role in determining the course of events, something they did not always feel in real life, similar to voter apathy today.

Finally, Twain's choice to change Colonel Sellers's first name to Mulberry was ripe with the sort of economically focused satire that was often exploited on the SFM's minstrel stage. Even in the 1870s, business and farm magazines still referred to the "mulberry mania" of the 1830s ("Silk" 230), when efforts to create a lucrative American silk industry had led to a "wild spirit of speculation" in silkworm eggs and the mulberry trees that were to provide the leaves to feed the worms (Reddall 362). Unfortunately, however, through the distribution of convincing circulars, "shrewd speculators" had created a market for a particular—and particularly inferior—species of mulberry tree, *Morus multicaulis*. Popular demand outrageously inflated its prices and, in the end, ruined thousands of farmers and investors who eschewed the more reliable mulberry species. They mortgaged their farms and sank their savings into trees that ended up useful only as firewood—a context that makes Mulberry Sellers's effort to mask his poverty by hiding a candle in his stove to create the "appearance of heat" even more poignant (133–34).

The San Francisco Minstrels' response to *Colonel Sellers* is, unfortunately, largely lost to history, as no extant script remains (if indeed there ever was one; see "Old Minstrels Days" on their improvisation). Yet by 9 November 1874, and probably earlier, the minstrels were running a play in the second part of their show called "There's Millions in It!"[15] starring Billy Birch—whose performance style is said to have influenced Twain's own (Knoper 149)—as "Col. Sell-us"; Charley Backus as "Mrs. Sell-us"; Add Ryman as "Mr. White"; and Carl Rudolph as "Mr. Green" (program, Harvard). These last two characters do not, of course, appear in Twain's play, and we can only imagine from their significant names that the character of "Mr. White" plays on aspects of race, honesty, or both, while "Mr. Green" likely has a key role in the money-making schemes, either as backer or manipulator or both.

The shift in Sellers's name to "Sell-us" offers a hint that the SFM's Colonel was less benign in minstrel-show blackface than on the "legitimate" stage, perhaps closer to the character in the novel. Or perhaps Charley Backus's early experiences lent an edge to their production, for his father had been one of the thousands financially ruined during the "mulberry mania." Backus had grown up in a house "full of silkworms, mulberry leaves," and wild and ruined "dreams." The contempt of wealthier family members and townspeople toward his immediate family was something Backus repaid with interest on stage throughout his career, his picture-perfect mimicry and mockery instantly recognizable to Rochester residents who caught the SFM's New York City shows ("The Minstrel Backus" 2).

The SFM poster on this date also alerts audiences, "Look out for [an upcoming] Great Society Drama, by Six of America's best authors," which may be a swipe at Twain's collaboration with Warner, or may simply be one of their many digs at pretension in the theater. This poster, too, is among many that make claims about the nature of the SFM's audiences: "Houses Crowded to the Doors, with delighted and enthusiastic audiences, composed of the ELITE OF THE CITY," but also proclaiming "The Insurrection begins at 8," rather than merely their customary "trouble." By the next week, posters show that the SFM had moved on from their burlesque of Twain's play, presenting new farces or parodies in its place. A tribute to Twain and the spirit of his character, though, remains in their poster, which adds a new subheading directly under their theater name, an ambivalent and raucous expression of both attraction and suspicion: "There's Millions in it" (Harvard programs).

"This at Least Shall be Sacred": Satire, Hope, and Character in Chaotic Financial Times

Mark Twain and the San Francisco Minstrels appealed to their respective audiences because they gave expression to the contradictory impulses and conflicting interests of the era, acknowledging and validating a widespread ambivalence and confusion. Gilded Age audiences realized that in this age of competition, no one beyond intimate circles was wholly on your side. Yet both Twain and the SFM also conveyed a sense of camaraderie with their audiences, seeming to welcome them into their intimate circles. In 1876 the SFM even replaced the traditional half-circle of the minstrel show with parlor furniture, welcoming their audiences as "friends" to their home, their theater: "They used to take their audiences into their confidence and make it sort of a family circle affair, and they would spring impromptu gags on one another about things that had happened during the day" (Horton 252). Twain's interactions with his lecture audiences were, similarly, unusually intimate. Rather than reading his works, he memorized and performed them, talking directly to his audiences, wholly absorbed in eliciting the responses he craved from them. As one reviewer put it, "it seemed as if he had just dropped in to tell a story" (*Newburgh Daily Journal* 21 November 1884: 2, qtd. in Holmes). His gift for strong characterization (however literary critics might see his flaws in plot or unity) made his characters come alive, reminding his audiences of real people that they knew. Audiences felt welcomed into these intimate worlds and, as a result, became invested in their success.

Equally important, Twain and the SFM offered a sense of "character" and honesty that was not limited to their attacks on corruption. Because of their self-deprecating humor, they rarely came across as judgmental or self-righteous, even in their most wicked and relentless satire. They evinced sympathy and empathy with the honest, hardworking, and compassionate members of all classes, but especially with those who increasingly were seen as the "deserving poor," as in Twain's *Adventures of Huckleberry Finn*, *The Prince and the Pauper*, and numerous other texts that present members of these classes as real people rather than as sentimental tropes for the amusement or palliation of the upper classes. Songs by the SFM asked audiences to "Put Yourself in His Place" (Howard) or "Never Go Back on the Poor" (Newcomb). But more, both Twain and the SFM were active in advocacy and charitable concerns—numerous newspaper clippings reveal that the SFM offered free performances in asylums and participated in or hosted benefit performances for local food kitchens and the destitute families of deceased actors (*NYT* 20 October 1865; 18 October 1874, 12 February 1882, et al.).

Family was important in character, and Twain and the SFM were family men. Twain protected the privacy of his family, but his devotion was clear. His wife and daughters also traveled extensively with him, and the hospitality of the Clemenses' Hartford home was legendary. Billy Birch's celebration of his silver wedding anniversary with Virginia Birch received significant coverage in the *New York Times* (29 September 1881:5). And while Charley Backus had been married briefly twice before, his third marriage was long lasting, and its quality was noted by fellow performers and occasionally the press. On his death in 1883, Backus, who had been careful with his money and determined that no benefit performance would be needed by his wife and child ("The Minstrel Backus"), left an estate worth over $350,000, equivalent to about $8.4 million today (Estavan 203). For his Gilded Age audiences, no taint touched wealth earned for such a purpose.

So, when in 1874, even as the economic depression was intensifying, the SFM opened their opulent theater uptown, audiences did not feel that the minstrels' success was undeserved. News articles instead proudly spoke of them as local boys who had done well. Built at a cost of over $100,000 ($2.1 million today)—a lush and extravagant house seating almost five hundred when it was built (*Souvenir*), renovated by 1880 to increase the seating capacity to eight hundred (United States, Census.)—the "opera house" seemed a home to its audiences, who visited regularly and gladly. After Charley Backus's death in 1883, the *New York Tribune* reminded its readers that their theater was not purchased on borrowed money or talent. The SFM owned their theater, worked for no one but their audiences, wrote their own material: "the leading minstrel owns his own theatre and built it out of laughs" (24 June 1883: 4). At the same time, Twain's successes were viewed internationally and at home as quintessentially American. His audiences and readers reveled in those successes. The Clemenses' building of their opulent and eccentric home in Hartford, also during the Panic of 1873 and the depression, seemed a confirmation of America's promise. And later, in the 1890s, when he faced financial ruin during an even more severe depression, Twain's decision to pay his creditors back in full, coupled with his protection of his family and the restoration of his fortune through a grueling international lecture tour, confirmed not only the content of his character, but also the viability of the American Dream even in times of great hardship.

The audiences who loved Twain and the SFM did not see their successes as exploitative, but as symbols of hope. Hard work, wits, and "character" were still "the best part[s] of capital." And it was reassuring to those audiences to know that success did not crown only the corrupt: in staying true to oneself, one's family, and one's talents, there really could be "millions in it."

Notes

1. While no comprehensive historical study of postbellum minstrelsy has yet been written, my research suggests that there are four distinct types of blackface minstrelsy. When Tony Pastor opened white variety houses in the 1860s, many white performers left the blackface stage, able to perform their own ethnic music and humor in their own skin to wide audiences for the first time. Their exodus opened spaces for actual African American blackface performers and female minstrel troupes. White blackface performers whose primary focus was to perform race and stereotype offered the third type of minstrelsy. And finally, there was the satiric blackface style exemplified by the San Francisco Minstrels.

2. During the postbellum era, economic or new sectional interests were increasingly at odds with moral or political ones. Neither political party, therefore, was able to develop sound or unified economic policy (Barreyre 409–16). By the Panic of 1873, both parties were internally split on economic questions and were unable to respond effectively to the financial crisis, contributing to the resulting long-wave economic depression and the collapse of Reconstruction. Fels was one of the early proponents of the "long-wave" theory; the core of his argument is that rather than thinking in "depression cycles," each should be taken in its specific historical context. In an essay that is profoundly revealing, Barreyre picks up this challenge, synthesizing specific economic and historical data and integrating these with the political and moral interpretations of Reconstruction and its demise.

3. "The Dying Brigand" was a tableau vivant (living tableau) worked into English playwright James Planchés's *The Brigand* (1829), popular on both sides of the ocean. "Arrah Na Pogue" is by Boucicault. Twain approached Boucicault about writing the script for a play based on *The Gilded Age*, but when Boucicault demanded one-third of the profits, Twain decided to write it himself (Thomason 56).

4. While no extant script exists, the Metropolitan Hotel was ripe for economic

and political satire. Across the street from the SFM's first theater, the hotel was rented by "Boss" Tweed and managed by his son William (Ackerman 2, 51). There Tweed celebrated the 1868 Tammany victories, when he successfully placed his candidates as governor (John T. Hoffman), New York City mayor (A. Oakey Hall), and state supreme court justice (George Bernard), along with Tweed's own reelection on the county board of supervisors (Ackerman 48–49, 56). It was a year of unprecedented voter fraud and economic chicanery, in which the "total votes cast in New York exceeded the number of possible voters—actual human beings of voting age, status and gender—by more than 8 percent" (58), and added significantly to Tweed's fortune.

5. I do not mean here to deny or question the significance of the cultural aspects of racial or ethnic identity. Yet legal definitions of race were hotly contested throughout the century. Those battles were fought over definitions of what made a person "white," conferring access to political rights and economic and social opportunities. "Race" is a social and legal construct in America, based in self-ownership, in the idea of self as property. Abolitionists, following Locke's discussion of slavery in his *Treatises on Government*, had argued that slavery was not tenable because self-ownership could not be alienated (see, for example, Finney 197; Brown 413–15).

6. Slavery was extremely lucrative for the wealthiest planters, and its products lucrative for other industries. While the South overall possessed a lower proportion of wealth than the North, the economic power of the wealthiest slaveowners was formidable. In 1850 and 1860, "southern planters were disproportionately among the wealthiest Americans" (Engerman 343). In 1860 five of the wealthiest ten states were southern (Dyer 59). The richest 1 percent of Americans (over half of them southern) owned 24 percent of the wealth in 1860 (Pope 134). For a comparison with the postwar corporate robber barons, in 1870 the wealthiest 1 percent owned 27 percent of the national wealth (136). When we further consider the financial impact of emancipation, we can begin to understand the economics of the postwar power shift and the centrality of race in that dynamic. Williamson and Cain show that almost half of southern wealth in 1850 and 1860 was in the aggregate value of human chattel: $3,059 *million*—almost $10 *trillion in 2011*—which would have been "roughly 70 percent of GDP" (9–10, esp. Table 4).

7. Throughout the chapter, comparison of dollar values will be offered using Williamson's "Relative Value" calculator. This figure uses the historical standard of living computation, the value of this income in its ability to purchase or pay for the necessities of life.

8. The figures presented are as reported to the Internal Revenue office, and are listed in a religious publication. In keeping with the era's ambivalence about wealth, corruption, and morals, the *Register* kept track of the moral measure of the city, its religious and charitable life—and its dissipations.

9. Some reviewers even found that subscription publishing itself contributed to corruption, offering "booksellers a premium on dishonesty in order to obtain for

their shelves copies of a book 'sold only by subscription'" ("The Stolen White Elephant," rpt. from the *Chicago Tribune* in the *Literary News* 1 [n.s., July 1882]: 207).

10. For more about Twain and the SFM, see McCoy, "The Trouble Begins at Eight" Blackface historians and contemporaries support Twain's assessment of the SFM's unique qualities. Robert Toll, Lawrence Estavan, and other historians of the genre and era acknowledge that the SFM were both the "pioneers" and exemplars of the postbellum satiric style. Stories, speeches, memoirs, letters, novels, and periodical pieces refer familiarly to the SFM for at least four decades after death and illness broke them up in 1883. Even as late as 1919, Bert Williams, the great African American blackface minstrel, found himself and his humor compared to the SFM by older audience members: "I am sure he prefers the San Francisco Minstrels, and he misses the banjo. He takes you seriously, and you wish he wouldn't" (Williams 348). Twain's greater status as an American icon has, of course, lasted much longer.

11. See, for example, Camfield 23–31. While Camfield brilliantly and eloquently lays out the central concerns of the era and the novel, he sees Twain's own speculation and pursuit of wealth as possibly "a mark of Twain's hypocrisy" (30), agreeing in the end with an early critic that Twain's and Warner's "hope of gaining a liberal heap of that money, whose worship" the novel "purports to ridicule," is hypocritical (Boston *Literary World*, January 1874, qtd. in Camfield 13). Critical discussion on this issue intensified when intellectual property was at stake, especially in collaborative efforts. Loving and others see that Twain's efforts to secure exclusive copyright to material in *Colonel Sellers*, "cutting out Warner," demonstrate that he was "a victim of the very Gilded Age" morals he and Warner expose (205). Thomason examines the texts in detail and concludes that the evidence "raises some question about the ethics of the proposal he made to Warner," giving "Twain exclusive possession to the play and its profits" (236–55). Yet the fact that Twain scrupulously compensated Gilbert Densmore, who had written an earlier script in violation of a copyright he did not know existed, suggests that Twain's view of Warner's contributions bears further scrutiny. Similarly, the SFM had no real blackface successors, largely because they defended their brand of satire by ruthlessly driving competitors out of the city and out of business—especially when members of those companies had previously appeared as members of the SFM company.

12. As W. T. Lhamon has argued effectively, to understand blackface, we must understand it in terms of economic and cultural disparity; it "has always existed in a pressure cooker of disdain. Raising cain is a response to that disdain" (*Raising Cain* 117). "Raising Cain" is a trope that Twain will play with in *Adventures of Huckleberry Finn*, as Huck says his pap "raised Cain around town" when he drank (29, ch. 6), not long before the elder Finn kidnaps his son, locks him in a cabin and leaves him there for three days. He returns "all mud" from the gutter—essentially an unconscious and impromptu blackface performance—in an effort to claim Huck's reward money and control over his person.

13. Thomason further argues in his dissertation that the importance of the play goes beyond the money it earned. He sees Twain's "development as a dramatist [as] intricately woven into his development as a novelist" (4). Without the "immediate personal and financial success" of the play, Twain "might have felt differently about his boyhood" as a topic for further exploration (267–68). Randall Knoper argues cogently that the play "deserves a more central place in accounts of Twain's writing" (69) and also connects the play's success with the writing of *Adventures of Huckleberry Finn* (71–77). Many of his arguments about performance dovetail provocatively with the specific consideration of the SFM's influence.

14. John H. Burnett was a minor actor of the period. While there is no definitive printed statement that he was a "white" actor in blackface when playing a "Negro role," such performance was the norm in the era. Because race is, in part, a social performance (and at the time, a legal one as well), the absence of racial designation in contemporary documents indicates that Burnett was considered a white man and would have played "ethnic" or "racial" roles with what was considered appropriate makeup. The *New York Times* "Amusements" column (17 August 1871) lists John Burnett as a part of Augustin Daly's company at the Fifth Avenue Theatre. The *Actors' Society Monthly Bulletin* also lists John H. Burnett as one of their "Reliable Actors" (1 March 1899: 2). No known African American actors appear in this listing, and again the absence of racial designation carries the presumption of whiteness. Further, later productions reveal that a "white" actor in blackface regularly played the role. A playbill from the Boston Museum, dated 17 May 1886, lists Mr. William Seymour as "Uncle Daniel, an old negro" (Jerome Lawrence and Robert E. Lee Theatre Research Institute). Seymour was the child of "The Irish Comedian," James (Cunningham) Seymour, an immigrant from Belfast, and Lydia Eliza Griffith, both actors (Jensen 8). William Seymour began his stage career at the age of seven; starting in 1879 he was the stage manager and artistic director for the Boston Museum, "occasionally also acting in productions" (11). Special thanks to Orville W. Martin and Nena Couch for their kind and thorough assistance in finding information about Seymour.

15. "There's millions in it" is a signature phrase for Colonel Sellers. It appears numerous times in the play and quickly became a widely recognized catch phrase in the era.

Works Cited

List of Periodicals (clippings are identified by date and page number within the text when possible; more significant articles are listed in the reference list that follows)

Actors' Society Monthly Bulletin
Chicago Tribune
Dramatic Magazine

Literary News

New Music Review and Church Music Review

New York Daily Tribune

New York Times (NYT in text)

Ackerman, Kenneth. *Boss Tweed: The Rise and Fall of the Corrupt Politician Who Conceived the Soul of Modern New York*. New York: Caroll and Graf, 2005.

Barreyre, Nicolas. "The Politics of Economic Crisis: The Panic of 1873, the End of Reconstruction, and the Realignment of American Politics." *Journal of the Gilded Age and Progressive Era* 10.4 (October 2011): 403–23.

Brown, William B. "Religious Organizations and Slavery." *Oberlin Quarterly Review* 4.4 (October 1849): 409–37.

Camfield, Gregg. "Afterword." *The Gilded Age* by Mark Twain and Charles Dudley Warner. New York: Oxford UP, 1996. 13–31.

Cooper, George, lyrics, and Harry Miller, music. "Specie Payment: Song and Chorus for the Times." New York: John L. Peters, 1870. Courtesy of the Lester Levy Collection, Johns Hopkins University.

Dumont, Frank, and W. S. Mullaly. "The Dandy Colored Waiters: March Song & Chorus / as sung by Birch and Backus." Boston: Oliver Ditson, 1880.

Dyer, G. W. *Democracy in the South before the Civil War*. Nashville: Publishing House of the Methodist Episcopal Church, South, 1905.

Engerman, Stanley L. "Slavery and Its Consequences for the South in the Nineteenth Century." *The Cambridge Economic History of the United States*. Ed. Stanley L. Engerman and Robert E. Gallman. New York: Cambridge UP, 2000. 2:329–66.

Engerman, Stanley L., and Robert E. Gallman, eds. *The Cambridge Economic History of the United States*. Vol. 2. New York: Cambridge UP, 2000.

Estavan, Lawrence, ed. *San Francisco Theatre Research: Minstrelsy*. Vol. 13, Monograph XXV. San Francisco: Works Project Administration, 1939.

Fels, Rendigs. "The Long-Wave Depression, 1873–97." *Review of Economics and Statistics* 31.1 (February 1949): 69–73.

Finney, Reverend Charles Grandison. *Skeletons of a Course of Theological Lectures*. Oberlin: James Steele, 1840. Google Books.

"Freaks of Fortune, and Their Lessons." *Harper's New Monthly Magazine* 47.99 (August 1858): 344–49.

Harvard Theatre Collection. Houghton Library. Harvard University. Cambridge.

"Hazing at the Stock Board" (5 April 1884). In *The Police Gazette*. Ed. Gene Smith and Jayne Barry Smith. New York: Simon and Schuster, 1972.

Holmes, B. Scott. *Promoting Huck Finn: The Twain-Cable Tour of 1884–85*. *<bscottholmes.com/content/promoting-huck-finn-twain-cable-tour-188485>*.

Horton, Judge William Ellis. *Driftwood of the Stage*. Detroit: Winn and Hammond, 1904.

Howard, Rollin. *Put Yourself in His Place*. New York: Charles W. Harris, 1871.

Howells, William Dean. "Review of *Colonel Sellers*" (1875). *Atlantic Monthly*. Rpt. *Mark Twain's Letters*: 652–54.

Jensen, Mary Ann. "The William Seymour Theatre Collection: A Curator's View." *Princeton University Library Chronicle* 48.1 (Autumn 1986): 6–12.

Jerome Lawrence and Robert E. Lee Theatre Research Institute. Thompson Library. The Ohio State University.

Jones, Willoughby. *The Life of James Fisk, Jr., Including the Great Frauds of the Tammany Ring*. Philadelphia: Union, 1872.

Knapp, Mrs. Shepherd (Emma Benedict). *Hic Habitat Felicitas: A Volume of Recollections and Letters*. Boston: W. B. Clarke, 1910.

Knoper, Randall. *Acting Naturally: Mark Twain and the Culture of Performance*. Berkeley: U of California P, 1995.

Lhamon, W. T., Jr. *Raising Cain: Blackface Performance from Jim Crow to Hip Hop*. Cambridge: Harvard UP, 1998.

Loving, Jerome. *Mark Twain: The Adventures of Samuel L. Clemens*. Berkeley: U of California P, 2010.

McCoy, Sharon D. "Cultural Critique in *Tom Sawyer Abroad*: Behind Jim's Minstrel Mask." *Mark Twain Annual: The Journal of the Mark Twain Circle of America* 4 (2006): 71–90.

———. "'The Trouble Begins at Eight': Mark Twain, the San Francisco Minstrels, and the Unsettling Legacy of Blackface Minstrelsy." *American Literary Realism* 41.3 (Spring 2009): 232–48.

"The Minstrel Backus." *New York Sun* 26 June 1883: 2.

Morrison, Toni. *Playing in the Dark: Whiteness and the Literary Imagination*. Cambridge: Harvard UP, 1992.

Newcomb, Bobby. "Never Go Back on the Poor." New York: Richard A. Saalfield, 1887.

"Old Minstrel Days: Billy Birch, the Veteran Comedian, Talks of Other Times." *Daily Alta California* (12 October 1890): 12.

Paine, Albert Bigelow. *Mark Twain: A Biography*. Vol. 3. New York: Harper and Brothers, 1912.

Pope, Clayne. "Inequality in the Nineteenth Century." *The Cambridge Economic History of the United States*. Ed. Stanley L. Engerman and Robert E. Gallman. New York: Cambridge UP, 2000. 2:109–42.

"Receipts of the New York Theatres, for the Last Season." *American Quarterly Church Review and Ecclesiastical Register* 18 (1867):139.

Reddall, Henry Frederic. *Fact, Fancy, and Fable: A New Handbook for Ready Reference on Subjects Commonly Omitted from Cyclopædias*. Chicago: McClurg, 1892.

Ryman, Add. Arr. Charles White. *Julius the Snoozer*. New York: De Witt, 1876.

"Silk and Silk Manufacture. No. V. The Morus Mouticaulis Mania." *Manufacturer and Builder* 5.10 (October 1873): 230.

Smith, Francis Hopkinson, with Frank Berkeley Smith. *Enoch Crane*. New York: Scribner's Sons, 1916.

Souvenir of Places of Amusement in New York City. [New York]: Annunciator Press, 1874. Hathi Trust Digital Library.

Thomason, Jerry Wayne. "'Colonel Sellers': The Story of His Play." Unpublished dissertation. University of Missouri–Columbia, 1991.

Thomason, Jerry, and Tom Quirk. "Introduction." "Col. Sellers, 'A Drama in Five Acts' by Saml L. Clemens." *Missouri Review* 18.3 (1995): 111–12.

Toll, Robert C. *Blacking Up: The Minstrel Show in Nineteenth-Century America*. New York: Oxford UP, 1974.

Twain, Mark. *Adventures of Huckleberry Finn*. 1885. Ed. Victor Fischer and Lin Salamo, with Harriet Elinor Smith and Walter Blair. Berkeley: U of California P, 2001.

———. *Autobiography of Mark Twain: The Complete and Authorized Edition*. 3 vols. Ed. Harriet Elinor Smith et al. Berkeley: U of California P, 2010, 2012, 2015.

———. "*Col. Sellers*, A Drama in Five Acts by Saml. L. Clemens." *Missouri Review* 18.3 (1995): 109–10; 113–51.

———. *Mark Twain's Letters, 1874–1875*. Vol. 6. Ed. Michael B. Frank and Harriet Elinor Smith. Berkeley: U of California P, 2002.

———. *Mark Twain's Notebooks and Journals, 1883–1891*. Vol VIII. Ed. Robert Peck Browning et al. Berkeley: U of California P, 1979.

———. *Mark Twain's Travels with Mr. Brown*. Ed. Franklin Walker and G. Ezra Dane. New York: Knopf, 1940.

———. "The Revised Catechism." *New York Daily Tribune* 27 September 1871: 6.

———. "A True Story, Repeated Word for Word as I Heard It." *Atlantic Monthly* 34.205 (November 1874): 591–94. Rpt. *Sketches, New and Old*.

Twain, Mark, and Charles Dudley Warner. *The Gilded Age: A Tale of To-day*. New York: Oxford UP, 1996.

United States. "Social Statistics of Cities." *Census Reports. Tenth Census*. 1 June 1880. 18: 568.

Wheeler, Andrew Carpenter. "The Park Theatre—'Colonel Sellers.'" New York *World* (17 September 1874). Also reprinted in *Mark Twain's Letters*. 650.

Williams, Bert. Interview. "Keeping Up with the Laughs." *Theatre Magazine* (June 1919): 346, 348.

Williamson, Samuel H. "Seven Ways to Compute the Relative Value of a U.S. Dollar Amount, 1774 to Present." *Measuring Worth*. 2014. <www.measuringworth.com>.

Williamson, Samuel H., and Louis P. Cain. "Measuring Slavery in 2011 Dollars." *Measuring Worth*. 2015.<www.measuringworth.com/slavery.php>.

Wineapple, Brenda. *Ecstatic Nation: Confidence, Crisis, and Compromise, 1848–1877*. New York: Harper Collins, 2013.

Wittke, Carl. *Tambo and Bones: A History of the American Minstrel Stage*. Durham: Duke UP, 1930.

10

"A House of Cards"

Fictitious Capital and *The Gilded Age*

Jonathan Hayes

Three decades before Thorstein Veblen described modern America as organized by business enterprise, Mark Twain's first novel, *The Gilded Age*, coauthored with Charles Dudley Warner, depicted the dramatic shift of the mid-nineteenth-century U.S. economy toward finance and the market for fictitious capital.[1] In *The Gilded Age* (1873), Wall Street investors exercise their social power through financial credit, which induces a "fever of speculation" (363) among the working and middle classes that fails to relieve them of their poverty. The novel depicts fictitious capital, or "money that is thrown into circulation as capital without any material basis in commodities or productive activity" (Harvey 95), as a source of illusion that distorts economic activity and disrupts social reality. The circulation of fictitious capital—the basis of the finance economy—is revealed to be dependent upon discourse that promises the fulfillment of material desires but which ultimately provokes economic collapse, outbursts of violence, and the reinforcement of poverty. In identifying finance as the motivator of such social phenomena, the novel criticizes the expansion of finance capitalism as it develops into the modern business enterprise economy.

The novel describes two Wall Street–based companies created with fictitious capital, the Salt Lick Pacific Extension and the Columbus River Slack-Water Navigation Company. Numerous other speculative endeavors, such as Squire Hawkins's Tennessee Land claim, Mr. Bigler's railroad and real estate companies, and Colonel Eschol Sellers's endlessly proliferating business plans, are either conceived as finance-based investments or viewed as potentially profitable as a result of the developing finance economy. In varying degrees, the profitability of these schemes depends upon the market for fictitious capital, by which investors anticipate profit from ownership of stock shares or from the sale and exchange of their claims. For the Salt Lick Pacific Extension and the Columbus River Slack-Water Navigation Company, the viability of each company hinges upon its capacity to develop infrastructure, attract other commercial ventures in its areas of operation, and continually expand its market. Promoters of both companies require vast outlays of money, which they seek in the form of credit from state sources, particularly the federal government, as well as from private investors.

In these finance-based enterprises, the circulation of fictitious capital and its enabling discourse mutually reinforce each other. The promotional language of financial speculation promises numerous benefits: economic expansion, advancement in social class, wealth, and luxury for working-class and middle-class investors, and stability for laborers. This discourse of capital and social gain strongly influences men and women desiring an escape from impoverished social conditions. The failure of financial enterprises to deliver on such promises reveals the discourse sustaining the financial economy as myth that occludes social and economic reality. The novel's characterization of the finance economy as sustained by mythic discourse is especially evident in its pivotal chapter 28, when novice speculator Henry Brierly visits the Wall Street offices of the Columbus River Slack-Water Navigation Company and questions whether the company's appropriation of capital from the federal government is "a myth" or "a reality" (205). While the firm's unnamed Wall Street president obscures the distinction between myth and reality to justify the firm's profits, his obfuscations rely upon the discourse that sustains finance capital. Newton Arvin, who faulted Twain for failing to adopt "a revolutionary philosophy of comradeship," ranked his depiction of the Wall Street–based firm—along with the beginning of *Adventures of Huckleberry Finn*—as among his most inspired passages (85).

The novel also situates the finance economy against a social realm where middle- and working-class characters seek wealth to make themselves romantically appealing, and where romance offers the potential for advancement in social class. Thus, the novel intertwines its narrative of finance with a sentimental melodrama. The latter describes a marriage market paralleling the finance economy that is sustained by romantic discourses promising fulfillment of desires, advancement in social class, and acquisition of material wealth and luxury. In the melodramatic plot, characters view romance, sex, and marriage as parallel if not as means to gaining material security. These characters calculate upon romance for social advancement, and they also utilize financial speculation to advance their romantic pursuits. The combination of romance and financial narratives reveals that both social domains are framed within the language of calculated exchange.

In the principal melodramatic narrative, romance discourse motivates Laura Hawkins, a young woman adopted as a girl by the Hawkinses, to seek greater material security and luxury through relationships with powerful, upper-class men, with the ultimate goal of marriage to one of them. In another romance narrative, financial speculation provides a basis for male characters to acquire sufficient wealth for them to qualify as worthy romantic partners for marriage. For example, Philip Sterling, who locates valuable coal deposits on land purchased as a speculative investment, achieves financial success that makes his marriage to Ruth Bolton likely. Through this narrative the novel affirms the ideology of financial capitalism. However, the discrepancy between sentimental romantic discourse and social reality in the tragic narrative of Laura Hawkins, a woman excluded from the male world of finance and business, reflects critically upon financial enterprise, particularly as her failure to advance socially through marriage parallels the defeats of middle- and working-class men in their attempts to achieve material security through finance-based investments.

The novel's melodramatic, sentimental narratives reveal a homology between the desire-based discourses of romance and financial enterprise, evoking criticism of the finance-based economy that has not yet been fully described in studies of *The Gilded Age*. Although critics have vigorously debated the novel's politics since at least the 1930s, these political readings have focused primarily on the novel's content rather than its discourses. The argument has generally turned upon whether the novel criticizes the financiers directing the post–Civil War economy, whether it expresses a working-class or petty-bourgeois point of view, or whether its criticism is sufficiently social and materialist.[2] Critic Bryant Morey French, who identifies the novel as the turning point in Twain's writing career that made him a "social novelist" (241), describes a particular nuance of this debate, noting Walter Fuller Taylor's objections: "[Taylor] maintains that 'the principal force' is an intangible one, 'the Spirit of Speculation.' He appears to believe that Mark Twain attributed the ills of the socio-economic system to the ideology born of that system rather than to the system itself. . . . In other words, the fact that Taylor leaves the Spirit of Speculation as the ultimate 'principal' implies an abandonment of social reality in favor of moral metaphysics" (216). French responds by emphasizing the historical and social basis of the novel's depiction of speculation. He notes, for example, the novel's sources in actual events, such as the expansion of railroad construction in the late 1860s and early 1870s. Notably, economic historians such as Alfred Chandler have identified the growth in railroad construction, beginning in the 1840s and escalating through the 1850s, with the expansion of finance capital. French also notes the novel's depiction of corporate interests controlling the political state, which he says dramatized "the headlong plundering of the national domain that was to lead to monopoly control of the economy" (219). French contends that critics of the novel who dismiss it for failing to criticize the U.S. political and economic system neglect its historical and social dimensions. He echoes labor historian Philip Foner, who argues that critics dismissing the novel overlook its depiction of Wall Street: "How anyone who reads the section dealing with the passage of appropriation bills can argue that *The Gilded Age* purposely avoids sketching 'the real leaders of the great barbecue,' is beyond comprehension. If the 'real leaders' were not the bankers, brokers, and presidents of Wall Street corporations, who were they?" (84). In countering critics of the 1930s such as V. L. Parrington, Foner emphasizes the novel's depiction of Wall Street financial power. Similarly, French's study contextualizes the novel at the turn of the U.S. economy to monopoly capitalism, marking an advance toward a more fully developed historicized critical approach.

However, scholarly criticism on *The Gilded Age* has ignored how the novel's literary strategies generate its critical representation of Wall Street and the financial capitalist system. In other words, criticism both for and against the novel's politics has treated its representation of speculative schemes apart from its literary form; critics have concentrated on *what* it represents rather than *how* it produces those representations. Ironically, it is the historian Foner who reminds literary critics that the book is not a historical essay, but rather a novel, and that Twain wrote first of all as a novelist. In fact, Foner argues that the novel's political criticism depends upon its fiction: "Twain was not, after all, writing a tract. He was performing the novelist's classic task—that of placing before us a group of characters and bringing them to life, causing the reader to say as he read, 'Yes. This is right. This is the way the corporations buy legislators'" (84). Foner's comments suggest the need for a more attentive literary critical practice to illuminate the novel's political dimensions.

In this chapter, I argue that financial narratives and sentimental melodrama narratives complement each other in *The Gilded Age*, revealing that the circulation of fictitious capital in the finance economy sustains itself through desire-based discourses, and that these discourses permeate the social domain. This is particularly evident in romantic relationships that men and women conduct as informal asset transactions in a virtual marriage market. The novel also reveals the vast discrepancy between financially driven discourses and social actuality as a source of uncertainty for middle- and working-class men and women. The description of the finance economy as a "house of cards," expressed in the words of Philip Sterling's romantic counterpart, Ruth Bolton, identifies the source of this uncertainty in the circulation of fictitious capital (and its corresponding desire-based discourses), which David Harvey observes to be "always in a precarious position precisely because it has no material basis" (95). As *The Gilded Age* shows, the discourses enabling the circulation of immaterialized capital occlude the uncertainty and instability of the finance economy.

While the finance economy requires myth-making discourse to sustain itself, classical economists do not acknowledge its guiding desire-based fictions. Instead, as literary historian Kurt Heinzelman has observed, classical economists claim to analyze economic phenomena on the basis of empirical science. In claiming rational and objective methodologies for their analyses, classical economists neglect observance of how imaginative language and subjective concepts guide and shape their descriptions of economic activity. Recalling Marx's criticism of Adam Smith's concept of "economic man" as a figure of speech, "an acceptable metonym for 'Man,'" Heinzelman notes, "In Marx's eyes, Smith and his contemporaries mistook the status of economic analysis by creating 'Robinsonades,' individualistic projections of an economy comprising (eighteenth-century) individuals just like themselves; their subjectively conceived evaluation of ethical process caused them to misunderstand the role of the economist himself in the broader social history of economic production" (47–48). Citing Adam Smith's theory of prices in *The Wealth of Nations*, Heinzelman further shows that classical economists construct ostensibly scientific models of the "market" that are nevertheless imaginative in origin. Heinzelman argues that modern economic theory has been built upon the "market value" of labor, despite "all its fictive fluctuations, its apparitional embodiment of nominal value." He says, "In the world of Smithian economics, we live and prosper—literally—by the force of imagination. But not even poetry places such a singular value on the accrediting value of the unmediated imagination" (98). Twain's and Warner's characters similarly live "by the force of imagination," mistakenly believing that their investments in enterprises whose existences depend upon fictitious capital will provide them with financial security if not financial abundance.

Referring to paper securities such as stocks and bonds, Marx famously called fictitious capital an "insane form" of capital due to its capacity to distort values (596). Paper securities duplicate what they represent: money invested in profit-seeking enterprises, as well as a claim on the future revenue of those enterprises. The quoted prices of these exchangeable securities fluctuate based on what investors believe to be the future profitability of an enterprise, and due to such fluctuations, the market price may not reflect the productive value of an enterprise. The securities market operates as a source of illusion, Marx says, because prices only approximate the value of productive enterprises, which may or may not be realized at a future time. Noting fictitious capital's tendency to produce "soap bubbles of nominal money capital," Marx adds: "All these securities represent nothing but accumulated claims, legal titles, to future production. Their money or capital value either does not represent capital at all, as in the case of national debts, or is determined independently of the real capital value they represent. . . . And an accumulation of money capital means for the most part nothing more than an accumulation of these claims to production, and an accumulation of the market price of these claims, of their illusory capital value" (599). While fictitious capital mobilizes surplus capital for productive ends, it also produces distortions about the actual productive value of an enterprise or industry. Speculative fevers ensue when prices exceed actual productive capacity, and economic crashes often follow.

Throughout *The Gilded Age*, the desire for greater material security motivates male characters to invest and perform labor for schemes based upon financial speculation. Squire Hawkins and Colonel Eschol Sellers are particularly driven in their expectations of profit from speculative investments. For Squire Hawkins, his failed investment in the Tennessee Land contributes to his family's experiences of poverty, which continue after he dies and his children inherit the title. Similarly, Colonel Sellers's wildly imaginative but comically unrealistic business schemes fail to provide his family with material security. When the Columbus River Slack-Water Navigation Company collapses, his illusions are dispelled, and "all in a moment his air-castles crumbl[e] to ruins about him" (211). In both instances, their desires to achieve greater material wealth and luxury through financial schemes encourage them to invest and perform labor for enterprises of no economic or productive value.

Expressing their desire for profit and greater material security, these male speculators describe business plans with inflated romantic language. Squire Hawkins purchases a title to 75,000 acres that he believes will result in great wealth for his children, Washington and Emily.[3] At the time Hawkins purchases the land, he proudly boasts of its potential to increase in value, saying, "the whole tract would not sell for over a third of a cent an acre now, but some day people will be glad to get it for twenty dollars, fifty dollars, a hundred dollars an acre! What would you say to . . . *a thousand dollars an acre*!" As Hawkins inflates these numbers, the narrator emphasizes the romantic quality of his assertions. Hawkins expresses "wonder" over possible future wealth, he expects the development of railroads will result in a "revolution" in the world "that will make men dizzy to contemplate," and he expects that profits derived from sale of the title will allow his children to "live like the princes of the earth; they'll be courted and worshipped; their names will be known from ocean to ocean!" (15–16).

Hawkins expects that major developments in transportation, mining, and agriculture, typical enterprises financed by Wall Street investment firms, will increase the value of the Tennessee Land. He especially identifies the potential for profit with the expansion of the railroads: "There's a bigger wonder—the railroad! These worms here have never even heard of it—and when they do they'll not believe in it. But it's another fact. Coaches that fly over the ground twenty miles an hour—heavens and earth, think of that, Nancy! Twenty miles an hour. It makes a man's brain whirl. Some day, when you and I are in our graves, there'll be a railroad stretching hundreds of miles—all the way down from the cities of the Northern States to New Orleans—and it's got to run within thirty miles of this land—may be even touch a corner of it" (15–16). Similar to the novel's large-scale financiers, such as Mr. Bigler of the Pennybacker, Bigler, and Small firm of railroad contractors, Hawkins's whirling brain envisions vastly expanded commercial and transportation industries across the United States and its frontier spaces. While Hawkins's purchase of the Tennessee Land could result in profit from the development of the land's natural resources, his greater expectation wagers on an increase in the land's market value based upon the expansion of the railroad industry.[4]

Hawkins's expectations of profit from the Tennessee Land are based on the historical development of the financial industry as both a product and a source of railroad growth. The expansion of fictitious capital that occurred with railroad development resulted in new stock markets as well as investment banks and brokerages, such as those of J. P. Morgan, Jay Cooke, Jay Gould, and Jim Fisk, which "bought and sold railroad securities, acted as financial agents for a number of roads, and served as investment advisers to men with surplus capital" (Chandler 45). By the 1860s and the early 1870s, when Twain and Warner wrote *The Gilded Age*, coordination between the financial industry and railroad companies was extensive. Historian Richard White writes, "Eventually, membership on railroad boards overlapped with membership on the boards of banks and trust companies, which become a kind of headquarters for organizing these linked investments" (50). Financial firms promoted railroads on the basis of a "virtual world of financial statements, prospectuses, newspapers accounts, and market values that at once stood in for and was inseparable from the actual railroads" (White 67). Hawkins's inflated expectations for profiting from the Tennessee Land as a consequence of railroad expansion are based on this finance-driven "virtual world." Without the fictitious discourses associated with railroad enterprise, expressed in prospectuses, market values, etc., Hawkins would have no plausible basis to imagine acquiring great profits from his Tennessee Land investment.

While Squire Hawkins is obstinate about the Tennessee Land, Colonel Sellers's descriptions of his business plans absurdly exaggerate the desires and hopes of financial speculators. When the story advances ten years to approximately 1860, Washington Hawkins turns to Sellers for help after the Hawkins family goes bankrupt. Sellers regales Washington with implausible business plans, describing financial speculation in romanticized terms:

"[S]oon he was building glittering pyramids of coin, and Washington was presently growing opulent under the magic of his eloquence" (61). Despite Washington's insistence upon his poverty, Sellers continues describing investment plans, each one more grandiose than the previous. When Sellers tells Washington of his nearly completed invention of a cure for "sore eyes," which he plans to market as "Eschol Sellers' Infallible Imperial Oriental Liniment and Salvation for Sore Eyes," he describes it in terms specific to financial enterprise. In describing these plans, Sellers mimics the speech of financiers such as Mr. Bigler as he absurdly tells the impoverished Washington: "Keep your money close and add to it. I'll make it breed." Sellers's scheme to build a company from a small initial investment and expand it to a global multimillion-dollar enterprise describes a typical finance-backed corporation: "All the capital needed is to manufacture the first two thousand bottles—say a hundred and fifty dollars—then the money would begin to flow in" (66). When Sellers tells Washington he would make Washington's money "breed," he expresses in frontier vernacular the claim that investment in stocks, bonds, and other forms of commercial paper—fictitious capital—necessarily results in productivity and financial profits.

While Sellers's fantasy of acquiring wealth through financial speculation is unrealistic, his assertions express the romantic, desire-based discourses of financial investment. Sellers's comments to Washington Hawkins especially exaggerate these discourses: "Washington was so dazed, so bewildered—his heart and his eyes had wandered so far away among the strange lands beyond the seas, and such avalanches of coin and currency had fluttered and jingled confusedly down before him, that he was now as one who has been whirling round and round for a time, and, stopping all at once, finds his surroundings still whirling and all objects a dancing chaos" (67–68). Sellers's fantastical narratives promise fulfillment of desires for material luxury despite the likelihood that the investments will not be profitable. The romantic imagery associated with Sellers's storytelling aptly captures the fictitious quality of his plans, which appear as only faintly plausible due to the circulation of fictitious capital driving the finance-based economy.

Squire Hawkins's and Colonel Sellers's speculative investment schemes are small-scale endeavors built on unrealistic hopes that nevertheless pale in comparison to the two Wall Street financial enterprises that set in motion much of the novel's action. The Salt Lick Pacific Extension is a firm that Wall Street executives create to build a railroad through the Missouri frontier, a railroad that its proponents assert will create commercial markets not yet in existence. Wall Street executives also create a second firm, the Columbus River Slack-Water Navigation Company, and they request an appropriation from Congress that will ostensibly fund the company's land and waterway projects. Created entirely through fictitious capital, each company's existence depends upon discourse—rhetoric to encourage the efforts of investors and laborers.

The Wall Street promoters of the railroad enterprise sustain the illusion of the firm's profitability through promises of material wealth that stoke the gullibility of novice speculators such as Henry Brierly and Philip Sterling. For these two young men, traveling with the company's railroad exploration crew is not merely a business endeavor but also an adventure, as the narrator notes: "Happy youth, that is ready to pack its valise, and start for Cathay on an hour's notice" (95). Henry, the nephew of a Wall Street manager, adopts the facile idioms of Wall Street as he describes the business to Philip: "'We lay out a line, spot the good land, enter it up, know where the stations are to be, spot them, buy lots; there's heaps of money in it'" (95). He also believes that business success will win him favor in his romantic pursuit of Ruth Bolton. Philip writes letters to her describing the perils of the frontier, bearing the message that "[i]f he returned with a fortune, perhaps and perhaps" (96). Philip's love letters to Ruth reveal the inseparability of his desire for profit from financial enterprise and his romantic hopes.

Ruth, the daughter of Philadelphia Quakers, contrasts sharply with Philip. Against his overeager search for wealth, her ambition is to study medicine, placing her at odds with her conventionally minded parents. She not only resists gender norms but also openly challenges the financiers who visit the Bolton home seeking money for speculation in railroad and mining enterprises. Additionally, Ruth's interest in science and her experiences as a medical student characterize her as practical and realistic. When Mr. Bigler asks for an investment from Ruth's father, Ruth challenges the plan as a scheme to cheat the middle class. The investment Mr. Bigler describes is a typical corporate-structured railroad enterprise:

> We'll buy the lands . . . on long time, backed by the notes of good men; and then mortgage them for money enough to get the road well on. Then get the towns on the line to issue their bonds for stock, and sell their bonds for enough to complete the road, and partly stock it, especially if we mortgage each section as we complete it. We can then sell the rest of the stock on the prospect of the business of the road through an improved country, and also sell the lands at a big advance, on the strength of the road. (112–13)

Skeptically, Ruth asks, "You'd sell the stock, I suppose, Mr. Bigler, to anybody who was attracted by the prospectus?" (113). Her uneasiness over her father's investment in the enterprise reflects upon the fictitious, illusory quality of financial capital: "[Ruth] could not have been more discontented if all the wealth about her had been as unsubstantial as a dream." Her observation "I feel . . . as if I were living in a house of cards" (194) identifies the finance economy as fundamentally precarious, and her metaphor presciently anticipates the collapse of the venture, which follows shortly.

The Columbus River Slack-Water Navigation Company epitomizes the operations of the finance economy. Its Wall Street managers deploy successive promises in order to sustain the circulation of fictitious capital, promoting the company to potential investors. They also petition Congress utilizing Sellers's fictitious map of a new town to be built on the site of Stone's Landing and to be called Napoleon, "with a perfect net-work of railroads centering in it, pictures of wharves, crowded with steam-boats, and of huge grain-elevators on the bank" (165). Notably, the map illustrates what Colonel Sellers and Mr. Brierly have imagined, converting Stone's Landing squalor—"a dozen log cabins, with stick and mud chimneys, irregularly disposed on either side of a not very well defined road" (129)—into a burgeoning center of economic and social vitality. In winning the $200,000 congressional appropriation, with an assist from the particularly corrupt Senator Abner Dilworthy, the financial managers spin an effective fiction. Their promises to build a future of projected productivity in a town that does not yet exist demonstrates how a commercial market driven by fictional representations can generate finance capital.

The collapse of the Columbus River Slack-Water Navigation Company reveals the fictional quality of the discourses from which the company was mythically built and the immateriality of the project's financial basis. Although the passage of the congressional appropriation sets in motion the work to redesign Stone's Landing as the town of Napoleon, the money to pay the workers fails to arrive from the company's Wall Street offices. To keep their dream aloft, Brierly and Sellers attempt to assuage the strapped workers by providing discounted credit to be used at local stores. They do so assuming the Wall Street office will provide them with money to repay the credit. When the money still fails to materialize, the discount orders lose their power as currency, and the workers rebel. Brierly sets out for New York to escape a "mob" of rioting workers, telling Sellers "*he* was bound east for money." Meanwhile, the workers "had gutted the Navigation office, then piled the beautiful engraved stock-books and things in the middle of the floor and enjoyed the bonfire while it lasted." Sellers manages to placate the workers by promising "every one of them a lot in the suburbs of Stone's Landing. . . . "[T]hings were blooming and pleasant again, but the men had no money, and nothing to live on." Soon enough the workers "hated themselves for letting [Sellers] beguile them with fine speeches" (188). The entire ordeal shows how the gap between the project's fictitious value and its real value is obscured by discourse that satisfies desire. Unfortunately, the project's hollow core makes each promise an empty echo that can only forestall, not prevent, the inevitable failure.

Although Sellers's speculative imagination has helped to create the company, and he has acted as the company's local manager along with Brierly, he is also a pawn of the Wall Street managers. Like the workers who are left penniless, Sellers fails to profit from the enterprise. Even after the workers have gone weeks and months without pay, Sellers tries to explain to his wife, Polly, that money from the company will arrive: "[T]hat will set things booming again." When Polly replies, "But Eschol, you've *been* expecting it every day," he insists not only that money from the company will arrive soon, but that even greater amounts than the congressional appropriation will be forthcoming. Polly replies, "In the future, Eschol?" (197–98). Polly's response opposes Sellers's finance-inspired illusions, and as with Ruth Bolton, her sense provides a counterpoint to the male-centered business of finance capital. When the Salt Lick Pacific Extension bypasses Stone's Landing in favor of Hawkeye, plans for the Columbus River Slack-Water Navigation Company collapse entirely. Stone's Landing is finally abandoned as a site of "deadly lethargy," where nature resumes its rhythms, reinforcing the immaterial quality of the company's financial activity.

Meanwhile, Brierly's errand to obtain funding to keep the project going turns into an education in the workings of fictitious capital. The unnamed president of the Wall Street investment company explains that the $200,000 from Congress is not a "real" appropriation. It "was never intended for anything but a mere nest egg for the future and *real* appropriations to cluster around" (205). Shocked at the disappearance of the anticipated "tangible thing" and the president's characterization of $200,000 as not quite "real," Brierly asks, "Well, was it a myth, or was it a reality? Whatever become of it?" The president obfuscates, answering that the appropriation did not cover the company's expenses to advertise bonds and to fund religious propaganda, which "makes our bonds go handsomely among the pious poor." The balance paid for lobbyists and bribes for U.S. legislators. In effect, the appropriation, less the amount that was skimmed off by this company president, went entirely to fund the discursive tools used to generate more investment, leaving no funds for the actual building of the project.

Capitalist discourses promising material security and social status shape the world of romance and marriage as well. The financial narratives inform the novel's romance narratives that endorse the marriage market, an arena of exchange in which characters seek partners not only for fulfillment of their intimate desires, but also for wealth and position. These romance narratives reveal a homology between the fictional sentimental melodrama and finance-inspired enterprises. The discourses of both the finance and romance narratives promise the fulfillment of desires, raising expectations that often fail to be met in reality.

Laura Hawkins's narrative develops in accordance with nineteenth-century sentimental melodrama conventions but emphasizes the intersection of romantic and financial discourses. French has noted that "the principal ingredients of the sensation novel are present: disaster (in the steamboat explosion), unknown parentage, adoption, false marriage, murder, self-sacrificing devotion, and hovering between life and death" (45). Orphaned as a result of a steamship explosion and adopted by the squire and Nancy Hawkins, Laura learns upon Squire's death that a man that may be her biological father has been looking for her and that he may be an "'aristocratic gentleman'" (78). But without further proof, rumors about her uncertain lineage spread throughout the town. Soon Laura experiences her first romantic disappointment, when the doctor Ned Thurston stops seeing her. She views the loss of Thurston's attention as a missed opportunity to advance in social class, noting that he "comes of one of the first families of the village" and that he is "prosperous" (83). But her reversal of fortunate expectations also causes her to question the discourse of the romance novels that had reinforced her hopes with Thurston; in her disappointment she asks herself, "[A]re all books lies?" (84). Despite her momentary skepticism about the status of romance narratives, they continue to guide her actions in seeking powerful men for marriage opportunities.

Laura's romantic imagination and desire to escape her family's poverty directly lead her to marry the ex–Confederate officer Colonel George Selby. This arc of her narrative emphasizes both the social circumstances of her family's poverty and her education through romance literature. Knowing all too well "the sting of poverty," Laura realizes that the power of her sexual appeal is an asset that she can trade on to rise above her condition, rather than settle for "the rather loutish young men who came in her way and whom she despised." Her reading, consisting of "romances and fictions which fed her imagination with the most exaggerated notions of life, and showed her men and women in a very false sort of heroism" (137), encourages her to set her sights on Selby when he visits the town of Hawkeye. Having attracted the attention of a man of higher class standing reconfirms her belief in the discourses of romance: "It was all true, then, the romances she had read, the bliss of love she had dreamed of" (138). Shortly after their marriage, however, Selby casts her off, revealing that he has a wife in New Orleans and dismissing their "romance [as] played out" (140). In keeping with the proverb about the fury of a woman scorned, Laura will later track Selby down in

New York and fatally shoot him in a hotel lobby. Like other violent scenes in the novel (e.g., workers burning down the Columbus River Slack-Water Navigation offices), Laura's act has been precipitated by her disappointment over unfulfilled desires for material security. At the conclusion of her trial for the murder of Selby, her defense attorney Mr. Braham pleads with the jury to acquit her, qualifying her action as a by-product of the couple's class differences. "Col. Selby, he said, belonged, gentlemen, to what is called the 'upper classes.' It is the privilege of the 'upper classes' to prey upon the sons and daughters of the people" (405). This rather peculiar defense reinforces the novel's depiction of upper-class opportunism.

However, the intervening plot of Laura's rise as a persuasive lobbyist shows her in control of political and romantic scenarios by capitalizing on her sex appeal. As Laura makes romance a means for social advancement, she resembles financiers making use of fictitious discourse in promoting their financial investments. Laura's coy flirtation with Senator Abner Dilworthy illustrates that she is no longer a dupe of romance; rather, she has learned to make strategic use of her sex appeal to advance her interests. Her power is evident in her rejection of Henry Brierly, who presumes that his relative wealth and higher social-class status will entice her. Laura uses Brierly's desires to her advantage as she calculates upon her romantic allure and its profitability, strategically quantifying how much of her youthfulness it would be "profitable to retain." Laura's "cool brain and exquisite art" combine the qualities of rational calculation and "artful" invention. Only such a combination "could have made [Brierly] lose his head in this way" (145), particularly because his sensibilities are attuned to financial enterprise.

Laura's calculations in her pursuit of men obscure any essential distinction between an imagination fueled by fictional romance stories and one fueled by business discourse. Her earlier naive reading of romances that promised a life of "happily ever after," enabling Selby to seduce her, has given way to a more cynical, avaricious kind of reading. Now romantic discourse directly shapes her desire for material and social advancement, instructing her that beauty and ambition will provide her with the means to attain such wealth and position. When Dilworthy arrives in town, she puts her calculations to use for social gain. Laura's efforts are not lost upon Brierly, who "was beside himself with rage . . . [and] declared that women were always ready to drop any man for higher game" (155). Laura's subsequent success in Washington social circles, facilitated by Dilworthy, is derailed only when Laura encounters Selby again and plots to take revenge upon him.

Laura's romance narrative stands in stark contrast to the stories of courtship by male characters. The first is the melodrama of Washington Hawkins's infatuation with Louise Boswell, the daughter of Washington's employer,

Gen. Boswell, an upper-class real estate businessman. The lower status of Washington's upbringing in the town of Hawkeye and his relative poverty present difficulties in achieving his goal of marrying Louise. He views the kinds of speculative investments proposed by Sellers as his only means to have sufficient income to make a marriage possible, thus confirming his view of the inseparability of love and business: "Some instinct taught Washington that his present lack of money would be an obstruction. . . . He longed for riches now as he had never longed for them before" (72). His desire for wealth through speculation in order to qualify for marriage to Louise Boswell, thus advancing in social class, suggests that romantic and financial discourses recursively complement and reinforce each other. In order to attain the wealth that will enable him to marry Louise and become part of the genteel Boswell family, Washington turns to his one remaining asset, the family's Tennessee Land. Colonel Sellers devises the scheme to sell the land to the U.S. government, and Senator Dilworthy introduces a bill authorizing the purchase. With the bill's anticipated passage, Washington imagines that, in addition to winning Louise's hand, his entire family will be socially elevated. Writing to his mother with unwitting irony, he rhapsodizes, "'Laura will be queen of America, now, and she will be applauded, and honored and petted by the whole nation'" (331). Although the bill fails and Washington does not ever acquire wealth, he wins the assent of Gen. Boswell for marriage to Louise, due in part to Boswell's own reversal of fortune when his railroad investments fail.

The final subplot that turns on the conflation of romance and finance advances Philip Sterling's prospects of marriage with Ruth Bolton, bolstered by his success in a mining enterprise in which his would-be father-in-law Eli Bolton has invested. After months of unsuccessful attempts to find coal, Philip discovers a large deposit with a double payoff: profit for Eli's investment, and proof of Philip's worth as a husband for Ruth. While this narrative directly links financial speculation and romance, it counters the earlier satires of finance capitalism and duplicitous romance. Here, Philip's initiative casts hard work and perseverance as means of achieving financial success, material security, and perpetuation of the bourgeois family. Philip's success in business also suggests that despite the uncertainty and crises of the new financial economy, initiative, intelligence, and effort ultimately determine the conditions of success and failure in modern American society.

Although the courtships between Washington and Louise and between Philip and Ruth affirm the finance economy through their successful resolutions, the denouement to Laura Hawkins's narrative contrasts with the male-centered romance narratives and critically reflects upon finance capital. After Laura's widely publicized trial for the murder of Colonel Selby ends in her acquittal, a promoter named J. Adolphe Griller offers her a business proposition as a traveling lecturer. Laura fantastically imagines dazzling audiences and assuming the romanticized role of a queen, seeming to confirm the role that Washington imagined for her: "She would array herself in fine attire, she would adorn herself with jewels, and stand in her isolated magnificence before massed audiences and enchant them with her eloquence and amaze them with her unapproachable beauty. She would move from city to city like a queen of romance" (433). Laura fantasizes that her "eloquence," her capacity to tell a compelling story, would result in personal profit. Her fantasy of success again reveals her similarity to Colonel Sellers, Henry Brierly, and Washington Hawkins, whose desires for material security are stoked by fictitious discourses promising wealth and luxury.

When Laura finally takes the stage on opening night, her view of the lecture hall reveals "[o]nly a vast, brilliant emptiness," in which not more than forty people are seated. Laura's vision of the "brilliant emptiness" of the hall not only reflects the authors' characterization of financial enterprise as similarly "brilliant" but empty but also shows the popular rejection of imaginative narrative for business profit. In a scene strikingly reminiscent of the unpaid, rioting workers at Stone's Landing, the audience turns upon Laura in a violent outburst: "[A] brutal laugh and an explosion of cat-calls and hisses saluted her from the audience. The clamor grew stronger and louder, and insulting speeches were shouted at her. A half-intoxicated man rose up and threw something, which missed her but bespattered a chair at her side, and this evoked an outburst of laughter and boisterous admiration" (435). Resembling the workers in their revolt, the "mob" pursues Laura as she flees the lecture hall. The public's violent rejection of Laura Hawkins and the business plan concocted by J. Adolphe Griller strongly contrasts with her expectations of success. The scene reveals a limit point for an economy increasingly dependent upon fictitious capital and its corresponding discourses for continued growth. This limit point is further evident in Laura's death immediately following her failure and flight from the lecture hall. The narrator's description of Laura's appearance in death lingers over the motionlessness of her figure: "When the spring morning dawned, the form still sat there, the elbows resting upon the table and the face upon the hands. All day long the figure sat there, the sunshine enriching its costly raiment and flashing from its jewels; twilight came, and presently the stars, but still the figure remained; the moon found it there still, and framed the picture with the shadow of the window sash, and flooded it with mellow light; by and by the darkness swallowed it up, and later the gray dawn revealed it again; the new day grew toward its prime, and still the forlorn presence was undisturbed" (436–37). For a character defined by romantic hopes and desires for material success, this concluding image of her body at the time of death pointedly reflects the failure of misguided imagination to overcome material reality. The stasis of the scene marks a dramatic end for the romantic imagination in a profit-based financial economy.

Although Twain and Warner undermine their criticism of the financial economy by concluding the novel with affirmative male-centered romances, their portrayal of workers rioting against a Wall Street–financed firm captures the precarious social and economic conditions of the early-to-mid-1870s. In light of the start of the 1873–1878 economic depression that coincided with the novel's publication, Ruth Bolton's comment that she feels as if she "were living in a house of cards" reads today as a journalistic observation. In showing the precarious quality of financial enterprise, the novel reveals the inherent limitations to the finance economy as described by the narrator: "[T]he Bolton household had no idea of the number of perils that hovered over them, any more than thousands of families in America have of the business risks and contingencies upon which their prosperity and luxury hang" (195). The comment aptly describes the problem for the middle and working classes with the finance economy, even if the authors do not imagine a noncapitalistic alternative to it.

Notes

1. Thorstein Veblen describes business enterprise as a particular organization of capitalism that developed in the late nineteenth century, which is identifiable by the expanded role of credit or finance in the productive process. Veblen differentiates business enterprise from other forms of capitalist production such as industrial capitalism. See Veblen, 1–4.

2. Critics of the 1920s and 1930s generally found the novel disappointing (Van Wyck Brooks, V. L. Parrington, Granville Hicks), while the critics of the 1950s and 1960s evaluated it favorably (Philip Foner, Bryant Morley French, and Maxwell Geismar).

3. Twain based Squire Hawkins's purchase of the Tennessee Land on a similar purchase by his father, John M. Clemens, who obtained thousands of acres of land in Tennessee as an investment. See *Autobiography of Mark Twain*, 1: 206.

4. David Harvey notes that with the development of financial markets, property rights to land may function as fictitious capital. See Harvey, 276.

Works Cited

Arvin, Newton. "Mark Twain: 1835–1935." *Critical Essays on Mark Twain, 1910–1980*. Ed. Louis J. Budd. Boston: Hall, 1983. 84–88.

Chandler, Alfred. *The Railroads: The Nation's First Big Business.* New York: Harcourt, 1965.

Foner, Philip S. *Mark Twain: Social Critic.* New York: International, 1958.

French, Bryant Morey. *Mark Twain and* The Gilded Age: *The Book That Named an Era.* Dallas: Southern Methodist UP, 1965.

Harvey, David. *The Limits to Capital.* London: Verso, 2006.

Heinzelman, Kurt. *The Economics of the Imagination.* Amherst: U of Massachusetts P, 1980.

Marx, Karl. *Capital.* 1894. Trans. David Fernbach. 3 vols. New York: Penguin, 1991.

Twain, Mark. *Autobiography of Mark Twain: The Complete and Authorized Edition.* 3 vols. Ed. Harriet Elinor Smith et al. Berkeley: U of California P, 2010, 2012, 2015.

Twain, Mark, and Charles Dudley Warner. *The Gilded Age.* 1873. New York: Library of America, 2002.

Veblen, Thorstein. *The Theory of Business Enterprise.* 1904. New Brunswick: Transaction, 1978.

White, Richard. *Railroaded: The Transcontinentals and the Making of Modern America.* New York: Norton, 2011.

11

"By and By I Was Smitten with the Silver Fever"

Literary Veins in *Roughing It*

Jeffrey W. Miller

> I found abundant enjoyment in being rich. A man offered me a three-hundred-dollar horse, and wanted to take my simple, unendorsed note for it. That brought the most realizing sense I had yet had that I was actually rich, beyond shadow of doubt. It was followed by numerous other evidences of a similar nature—among which I may mention the fact of the butcher leaving us a double supply of meat and saying nothing about money.
>
> —Mark Twain, *Roughing It*

The above passage—from Mark Twain's 1872 novel *Roughing It*, touches on a key ontological distinction—that of "being rich" versus acting rich. What makes one "actually rich"? Is it having cold, hard cash on hand, or does it require changed social and economic relations? In the mining world of Washoe depicted in the novel, how does one acquire this status? How does one go about getting rich? Arguably, this is the single question that motivates the narrator more than any other. Over the course of the novel, he goes West in order to get rich—first by prospecting for silver, then by writing about it. Neither attempt is successful, but the object of making money remains at center stage throughout. And, all due respect to the butcher, our narrator can't go two pages without saying something about money.

I argue that the act of mining—the archetypal act of taking money out of the earth—is a symbol for literary production in *Roughing It*. This symbol takes a number of forms, but most commonly it associates literary production with mining for precious metals and correlates both of these acts with financial success. *Roughing It* offers a number of significant juxtapositions of mining and writing, because it contains extensive descriptions of actual mining and because it was written as Twain was polishing the image of himself as a literary man.

Critics have often read *Roughing It* as a bildungsroman. Indeed, the education of the naive narrator grants a familiar coherence to the book. However, this reading necessitates the construction of a dichotomy between the "rough" world of mining and the "civilized" world of letters. In this view, as Twain fails to become a miner, he initiates his identity as a literary man. In contrast, my reading of *Roughing It* collapses that dichotomy, arguing that Twain can conceive of what it means to be a literary man only through the rhetoric of mining. In fact, that literary identity is possible only as far as it is able to depict the culture of mining and, more broadly, the culture of financial possibility in the American West. Ultimately, I demonstrate how Twain's vision of the literary is dependent upon the narrative of (literally) striking it rich. This vision is realized in three ways. First, he inverts the standard western narrative of mining success. Second, he conflates writing, mining, and money throughout the novel. Third, he emphasizes the commodification of writing.

Inverting the Narrative of Mining Success

While *Roughing It* adheres to several patterns common to the narrative of western American success, ultimately the novel inverts that narrative by depicting failure rather than success. Ironically, however, failure in mining is a necessary component to Twain's successful writing and, specifically, successful humor. Thus, Twain succeeds by depicting failure. This is not just a matter of the text's bildungsroman aspect—that is, our protagonist does not fail at mining so he can succeed at writing. He succeeds in writing by depicting his failure as a miner and his failure as a writer.

Gregg Camfield asserts that *Roughing It* is "virtually a hymn in praise of the enterprising spirit of the West" (97). Indeed, the potential for enterprise is ever present, but other critics offer a more tempered view. Peter Messent, for instance, has recognized that while the novel tells the story of western economic opportunity and rebirth, it also "complicates and undermines" that story (49). Messent claims that the tensions of *Roughing It* are a result of the interplay of the individualist West and the capitalist East.

My reading of *Roughing It* shifts focus away from the growth of the narrator and the novel's plot. Although I agree that the narrator seems to move generally from innocence to experience, I do not see this movement as significant enough to inform the structure of the novel. Instead, I assert that a single idea runs through the novel, thus offering a unifying focus. That idea is one that remains near and dear to Sam Clemens throughout his life: money. The protagonist in *Roughing It*, through his various adventures and travels, through his confusions and epiphanies, consistently searches for economic opportunity. The protagonist's two main endeavors are mining and writing, and money is the stated object of both. That mining and writing connection also serves to ameliorate what Messent calls the "epistemological uncertainty" of the narrator, as he finds purpose in the capitalistic enterprise.

One of Twain's standard patterns is that of simultaneously confirming and undermining traditional narratives. This pattern has often been identified as a source of his humor, especially through the lens of thwarted expectations (Bassett; Hill; Justus; Messent). This pattern appears in *Roughing It*, as the narrator is constantly depicting success in the world of mining—the traditional narrative. However, that narrative is continuously undermined because it is a success that is never realized.

The standard narrative of the mining West represents the trajectory of possibility, success, and transformation. Janet Floyd explains that this is so in part because of the intertwined nature of journalism and mining in the Washoe Big Bonanza era: "The newspapers where these writers found, or developed, work were organs owned or sponsored by mining companies and supported by communities of migrants whose working lives were directed toward prospecting and mining silver" (57). Therefore, the papers often depicted successful mines and affluent miners. However, even eastern journalists—those not employed by mining companies—tended to tell similar stories of possibility and success. One reason for this consistency is that eastern newspaper editors rarely sent their own correspondents out West to write firsthand reports. Instead, they clipped copy directly from western papers and became sites of extension for the corporate story.

When an eastern correspondent did go out West and report on the experience, he often did so as an outsider rather than as a participant. Perhaps the best-known of these outsiders is J. Ross Browne, who wrote a series of articles on Washoe for *Harper's* in 1860. Henry Wonham points out that this series of articles was influential upon Twain as he was writing *Roughing It* (93). Even though Browne highlights the difficulties inherent in striking out West in search of success, he never questions the existence or availability of that success. For instance, he characterizes the ubiquity of silver ore in Washoe and its easy accessibility: "SILVER—solid, pure SILVER! Beds of it ten thousand feet deep! Acres of it!—miles of it! —hundreds of millions of dollars poking their backs up out of the earth ready to be pocketed!" (5). He asserts that the silver in Washoe is "solid" and "pure" (neither was true) and converts it into "dollars" that are visible and ready to be picked up and pocketed as easily as a dime on a street corner.

Those critics who read *Roughing It* as some sort of bildungsroman read Twain's inversion as a necessary step in the progress of the narrator from innocence to experience—from failure as miner to success as writer (Caron; Gunn). However, one could just as easily read Twain's writerly success as preliminary and uncertain. Furthermore, the narrator displays evidence of the failure of writing throughout the novel. For Twain, though, failure is success, because it makes a better story; mock mining success couched in failure creates literary success.

If the standard narrative can be divided into looking for a vein, staking a claim, and mining the ore, Twain includes only the first two of these stages, as he does not engage in mining—he engages only in the prospect of mining. Twain could have easily constructed a narrative of the third stage, as there is evidence that Sam Clemens worked hard at mining. In a letter to Orion, he claims, "[M]y back is sore and my hands blistered" from handling the pick and axe (SLC to Orion Clemens). However, the novel tells a different story: he looks but does not find; he stakes but does not mine. His record of the mining life is a record of incompletion: "We took up various claims, and commenced shafts and tunnels on them, but *never* finished any of them. . . . We were always hunting up new claims and doing a little work on them and then waiting for a buyer—who *never* came. We *never* found any ore that would yield more than fifty dollars a ton; and as the mills charged fifty dollars a ton for working ore and extracting the silver, our pocket-money melted steadily away and none returned to take its place. We lived in a little cabin and cooked for ourselves; and altogether it was a hard life, though a hopeful one—for we *never* ceased to expect fortune and a customer to burst upon us some day" (251, emphasis added). The repetition of "never" in this short passage emphasizes the incompletion that characterizes Twain's prospecting life. His best chance at success appears to be the "curious episode" of Higbie's discovery of the "blind lead" in chapter XL, but it is marked by another "never"—he and his companions never complete the necessary work on the claim that would secure their ownership of the lead, and so it becomes public property.

In the context of traditional "greenhorn" interpretations of the novel, these "nevers" are examples of Twain's unfitness for the life of mining. In my interpretation, however, these "nevers" are manifestations of Twain's narrative imperative to delay. Thus, Twain's looking but not finding, planning to work but not working, spending money before having money, and so on, parallels his humorist's instinct to delay, pause, and defer a story.

Twain's humor relies on what he calls the "pause" before the snapper—the "most important thing in the whole story," he asserts in "How to Tell a Story" (*Collected Tales, Sketches, Speeches, and Essays* 2:204). This delayed gratification is parallel to the delayed strike (or delayed work) in mining. The story of Jim Blaine's ram is perhaps the best example of this delay in the novel. Twain recounts how his compatriots urge him to ask Jim Blaine about his grandfather's ram while he is drunk (383). After a long series of incomprehensible digressions, he falls asleep. Twain leaves the story untold, "a dark mystery to this day" (390).

2. Conflating Mining, Writing, and Money

In addition to depicting the failure of mining alongside the failure of writing, Twain conflates mining and writing most notably in his depiction of silver fever, in which he recognizes that language—both oral and written—shapes the success of mines; in his use of jargon; and in his serial depiction of the "lost mine."

Twain recognizes that language is the contagion of silver fever—the lightning communication of vein information is the first necessary step of spreading the news. His first extended description of prospecting in chapter XXVI contains a number of key elements illustrating language as this kind of conduit:

> By and by I was smitten with the silver fever. . . . Plainly this was the road to fortune. . . . Not a mine could be named that had not experienced an astonishing advance in value within a short time. Everybody was talking about these marvels. Go where you would, you heard nothing else, from morning till far into the night. . . . The "Last Chance" had found a "clay casing" and knew they were "right on the ledge". . . . And so on—day in and day out the talk pelted our ears and the excitement waxed hotter and hotter around us. . . . Cart-loads of solid silver bricks, as large as pigs of lead, were arriving from the mills every day, and such sights as that gave substance to the wild talk about me. (193–94)

The common denominator of this fever is the influence of "talk"; Twain expertly places jargon in the middle here, and it is jargon that carries an unmistakable sense of value. Even the mine's name—Last Chance—implies an urgency toward action. Although the "wild talk" is rooted in concrete reality ("cart-loads" of silver!), there is no evidence that the Last Chance (or any other mine) is the specific source of that silver glimpsed by the cart-load, and it is plain that the talk itself is what ascribes value to a particular mine. The mining conversation is omnipresent ("go where you would"), omnitemporal ("day in and day out"), and omniscient ("everybody was talking").

The "silver fever" passage emphasizes the continuity between East and West. Rather than depicting a crazy frontier in which capitalism has gone out of control, Twain depicts a version of the typical market economy, in which value is constructed through the notion of exchange—just as it is back East. Further, the passage underscores the relationship between language and value in that market economy, a relationship that is well documented by economic historians. The booms and bubbles of capitalism are accompanied by the narrative of potential value, and the busts and crashes are accelerated by the narrative of uncertain value. The bank runs so typical of an economic crisis are a function of the transmission of a "contagion"—bad news that is spread socially until it becomes an information epidemic (Kelly and Ó Gráda; Aspers; Calomiris and Schweikart; Kindleberger and Aliber). In Twain's depiction of the boom years of Washoe, the narrative of potential value—"wild talk"—acts as a kind of paper money that stands in for the silver bricks, imputing value to the mines that (might) provide them. Hence, the circulation of that talk is the "currency" of the frontier. Unlike silver bricks or even paper money, however, talk is in unlimited supply and thus inflates itself and destabilizes itself when it becomes omnipresent. In his wide-ranging study of the connection between language and money, Marc Shell asserts that credit money and paper money allow an "idealist transcendence" of commodities (108). In other words, paper money transforms a market as a site of the exchange of things into a site of the exchange of ideas. Twain depicts this transformation in the market of mine "feet."

The practice of selling "feet"—essentially shares of a mine—illustrates the relationship between narrative and mining in terms of value, as the feet acquire value through reputation and the exchange of ideas. The name itself connotes regularity and fairness—a foot is a foot, after all, but the actual value of feet in particular mines varies wildly. Twain recounts how men would sell and trade feet by attempting to construct value for the mine through building a narrative:

> Every man you met had his new mine to boast of, and his "specimens" ready; and if the opportunity offered, he would infallibly back you into a corner and . . . exclaim: "Look at that! Right there in that red dirt! See it? See the specks of gold? And the streak of silver? That's from the Uncle Abe. There's a hundred thousand tons like that in sight! Right in sight, mind you! And when we get down on it and the ledge comes in solid, it will be the richest thing in the world! Look at the assay! I don't want you to believe me—look at the assay!" (215)

As before, the story begins rooted in material—here, instead of silver bricks, the man carries a "specimen" ready for inspection. However, once he understands that the "specks of gold" are not visible, he turns to the authority of the "assay," which Twain describes as "a greasy sheet of paper" that offers evidence from the "richest piece of rock" in the mine. In other words, the prospector wants our narrator to treat the assay as paper money.

Peter Messent points out that Twain's particular references to "greenbacks" in the novel indicate that he had a distrust of paper money that was reflective of the national dependence upon the "intrinsic value" of hard money. However, Messent may overstate the sway of hard-money advocates in the nineteenth century, as the greenback issue was hardly settled into a national consensus. As Gretchen Ritter outlines in her history of finance politics in postbellum America, the "soft money" crowd mounted regular and vigorous opposition to hard-money policy (47–58). Furthermore, greenbacks were the "routine medium of exchange" (Greenfield and Rockoff 905).

There is a scattering of references to greenbacks in his letters of this period, at least one of which is derogatory: "[W]hat do you suppose I could do with greenbacks here?" (SLC to Jane Lampton Clemens). In this context, it is possible to read Twain's satirical stab at paper feet as some sort of goldbug commentary. It certainly seems as if he is mocking the general Washoe acceptance of economic potential in place of hard money. On the other hand, greenbackers were believers in "democratic promise" and "equal economic opportunity" (Ritter 96). Even though Twain is satirizing the too-easy acceptance of feet for silver, there is something exhilarating in the possibility that "every man . . . had his new mine." In fact, a few pages later, Twain himself becomes "every man": "[W]e had learned the *real* secret of success in silver mining—which was, *not* to mine the silver ourselves by the sweat of our brows and the labor of our hands, but to *sell* the ledges to the dull slaves of toil and let them do the mining!" (217). The business of selling, and thus the business of narrative, has fallen under his purview.

Once Twain begins to relate his experience as a journalist, it becomes clear how much the narrative surrounding feet, mines, and assays impacts the determination of value in the Nevada marketplace. Floyd indicates that most journalists were "company men," but Twain illustrates how the construction of a narrative around a mine was more important than the construction of a shaft or the locating of actual ore:

> New claims were taken up daily, and it was the friendly custom to run straight to the newspaper offices, give the reporter forty or fifty "feet," and get them to go and examine the mine and publish a notice of it. They did not care a fig what you said about the property so you said something. . . . If the rock was moderately promising, we followed the custom of the country, used strong adjectives and frothed at the mouth as if a very marvel in silver discoveries had transpired. If the mine was a "developed" one, and had no pay ore to show (and of course it hadn't), we praised the tunnel; said it was one of the most infatuating tunnels in the land; driveled and driveled about the tunnel till we ran entirely out of ecstasies—but never said a word about the rock. We would squander half a column of adulation on a shaft,

> or a new wire rope, or a dressed pine windlass, or a fascinating force pump, and close with a burst of admiration of the "gentlemanly and efficient Superintendent" of the mine—but never utter a whisper about the rock. (307–8)

The formulas Twain uses as a reporter are similar to his earlier descriptions of silver fever, although the "wild talk" has become controlled propaganda. Now, however, Twain is a generator of the narrative rather than a receiver of it. The repetition of "never said a word about the rock" is effective, as are the deprecatory synonyms for "write" (frothed, driveled, squander) and the focus on the tools of the trade as a substitute for success. Because so much value is placed on potential through the selling of stock, the actual value of the rock in a mine is not as important as its perceived value, and its perceived value is constructed through language. As with the "silver fever" episode, the exchange of things has been transformed into the exchange of ideas; here, the paper money of mine feet is exchanged for inches in the newspaper column. In this case, the inches are put in circulation in order to increase the circulation of the feet. This perpetual circulation evokes Marx's claim in *Capital* that the circulation of money is an "end in itself . . . [and] therefore limitless" (253). For Twain the new journalist, this limitless circulation creates winners all around—the miner inflates the currency of his mine (feet, not silver), and the reporter meets his deadline with a few inches of news, along with a few feet of mining stock. As a "company" reporter, Twain becomes practiced at building enticing narratives around individual claims, although in this passage he reveals the trade secret of avoiding the hard facts of the mine's hard money (or lack thereof).

In order to construct these narratives, Twain needs to familiarize himself with the vernacular of the mines, first when he becomes a miner, then when he becomes a journalist. The motivation for this is twofold; of course, in order to negotiate success in the West, he must be able to speak its language. More importantly, however, he understands the role of language and the exchange of ideas in shaping identity. One cannot be a miner if one cannot speak like a miner. As a writer, he must wield the language of his subject expertly. Using jargon authenticates his authority as expert, even as he is depicting his failure to flourish in that environment. Furthermore, there is an aspect of camaraderie to the insider status granted to those who master the language—what Stephen Fender calls "the manly jargon of the mines" (746).

Henry Wonham claims that Twain's transformation in *Roughing It* centers on the acquisition of a "new language" (95). He is right that the narrator acquires the art of western "tall narrative"—the naive romanticist becomes an experienced "yarn spinner" (101). However, we should not overlook the new mining language that he acquires. In fact, the narrator is somewhat self-conscious of his knowledge, as is evidenced by an oddly placed footnote late in the book. Through this note, appearing three-quarters of the way through the narrative, the narrator seems intent upon sharing his knowledge with the reader, pointing out his use of "mining technicalities" that "may be a little obscure to the general reader" (443). This is out of character for Twain, who generally prefers surprise over clarification.

In addition to learning the jargon of the mines, Twain learns its folklore as well. Certainly, the tall tale is part of the expected repertoire of a frontier storyteller, but miners have tales of their own, some of which fit well into Twain's penchant for delay and diversion. One such tale is the story of the "lost mine," or the "one that got away" (Rosenberg 295–96). Commonly in these stories, the lost mine is literally lost; that is, a prospector finds a lead, wanders back to town, and is unable to relocate the vein. In *Roughing It*, Twain offers the tale with multiple narrative layers, and in doing so he illustrates how the connection between mining and language structures the book. The "lost mine" (or mines) in the novel is both literal and figurative. Twain depicts a series of lost mines, beginning with the story of the Whiteman cement mine—a mine literally lost: "[Whiteman] had been hunting for the lost mine, in hunger and thirst, poverty and sickness, for twelve or thirteen years" (261). Whiteman is the archetypal prospector, the continual searcher, who seems to misunderstand the mining market of ideas in Washoe. He is a hard-money man in search of intrinsic value in a world of soft-money paper stocks.

More seriously, Twain relates a mine that is not physically lost, but legally lost: his missed opportunity to gain millions through the assisted sale of a Washoe mine back East. Unfortunately, he misses his train, and another takes his place. Twain associates this failure with the original "blind lead" failure, and the two stories are connected by more than just failure. Essentially, Twain misses out each time because of a paper-bound technicality, and each event underscores the transformation of real mines—actual holes in the actual ground—to words on paperstock.

Finally, at the furthest end of the figurative spectrum, the lost mine of meaning becomes a common theme. Others have argued that the unabridged dictionary, which makes itself conspicuous during the stage trip to the West, serves as a symbol of the linguistic gap between East and West (Gunn; Messent; Michelson). Messent, in particular, claims that its value out West is marginal, because it does not depict the vernacular speech that Twain so often encounters. Michelson goes further, pointing out that it represents language as a "dangerous business" by becoming a projectile (46). I see it as representative of a more general failure of language in the novel. It sets up the serial failure of Twain the writer that accompanies the failure of Twain the miner. As the ostensible authority on language, the dictionary offers a tangible reference point that connects "reality" to words. However, our narrator feels that this link is broken, and he lacks the skill to go beyond what it offers: "It was hard to bring the comprehension away down to such a snail-pace as [two miles an hour], when we had been used to making eight and ten miles an hour. When we reached the station on the farther verge of the desert, we were glad, for the first time, that the dictionary was along, because we never could have found language to tell how glad we were, in any sort of dictionary but an unabridged one with pictures in it. But there could not have been found in a whole library of dictionaries language sufficient to tell how tired those mules were after their twenty-three mile pull" (144–45). This whole passage is riddled with a subtext of lost meaning. He equates comprehension with physical speed, and as they slow, they also cannot generate meaning without the help of pictures. Ultimately, however, language fails, as the exhaustion of the mules remains beyond the ability of the narrator to relate. This bit with the dictionary begins a long string of passages where the narrator is dissatisfied with the quality of his writing, and he repeatedly apologizes for his shortcomings.

Mining the Literary Vein

In addition to the role that writing might play in enhancing the value of mines and mining stock, *Roughing It* makes a case for writing itself as a commodity. That is, writing pays, and virtually every depiction of writing in the novel is accompanied by an explanation of how it will pay. The commodification of writing works both metaphorically (ideas as a resource to be mined through writing) and literally (writing as a product to be sold). This commodification of writing creates an intersection between Twain's consciousness of the possibilities of language and the narrative of mining that permeates the novel superficially and structurally.

The basic metaphor is that of ideas as precious metals that must be prospected and found, then worked out from a primitive state into finer stuff. There is nothing new in this; Floyd asserts that this metaphor has been commonplace since the Renaissance (33), and Shell traces it all the way back to Plato (131ff). For Twain, however, the metaphor takes on additional weight because of the mining context of *Roughing It*. Twain the journalist makes much of prospecting for copy to fill his columns. Part of that copy is filled by literally writing about the mines, carefully employing mining jargon throughout the novel. In addition, he also utilizes that jargon figuratively in a variety of ways.

"Rich," for instance, is most often used in the novel to describe the economic state (of a person or a mine), but Twain also uses it to describe language: "enriching your minds" (164); "rich" slang of Nevada (330); a "rich brogue" (362); a "rich voice" (472); "enriching his mind with information" (506); "the richest specimen of journalistic literature" (580). While "rich" is not proper mining jargon, Twain uses it so often in connection with Washoe that it becomes so by association.

One of the most extended (and noteworthy) episodes in the novel that bears relation to the usage of language and its connection to meaning is that of Scotty Briggs and the minister, who discuss the prospect of Buck Fanshaw's funeral. Many critics have analyzed this passage, almost always with the notion that Scotty and the minister represent two poles of language—Scotty's western slang and the minister's eastern formal English (see Bassett 229; Beidler 46–47; Bird 24; Coulombe 62; Florence 111). Beidler rightly calls attention to the way in which language structures thought, claiming that the two men exhibit "two discourses [and] two complete and separate ways of knowing" (46). It is important to add that Scotty speaks not just western vernacular, but mining camp vernacular that is suffused with economic references. He imputes industry to the church (the minister is the "head clerk" of the "doxology-works" 332), he frames the conversation around gambling, speaking of antes and raises, and he sees the minister as a prospector searching for meaning ("you see my blind" 333). Most significantly, he has come to conduct a business transaction—to hire the minister to officiate at the funeral: "[W]e'll take care of *you*, pard. We'll fix you all right . . . whatever you want" (334). Thus, the episode is simultaneously a negotiation of meaning between East and West and a negotiation of exchange-value between the spiritual and the material.

After *Roughing It* appeared, various readers were quick to assert that Twain engages in figurative mining. As George Plimpton reports, Howells calls Twain's experiences in Nevada "gold under his hand," and the *Territorial Enterprise* announces *Roughing It* by claiming Twain as a native son: "[I]t was while a resident here and associated with the Enterprise that he assumed the name Mark Twain and developed that rich and inexhaustible vein which has made the title famous" (xxxvi, xli). Both of these references speak to the limitless nature of the realm of ideas and the circulation of money. Howells obliquely crowns Twain as a Midas-figure, implying that his ideas (and thus his writing) will create value as long as he can continue to produce them. According to the *Enterprise*, that production goes beyond the borders of time and space—not unlike the silver fever discussed earlier.

This literary production is depicted in the novel itself as a commodity—in the language of Marx, a thing that has a use-value and an exchange-value (125–26). The use-value of Twain's literary production might be to provide entertainment, but Twain seems much more interested in the potential exchange-value of his work, constantly connecting words to money (or trying to do so). In describing his first lecture—a form of merged writing and performance that provided him with much-needed income throughout his life, Twain connects it to mining and money. First, he recognizes the economic potential of the lecture: "I had the field all to myself, for public lectures were almost an unknown commodity in the Pacific market" (564). He conceives of the operation from the perspective of a businessman—investigating the market and enlisting ringers to laugh on cue, so as to offer the infectious illusion of satisfied customers. Once he commits to the lecture, he describes the audience response in language befitting a miner: the biggest laugh is an "explosion" and his compatriots worked like "pile-drivers" (563). He doesn't even seem to care that his meaning has been thwarted; he intended a "morsel of pathos," but one of his ringers took his wry smile as a signal and set the house laughing at the "joke" that was meant to be serious. This passage reverses the transformation of the silver-fever passage, where the exchange of things became the exchange of ideas. Now the "abundance of money" earned from the lecture allows Twain to "wisely let . . . go" of his intended meaning.

There is a striking passage from his autobiographical dictations in which Twain relates an early memory that illustrates his understanding of how his identity as a miner, however brief, structures his identity as a storyteller: "[A]ll through my life my facts have had a substratum of truth, and therefore they were not without preciousness. Any person who is familiar with me knows how to strike my average, and therefore knows how to get at the jewel of any fact of mine and dig it out of its blue-clay matrix" (*ATM* 1:268). Notice the monetary value that Twain attaches to fact here: it is "the jewel." Not exactly silver, but the implication is similar. The episode indicates that Twain still thought of mental processes as akin to mining—even forty years after laying down his pickax. Here, the value of truth (the "substratum") seems to be the intrinsic value—the hard money—at the heart of his literary project.

Twain understands the relative value of commodities, and in *Roughing It* he outlines how "trifles" in the West are much more expensive than the same items in the East, listing everyday items that he balances with their economic value—as the items accrue, his "bag of silver" lightens (137–38). However, we can see that Twain addresses his writing using the same sort of "expense account" rhetoric. Sometimes this correlation is tossed off as a humorous aside: "no additional charge for this joke" or ascribing a worth of "millions" to a statement (267, 269).

Michelson reads Twain's frontier as an escape from civilization and sense.

While this is true to an extent, it is also true that the logic of capitalism—which marries language and money in multiple ways—acts as the ultimate ordering principle of the frontier. Thus, Twain is not really escaping civilization; rather, he is helping to construct a version of eastern capitalism in the West—an exaggerated version, yes, but one that clearly follows the rules and logic of the eastern system. In broader terms, Twain offers a version of the West to eastern readers, and as he developed a sense of himself as a commodity in the literary marketplace, he became more aware of how that commodity ought to be marketed for the general marketplace. His solution, of course, was to begin publishing his books by subscription with Elisha Bliss and the American Publishing Company, because he felt that doing so would give him the best chance of making the most money (Kaplan 61). In this context, Twain was cognizant that "facts" have a different relative value in the world of subscription publishing (Hill 28; Wuster 7–8). But even more important, subscription publishing allowed Twain to reach a different class of customer and have greater control over how his literary self was being sold to the world. His letters to Bliss frame his literary productions almost entirely in economic terms. His highest praise for his own work is that "it will sell," and he compares his books to each other similarly—"it will outsell . . ." (SLC to Elisha Bliss, 10 July 1871 and 26 February 1873). Granted, these are letters to his publisher, which are naturally concerned with business matters, but it is striking how much his vision of the literary is so clearly connected to his ability to generate and accumulate money.

Works Cited

Aspers, Patrik. "Knowledge and Valuation in Markets." *Theory and Society* 38 (2009): 111–31.

Bassett, John. "*Roughing It*: Authority through Comic Performance." *Nineteenth-Century Literature* 43 (1988): 220–34.

Beidler, Philip. "Realistic Style and the Problem of Context in 'The Innocents Abroad' and *Roughing It*." *American Literature* 52 (1980): 33–49.

Bird, John. *Mark Twain and Metaphor*. Columbia: U of Missouri P, 2007.

Browne, J. Ross. "A Peep at Washoe [Second Paper]." *Harper's New Monthly Magazine* 22 (January 1861): 145–62.

Calomiris, Charles W., and Larry Schweikart. "The Panic of 1857: Origins, Transmission, and Containment." *Journal of Economic History* 51 (1991): 807–34.

Camfield, Gregg. "A Republican Artisan in the Court of King Capital: Mark Twain and Commerce." *A Historical Guide to Mark Twain*. Ed. Shelley Fisher Fishkin. Oxford: Oxford UP, 2002. 95–126.

Caron, James E. "The Comic Bildungsroman of Mark Twain." *Modern Language Quarterly* 50 (1989): 145–72.

Coulombe, Joseph. *Mark Twain and the American West*. Columbia: U of Missouri P, 2003.

Fender, Stephen. "The Prodigal in a Far Country Chawing of Husks." *Modern Language Review* 71 (1976): 737–56.

Florence, Don. *Persona and Humor in Mark Twain's Early Writing*. Columbia: U of Missouri P, 1995.

Floyd, Janet. *Claims and Speculations: Mining and Writing in the Gilded Age*. Albuquerque: U of New Mexico P, 2012.

Greenfield, Robert L., and Hugh Rockoff. "Yellowbacks Out West and Greenbacks Back East: Social-Choice Dimensions of Monetary Reform." *Southern Economic Journal* 62 (1996): 902–15.

Gunn, Drewey Wayne. "The Monomythic Structure of *Roughing It*." *American Literature* 61 (1989): 563–85.

Hill, Hamlin. "Mark Twain: Audience and Artistry." *American Quarterly* 15 (1963): 25–40.

Justus, James H. *Fetching the Old Southwest: Humorous Writing from Longstreet to Twain*. Columbia: U of Missouri P, 2004.

Kaplan, Justin. *Mr. Clemens and Mark Twain: A Biography*. New York: Simon and Schuster, 1966.

Kelly, Morgan, and Cormac Ó Gráda. "Market Contagion: Evidence from the Panics of 1854 and 1857." *American Economic Review* 90 (2000): 1110–24.

Kindleberger, Charles P., and Robert Z. Aliber. *Manias, Panics, and Crashes: A History of Financial Crises*. 5th ed. Hoboken: Wiley, 2005.

Marx, Karl. *Capital: A Critique of Political Economy*. Vol. 1. Trans. Ben Fowkes. New York: Penguin, 1990.

Messent, Peter. "'It's a Great Country, Ma'—Blind Leads and Shifting Ground: The West in Mark Twain's *Roughing It*." *Canadian Review of American Studies* 26 (1996): 49–78.

Michelson, Bruce. *Mark Twain on the Loose: A Comic Writer and the American Self*. Amherst: U of Massachusetts P, 1995.

Mitchell, Lee Clark. "Verbally Roughing It: The West of Words." *Nineteenth-Century Literature* 44 (1989): 67–92.

Plimpton, George. "Introduction." Twain, *Roughing It*. xxxi–xliv.

Ritter, Gretchen. *Goldbugs and Greenbacks: The Antimonopoly Tradition and the Politics of Finance in America, 1865–1896*. New York: Cambridge UP, 1997.

Rosenberg, Bruce A. "The Folklore of the Gold Rush." *Huntington Library Quarterly* 44 (1981): 293–308.

Shell, Marc. *Money, Language, and Thought: Literary and Philosophical Economies from the Medieval to the Modern Era*. Berkeley: U of California P, 1982.

Twain, Mark. *Autobiography of Mark Twain: The Complete and Authorized Edition*. 3 vols. Ed. Harriett Smith et al. Berkeley: U of California P, 2101, 2012, 2015.

———. *Collected Tales, Sketches, Speeches, and Essays.* 2 vols. Ed. Louis Budd. New York: Library of America, 1984.

———. *Roughing It.* 1872. New York: Oxford UP, 1996.

———. SLC to Elisha Bliss, Jr., 10 July 1871, Elmira, N.Y. (UCCL 11312). <http://www.marktwainproject.org/xtf/view?docId=letters/UCCL11312.xml;style=letterletter;brand=mtp>.

———. SLC to Elisha Bliss, Jr., 26 February 1873, Hartford, Conn. (UCCL 00876). <http://www.marktwainproject.org/xtf/view?docId=letters/UCCL00876.xml;style=letterletter;brand=mtp>.

———. SLC to Jane Lampton Clemens and Pamela A. Moffett, 25 September 1864, San Francisco, Calif. (UCCL 00087). <http://www.marktwainproject.org/xtf/view?docId=letters/UCCL00087.xml;style=letterletter;brand=mtp>.

———. SLC to Orion Clemens, 17 and 19 April 1862, Aurora, Nevada (UCCL 00043). <http://www.marktwainproject.org/xtf/view?docId=letters/UCCL00043.xml;style=letterletter;brand=mtp>.

Wonham, Henry B. *Mark Twain and the Art of the Tall Tale.* New York: Oxford UP, 1993.

Wuster, Tracy. "'There's Millions in It!' *The Gilded Age* and the Economy of Satire." *Mark Twain Annual* 11 (2013): 1–21.

12
The Art of Arbitrage
Reimagining Mark Twain, Business Man

Henry B. Wonham

> OCTOBER: This is one of the peculiarly dangerous months to speculate in stocks in. The others are July, January, September, April, November, May, March, June, December, August, and February.
>
> —"Pudd'nhead Wilson's Calendar"

> There are two times in a man's life when he should not speculate: when he can't afford it and when he can.
>
> —*Following the Equator*, "Pudd'nhead Wilson's New Calendar"

Setting Henry's Hen

Among American writers, only one holds the distinction of having lent his name to the jargon of Wall Street traders, who refer to the "Mark Twain Effect" when they describe the oddly regular phenomenon of declining stock prices in the month of October. Despite this personal association with the occult operations of Wall Street, Twain could muster little enthusiasm for the folly of speculation as he crafted Pudd'nhead Wilson's witticisms throughout the period that climaxed with his bankruptcy proceedings in 1894. Speaking through Pudd'nhead's sardonic voice, he conveys some of the constitutional bearishness that had made *The Gilded Age* such an effective send-up of frontier investment schemes and the shady movements of capital in Washington, D.C., twenty years before. Skepticism about high finance was indeed the consistent theme of Twain's statements about speculation, and yet—as critics and biographers have always lamented—he rarely applied this sober wisdom to his own financial decision making. Years after bankruptcy, having turned his business affairs over to a far more prudent investor, Henry Huttleston Rogers, he was still prone to lose his head over speculative opportunities, such as Plasmon, the powdered milk product that cost him a large portion of his recovered fortune. Robert Sattelmeyer captures the well-known paradox, itself a cornerstone of Twain studies, in explaining that whatever Mark Twain "may have said about the American economic system in satirical works such as *The Gilded Age*, his own practices constituted an uncritical endorsement of it" (89). Indeed, the record of Twain's investment career almost tempts one to wonder if it was his collaborator, Charles Dudley Warner, who supplied the novel's cynical attitude toward financial risk. Years later, in 1889, while Twain's Yankee is pinning the hopes of Camelot to a new patent office and a fledgling stock market, Warner's latest novel, *A Little Journey in the World*, took a dim view of futures trading and other business innovations "of the higher and almost immaterial sort," innovations that required "an element of faith" and "a belief in the unseen" (37).

Of course, in certain moods, Mark Twain could outdo Warner as a critic of capitalism's unseen operations. Whatever the latter contributed to the novel's plan, no one questions Twain's authorship of the most endearing financial crank in American literature, Eschol Sellers, whose money-making schemes in *The Gilded Age* depict speculation as nothing but the name for an insane faith in the ability of money to reproduce itself. To the naive investor, "the Colonel's tongue was a magician's wand that could change . . . water into wine as easily as it could change . . . present poverty into imminent future riches" (83). What promises to fuel the magician's wand is capital, which never arrives from Washington or Wall Street in quantities sufficient to perform the Colonel's imagined miracles. "How much money have you got," Sellers asks his impoverished protégé, Hawkins. "I'll make it breed" (87). Yet money refuses to procreate in *The Gilded Age*, and, as a financial operation, speculation serves only to enrich the bankers and politicians who know this better than investors.

In practice, Sellers's brand of financial magic may be no better than Merlin's inept wand-waving in *A Connecticut Yankee*, and yet Mark Twain's profound skepticism about speculation never quite penetrated his even more profound faith in the unseen generative power of money. His own investments usually refused to multiply, just as Sellers never actually succeeds in converting "present poverty" into "future riches," but Twain never abandoned the idea that a kind of real magic underlies certain financial operations. In a euphoric letter to Rogers, whose careful management had substantially rebuilt the Clemens fortune by the turn of the century, he described the notorious financier and Standard Oil director as "a magician who can turn steel and copper and Brooklyn gas into gold" (*Mark Twain's Correspondence with Henry Huttleston Rogers* [*MTHHR*] 389). Pudd'nhead Wilson might rail against the false alchemy of dreamers like Eschol Sellers, but, under the right incubatory conditions, Mark Twain always believed, money really is capable of breeding money. Thanking Rogers almost giddily for his stewardship, he wrote: "Why, it is just splendid! I have nothing to do but sit around and watch you set the hen and hatch out those big broods and make my living for me" (*MTHHR* 389).

In suggesting that Mark Twain was both an avid enthusiast and a trenchant critic of speculative finance, it might seem that I am merely reframing the paradox outlined in Sattelmeyer's comment, the idea that Mark Twain's business activities exemplified the very behaviors he satirized so effectively as a writer in *The Gilded Age* and elsewhere. In fact, a version of this paradox informs virtually all commentary on Mark Twain's twin careers as writer and businessman, receiving perhaps its most eloquent expression in Justin Kaplan's *Mr. Clemens and Mark Twain*. Following Kaplan's lead, biographers and critics have generally concurred in portraying Clemens/Twain as a chronically divided personality, one part reckless business man, given to building castles in the air, the other part worldly-wise writer, skeptic, and ironist, ever alert to sham and fraud. The bohemian side of his personality never stopped believing that the next risky investment would make him incomprehensibly rich, while Mark Twain of Hartford crafted a literary persona by poking fun at human foolishness in all its forms, including especially that of *homo economicus*. The binary story of opposed and only occasionally reconciled personalities—one wisely literary, the other naively economic—has had such staying power because it is largely true, and yet my reason for invoking a version of the classic account is to suggest that "Mark Twain, Business Man" (a moniker borrowed from Samuel Webster's pioneering biographical study) is more intricately related to Mark Twain the writer and ironist than we have been capable of appreciating. In fact, while speculators and magicians inevitably turn out to be fools or frauds in Twain's fiction, a particular kind of procreative magic pervades his imaginative world, a magic closely linked to the alchemy that turns steel and copper into gold and that incubates money itself. Speculation is one word for this magic, but, as Twain's campy image of himself, seated comfortably in the Rogers chicken coop, suggests, this kind of speculation entails no risk. Henry's hen lays its eggs without fear of inflation or economic panic. Once she is "set," money begets money as a process of natural accretion, a magic that requires no magician, and so, in fact, speculation is not exactly the right term. What Twain enjoys in this image of sedentary, even passive, financial accrual is better described as steady source of unearned income.

In the discussion that follows, I argue that an image of regular returns on invested capital, or of the reliably procreative Rogers hen, played a profound role in Mark Twain's imagination, informing not only his conception of financial well-being for himself and his family, but his understanding of literary creativity itself. Indeed, powdered milk and typesetting machinery aside, the most significant investment of Twain's business career was unquestionably the literary persona he crafted with such care, and over which he asserted rights of "ownership" that tested the era's understandings of both authorship and copyright law. The contributors to this anthology have begun to explore this largely uncharted commercial terrain, and in so doing they have sketched the outlines of a different version of Mark Twain, Business Man than the one we thought we knew.

The writer I am describing understood his art in terms of an effort "to make comic capital out of everything [he] saw and heard," an effort designed to culminate in another chicken coop image of sedentary contemplation (Henderson 43). In a characteristic huff, he complained that Routledge and Sons "are the only English publishers who pay me any copyright, & therefore, if my books are to disseminate either suffering or crime among readers of our language, I would ever so much rather that they did it through that house, & then I could contemplate the spectacle calmly as the dividends came in" (*Mark Twain's Letters* 5:163–64). This idea of sedentary accumulation of authorial dividends played a central role in Twain's understanding of his own creative process, and it animates (ironically enough) some of the most suggestive moments in his fiction. An uncanny foreshadowing of the comfortably seated Routledge author, in fact, appears at the close of the iconic whitewashing scene in *The Adventures of Tom Sawyer*—a scene to which I will return—in which Tom, perched on "a barrel in the shade," quietly contemplates his transformation from "a poverty-stricken boy" into a child financier, who is "literally rolling in wealth" (31). Such transformations, I will argue, and the seemingly magical financial transactions that instigate them, are to a significant degree the purport and the purpose of Mark Twain's art.

Of course, several generations of economically minded critics, such as William Charvat, Daniel Borus, and Walter Benn Michaels, long ago taught us to read late-nineteenth-century American fiction in relation to the market culture of which it was an essential part. Today, that work remains as fresh and relevant as ever, and yet I want to present Mark Twain's relation to the market—specifically the market for those "higher and almost immaterial" financial instruments, such as stocks and futures—as a special case. William Dean Howells, arbiter and defender of so many of the tastes and values that characterize the period's creative zeitgeist, provides a useful point of contrast when he describes the Wall Street tycoon Jacob Dryfoos in *A Hazard of New Fortunes* as "a "hardened speculator" (234). According to Howells's narrator, Dryfoos's "moral decay began with his perception of the opportunity of making money quickly and abundantly." It would not be too much to say that two entirely different kinds of money circulate in *Hazard*, the kind that is "earned painfully, slowly, and in little amounts," and the kind that is "won suddenly and in large sums," "without effort and without merit." The prospect of unearned income, or of money that corresponds to nothing but itself, leads the hapless Dryfoos family from their farm in Ohio to New

York, "whither the men who have made money and do not yet know that money has made them, all instinctively turn." Here, from his office on Wall Street, Dryfoos can sit at his desk and "watch his money breed more money, and bring greater increase of its kind in an hour of luck than the toil of hundreds of men could earn in a year. He called it speculation, stocks, the street; and his pride, his faith in himself, mounted with his luck" (234).

Needless to say, Mark Twain's disposition toward the reproductive capacity of money, not to mention his relish for sedentary contemplation of the spectacle, is of an entirely different sort. If Howells's speculator is nothing but a hollow man, constituted through and through by an all too easily won self-referential currency, Twain's most successful speculators are anything but hollow; in fact, they enjoy an impression of "weight" or "substance" precisely as a result of their speculative prowess. Perhaps this is most obviously the case when Huck and Tom strike it rich at the end of *The Adventures of Tom Sawyer* by finding a hidden treasure under circumstances that more closely resemble a high-stakes currency transaction than a feat of excavation. In fact, the image of money that breeds more money could not be more literally brought to bear than when Injun Joe begins digging a hole in the ground to hide his bag of $600 in silver coins, only to find $12,000 in gold coins already buried there. In a seemingly pointless plot twist, one that changes nothing except the story's bottom line, $600 suddenly becomes $12,000. Yet the switch is not altogether haphazard, for the two treasures have quite different economic meanings. The silver represents a sudden windfall in disposable income, in that "six hundred dollars was money enough to make half a dozen boys rich," but $12,000 is not the sort of money one spends on candy and marbles; it is the sort that begets more money, as the narrator explains: "The Widow Douglas put Huck's money out at 6 per cent, and Judge Thatcher did the same with Tom's at Aunt Polly's request. Each lad had an income, now, that was simply prodigious—a dollar for every week-day in the year and half of the Sundays. It was just what the minister got—no, it was what he was promised—he generally couldn't collect it. A dollar and a quarter a week would board, lodge and school a boy in those simple days—and clothe him and wash him, too, for that matter" (269). The second treasure makes Huck and Tom rich, not just for the moment, but in perpetuity, and this difference meant a great deal to Mark Twain, both as a financial consideration and, as we shall see later, as a precondition for literary creativity. Howells, Dreiser, or Hamlin Garland would surely have played the scene differently, but for Twain the only thing more fascinating than a large bag of spendable cash is the even more enticing prospect of a steady, uninterrupted flow of healthy returns on investment. Moreover, the fact that such income is *not* remuneration for work is as crucial for Twain as it is morally problematic for Howells. Work for wages is virtually always a raw deal for the worker in Twain's fiction, as it is for the unlucky minister, who should be as well-off as the boys, but who rarely collects *his* dollar a day. Wages simply cannot compete with dividends as a form of reliable income, a point Twain playfully reiterates when a character named Mr. Jones offers to help Tom and Huck haul the wagonload of gold and silver:

> "Why, it's not as light as it might be. Got bricks in it?—or old metal?"
> "Old metal," said Tom.
> "I judged so; the boys in this town will take more trouble and fool away more time, hunting up six bits' worth of old iron to sell to the foundry than they would to make twice the money at regular work. But that's human nature—" (262)

This invocation of a familiar work ethic is purely ironic, for it is by watching patiently, like the calmly sedentary Dryfoos, rather than toiling laboriously, that the boys have amassed a larger fortune "than anyone present had ever seen at one time before" (267). St. Petersburg may never have beheld such piles of gold and silver, but as if to remind us what kind of money this is—not disposable income, honestly earned, but investable capital, suddenly won—the narrator concludes this sentence with a seemingly unnecessary qualification: "though several persons were there who were worth considerably more than that in property."

Perhaps Walter Benn Michaels goes too far in aligning Howells and American realism with a "pre-capitalist domestic economy," one that understands speculation as the economic equivalent of dissipating romance, but his reading of Howells in *The Gold Standard and the Logic of Naturalism* helps to signal Twain's outlier status as a proponent of what Howells considers immoral money (40). "The goal of realism," as Michaels describes it, is to "minimize excess," including the vastly excessive returns enjoyed by realism's wayward financiers, such as Dryfoos, Lapham, and Cowperwood, beside whom we might be justified in listing Tom Sawyer and Huck Finn (38). Yet, for Twain, those unearned returns mark a beginning rather than an end of literary art, which is to say a beginning of "realism" in a notably different key. Indeed, it would not be too much to say that a steady flow of unearned income is linked in Mark Twain's imagination to the very possibility of verbal meaning. Money accrues to money, it should be noted, not only by generating 6 percent interest, but by imbuing the words of its possessor with something that closely resembles monetary value. Once their cash is put to work, Huck and Tom notice a change in the effect of their words: the boys "were not able to remember that their remarks had possessed weight before; but now their sayings were treasured and repeated" (268). Because they possess interest-bearing treasure, the remarks of the boys are now treasured, and words that once traded at a steep discount, like the privately issued paper currency that circulated as money in antebellum communities like St. Petersburg, now sell at par or better than par. The miraculous operations of capital, as distinguished from wages, have made the difference.

"Thou Shalt Always Find the Same Treasure"

Throughout his career, Twain repeatedly worked two jokes about the elusiveness of wealth. One of these jokes might be called the fiasco of the Tennessee land, those 75,000 acres of undeveloped woodlands in the Knobs of Tennessee that Sam Clemens's father, John Marshall Clemens, thought would make his progeny rich.[1] As the joke unfolds in various autobiographical writings and in the plight of the penniless Hawkins family in *The Gilded Age*, the point is that the vast hypothetical wealth embedded *in* the Tennessee land in the form of undiscovered coal, copper, and iron ore will never be extracted *from* the Tennessee land and will therefore never do the Clemens family or the Hawkins family any good. The problem is always that no capital exists to perform the magical transformation of material objects into tradable commodities, and so the tremendous potential value of the Tennessee land remains locked up in the land itself. Like the silver and quartz mines that thwart the narrator's get-rich-quick schemes in *Roughing It*, the Tennessee land consists of all-too-solid matter that refuses to be converted into liquid currency or commodity, with the result that the owners of such vast mineral wealth *feel* and *act* immensely rich—so rich that they cannot conceive of selling out at any price—while in fact they possess nothing of exchangeable value.

Twain relished the absurdity of this situation both for the physical comedy it entails in scenes of financial and bodily hardship, especially in *The Gilded Age* and *Roughing It*, and for the more serious psychological and ethical considerations suggested by the problem of wealth that refuses to manifest itself as something that can be used or exchanged. The absurd economic logic of slavery provided a steady source of material for this kind of joking, as when Jim predicts that he will someday be rich, and then theorizes: "I's rich now, come to look at it. I owns mysef, en I's wuth eight hund'd dollars" (73). Jim is an exchangeable commodity, of course, and Miss Watson can sell him for $800, but the idea that he might pocket the cash himself is as ludicrous as the idea that the Clemens family will ever convert the Tennessee land into what they consider its astronomical cash equivalent. The cupidity of the family tradition thwarts the Tennessee transaction, while Jim's wish to collect on his own value is just as surely doomed by the legal illogic of slavery. Indeed, his concluding remark, "I wisht I had de money, I wouldn' want no more," can be understood as a pathetic elaboration of the basic dilemma of the Tennessee land, the dilemma of hypothetical wealth that exists beyond the reach of its ostensible "owner."

If Twain's first money joke is about all-too-physical entities that resist commodification and exchange, producing comically false impressions of wealth, his second favorite joke about the elusiveness of riches moves in the opposite direction by focusing on the absurdity of financial symbols that have lost most or all of their connection to the real assets they pretend to represent. The career of Eschol Sellers is again relevant here, for Sellers specializes not only in far-fetched land development schemes, but also in the cultivation of a very different kind of phantom wealth, the kind that exists strictly on paper, as when he promotes a scheme to buy up 113 wildcat banks in Ohio, Indiana, Kentucky, Illinois, and Missouri, banks whose privately issued paper notes are worth a mere 44 percent of their published value. Sellers predicts that depressed bank stocks will "spin up to a tremendous premium" when customers realize that he has cornered the market on bad paper currency, and he estimates his future profit at "not a dollar less than forty millions" (86). Here, in the realm of paper notes unsupported by physical assets or metal coinage, money bears no relation to anything real. Unlike the stubbornly intrinsic value of undeveloped land, the value of privately issued paper is perfectly extrinsic to any stabilizing institution or thing, such as precious metal or a federal guarantee, and such money is therefore subject to wild and potentially comic fluctuations in value. Frustrated by the recalcitrance of solid rock, the narrator of *Roughing It* also shifts his focus to stock speculation, which results in a magnificent paper fortune and a predictable series of humorous disappointments.

As with the fiasco of the Tennessee land, Twain replays this second joke—what might be called the joke of mere sign-money—to various comic ends and in a variety of fictional settings, such as the hairball episode in *Huckleberry Finn*, where Jim cleverly manages to restore the exchange-value of "an old slick counterfeit quarter," or what Huck calls "pretty bad money," by sticking it overnight in a raw Irish potato (37). Bad money generally fails to pass for good, however, and the joke of mere sign-money typically ends, as in *Roughing It*, with a handful of paper notes or stock certificates that refuse to signify wealth. While the value of land remains trapped in the land itself, the value associated with written promises also fails to serve reliably as a medium of exchange.

Twain loved this back-and-forth between a materialist conception of money and scenarios in which money serves as a comically abstract symbol of wealth, twin explanations for the persistent hardship his most acquisitive characters always experience under frontier economic conditions. In fact, although concerns about obdurate natural resources and wildcat banking might seem especially pertinent to the American frontier, these concerns are as old as money itself. Serious theoretical debates on these issues date at least to the early eighteenth century, when European governments and their colonies began experimenting on a large scale with paper currency, or explicit sign-money, calling into question the traditional definition of money as a commodity with intrinsic value. Sign-money can be understood as any currency in which the symbolic value stamped upon the coin, bill, or other material token of exchange does not coincide with its real value as precious material. Linguist and economic historian Richard T. Gray explains that "in ancient times the currency used to measure value was presumed to contain its own inherent worth, established intrinsically by the preciousness of the material that represented it. In the modern age, by contrast, value becomes extrinsic and systematic; it no longer resides in the material through which it is expressed, but has become instead purely symbolic, lent currency by the arbitrary stamp imposed by political authority" (100). For the eighteenth century's economically progressive theorists, such as Adam Smith, this paradigm shift from a materialist to a symbolic or functionalist understanding of money was an essential stimulus to economic activity and a key to the wealth of modern nations. Conservatives and physiocrats, who linked economic value directly to land, warned that widespread use of sign-money was "a mere deceptive sleight of hand, an economic edifice built without a foundation" (Gray 99).

Such theoretical debates must have seemed as freshly relevant as ever one hundred years later on the American frontier, as large quantities of precious metal began flowing out of California and Nevada, while shaky credit schemes and privately issued currencies popped up across the nation to finance an unprecedented boom in industrial development. Although the paradigm shift from a materialist to a symbolic understanding of money had been under way for generations, or perhaps centuries, already, Gilded Age America offered rich contemporary imagery for both conceptions of currency, and Twain's money-tinged frontier humor makes full use of this imagery in describing the phantom riches he associated with both land ownership and sign-money. Yet somewhere between these comic scenarios lies a conception of money that holds its value and even accrues over time, an image of viable, enduring wealth. The stories of Tennessee land and wildcat banking are parables of economic futility, after all, comic explorations of the tricks that money refuses to play. Twain was at his humorous best in narrating such economic mishaps, but at a personal level he was also profoundly interested in the tricks that well-trained money *can* perform, and his thinking on this question centers on a particular account of wealth creation, one that entails neither physical work nor undue speculative risk.

One might look in any of several directions for an image of the sort of spontaneous fiscal accrual I have in mind, but a curious episode in *The Prince and the Pauper* provides a useful point of departure. The young pauper Tom Canty of course dreams constantly of becoming a prince at the beginning of the novel, and later, once mistaken for a prince, he dreams just as constantly of returning to his mother and sisters in the squalor of Offal Court. To be an actual pauper or a false prince is to long perpetually for the other condition. Yet midway through the novel, Tom as the false prince awakens from his dreams of Offal Court and then drifts off into yet another dream, a second-order fantasy that bears no apparent relevance to the novel's otherwise quite formulaic story line. Like the compounding of Tom Sawyer's treasure from $600 in silver to $12,000 in gold, this narrative interlude contributes nothing of significance to the development of either character or plot, nor is there anything funny to explain its presence in the text. Moreover, as with his namesake's inexplicable windfall of investable capital, Tom Canty's dream evokes an image of money that breeds money: "Tom slept again, and after a time he had this pleasant dream. He thought it was summer and he was playing, all alone, in the fair meadow called Goodman's Fields, when a dwarf only a foot high, with long red whiskers and a humped back appeared to him suddenly and said, 'Dig, by that stump.' He did so, and found twelve bright new pennies—wonderful riches! Yet this was not the best of it; for the dwarf said—'I know thee. Thou art a good lad and a deserving; thy distresses shall end, for the day of thy reward is come. Dig here every seventh day, and thou shalt find always the same treasure, twelve bright new pennies'" (161–62).

Perhaps the first thing to say about this episode is that it does not represent Mark Twain's finest moment as a novelist. Indeed, Tom's dream seems like the author's somewhat forced effort to imagine a condition of economic existence that the novel's comic logic flatly precludes. One can be a prince in this book, which means to command unlimited wealth of the sort that is "lent currency by the arbitrary stamp imposed by political authority," or one can be a pauper, which is to suffer the all-too-physical discomforts of abject poverty. These are the novel's equally untenable conditions, like the opposed frontier hardships that animate the comedy of *The Gilded Age* and *Roughing It*, and yet Tom Canty's dream provides an image of what Twain's comedy of fiscal disappointments usually makes unthinkable, namely, a regular flow of unearned income.

Different versions of this image recur with increasing frequency in Twain's fiction after *The Prince and the Pauper* (1882): Tom and Huck, of course, enjoy steady returns on their invested fortune throughout *Adventures of Huckleberry Finn* (1885), although Huck chooses not to collect his "dollar a day"; acting with ingenuity comparable to that of today's Federal Reserve Bank, Hank Morgan dilutes Camelot's currency, in effect lining his treasury with money created out of thin air in *A Connecticut Yankee* (1889); Roxy connives to receive a pension of $35 per month, or roughly another dollar a day, in *Pudd'nhead Wilson* (1894); and even Colonel Sellers, reincarnated as Mulberry Sellers in *The American Claimant* (1892), manages to marry his daughter into solid old money and a landed estate. The idea that money might incubate and breed more money receives perhaps its most indulgent treatment in the 1893 story "The £1,000,000 Bank Note," which Malcolm Bradbury has insightfully described as "a dream fantasy about the ambiguous space that lies between destitution and wealth" (xl). The hero of that story, outlandishly named Henry Adams, finds that he can do without a salary and a daytime job when he learns to convert his reputation as "the vest-pocket million-pounder" into income-producing capital (23).

It should not be surprising that, as bankruptcy approached in the years leading up to 1894, and as its humiliation lingered afterward, Twain's fiction often served as a site for this sort of wish fulfillment, and yet the idea of unearned income—of twelve pennies that appear every seventh day, or of "a dollar a day the year round"—was more than a dream of fiscal safe haven. Indeed, one of the central claims of this chapter is not only that an image of passive accrual underlies Twain's increasingly strained financial ruminations, capturing his sense of the way money *might* be capable of working under ideal circumstances, but that such an image informs his understanding of literary creativity itself—of the way words work.

I have already suggested that words and money bear a striking kinship in Twain's thinking about both economy and fiction. As many critics have noticed, he consistently figured words as a form of symbolic currency, often to be "discounted" according to their uncertain correspondence with reality, occasionally to be valued at par or better than par, as when Tom Sawyer or other characters of financial substance speak with words that are "weighted" and "treasured," like precious coins. Camelot's knights errant are "not persons to be believed," according to Hank Morgan, who calculates that the tales of heroism narrated by these chronic liars need to be "scaled" and "discounted . . . ninety-seven percent; the rest was fact" (189). The narrator of *The Innocents Abroad* applies a version of this familiar trope in admitting that his descriptions of Lake Tahoe regularly test the limits of European credulity: "I have tried to get this statement off at par here, but with no success; so I have been obliged to negotiate it at fifty percent discount" (204).

In repeatedly deploying the analogy between words and money, Twain placed himself in good company. Nietzsche's comparison of diluted contemporary words with coins that have lost their impression due to overcirculation is perhaps the most famous modern application of a trope that was already common in antiquity. In fact, Nietzsche would surely have enjoyed Twain's fictional development of the idea in *A Connecticut Yankee*, where Hank not only revitalizes the national idiom by starting a newspaper but replaces "the old gold and silver coins of the country," which were "so worn with use that the devices upon them were as legible as blisters, and looked like them" (334–35). According to Jean-Joseph Goux, the "organic" nature of the relation between words and money is so profoundly rooted in western thinking about value and meaning that it constitutes less a "mere analogy" than "a deep-seated isomorphism between the domains of money and language" (110).

Twain's comic haggling over the exchange-value of words thus belongs to a long intellectual tradition, and yet his conception of the isomorphism between language and money attributed special significance to a certain kind of money, namely, the kind that is unearned and that proliferates of its own accord. Personal finances played a role here, to be sure, and yet so did his sense that the imagination behaves like a well-managed investment portfolio, continually regenerating itself, not through intellectual effort, but as a process directly akin to the accumulation of capital. One might be compelled by circumstances to work for wages, but real money—the kind that trades at par or better—accrues to the passive fiscal spectator who, Dryfoos-like, "watch[es] his money breed more money" (*Hazard* 234). Applying this principle of accumulation to his own creative process, Twain famously described his struggle with writer's block while working on *Tom Sawyer*, a struggle that ended only after a "profitable" hiatus from work that came to serve as his basic theory of composition: "When the manuscript had lain in a pigeon-hole two years I took it out one day and read the last chapter that I had written. It was then that I made the great discovery that when the tank runs dry you've only to leave it alone and it will fill up again in time, while you are asleep—also while you are at work on other things and are quite unaware that this unconscious and profitable cerebration is going on" (*Autobiography* 2:97).

Fiction, here, is unearned profit that accumulates in the writer's imagination, like twelve bright new pennies one can count on finding under a stump every week. Interestingly, the image of a "tank" that refills itself unaided also suggests a scene of industrial productivity, something like a working mill that is powered by an inexhaustible supply of naturally flowing water. For

Twain, this paired conception of monetary and technological productivity—a profitable tank of the imagination—was ultimately a way of describing the real magic he persisted in believing to underlie both the procreative power of money and the closely related potential of machines to eliminate work. Of course, he was not alone in imagining such an extravagant linkage, as John Kenneth Galbraith confirms when he tells of an amusing episode in the early history of the Bank of England, whose speculative investment in the South Sea Company included plans for "a wheel for perpetual motion" (33). Fiscal and technological magic have always been closely associated in the minds of speculators and entrepreneurs, and one can scarcely distinguish between the two forms of faith in most investment schemes. According to Kaplan, throughout his life Twain was fascinated by labor-saving technologies that promised to minimize or eliminate work from the process of writing and communication (285). The Paige typesetter was of course to have been such a marvel of literary automation, as well as a fountain of perpetual dividends for its principal investor. Twain's comedy of elusive wealth usually dwells on his twin recipes for economic failure, crushing physical work and reckless speculation—Tennessee land and paper money—but a reliably "profitable" alternative exists, at least in theory. That alternative, so elusive in his own economic experience, centered on an image of dividends rolling in, an image that had as much to do with financial security, for Mark Twain, as it did with the nature of literary productivity.

The Art of Arbitrage

If literary fiction for Mark Twain was a kind of unearned income, a profit that accrues to the writer specifically *not* as compensation for work, writing was also a means to imagine the conditions under which unearned income might really come to bear. Where do those twelve shiny new pennies come from? The dwarf in Tom Canty's dream seems like an implausibly forced account of the way money might be imagined to be capable of breeding itself, and yet Mark Twain required such an account. After all, if unearned income is an unthinkable economic illusion or an exclusive prerogative of the already-rich, then work is the only way to make a living, and the tank of imagination can no longer be counted upon to refill itself perpetually. Both Twain's art and his sense of economic well-being, those inseparable aspects of his dual career as writer and business man, depended upon a conceivable story about the way twelve pennies or a dollar a day might materialize with no input of work. His fiction repeatedly stages this account, occasionally in strained moments, such as Tom Canty's dream, and sometimes in more compelling explorations of the generative possibilities of money. Among such fictive explorations, none is more suggestive than Tom Sawyer's financial maneuvering in the famous whitewashing scene.

Tom's exuberance for deal making, to be sure, sometimes makes him look like no more than a child-size version of Colonel Sellers, as in the forgettable sequel, *Tom Sawyer Abroad*, where he proposes a joint venture in sand. In that episode, Tom, Huck, and Jim are flying over the Sahara in a balloon, when Jim comes up with the idea of transporting the desert sand home to St. Petersburg to sell there as an industrial commodity for twenty-five cents per ton. Tom objects that Jim's plan is impractical, but he theorizes that the sand would be worth infinitely more if minute quantities were neatly bottled and marketed as "genuyne sand from the genuyne Desert of Sahara" (82). Such flat comedy echoes the outlandish schemes of Eschol and Mulberry Sellers, and yet even here Tom betrays some of the economic savvy that distinguishes him from Twain's less charismatic fiscal manipulators. For Tom understands, as Jim and Huck cannot, that the commodity in question has one value associated with its material utility and a very different value associated with its status as a symbolic object. To put the situation another way, Tom's inspiration here, as in the far more compelling whitewashing scene, lies in recognizing that there are two markets for sand: an industrial market for mere useful things, and a souvenir market for symbols; the discrepancy between the two creates an opportunity for *arbitrage*.

That term has a technical ring to it, and yet the basic concept is disarmingly simple. In contrast with speculation, which usually involves buying something with the expectation that its value will subsequently increase, arbitrage in its purest form names a riskless transaction that takes advantage of an existing discrepancy in prices. There are a variety of ways to introduce risk into arbitrage, and economists actually define certain transactions as instances of "risk arbitrage," but in theory, at least, the term refers to what economist Geoffrey Poitras calls "a riskless trading strategy that generates a positive profit with no net investment of funds" (2). What mitigates risk is the arbitrageur's tactic of buying and selling the commodity in question simultaneously, thus capitalizing not on some hoped-for future change in prices, which may or may not occur, but on an existing inconsistency in the way the commodity is valued in more than one marketplace. Tom's scheme is not a pure example of the strategy, for he lacks the wherewithal to buy real sand and sell symbolic sand at the same moment, and indeed it is difficult to imagine such an instantaneous transaction without modern systems of communication and transportation. Nevertheless, Tom cleverly harnesses the basic idea by noticing that a single commodity is valued differently in two marketplaces, a realization that awakens Mark Twain's incessant fascination with the way money might be coerced into procreating without risk or the investment of work.

It is worth pointing out, as well, that Tom's insight into discrepant values animates a familiar dyad. In fact, the juxtaposition of sand-as-useful-material with sand-as-souvenir is just another deployment of the comic formula that pits the stubborn materiality of Tennessee land against the flimsy abstractness of sign-money. Twain never got tired of a good joke, and the comic positions at play in the debate between Tom and his fellow balloonists are entirely familiar. The world of work, inadequate wages, and exaggerated material discomfort stands opposed to the world of play, pleasure, and hypersymbolization. Tom Sawyer's distinction among Mark Twain's many con men and hucksters—and his unparalleled economic prowess—lies in grasping that the juxtaposition of these untenable extremes is a potentially endless source of both humor and profit, a tank that always refills.

In describing Tom as what might be called a humorist-arbitrageur, I have already run afoul of a distinguished critical tradition that understands him as an unambiguous partisan in the struggle between the worlds of work and play. To be sure, the prefatory note to *The Adventures of Tom Sawyer*, which invites adult readers to remember what it was like to be a child, positions Tom's story explicitly as an exercise in nostalgia and an attempt to reclaim the childhood experience of freedom, leisure, idleness, and mischief from the clutches of an adult perspective dominated by physical work, tedious convention, and religious conformity. And Tom's succession of triumphs in the novel, as generations of readers have affirmed, amounts to the triumph of play.

But Tom's commitment to play requires scrutiny. Ben Rogers, it is worth remembering, is deeply immersed in play when he "hoves" into Tom's sight beside the unpainted fence. Whereas Tom cleverly pretends to play at whitewashing, Ben is *actually* playing, having given himself over imaginatively to the idea that he is both a riverboat pilot and his ship. Tom, meanwhile, feigns enjoyment of his whitewashing task, and his deception is so successful that it convinces Ben to stop playing at one kind of labor and begin performing another. James M. Cox and many other readers consider Tom the champion of play, citing his ability to "convert" work into play, but Ben and the other boys need little advice on this process (*Fate* 100). Moreover, Tom is conspicuous among his pleasure-seeking friends in refraining from Ben's sort of immersion in play. When the boys later abandon themselves to various literary scenarios under Tom's direction, he alone remains notably conscious that they are acting parts. In the whitewashing scene, he offers his brush to the highest bidder and then sits in the shade, perfectly idle—neither working nor playing. Tom clearly abhors hard work, but it is not accurate to say that he prefers play, or that his inspiration results in the triumph of play over work, for as he sits quietly in the shade, munching Ben's apple and rolling in his newfound wealth, he is doing precisely neither. Instead, with a placidity that rivals Dryfoos's own, he is sitting at the rural equivalent of his Wall Street desk, watching his assets multiply.

Readers have always recognized something ominous in this behavior, although an accurate name for it has proven elusive. Peter Messent views Tom warily as "an emergent businessmen" ("Tension" 139), and William Spengemann describes him as an "unscrupulous entrepreneur," who "takes advantage of his fellows for personal gain" (117). Cox shares some of the same reservations, calling Tom an "embryo businessman," who has "a bright future in the society of commerce and advertising" ("Tom Sawyer" 74). Such comments suggest that Tom's gift for turning a profit has a dark side, but his activities are "unscrupulous" only from the perspective of a Howellsian work ethic that Mark Twain clearly did not share. Work for wages is simply not a viable path to wealth in his fiction, especially in a situation like Tom's, in which a term of "captivity at hard labor" (25) is being exacted as payment for luxuries already purchased and enjoyed. Tom is no worker, to be sure, for he knows perfectly well that those who perform actual work in the novel either receive nothing for their efforts, like the slaves of St. Petersburg, or they receive a meager hourly wage, like Muff Potter or Injun Joe, who murders the young doctor after a dispute over inadequate payment for manual labor. He also knows that those who play at working must pay handsomely for the privilege, like Ben and the rest of the boys, who would have been bankrupted, according to the narrator, if the whitewash had held out a little longer (32).

Instead of either working or playing at work, Tom engages in what can best be understood as a form of arbitrage, capturing the discrepant value generated when something as mundane as painting a fence is reimagined and remarketed as a coveted form of recreation. As with his scheme to sell symbolic sand from the "genuyne desert of Sahara," Tom recognizes that the same commodity has two entirely different price tags attached to it, depending on whether it is suffered as work or enjoyed as play. He is an embryonic businessman, as Cox suggests, but his financial strategy should not be confused with speculation, which entails making bets on future price movements. In fact, Tom's approach to making assets grow is essentially risk-free, for he sells the job of whitewashing at a steep premium in the very act of paying for his day of hooky. His unearned profit is the difference—a fortune in trinkets—between what whitewashing costs as physical work and what it sells for as recreation, a difference the novel playfully elaborates when Aunt Polly, stunned by Tom's apparent efficiency, gives him yet another apple as his reward, "along with an improving lecture upon the added value and flavor a treat took to itself when it came without sin through virtuous effort" (34). Whereas Karl Marx believed that the worker who pours his labor into the commodity is the source of added value, Aunt Polly attributes this surplus to a misapplied notion of virtue. For Mark Twain and Tom Sawyer, these well-worn accounts of where added value comes from and how it accumulates are ridiculous. As Tom's budding career demonstrates, a surplus of a very different order awaits the arbitrageur who notices a discrepancy in the way two marketplaces assess the value of whitewashing, or sand, or anything else that might serve the purposes of both work and play, and Tom pockets this surplus in the form of unearned income. Like Tom Canty's spontaneously regenerating pennies, but with a more compelling economic backstory, this wealth also comes out of thin air and accumulates with no investment of hard work or speculative risk. As if to emphasize that his actual reward is payment neither for labor invested, as Marx would have it, nor for virtue displayed, as Aunt Polly might prefer, Tom hooks a doughnut on his way out of the kitchen at the close of her sermon, a little white-collar theft that reminds us of the purely gratuitous nature of the added value the arbitrageur has coaxed into his pocket.

The significance of this reading of the whitewashing scene lies less in what it might say about Twain's economic sophistication than in what it can tell us about the sources of his art. When placed in the right incubator, money begets money, as his fiction repeatedly tries to show, and his real heroes are the characters clever enough to sit idly in the shade while it accumulates in front of their eyes. This is also the sedentary posture of the novelist, who does not "work" at producing fiction, but who watches it accumulate from a distance. Writing to an admirer, Twain admitted to having deliberate methods of composition, but he insisted that, like Tom Canty's pennies, "they begot themselves, in which case I am only their proprietor, not their father" (*Selected Shorter Writings* 225). The novelist, as Twain pictures his vocation in "What Paul Bourget Thinks of Us," is literally a financier of representation, whose "whole capital . . . is the slow accumulation of *un*conscious observation" (*Collected Tales* 167). If "capital" is a metaphor here, the term attains a quite literal sense when the slow accumulation of observed detail begins producing assets in the form of copyrighted works, which serve as capital in the economic realm, allowing the comfortably reclining author to contemplate the spectacle of his success calmly, as the royalty dividends roll in.

As the "proprietor" of his own art, rather than its "father," Twain felt justified in claiming as many dividends as copyright law would permit, and yet he was curiously adamant about disowning the work involved in creating his literary assets. "As long as a book would write itself," he explained, "I was a faithful and interested amanuensis and my industry did not flag, but the minute that the book tried to shift to *my* head the labor of contriving its situations, inventing its adventures and conducting its conversations, I put it away and dropped it out of my mind" (*Autobiography* 2:97). The work of the novelist went on in a "mill whose helpful machinery never stands idle," a machine perhaps something like a perfected version of the Paige compositor (Mark Twain Project, SLC to Emily G. Hutchings, 14 November 1902, quoted in *Letter Writer* 25). The writer himself, like Tom Sawyer sitting in the shade, is explicitly idle as the industrial-compositional process goes on, generating words in the same way a pension or a bank account generates returns. As with the profitable tank of the imagination, technological magic is interwoven here with the financial magic that allows both money and words to come from out of nowhere, without speculative risk or input of labor. Both forms of magic are at the heart of Twain's understanding of his own creativity.

A Capitalist of High Character

One familiar way of thinking about the arc of Mark Twain's career holds that, in his later years, he outgrew the bohemian sensibilities that had made him famous around the world as the self-proclaimed American Vandal, embracing instead the values of a wealthy corporate elite. Justin Kaplan's biography paints a vivid picture of the transition through which "the people's author," as he calls Mark Twain, gradually became "the pet and the peer of the moguls," and other biographers, Ron Powers in particular, have explored Twain's quickening friendships with Rogers, Andrew Carnegie, and other titans of industry as an explanation for the uncertain creative efforts of his final years (Kaplan 384; Powers 562). Kaplan surmises that by 1906, "Mark Twain had outlived not his fame but the identity that had made him famous. The stage-coach and the river boat, symbols of the Western Mark Twain, had become the motor-car and the steam yacht, symbols of the plutocracy. . . . Stretched out on the sofa in Rogers's private office in the Standard Oil Building, smoking or reading while Rogers conducted his daily affairs, Clemens was completely at home and completely trusted" (383–84).

It had taken some time to achieve this comfortably sedentary pose on the sofa in capitalism's inner sanctum. Still knocking at the door in 1899, he had written to Rogers about an investment opportunity: "Don't leave me out; I want to be in, with the other capitalists" (*MTHHR* 409). A year earlier, after grilling a banker about a possible stake in a new venture, he was tickled to be regarded as an old hand at business negotiations, informing Rogers of what the banker had said: "I could get my living as a financier if authorship should fail me—a very nice compliment and quite true, though you probably don't believe it" (*MTHHR* 328). Whether Rogers was ready to believe it or not, the one-time Sage-Brush Bohemian and Wild Humorist of the Western Slope now described himself, with at least some justification, as "a capitalist of high character" (*MTHHR* 390).

In a provocative study of Twain's male friendships, Peter Messent has begun to revise this account of a late-life turn toward plutocracy by suggesting that "Clemens had—from early in his career—always enjoyed the company of those who possessed social authority and prestige" (*Friendship* 152). Messent's persuasive reassessment encourages us to date the transition in Twain's personal attitudes toward the moneyed elite from a much earlier period, and the present chapter has a corresponding aim. Indeed, while Twain may have begun calling himself a capitalist only late in life, I have argued that what might be understood as a capitalist imaginary was at work from the very beginning. In effect, Mark Twain was always trying to set Henry's hen, perhaps most interestingly in the early fiction, where feats of imaginative arbitrage and dreams of freshly minted coinage sometimes made it possible to conceive of literary art as a process of passive accrual, one that results in the slow accumulation of unearned intellectual and financial dividends.

Such an instance of what I am calling imaginative arbitrage occurs in *Roughing It*, when the narrator and his friend Johnny travel on foot from Virginia City to the shores of Lake Tahoe. The narrator explains that the two are on vacation, and much of the episode concerns the amazing healthiness of the high-altitude climate and the therapeutic benefits to be enjoyed from "roughing it" as a form of recreation. As with the playful juxtaposition of Mont Blanc as a site of exhausting work and of pleasurable sport in *Tom Sawyer*, the fun here lies in appreciating that the same experience has one value attached to its associations with physical privation, and another to its potential as sumptuous leisure. Tom Sawyer specializes in capturing the "added value" that measures this difference in economic terms, and the narrator of *Roughing It* also hopes to turn a large profit by reimagining wilderness in terms of recreational space.

In this case, it is homestead law, rather than Tom's economic savvy, that provides a blueprint for what can be thought of as an arbitrage transaction. Pure arbitrage, as I have said, describes the simultaneous buying and selling of a single commodity in more than one marketplace, such that the arbitrageur is able to capitalize on a difference in prices without exposure to risk. The narrator of *Roughing It* is incapable of such a transaction for many reasons, not least because he lacks capital, and yet his plan to transform a single tract of public land, worthless in its current state, into valuable personal property recognizes that a significant discrepancy in valuation awaits the frontier arbitrageur. He explains that he and Johnny have gone to Tahoe both for their own recreation and, in a closely related gesture, to become wealthy property owners by laying claim to virgin timber lands on the shores of the lake, lands they have no intention of harvesting by the sweat of their own brows, but which they hope to sell to a more risk-oriented speculator after establishing a legal claim. In order to assert their claim, the two men must engage in a minimal amount of what the narrator whiningly calls "heart-breaking work," work that turns out to be mainly symbolic, however, in that the timber enclosure they establish to define the borders of their property amounts to little more than a few haphazardly felled pines (171).

According to homestead law, the pair must also establish a dwelling and live on the property in order to secure their claim. They do so by building a makeshift bivouac out of fallen branches, a shelter the narrator is again careful to identify as more symbolic than actual, given that the two friends continue to sleep under the stars on the beach. For one of the few times in Mark Twain's writing—the whitewashing scene is another conspicuous example—the minimal requirements of physical "work" seem consistent with chronic laziness and evasion of responsibility. To describe the situation another way, profit in this scene, generated through the creation of personal property, accrues to the narrator by virtue of his ability to do nothing but stay in one place, and, like Tom, have "a nice, good, idle time all the while." As in the whitewashing scene, work blends seamlessly with recreation in the narrator's pastimes on the lake, where what he calls his "job" consists of occupying a pristine recreational space, and where his daily "business" amounts to drifting around in a boat and admiring the scenery (174). The two friends are actively engaged in establishing what they hope will be a lucrative timber claim, and yet their occupation is inseparable from perfect idleness. Describing their daily labor, the narrator says: "We usually pushed out a hundred yards or so from shore, and then lay down on the thwarts, in the sun, and let the boat drift by the hour whither it would" (174).

This image of directionless drift should be full of suggestion for Twain's readers, some of whom will immediately think of Huck and Jim floating along the mile-wide river, while others will recall the "pathetic drift between the eternities" that Hank Morgan's darker vision evokes (217). The same image resonates with special intensity in Mark Twain's thinking about money—about where it comes from, how it grows, and what inspires it to beget itself. In those rare fictional instances in which work blends ambiguously with perfect idleness, as on Lake Tahoe, profit comes not as the reward for exposure to risky investments or as compensation for actual labor, but as an almost magically "added value" that awaits the writer-arbitrageur, who controls the conceptual and economic difference between work and play. Of course, Twain creates this image of a capitalist Eden in *Roughing It*—a place where money, in an almost literal sense, grows on trees—only to recoil at the shock of its destruction. The narrator awakens from one of his lazy drifts across the lake to notice that his campfire has ignited a terrible inferno, which consumes the timber claim, along with the book's most probing and promising image of a productive idleness. *Roughing It* manages to go on making readers laugh, but this scene of destruction is an eerie foreshadowing of the nightmare stories of Twain's late career, in which happy homes are suddenly burned to the ground, prosperity is dashed overnight, and stunned victims are left wondering whether they are awake or asleep. Twain never stopped searching for a viable image of the sort of spontaneous accrual of property he described in the Tahoe episode, and yet that episode's violent undoing suggests that he harbored misgivings from the very outset that Henry's hen would ever "hatch out those big broods."

It was only as an elderly writer that Twain stretched himself out on the Standard Oil sofa and began enjoying the literal unearned income that Rogers's financial stewardship ensured, but this image of sedentary reception had already served for decades as an account of the creative process. Writing in 1884 of his long-standing interest in mental telegraphy, he explained that, "all my powerful impulses come to me from somebody else." He had the sensation that "the other person is supplying the thoughts to me, and that I am merely writing from dictation" (SLC to William F. Barrett, 4 October 1884, quoted in Robinson 366). Much as Rogers, by 1906, was quite literally supplying dividends to the elderly friend who was lounging on his sofa, a younger Mark Twain already understood his compositional process in terms of the passive reception of literary returns from "somebody else." As a writer, in other words, he had been on the sofa all along.

In certain respects, this image of sedentary accumulation of unearned literary and financial assets is entirely consistent with the carefully wrought persona Twain cultivated over the course of his career. It hardly seems coincidental that he positioned himself in various states of repose for some of his most iconic photographic portraits. Yet the image of a risk-averse "capitalist of high character" does not square as well with the portrait criticism has handed down of "Mark Twain, Business Man," who is presumed to have been a reckless speculator and general pudd'nhead in financial matters. There is no question that he took enormous and ill-considered risks as an investor, and the biographical record is accurate in understanding him as a quixotic financier. What is less appreciated, however, is the role of Tom Sawyer's inspiration in Mark Twain's creative life. The lesson of Tom's adventures, which speaks directly to the sources of Twain's art, is that workers and players are destined to remain poor, while profit awaits the arbitrageur who sits idly in the shade, ready to capture the surplus value generated when "work" is revalued as "play." Mark Twain's entangled careers as writer and business man actually strike a surprisingly harmonious chord in imagining this risk-free "added value" as the elusive return on investments of intellectual and financial capital.

Note

1. See Lawrence Howe's chapter in this collection for a significant reassessment of the actual size and value of the Clemens family's real estate holdings in Tennessee.

Works Cited

Bradbury, Malcolm. "Introduction." *The £1,000,000 Bank-Note and Other New Stories*. 1893. New York: Oxford UP, 1996. xxxi–xliv.

Cox, James M. *Mark Twain: The Fate of Humor*. Princeton: Princeton UP, 1966.

———. "Tom Sawyer: Performer and Chief Entertainer." *Readings on* The Adventures of Tom Sawyer. Ed. Katie de Koster. San Diego: Greenhaven, 1999. 68–76.

Galbraith, John Kenneth. *Money: Whence It Came, Where It Went*. Boston: Houghton Mifflin, 1975.

Goux, Jean-Joseph. *Symbolic Economies: After Marx and Freud*. Trans. Jennifer Curtis Gage. Ithaca: Cornell UP, 1990.

Gray, Richard T. "Buying into Signs: Money and Semiosis in Eighteenth-Century German Language Theory." *The New Economic Criticism: Studies at the Intersection of Literature and Economics*. Ed. Martha Woodmansee and Mark Osteen. London and New York: Routledge, 1999. 95–113.

Henderson, Archibald. *Mark Twain*. New York: Frederick Stokes, 1912.

Howells, William Dean. *A Hazard of New Fortunes*. 1890. New York: Oxford UP, 1990.

Kaplan, Justin. *Mr. Clemens and Mark Twain: A Biography*. New York: Simon and Schuster, 1966.

Messent, Peter. *Mark Twain and Male Friendship: The Twitchell, Howells, and Rogers Friendships*. New York: Oxford UP, 2009.

———. "Tension over the Changing American Culture." *Readings on the Adventures of Tom Sawyer*. Ed. Katie de Koster. San Diego: Greenhaven, 1999. 136–43.

Michaels, Walter Benn. *The Gold Standard and the Logic of Naturalism*. Berkeley: U of California P, 1987.

Poitras, Geoffrey. "Arbitrage: Historical Perspectives."<www.sfu.ca/~poitras/EQF_ARB$$.pdf>.

Powers, Ron. *Mark Twain: A Life*. New York: Free Press, 2005.

Robinson, Forrest G. "An 'Unconscious and Profitable Cerebration': Mark Twain and Literary Intentionality." *Nineteenth-Century Literature* 50.3 (1995): 357–80.

Sattelmeyer, Robert. "Steamboats, Cocaine, and Paper Money: Mark Twain Rewriting Himself." *Constructing Mark Twain: New Directions in Scholarship*. Ed. Laura E. Skandera-Trombley and Michael J. Kiskis. Columbia: U of Missouri P, 2001: 87–100.

Spengemann, William C. "A Celebration of Innocence." *Readings on the Adventures of Tom Sawyer*. Ed. Katie de Koster. San Diego: Greenhaven, 1999. 112–19.

Twain, Mark. *Adventures of Huckleberry Finn*. 1885. New York: Oxford UP, 1996.

———. *The Adventures of Tom Sawyer*. 1875. New York: Oxford UP, 1996.

———. *The American Claimant*. 1892. New York: Oxford UP, 1996.

———. *Autobiography of Mark Twain: The Complete and Authorized Edition*. 3 vols. Ed. Harriet Elinor Smith et al. Berkeley: U of California P, 2011, 2012, 2015.

———. *Collected Tales, Sketches, Speeches, and Essays, 1891–1910*. Ed. Louis J. Budd. New York: Library of America, 1992.

———. *A Connecticut Yankee in King Arthur's Court*. 1889. New York: Oxford UP, 1996.

———. *Following the Equator and Anti-Imperialist Essays*. 1897. New York: Oxford UP, 1996.

———. *The Innocents Abroad*. 1869. New York: Oxford UP, 1996.

———. *Mark Twain, Letter Writer*. Ed. Cyril Clemens. Boston: Meador, 1932.

———. *Mark Twain's Correspondence with Henry Huttleston Rogers, 1893–1909*. Ed. Louis Leary. Berkeley: U of California P, 1969.

———. *Mark Twain's Letters, Volume 5: 1872–1873*. Ed. Lin Salmo and Harriet Elinor Smith. Berkeley: U of California P, 1997.

———. *The £1,000,000 Bank-Note and Other New Stories*. 1893. New York: Oxford UP, 1996.

———. *The Prince and the Pauper*. 1882. New York: Oxford UP, 1996.

———. *Roughing It*. 1872. New York: Oxford UP, 1996.

———. *Selected Shorter Writings*. Ed. Walter Blair. Boston: Houghton Mifflin, 1962.

———. *Tom Sawyer Abroad*. 1894. New York: Oxford UP, 1996.

———. *The Tragedy of Pudd'nhead Wilson and the Comedy of Those Extraordinary Twins*. 1894. New York: Oxford UP, 1996.

Twain, Mark, and Charles Dudley Warner. *The Gilded Age*. 1873. New York: Oxford UP, 1996.

Warner, Charles Dudley. *A Little Journey in the World*. 1889. New York: Johnson, 1969.

Webster, Samuel Charles. *Mark Twain, Business Man*. Boston: Little, Brown, 1946.

Coda

"Follow the Money"

Lawrence Howe

"Follow the money": the now-famous line from the film *All the President's Men* (1976), uttered by the Watergate informant, alias "Deep Throat," has become a cultural touchstone. Whenever scandal breaks, this shrewd maxim is bound to follow. And yet for all of its seeming simplicity, the line itself contains a threefold irony:

1. Mark Felt, revealed in 2005 as the source that led Woodward and Bernstein to their award-winning exposé of the Nixon administration's darkest hour, probably never said the words attributed to him by the screenwriter William Goldman;
2. Hal Holbrook, the actor who so ominously delivered the line in his portrayal of Felt, is far more famous for uttering the words of Mark Twain over the last fifty years; and
3. If ever there was a figure in American history for whom the phrase "follow the money" was especially meaningful, it was Mark Twain.

Twain's relationship to money and its diverse areas of influence—finance, marketing, commerce, politics, class status, marriage, social mobility, patronage, philanthropy—was a complex, lifelong affair. The well-known biographical outline of Samuel Clemens's interest in wealth might be more aptly captured by the slogan "chase the money," but as Mark Twain he was far more circumspect, astute, and wry than this pejorative phrase suggests.

Mark Twain and Money takes Deep Throat's prescription to heart. Although the contributors speak independently on various aspects of Mark Twain's interest in economics, we all find it curious, if not troubling, that critical accounts of his cultural significance have generally glossed over his thoughts on economics. When scholars have addressed his financial matters, their narratives have taken a fairly uniform shape. And so, from one angle or another, the essays in this collection attempt to answer a long-overdue question. Namely, given Twain's celebrated wisdom on important cultural issues and his ability to lend his distinctive voice to a skeptical analysis of how those issues influence American experience, why has his concern with money been relegated to a narrow and frequently repeated footnote about bad investments and bankruptcy, a footnote typically couched in equal parts embarrassment and ridicule?

In addressing this question, the chapters in this collection "follow the money" in the most inclusive sense, considering the meanings embedded in the texts and contexts of economic flux. This seems only fitting: he was always forthright about the fact that literature was a business for him; and he wrote incisively about shifting economic conditions and behaviors with inventive playfulness and philosophical sophistication. Shouldn't we treat Twain's interest in economics as openly as he did? This volume axiomatically assumes that, far from a footnote, economics should be an essential area of inquiry in Twain scholarship; it informs us about how America's most well-known writer understood the dynamics of power that come into play whether money flows freely or eddies in pools away from the mainstream.

Analyzing a wide range of economic principles and practices, the contributors acknowledge Samuel Clemens's enthusiastic financial activities and scrutinize Mark Twain's wary skepticism about economics, both macro and micro. The tension between the restive desires of the man and the more thoughtful suspicions of his authorial persona provides interpretive traction. Nuanced analysis of this tension involves resisting assumptions that Clemens's transactions were straightforward and that Twain's writings were unequivocally critical of economic affairs. Rather, following his lead, shrewd readers account for the complexity involved in economic exchanges, as well as in Twain's sometimes conflicted manner of analyzing them. So the essays collected here offer a corrective for the biographical habit of judging Twain as an artist who had no business thinking of himself as a businessman, and condemning him for putatively betraying his artistic integrity when his attention turned, as it so often did, to commercial affairs.

In applying various strategies to tease out economic meanings in Clemens's life and Twain's texts, *Mark Twain and Money* draws upon and contributes to what was called New Economic Criticism when it first appeared a couple of decades ago. Although the adjective "new" may now seem outdated, scholars who analyze the interrelation between economics and narrative continue to generate new insights about the framing of economics in literary texts. Indeed, economic interpretation highlights two frequently overlooked factors: first, the theories and rules of economic exchange are established in language, and thus language conditions our grasp of all economic operations; and second, discourse itself—and especially narrative discourse—is a form of transaction between parties, an implicit contract with expectations and obligations.

Acknowledging the essential role of language in both economics and literature—and that writing itself is central to economics—gives the lie to romantic notions of the literary artist as occupying a rarefied arena divorced from the market. Twain unabashedly understood that he was an agent in the literary marketplace, and his texts *speculate*—to borrow from the vocabulary of investment—about the nature and effects of economic exchange with the hope of valuable return. Of course, in an entry to "Pudd'nhead Wilson's New Calendar," he mused, "There are two times in a man's life when he should not speculate: when he can't afford it and when he can" (*Equator* 535). But privately he admitted to William Dean Howells that he had an irremediable penchant for speculation, a comment that ambiguously conflates his attraction to business investment and to the essential business of writing fiction (22 August 1883, *Mark Twain–Howells Letters* 439). The degree to which he was drawn to both forms of speculation is an index of how business activities and imaginative narratives intersected throughout his career. Thus, *Mark Twain and Money* assesses how Twain's own literary practices are bound up in the dynamics of economic exchange, just as those dynamics are themselves subject to the discursive conditions of the verbal acts in which they are performed.

The illuminating perspectives that these critical readings bring to the meaning of economics in Twain's writing signal the potential for criticism that lies ahead. For example, in addition to the prospect of bringing new interpretive clarity to Twain's explicitly economic thought-experiments, such as "The £1,000,000 Bank Note" and "The Man That Corrupted Hadleyburg," this methodology can shed light on Twain's recurring fascination with figures like Colonel Sellers, the harebrained schemer based partly on Samuel Clemens's eccentric uncle Jesse Leathers. First appearing in *The Gilded Age* and later in Twain's dramatic forays, as well as in the novel *The American Claimant*, Sellers hatches increasingly impractical plans that he is certain will reap millions, if only the right backing would come along. Many critics and biographers have understandably drawn an analogy between Sellers's absurd fiscal optimism and the reckless judgment that led to Clemens's disastrous investments in the Paige typesetter, but a more nuanced appreciation of economic circumstances suggests that conflating the two is somewhat unfair for several reasons.

First, Clemens was not the inventor, like Sellers, but the investor, the money behind the idea; second, as Bruce Michelson has persuasively shown, having been a printer, Clemens had an informed understanding of the machine's efficiency advantages (10); third, he was among a number of investors in Paige's device (H. H. Rogers, the epitome of the hardheaded businessman, who assisted Clemens through his financial debacle, invested thousands rather late in the life of the typesetter); and last, as demoralizing as the typesetter fiasco was to him, this particular event was somewhat of an outlier. When Clemens tried his own hand at invention, the devices he envisioned were far more modest, and hence less risky and, in the case of the self-adhesive scrapbook, even successful. Although I differ with some of the other contributors, in my view most of Clemens's investments were not outlandish schemes and reflected his awareness of popular trends and run-of-the-mill financial opportunities. More to the point, for every patent application for a bed clamp or a scrapbook or a history game, for every investment in a health food product like Plasmon or an insurance company or efficiency improvements for jacquard looms, there was writing—a novel, a travel narrative, a story, a magazine sketch, an autobiography—in which he invested his imagination with an equal or greater interest and a fully warranted expectation of value. Economic criticism is uniquely equipped to elucidate the subtle ironies in the career of a man who, in multiple letters to his business manager, insisted on calculating the "commercial value" of his magazine writing at $200 per 1,000-word page (SLC to Fred Hall, Mark Twain Project) and simultaneously wrote "The $30,000 Bequest," a biting satire about the powerfully dangerous allure of imaginative speculation.

Economic analysis of the U.S. Mint's recent release of two commemorative Mark Twain coins might also point out that this event appears to turn the phrase "follow the money" on its head: the money seems to be following Twain. The $5 gold coin available for purchase at $371.15 and the $1 silver coin retailing for $44.95 highlight the fact that market value detaches from the material of a commodity. Granted, the price includes a surcharge that goes to support the Mark Twain Project at UC Berkeley's Bancroft Library, the Mark Twain House in Hartford, and the Mark Twain Boyhood Home and Museum in Hannibal. So an economic interpretation of these Twain-related spin-off products would certainly acknowledge the benefits accruing to worthy institutions dedicated to maintaining awareness of Twain and his literary work as important cultural contributions. However, the coins themselves are open to further interpretation. The motto "In God We Trust," required on all U.S. currency since the days of fervent anti-Communism in 1957, makes for unintended irony when commemorating a notorious religious skeptic like Mark Twain. Further ironies abound when we recall that one of Twain's most famous stories, "The Man That Corrupted Hadleyburg," a pointed satire of avarice, closes with the image of a coin whose revised motto reads: "LEAD US INTO TEMPTATION" (83). One is tempted to read Hadleyburg's emphatic coinage as a sardonic comment on the marketing savvy that has found yet another way to sell Mark Twain's image and to transform the iconography of his most well-known works, quite literally, into cash. One is also tempted to suspect that Mark Twain would have approved.

In somewhat broader terms, the merits of economic criticism suggest that its methodologies hold promise beyond the scope of Mark Twain. Interrogating how economic exchange gives shape to society and direction to its practices—including literary and scholarly practices—can yield knowledge about our current moment, which in the wake of Thomas Piketty's *Capital in the Twenty-first Century* is being called the "New Gilded Age." For obvious reasons, wealth is generally viewed positively; however, criticism that follows the money, in all of its forms and implications, promises a greater understanding of how money both expands and curtails freedom in ways that are equally consequential. Although the flood of virtually unlimited and undisclosed campaign cash has made Deep Throat's directive seem like a quaint anachronism in contemporary politics, literary criticism that follows the money can provide insights that increase our common stock of cultural capital.

Works Cited

All the President's Men. Dir. Alan Pakula. Perf. Dustin Hoffman, Robert Redford, Hal Holbrook. Screenwriter William Goldman. Warner Bros., 1976.

Michelson, Bruce. *Printer's Devil: Mark Twain and the American Publishing Revolution*. Berkeley: U California P, 2006.

Piketty, Thomas. *Capital in the Twenty-first Century*. Cambridge: Harvard UP, 2014.

Twain, Mark. *Following the Equator*. New York: Oxford UP, 1996.

———. "The Man That Corrupted Hadleyburg." *The Man That Corrupted Hadleyburg and Other Stories*. New York: Oxford UP, 1996: 1–83.

———. *Mark Twain–Howells Letters*. Ed. Henry Nash Smith and William M. Gibson. Cambridge: Belknap-Harvard UP, 1960.

———. SLC to Fred Hall, 22 July, 24 July, 23 August 1892. Mark Twain Project, University of California, Berkeley.

Contributors

M. Christine Benner Dixon earned her Ph.D. at Drew University and now teaches English at the Winchester Thurston School in Pittsburgh, where she also serves as department chair. Her 2014 dissertation is entitled *The Pain Economy: Mark Twain's Investment in Pain.*

Gregg Camfield is Professor of English at the University of California, Merced. He has published widely on the works of Mark Twain, American literary humor, literary sentimentalism, and domesticity. He is the author of *Sentimental Twain: Mark Twain in the Maze of Moral Philosophy* (Pennsylvania, 1994), *Necessary Madness: The Humor of Domesticity in Nineteenth-Century American Literature* (Oxford, 1997), and *The Oxford Companion to Mark Twain* (2003).

Joseph Csicsila is Professor of English at Eastern Michigan University. He has published widely on Mark Twain and other American literary figures. Csicsila is the author of *Canons by Consensus: Critical Trends and American Literature Anthologies* (2004), coauthor of *Heretical Fictions: Religion in the Literature of Mark Twain* (2010), and coeditor of *Centenary Reflections on Mark Twain's* No. 44, The Mysterious Stranger (2009), and the *Prentice Hall Anthology of American Literature* (2011).

Jonathan Hayes is currently a full-time instructor of English at Southeast Missouri State University in Cape Girardeau. He received his Ph.D. in English from the University of Pittsburgh in 2013. His research interests include nineteenth-century American literature and transnational literature of the Americas.

Lawrence Howe, Professor of English and Film Studies at Roosevelt University, is the author of *Mark Twain and the Novel: The Double-Cross of Authority* (Cambridge University Press, 1998) and a contributor to the

Oxford Mark Twain. He is currently writing a book on property in Mark Twain and American culture. His recent scholarly work in film studies covers a wide range of topics, including the volume *Refocusing Chaplin: A Screen Icon through Critical Lenses* coedited with James Caron and Benjamin Click.

Judith Yaross Lee is an award-winning teacher and scholar at Ohio University, where she serves as Professor of Rhetoric & Public Culture and Director of Honors Tutorials in the School of Communication Studies. Her newest book, *Twain's Brand: Humor in Contemporary American Culture* (2012), shows how recent American humor offers insights into the post-industrial culture created by the information economy. She is also the author of *Garrison Keillor: A Voice of America* (1991) and *Defining New Yorker Humor* (2000).

Sharon D. McCoy is the past executive coordinator of the Mark Twain Circle of America, the past president of the American Humor Studies Association, and an academic free agent. She has been teaching writing and American literature at the University of Georgia since 2004 and is currently completing a book-length manuscript on Mark Twain and postbellum blackface minstrelsy, "Nothing But Trouble: Blackface in Mark Twain's America." McCoy is the editor of *All Things Twain: An Encyclopedia of Mark Twain's World* (Greenwood Press).

Jeffrey W. Miller is Associate Professor of English at Gonzaga University. He has published articles on a variety of authors associated with American realism and naturalism, including Mark Twain, Charles Chesnutt, Pauline Hopkins, and Rebecca Harding Davis. He is currently completing a monograph on citizenship in nineteenth-century United States literary culture.

Ann M. Ryan is Professor of English at Le Moyne College. With Joseph B. McCullough, she is the coeditor of *Cosmopolitan Twain* (Missouri, 2008), an anthology of critical essays that situate Mark Twain within the context of an evolving international and cosmopolitan community.

Mark Schiebe is Assistant Professor at Queensborough Community College of the City University of New York. His work on Flannery O'Connor appears in the collection *Wise Blood: A Re-Consideration* (2011), and he is currently finishing an article about optical instruments in the fiction of Henry James.

Susanne Weil is Associate Professor of English and Humanities at Centralia College in Centralia, Washington. In addition to her scholarly interests in Mark Twain and late-nineteenth-century American literature, she is a passionate beekeeper.

Henry B. Wonham is the author of *Mark Twain and the Art of the Tall Tale* and *Playing the Races: Ethnic Caricature and American Literary Real-*

ism, both published by Oxford University Press. His other books include *Charles W. Chesnutt: A Study of the Short Fiction* and an edited volume, *Criticism and the Color Line: Desegregating American Literary Studies*. He is Professor of English at the University of Oregon.

Index